Freedom of Speech Under Attack

Freedom of Speech Under Attack

Afshin Ellian and Gelijn Molier (Eds.)

eleven
international publishing

Published, sold and distributed by Eleven International Publishing
P.O. Box 85576
2508 CG The Hague
The Netherlands
Tel.: +31 70 33 070 33
Fax: +31 70 33 070 30
e-mail: sales@budh.nl
www.elevenpub.com

Sold and distributed in USA and Canada
International Specialized Book Services
920 NE 58th Avenue, Suite 300
Portland, OR 97213-3786, USA
Tel.: 1-800-944-6190 (toll-free)
Fax: +1 503 280-8832
orders@isbs.com
www.isbs.com

Eleven International Publishing is an imprint of Boom uitgevers Den Haag.

ISBN 978-94-6290-027-1
ISBN 978-94-6274-233-8 (E-book)

Cover photo: Eustache Le Sueur, *La prédication de Saint Paul à Éphèse* (1649). Louvre, Departement des Peintures, INV. 8020. 'When St. Paul entered Ephesus "a number of those who practiced magic collected their books and burned them publicly" (Acts 19:19).'

Printed in The Netherlands

Preface

This book is a 'follow-up' to and expansion of a book that appeared in 2011, in Dutch, entitled *Mag ik dit zeggen? (May I say this?)*. That year saw the trial of Geert Wilders, parliamentarian and party leader of one of the largest political parties in The Netherlands. Several prominent scholars contributed to *Mag ik dit zeggen?*, discussing matters in the domains of penal law, constitutional law, comparative law and philosophy of law, approaching the issues surrounding freedom of expression, particularly its meaning and scope, from these varied but related perspectives. Central questions are: Should a parliamentarian be allowed more freedom of expression than an 'ordinary citizen'?; How should 'group insult' and 'incitement to hatred and discrimination' be interpreted?; What is the significance of the European Convention on Human Rights for freedom of expression?; What should the dimension of freedom of expression in a modern democratic state of law be? These questions have lost none of their import and actuality, in particular in light of the fact that a decision to prosecute Geert Wilders has been made again, this time not for his remarks about Islam, but for what he has said about a group of people: Moroccans.

On that basis, the editors of the Dutch volume have seen fit to realize a volume in English. Still, the present volume is not limited to an exposé of Dutch law regarding freedom of expression and, in particular, in which cases it may be curtailed. The Wilders case is merely a symptom of a development on a larger scale, namely at the European level: The rise of nationalistic and populist (extreme right) politicians who willingly confront the limits of freedom of expression in the discussion about the immigration and integration of aliens and refugees. At the same time, radicalized Muslims who sympathize with terrorist acts increasingly make use of Facebook and other social media to glorify Jihad and other acts of violence. These developments necessitate, in our view, a closer reflection of freedom of expression in all its dimensions. In accordance with this observation, a number of (new) contributions to this volume explicitly deal with the issues of 'religious extremist speech,' 'terrorism-related speech' and 'religious/racist hate speech.' In addition, the theoretical aspects of the relation between freedom of expression and democracy are given ample attention, making it clear how heavily this relation bears on the question of limiting the scope of this fundamental right. The significance of the latter issue becomes clear if one considers the sometimes incoherent and inconsistent case law of the ECtHR. One of this book's aims is, accordingly, to encourage a renewed discussion with respect to freedom of expression, in which all starting-points are allowed to be questioned, so that this fundamental right is also 'theoretically' provided with the proper support.

We would, in conclusion, like to thank our colleague Jasper Doomen for his tireless efforts in realizing this book. Jasper has translated our jointly written first chapter and our individual contributions. In addition, he has made corrections to some of the other contributions. Without his speedy work, it would have taken much more time to conclude the final stage of this book.

The editors
Professor Afshin Ellian,
Gelijn Molier, PhD, LL.M.

A note by the editors

alles van waarde is weerloos
wordt van aanraakbaarheid rijk
en aan alles gelijk
als het hart van de tijd
als het hart van de tijd

all that has value is defenseless
will grow rich from touchability
and become equal to everything
like the heart of time
like the heart of time
Lucebert (Dutch poet)

On January 7, 2015, Europe was struck at its heart. Two jihadists, ordered by Al-Qaeda, attacked the office of the satirical magazine *Charlie Hebdo*. The first thing they did was execute the policemen, one of whom was a French citizen with an Islamic background. They proceeded to storm the building, where they murdered 10 cartoonists: the editors of *Charlie Hebdo*. In addition, a main editor was killed. Another jihadist, who sympathized with Islamic State (ISIL), charged a Jewish grocery store, where he killed four Jews just for being Jewish. Paris was effectively held hostage for 48 hours by these terrorists. In the end, the French police managed to cease these terrorist acts. The offenders died in the process. Sorrow and joy were abundant in Europe.

Citizens demonstrated in the European cities with the slogan *Je suis Charlie* ('I am Charlie'). This epithet was appropriated in the demonstrations in order to show one's disgust at what had happened. In Amsterdam, thousands of citizens gathered in order to commemorate the victims. That was not the sole reason for their presence, though. They also wanted to make it clear to the world that freedom of speech is an unshakeable foundation of the European legal order and civilization. The Dutch Prime Minister Mark Rutte addressed the gathered crowd on Dam Square. He stressed the crucial import of freedom of speech:

'Yesterday in Paris twelve people were murdered in cold blood. Twelve gatekeepers of freedom. Including our freedom. (…) And we are not alone. Everywhere in Europe, people are standing side by side, shoulder to shoulder. In solidarity with France, with the victims and with the victims' loved ones. We are here to say that hatred and violence must never and will never defeat respect and tolerance. We are here because freedom and democracy are non-negotiable. There is simply no such thing as being half free. And while freedom implies responsibility, it must never mean self-censorship. We will not let fear govern our lives. We will not let anyone take away our freedom. (…) Our country and its neighbors have room for everyone's beliefs and everyone's convictions. This freedom is not always easy to live with. Because it does not only protect opinions we are comfortable with, compliments and innocuous commentary. Freedom also protects unwelcome and caustic criticism, sharp disagreement and sarcastic mockery. That is the essence of democracy. It is at the heart of true freedom.

After all, what is the first thing that dictators forbid? Making fun of authority. The freedom to criticize and make fun of authority is the ultimate proof that we are civilized people. That we never try to silence each other. The murderers tried to kill free speech yesterday by taking aim at journalists. We must answer them with words: loud words, strong words, free words. The murderers tried to kill our sense of security yesterday by executing police officers. We must answer them by showing solidarity with our police. By protecting one another. By cherishing mockery, satire and jokes about everyone and everything. There is no place in our society for fundamentalist violence and intolerance. And this cowardly murder of twelve people only strengthens us in this conviction. What happened yesterday in Paris shows how real and close the threat of terror is. We are and will remain alert. Together, we are and will remain vigilant. What it comes down to is this: yesterday fanatics carried out a barbaric attack, which touches us all. Today we are responding in the thousands: Keep your hands off our freedom. Since yesterday, the voice of *Charlie Hebdo* is more pervasive and more powerful than ever. And that is the best answer we can give.'

These almost historic words were uttered with the fitting calmness and composure and were received with great enthusiasm by the crowd. Liberté, Égalité, Fraternité! Those are the values of the First Republic, which are still promoted by present-day France and, in fact, the whole of Europe. It is these values the terrorists in Paris and their kindred spirits from the Middle East sought to sacrifice upon the altar of fanaticism. On January 11, millions of people joined together in Paris and other French cities, marching down the streets in order to send an unmistakable message: they would not capitulate to acts of violence and terror. Over 40 of the world's leaders were present at this demonstration.

'Tout est pardonné' ('all is forgiven') could be read on the cover of *Charlie Hebdo*. Below it a cartoon was printed of the prophet Muhammad, displayed in tears. One wonders, though, who or what it is that must be forgiven. The bullets in Paris were a reminder of the deadly force of the depiction interdiction. The majority of the casualties of Islamic terrorism are themselves Muslim. In Islamic countries, dozens of Muslims are killed by jihadists on a daily basis. Writers, lawyers, artists and reporters are not secure in those areas.

This edited volume deals with freedom of speech. In the context of the Paris attacks, it has gained a grim connotation.

Tout est pardonné, all is forgiven; this locution may now be associated with the lines in Lucebert's poem: all that has value is defenseless.

Afshin Ellian and Gelijn Molier
Leiden, January 2015

Table of Contents

Part II The International Dimension of Freedom of Speech

1 The Various Aspects of Freedom of Speech

Afshin Ellian and Gelijn Molier

Introduction

This book is a follow-up and an elaboration of the book *May I say this?*, which appeared in Dutch (the original title being *Mag ik dit zeggen?*) in 2011.[1] In that year, the trial against Geert Wilders, parliamentarian and political leader for one of the largest parties in The Netherlands, took place. The trial of Wilders was a focal point in a line of trials concerning freedom of expression. Imams, reverends, members of parliament, artists and writers were all tried over the last decade because of what they expressed, in some cases leading to convictions. In 2002, politician Pim Fortuyn was murdered; he had pleaded for the abolishment of the ban on discrimination of article 1 of the Dutch constitution, in order to expand freedom of expression. In 2004, a Dutch filmmaker and columnist, Theo van Gogh, was murdered, for supposedly having offended the prophet Mohammed in his movie *Submission*, which dealt with the suppression of women in Islamic cultures. These events culminated in heated debates in The Netherlands over the last years about the multicultural society in general and Islam in particular. Geert Wilders' acquittal in 2011 seemed to have created, at least in a legal sense, some clarity: Expressions about a religion and its sacred symbols, as well as acts and beliefs of religious people, are allowed, however crude and offensive they may be, but if the expressions concern religious people themselves, the penal code applies.

In the following period, Wilders abode by the limits demarcated by the judiciary. Moreover, he was no longer focused on Islam but rather on the European Union. The debate on the limits of freedom of expression seemed to be over and peace seemed to have returned to society, until Wilders submitted a question to those of his adherents who had gathered in a room in The Hague, on March the 19th 2014, the night after the municipal elections. He asked whether they would rather have 'more or fewer Moroccans in this city and in The Netherlands.' His fellow party members chanted 'fewer, fewer, fewer,' whereupon Wilders replied 'then we will make the necessary arrangements.' A few days earlier he had already let slip that he sought to make sure, if possible, that for the residents of The Hague

1 A. Ellian, G. Molier and T. Zwart (Eds.), *Mag ik dit zeggen? Beschouwingen over de vrijheid van meningsuiting*, The Hague Haag: Boom Juridische uitgevers 2011.

there would be 'lower taxes and fewer Moroccans.' On this occasion, the indignation from the majority of the Dutch population was significant and even the mass media, which had supported Wilders up to that point, publicly dissociated themselves from him. Over 6,400 people filed a complaint for insult and (incitement to) discrimination. The district attorney took over half a year to reach the decision that Geert Wilders was once again to be prosecuted, this time for insulting a group of people on the basis of their *race* (article 137c of the Dutch Criminal Code) and incitement to hatred and discrimination against people on the basis of their *race* (article 137d).

As a consequence, the question 'may I say this' once again became a hot topic in The Netherlands. Even though the contributions to this edited volume regard the Wilders trial of 2011, and none of them discuss the recent decision of the district attorney to once again prosecute Wilders, none of the questions put forward here have lost any of their merit in terms of actuality. One may even go so far as to say that the decision to prosecute Wilders for a second time makes it all the more clear that a renewed reflection on freedom of expression in all of its dimensions is of the utmost importance. With the rise of nationalistic and extremist political parties in Europe on one side and radical Islamic groups on the other, the principled question to the meaning and limitations of freedom of expression in a democratic state of law has a greater dimension than ever before. Do we opt for a system in which politicians are muffled if they say things that infringe upon the values for which democracy stands, or should the American model be preferred, in light of the fact that the European nations have by now all become multi-religious and multicultural societies? What are the reasons for choosing one model of democracy over the other? There are various conceptions of democracy from which to answer the question whether a parliamentarian should have more or less room to say what he wants than an ordinary citizen.

The role and position of the judiciary also needs to be taken into consideration in reflecting on these matters. Adjudication is essentially characterized by an impartial settlement of disputes by a neutral authority that has no stake in the outcome. Trying politicians because of what they say continually brings with it the danger of the reproach of a political trial, as the recent trials of Wilders, Le Pen and Féret have shown. This brings with it the danger that the legitimacy of the judiciary may be questioned, so there is good reason to carefully consider prosecuting politicians because of what they say. The issue is all the more pressing considering the fact that crimes of expression often contain vague terms that provide the judiciary with a lot of room to maneuver, to which may be added that the jurisprudence of the European Court of Human Rights (ECtHR) does not offer much support to national judges, since it is not a paragon of clarity and consistence in rulings concerning 'hate speech.' These matters will all be discussed in this book. So as to provide the necessary structure, we have decided to order the contributions along the following three lines.

First of all, there is the dimension of national law. The Dutch (penal) law is the focal point here, with some excursions to the laws of other nations (Germany and the United States). Second, the international legal dimension is discussed. The main topics of interest here are the European Convention on Human Rights (ECHR) and the jurisprudential framework realized by the European Court of Human Rights (ECtHR) with respect to freedom of expression as laid down in article 10 of the ECHR. In addition, the global level is dealt with, notably, the International Covenant on Civil and Political Rights (ICCPR) and the United Nations Human Rights Council. Finally, the legal philosophical or legal theoretical dimension of freedom of expression is examined. The editors of this volume believe that it is only possible to say something meaningful about the question 'may I say this?' from a legal philosophical reflection on freedom of expression. The fact that the contributions to this edited volume have been ordered along these three lines takes nothing away from the fact that the aforementioned classification is not always strict, with individual contributions often dealing with topics covering more than one of these dimensions.

GENERAL

In his work *The Spirit of the Laws*, from 1748, Montesquieu spoke the following grand words on freedom: 'The political liberty of the citizen consists in the tranquility of mind that arises from the conviction everyone has of his safety; and in order to possess this liberty it is requisite that the government be so constituted that one citizen need not fear another.'[2] Even several centuries later, in the era of Facebook and Google, these words are still conceived to constitute truth, logic and necessity.

The Arab Spring of 2011 would have been nearly inconceivable if television networks such as Al Jazeera, CNN and Fox did not have the opportunity to continually report on the mass gatherings on Tahir Square in Cairo. The social media have been important in contributing to the protests in the Arab world and the realization of the Iranian Green Movement in the summer of 2009. The tyrants realize all too well wherein the dangers of liberty lie: the exercise of power would be exposed to public control.

While the situation in the Arab world has dramatically changed since then, the limits of freedom of speech are hotly debated in the Netherlands. It is obvious that no freedom is unlimited, but where should the limits be drawn? At what point should the government be allowed to intervene?

2 Ch. de Montesquieu, *De l'Esprit des Lois*, Book 11, Ch. 6, p. 129, Paris: Librairie de Firmin Didot Frères, 1849 [1748]. The original text reads: 'La liberté politique, dans un citoyen, est cette tranquillité d'esprit qui provient de l'opinion que chacun a de sa sûreté ; et, pour qu'on ait cette liberté, il faut que le gouvernement soit tel qu'un citoyen ne puisse pas craindre un autre citoyen.'

A number of widely discussed trials in the 20th century, involving artists and writers in particular, led many to believe that the limits of freedom of speech had – on the whole – been decided. The criticism of Christianity was and is experienced as something normal in Dutch media, politics and art, the implication being that the potential to offend Christians is accepted and not considered to constitute a problem. Ever since the 9/11 attacks, the Western world has been involved in a debate on Islam and immigration policies. Multicultural society has been the subject of debate ever since the last decade of the previous century. Frits Bolkestein, the Parliamentary leader for the People's Party for Freedom and Democracy (a liberal political party) in the House of Representatives, was one of the early critics of the idealism associated with multiculturalism. Even at that time, this debate was generally marked by a sense of unease. Yet, at the same time, the way in which the public debate was conducted was the topic of discussion. For nearly a decade, The Netherlands was occupied by the question: 'May I say this?'

In order to answer this question, a penal approach was opted for in the end. Certain participants of the debate, rather than the government, have appealed to the judiciary in order to let the penal legal limits of freedom of speech be determined. The most conspicuous trial in that respect took place in 2011, against Geert Wilders, the Parliamentary leader in the House of Representatives for the Party for Freedom, one of the largest parties in The Netherlands. This trial, which was initiated in the wake of those who expressed their misgivings with respect to his statements on Islam, led to a great upheaval in Dutch society.[3] Freedom of speech is a human right. Western governments protest on a regular basis against penal repression of freedom of speech in other parts of the world. On that basis, it is at least ironic that we ourselves need to debate the penal limits of this freedom.

Freedom of speech is not only limited by the law. In addition, there are moral limits, standards of decency and even aesthetic limits. An expression or a work of art may contravene the law and yet not meet the standard of morals or aesthetics. When certain expressions or works of art are deemed immoral, indecent or ugly, their power of persuasion is diminished accordingly. Within the domain of freedom of speech one often underestimates the corrective force of moral and aesthetic debates.

A society that lacks the moral ability to discuss and judge the sense and nonsense of certain expressions tends to resort to the law, as if the law had some miracle cure at its disposal to resolve social disputes. Accordingly, authoritative lawyers frequently warn politicians and crusaders against expecting too much from the law in settling social disputes. Education and upbringing as well as the media are the institutions that should give some direction on how to debate political, moral and aesthetic issues. The law, and the Criminal

---

3 In this case, the so-called article 12 procedure (referring to article 12 of the Dutch Code of Criminal Procedure) was involved, meaning that if the District Attorney decides, as he is allowed to do, on the basis of the 'nolle prosequi' principle, not to prosecute, anyone whose interest is involved and who disagrees with this decision may request that prosecution should still take place.

Code in particular, should only be resorted to as a final recourse (the proper 'ultimum remedium').

Now that the smoke of the Geert Wilders trial is clearing, the time has come to take stock of the debate on the penal aspects of freedom of speech, especially since Wilders will, as was mentioned above, be prosecuted again. In this academic edited volume, a number of eminent legal scholars take a stance from differing perspectives on the issue of freedom of speech and in particular what penal limits should be observed.

About this book

Whatever one may think about the Geert Wilders trial, the question with regard to the meaning and limits of freedom of speech has, as a consequence of this event, been at the center of attention. In newspapers, (academic) journals, television broadcastings, lectures and gatherings, the topic of freedom of speech was frequently debated. It is ironic that the topic of discussion was simultaneously the precondition for it to be possible in the first place. After all, without freedom of speech, no discussion on its content and limits would be possible.

This makes it clear just how strongly interrelated freedom of speech and democracy are: a democratic form of government presupposes individual equality, while individual equality in turn presupposes that everyone must be allowed to express his or her view on a subject matter, even if the majority is in disagreement. In order to be *able* to do so in freedom, the state must thus guarantee to each person freedom of speech, which may in that sense rightly be dubbed a *basic* right. Although one may, then, say what one wants in The Netherlands, freedom of speech is not an unlimited freedom. It will become apparent from the contributions in this volume not just that no state or legal system supports unrestricted freedom of speech, but also that no author – however liberal he or she may be – would promote unrestricted freedom of speech. Each of them defends some limits on this freedom.

Where these limits should, in concrete cases, lie depends on the relative weight one attributes to freedom of speech in light of other elements, such as the position and task of the government, the protection of minorities, the position and the function of religion and the interest of protecting public order or the 'societal sphere.' Whether one decides in favor of optimally extended freedom of speech (the American system) or restricts it in significant respects (the German system), is determined in the end by the values that one considers fundamentally intertwined with the democratic state of law. Those values are, in turn, determined by theories in the field of legal and political philosophy regarding the state, democracy, the individual and the community. Communitarians will, with the framework of the community as a whole in mind, have fewer problems with restricting freedom of speech in favor of the protection of minorities than (classical) liberals, who do not promote group interests but rather the freedom of the individual. This also makes it clear that the question whether one is allowed to say something or not cannot be answered in the abstract once and for all, irrespective of the context. After all, the limits individuals define are the results of their own necessarily partial view on people and the world, which is, accordingly, necessarily subjective and arbitrary. In the words of the German philosopher Arthur Schopenhauer: 'The world is in every instance my representation of it.'[4]

An edited volume on the meaning and extent of freedom of speech seems to be an impossible mission in light of the previous remarks: What one person considers a stern criticism of religion that must be protected by freedom of speech another may deem punishable insult of one or more religious minorities. The question where the line should be drawn should be answered by the legislator. The most important and simultaneously most controversial restrictions of freedom of speech in this regard are the following articles from the Dutch Criminal Code: 137c (group insult on the basis of race, religion or world-view, sexual orientation and physical or mental disability) and 137d (incitement to hatred, discrimination and violence towards groups on the ground of race, religion or worldview, sexual orientation, gender and physical or mental disability).[5] These are also the criminal offences of which Geert Wilders was prosecuted and will be prosecuted again (see Introduction). The problem with these articles is that, on account of the vague terms they contain, they leave too much room for interpretation, enabling the individual judge to decide the case based on these terms. Many of the contributions to this volume deal with a (critical) assessment of these articles and the related jurisprudence.

The contribution by *Sackers* deals with article 137c and its history. He concludes that the legislative history is particularly surprising, since the article has been changed four times and, as a result, seems to serve as a general, 'all-purpose' concept. This means that the *ratio legis* of this provision is in peril of being obscured; from the perspective of the judiciary, article 137c is also surprising according to Sackers. He further maintains that the term 'contribution to a social or public debate', which the judiciary has developed in line with contextual review, adds to the danger of the previously mentioned all-purpose concept: Nowhere is it clarified what a 'public debate' actually is.

Nieuwenhuis considers, in his contribution, the meaning of article 137d; in particular, he inquires into the meaning of 'causing hatred,' and how it is to be interpreted in light of freedom of speech. He opts for a comparative legal approach. His analysis leads him to the conclusion that judges are, in interpreting 'causing hatred,' faced with several problems, which is unfortunate: While hatred may be indeterminate, this applies to a lesser extent

4 'Die Welt ist meine Vorstellung (...).' A. Schopenhauer, *Die Welt als Wille und Vorstellung*, vol. 1 (Ed. P. Deussen), Munich: R. Piper & Co.: 1911 [1819], § 1, p. 3.

5 In the remainder of this text, articles without further qualification will refer to the Dutch Criminal Code.

to a penal provision. A citizen who expresses him- or herself must be able, to a certain degree, to predict whether the expressions will, according to Nieuwenhuis, cause difficulties.

Molier and *Ellian* reach similar results with respect to both article 137c and article 137d. Molier maintains that the combination of vague terms, along with the relatively indeterminate criteria that have been developed in the jurisprudence to combat this problem, has led to the legal certainty of citizens being in jeopardy. Ellian points, in this regard, to the Janmaat case; Janmaat was a Dutch politician who was convicted for (being an accomplice to) incitement to discrimination. They consider the way in which the judiciary came to convict him hardly satisfying the standards of legal criticism. There is a great contrast, then, between this case and the acquittal in the Wilders case. It is of course characteristic of the law that the judge may decide either way in the case of vague notions, but where crimes of expression are concerned, this is an unwelcome situation. For Molier, the main danger consists in the continual threat of the reproach of a political trial.

Apart from this national penal context of freedom of speech, the European legal context, and more specifically the context of the European Convention on Human Rights (ECHR), plays an important part in confronting the question whether a certain restriction of freedom of speech by the national legislator is in accordance with the ECHR, in particular with article 10 of this treaty. The contributions by Zwart, Lemmens, Loof, Van Noorloos, and – again – Nieuwenhuis discuss this 'European legal dimension' of freedom of speech in detail. Nieuwenhuis argues that article 10 of the ECHR does not necessarily rule out a relatively broad interpretation of article 137d.

Zwart provides a general overview of the jurisprudence of the ECtHR with respect to article 10 of the ECHR, which guarantees freedom of speech. He observes that there are two contradictory interpretations in the jurisprudence. The first was adopted by the Court during the last forty years; it holds, *in nuce*, that political expressions must be protected as much as possible. The other interpretation was started in 2008; it appears to provide less protection to freedom of speech, in favor of the protection of (parts of) the population against insult, ridicule, incitement to hatred and discrimination, even if this was not accompanied by an actual call for violence or other criminal acts. Zwart observes that after adopting a staunch libertarian position for decades, ECtHR has become less tolerant towards insulting, blasphemous and spiteful remarks made as part of the political debate. Although Zwart recognizes that there may be good reasons to reconsider whether the robustness of the political debate should be preserved in light of the growing importance of values like harmony and respect, he concludes that such a reconsideration should be conducted by the political organs which enjoy an electoral mandate and not by the Court.

Lemmens's reflection ties in closely with Zwart's. He is focused on the way in which the ECtHR deals with 'hate speech' in general rather than with the protection of 'political speech' in particular. Before discussing the ECtHR's case law, he explores in detail the reasons provided in scientific studies to justify hate speech bans, as well as the criticism leveled against them. Subsequently, he presents the three ways in which the ECtHR approaches the problems involved in hate speech. He distinguishes between five varieties of hate speech, namely, political hate speech, racist hate speech, religious hate speech, sexual orientation and hate speech and, finally, incitement to violence. He shows that religious hate speech and hate speech related to sexual orientation in particular are problematic categories, which may lead to an unnecessary restriction of the free public debate. The next item that is discussed is the problem of denialism, especially Holocaust denial. While penalization of Holocaust denial may be argued on the basis of the historical context in which the European Convention on Human Rights was realized, a similar course of action is more difficult to take where other forms of genocide are concerned. Lemmens pleads for a clear distinction between denying genocide and justifying or glorifying it. He concludes that the development of ever more groups of people being characterized as hate speech victims is unwelcome; a broad interpretation of 'hate speech' brings with it the danger of free political debate being restricted. Maybe, as a society, we should ask ourselves whether we are not exaggerating and perhaps falling into the trap of the heckler's veto. At a certain point, protecting the sensibilities of a growing number of groups in society can boil down to creating new taboos, whereas the very idea of freedom of speech is to have as little taboos as possible.

Van Noorloos deals with the jurisprudence of the ECtHR regarding religiously motivated extreme expressions and political parties. So in this case, 'antidemocratic' expressions in a religious context are the topic of concern. Her conclusion is that the ECtHR in such cases tends to protect democracy and fundamental rights. Restrictions of freedom of speech in the case of religiously motivated extreme expressions are thus acceptable. In other words, the ECtHR tends to restrict pluralism in people's outlooks in order to protect pluralism and fundamental rights themselves. Subsequently, she discusses this theme from a legal theoretical perspective. The central questions here are: For what reasons, if any, may extreme expressions be forbidden, and with what ideas regarding democracy and toleration are they buttressed?

Loof, finally, endeavors to analyze the standards of the ECHR and the case-law of the ECtHR with respect to permissible restrictions on freedom of expression on public order, national security or other grounds in cases relating to terrorism. He investigates what room they leave for the criminalization of – or other ways of restricting – terrorism-related extremist speech. With regard to the prosecution for the offence of glorification of (or apology of) terrorism, Loof concludes that the ECtHR does not consider this incompatible with Article 10 of the ECHR, although the cases so far each time concerned publications in politically tense regions, where actual terrorist attacks were not uncommon. His analysis also makes it clear that the link between the publication and the potential consequences does not need to be a strong or direct one, nor does the author have to show a clear intent to incite. However, contextual factors are important here: the personal stature of the author (public figure or not), the size of the audience (mass media or not), the form of the expression and, last but not least, the security situation in a certain region. Nevertheless, his overall conclusion is that as far as terrorism-related speech is concerned, the Court is prepared to accept far-reaching restrictions of freedom of speech, especially in a sensitive security situation.

The European legal context, which generally provides room to impose far-reaching restrictions of freedom of speech, is usually contrasted with the American legal context, which provides virtually no room to restrict it. The mere fact that the American system is frequently referred to in the debate in The Netherlands is sufficient justification to pay attention to this. In his contribution, *Guiora* provides a general overview of the history and jurisprudence of the American Constitutional right to freedom of speech. His elaboration demonstrates that this freedom was not always equally extensive. In times of crisis, such as the First and Second World Wars, as well as the Cold War, freedom of speech *was* curtailed by the legislator and the judiciary. 'Political' opinions in particular lost the battle against national safety and public order. The contributions by Nieuwenhuis and Zwart referred to above also deal with the American jurisprudence concerning freedom of speech, from a comparative legal perspective.

Freedom of expression is not only guaranteed at the European level, but also internationally or globally. Article 19 of the International Covenant on Civil and Political Rights, adopted by the United Nations, states: 'Everyone shall have the right to freedom of expression.' *Awesta's* contribution regards this 'global' right to freedom of expression and the pressure this right has come under within the system of the United Nations as a consequence of the tensions between Islamic countries on the one hand and Western countries on the other, especially in the wake of the events of 9/11. He demonstrates how Islamic countries have tried, from the nineties of the last century, initially in the United Nations Commission on Human Rights and later in the United Nations Human Rights Council, to remove offending or defaming religions from the range of freedom of expression. The accent was shifted from protecting individuals against discrimination on the basis of their religious convictions to protecting religions as such. Freedom of religion was, accordingly, expanded with the right not to be harmed or offended in one's religious feelings. As understandable as this development may be in light of the clashes between different civilizations and groups of people resulting from the process of globalization, it is sharply opposed to the original intentions of the ICCPR, which is based on the ideal of protecting the human dignity of the *individual*. Awesta argues that the recent years, fortunately, show a transformation, the emphasis once more being placed on the restrictions of freedom of expression that have from the outset been acknowledged, namely, the ban on 'hate speech' and on incitement to discrimination. At the same time, he observes that the distinction between defaming a religion and incitement to hatred against individuals who adhere to that religion is quite indefinite, making it difficult at times to distinguish between them.

As a consequence, in a globalized society in which offensive expressions are rapidly spread on a global scale through the Internet, freedom of expression is continually under pressure. It is necessary to be vigilant in this respect, while it must be endeavored by all means at the global level of the United Nations to make sure that the range of this fundamental human right is not further restricted under pressure of non-Western countries.

The cartoon riots in Denmark and elsewhere in the world have put another aspect of freedom of speech at the forefront, namely the relationship between words and (the use of) violence. This may be called the sociological or empirical context of freedom of speech. The contribution by *Cliteur, Herrenberg* and *Rijpkema* examines this issue, and is particularly relevant with the recent attack on *Charlie Hebdo* in mind. They do not focus on the impact of words on the group of people addressed or attacked but rather on its counter: Violence directed against those who have expressed themselves in an insulting or derogatory way. They are interested in the difference between the freedom of speech of people like the politician Geert Wilders, the writer Salman Rushdie and the cartoonist Kurt Westergaard, *de iure* and *de facto*. It will become clear how one may rightfully have the freedom to say or publish what one wants while not using this freedom in practice, under pressure of groups that are not allied to the state. After a study of five cases, namely, the Carrell Affair, the Cartoon Affair, the Rushdie Affair, the Terry Jones Affair and the Youssef Affair, they conclude that the limits of free speech are, to an increasing extent, not established by the legislature or the judiciary, but rather by terrorist organizations and terrorist individuals, in such a way that it amounts to a new kind of censorship, at least with regard to a particular kind of speech: Religious criticism or religious satire.

One aspect has been of major importance in the Wilders case, namely the fact that it was a political representative who made the remarks in question, and that he made them in the context of a public debate. The fact that the remarks stemmed from a member of parliament has led to a debate on whether members of parliament should be privileged in this regard, meaning that they should, as representatives of their constituency, be allowed to express any opinion shared by this constituency, or that they should at least have parliamentary immunity in this regard both inside and outside parliament. Such a privileged position may be supported by the fact that in a democratic state, no vote should be suppressed. One may argue against this stance by saying that the position of a parliamentarian outside parliament and that of an 'ordinary citizen' do not differ to such a degree that a separate legal treatment of the former would be justified. Opponents of such special treatment emphasize, moreover, the duties of politicians to take responsibility for what they say, considering the fact that the impact on society and societal relations is, or may be, far greater than in the case of an 'ordinary citizen.' In their contribution, *Nehmelman* and *Vetzo* provide an overview of the tenet of parliamentary immunity and explore the pros and cons of extending this (to extra-parliamentary immunity) in detail. They advocate the extension of the current limited system of parliamentary immunity as laid down in article 71 of the Dutch Constitution. The special position of a politician is also dealt with in the contributions by Ellian, Rummens, Zwart, Sackers and Kwak.

As was mentioned in the foregoing, studying the (penal) legal limits of freedom of speech inevitably leads to the question: What is the purpose of freedom of speech? This is a meta-legal question that cannot be answered if one limits oneself to positive law. Studying positive law (i.e., legislation and jurisprudence) will at best yield a response to the question of what one may and may not say at a certain time, but will not indicate on what basis this is the case. That is the reason why a significant portion of a large number of the contributions are dedicated to legal theoretical and legal philosophical reflections on freedom of speech. In the contributions by Rummens, Molier, Van Noorloos, Nieuwenhuis, Ellian and Kwak, this so-called legal theoretical or legal philosophical context of freedom of speech is explicitly discussed.

Molier argues that freedom of speech cannot be considered an isolated principle, but is part of a political system characterized by the term 'liberal democratic constitutional state.' That does not mean that freedom of speech *itself* is a neutral principle; it is rather part of a certain political system that by definition entails a choice for a certain type of society. Its pillars are individual freedom and equality. The moment freedom of speech is used to realize a type of society that contravenes these individual values of equality and freedom, it undermines, accordingly, its own system. Or, in the words of Noorloos: 'A democratic constitutional state can hardly relativize the value of freedom itself.' In order to subsist as a political-societal legal system, the legal system must, then, necessarily place limits onto freedom of speech, to wit, to the point where said values are in danger of being corrupted by means of freedom of speech. With that in mind, freedom of speech *cannot* be an empty, void principle, but has content. For freedom of speech, this means, in Molier's view, that the line must be drawn at the point where it is used to discriminate against (groups of) persons because of their race, sexual orientation, physical or mental disability, gender or religion. After all, such actions contravene the core values of a liberal democratic constitutional state, to wit, individual freedom and equality (in the sense of individual equal value). In that respect, Molier is a proponent of substantive democracy, or, more accurately, of the theory that states that the liberal democratic constitutional state presupposes some form of militant democracy.[6]

In *Van Noorloos's* contribution, this conception of militant democracy is considered in detail; Nieuwenhuis, too, discusses it in his contribution. Many states have incorporated some sort of militant democracy into their constitutions or laws. In the German legal system, the most elaborate and detailed form of militant democracy can be found. The ECHR is also based on a substantive conception of democracy, evident in article 17, which stipulates

6 About militant democracy in general see: A. Ellian and G. Molier (Eds.), *The State of Exception and Militant Democracy in a Time of Terror*, Dordrecht: Republic of Letters Publishing 2012.

that 'nothing in this Convention may be interpreted as implying for any State, group or person any right to engage in any activity or perform any act aimed at the destruction of any of the rights and freedoms set forth herein or at their limitation to a greater extent than is provided for in the Convention.'

Opposed to this conception is a formal or procedural conception of democracy, as is familiar in the United States of America. This formal conception starts from an alternative approach, maintaining that the government should not judge political convictions, leaving it rather to individuals to decide for themselves whether to do so, or not. Related to this perspective is the idea that in a democracy anything should be allowed to be discussed. Every citizen should, accordingly, be allowed to present his or her viewpoints, whether these should be liberal, racist or anarchistic. In contrast to the substantive conception of democracy, constitutional stipulations and values may not draw a line where political opinions are concerned.

Ellian evinces, in his contribution, to be a supporter of this formal conception of democracy: 'repressive measures do not repel malicious ideas. They can merely restrict the actions of malevolent people. Words and ever more words are like the gladiators that must cross swords in the arena of law and politics.' Freedom of speech should be available to anyone, including the radical defenders of Islam. He draws the line of the penal legal limit of freedom at the point where calls are made to violence or where threats of the same nature are made. His focus is the meaning of politics and the interest of the *possibility* of politics for a liberal democratic constitutional state. Acting and speaking (including writing) are the ways in which politics are shaped in a democratic legal order. In his opinion, the political creates the necessary conditions for freedom to appear, while freedom is an inherently ultimate goal for the political realm. In other words, without a political order, including a legal order, freedom in word and action is unimaginable. Ellian argues that it is precisely because politics in the sense just outlined is so important that the 'responsibility' of parliamentarians does not entail that they should be faced with more restrictions in freedom of speech than artists and columnists.

According to Kwak, politics and law in a democratic society have a different logic. Politicians and lawyers accordingly tend to see the right to freedom of speech in different terms, which is well illustrated by the Wilders case. Kwak refers to Carl Schmitt, who famously presented the distinction between friend and enemy as characteristic of the political domain. Schmitt thought of politics in terms of what later came to be known as *identity politics,* the kind of politics involved when identity-defining characteristics such as race, ethnicity or religion are at stake. In the first part of his contribution, Kwak explores the logic of such politics of recognition and the implications for basic democratic values such as the right to freedom of speech. In the second part of his article, he contrasts this with the egalitarian culture that seems intrinsic to democracy. With Ronald Dworkin, he argues that this egalitarianism comes with the moral obligation to respect the equal dignity of fellow citizens and human beings generally. In The Netherlands, however, this moral obligation has been made into a *legal* obligation as the Dutch Criminal Code penalizes hate speech and incitement to violence and, especially, discrimination against individuals and groups. This latter provision can very well be understood as motivated to make the world safe for democracy by protecting individuals and groups from humiliation and exclusion. In that sense, Kwak appears to be an adherent of a substantive conception of democracy. He is wary, however, of the use of the criminal justice system to defend the egalitarian democratic culture in society, as the use of force and democracy are hard to reconcile.

Rummens, finally, adheres to a substantive conception of democracy as well; however, this does not entail, in his opinion, a conception of militant democracy. Instead, he pleads for a concentric model of democracy, which is capable of dealing with the 'paradox of tolerance' in an original manner, whereby extremists are given much leeway at the periphery of the political system but face decreasing tolerance as they approach the more formal centers of decision-making, such as parliament and government. As a result, the concentric model of democracy endorses a far-reaching legal protection of political speech, but this protection is not unlimited. Adjudication of free speech should focus on real threats posed to the democratic system. According to Rummens, only this threat can constitute a legitimate constraint on the political use of freedom of speech.

Part I
The National Dimension of Freedom of Speech

2 The Curious History of Group Discrimination in the Netherlands

Henny Sackers

Introduction

Most countries have criminal law provisions to avoid public disturbances caused by frictions between population groups. Many Western European countries have opted for a general criminal provision which typically ensues from the constitutional rights to human dignity and equal treatment. In addition, there are often separate criminal provisions making certain aspects of such group discrimination punishable. Traditionally, these have been related to prohibiting blasphemy and/or religious insult. Nevertheless, the development of the more general offence of group discrimination differs sharply from one country to the other and is largely determined by a country's legal and other history, as the following examples show. Under the common law in England, for instance, 'seditious libel' and 'blasphemous libel' have long been crimes, but racial discrimination was not addressed until the Race Relations Act of 1965.[1] Though religious insults and incitement have been offences in Belgium since the 19th century, that country did not adopt separate legislation to combat discrimination until relatively late. A law penalizing specific acts motivated by racism or xenophobia took effect in 1981, followed by the Anti-Discrimination Act in 2003. Yet in no other Western European country does the legal history play such a dominant role as in Germany, where legislation and case law are strongly influenced by Germany's complicated history in the 20th century.[2] Besides including a ban on group defamation, German post-war criminal law contains extensive prohibitions on incitement against population groups and incitement of racial hatred. Religious insults constitute a separate offence in Germany, having already been made punishable in the component German states' criminal law in the 19th century.[3]

Remarkably, none of the above-mentioned countries has made a clear choice to protect minority groups. And except for England, no position has been taken on limiting the

1 Prior to this, excesses could be prosecuted under the Public Order Act 1936, provided the public order was affected.

2 A.J. Nieuwenhuis, *Over de grens van de uitingsvrijheid*, Ars Aqui Libri, Nijmegen, 2011.

3 B.A.M. van Stokkom & H.J.B. Sackers, *Godslastering, discriminerende uitingen wegens godsdienst en haatuitingen*, Boom Juridische uitgevers, The Hague/Meppel, pp. 139-181.

freedom of speech to further the protection of population groups. Contrary to, say, the First Amendment rights in the United States, freedom of speech in Europe is not as protected. In the Netherlands, this has resulted in a diffuse compromise between freedom of speech and non-discrimination. The rather curious history of the Dutch ban on group defamation will be discussed below.

'Roaring Thirties'

Discrimination directed against a particular group of people was made illegal in the Netherlands in Article 137c of the Dutch Penal Code. The provision came about during a tumultuous period in the previous century. Periods such as these sometimes compel legislators to take quick action. That was true for Article 137c. In itself, a fast response by the legislature is not a problem. Every now and then, though, this leads to statutory provisions being formulated which obscure the lawmakers original intentions. The 1930s era was a tumultuous period. The Roaring Twenties were definitely over in Europe, and the continent was on the threshold of a politically uncertain era. Several criminal provisions were enacted in that period which had not previously appeared in the Dutch Penal Code. While the conduct in question had been around for a long time, only then was it included in the Penal Code because the turbulent period had given rise to a need to fight the conduct. Blasphemy, for example, had not been illegal in the Netherlands. However, in the 1930s, serious fear arose around militant Catholics taking the law into their own hands to fight statements, made by Communists, that were increasingly and unmistakably directed against Christian beliefs. This is when the prohibition of blasphemy was included in the Penal Code in 1932. Of course, this did not merely have to do with curbing the threat of 'mob justice'; the social conditions at the time were a major factor, too. Unemployment, poverty and above all political uncertainty were prevalent in the Netherlands, just like elsewhere in Europe. Against this backdrop, a new criminal provision limiting freedom of expression followed shortly after blasphemy was made illegal. The Act of 19 July, 1934 (titled 'Further Regulations to Protect Public Order'), brought on Article 137c, which, in short, made group defamation based on race a criminal act.

It does not seem unreasonable to say that the legislature may have been instrumental once.[4] Although it is doubtful that lawmakers appreciated the seriousness of the developments in Germany, it cannot be denied that portions of the population in the Netherlands were not completely unsympathetic to the core ideas of the new German leaders. Actually, it was only the Jewish community in the Netherlands which perceived the dangers of the

4 The minister later talked about a 'provision which reeked of somewhat opportunistic legislation' (Parliamentary Papers I, Proceedings 1970/71, p. 558).

harsh anti-Semitism. Through a powerful lobby (presumably bolstered by the emergence in 1933 of the National Socialist Movement, a Dutch political party which was openly sympathetic to the German Nazis), they were able to interest the political world in a legislative bill penalizing racial discrimination. The bill was introduced, but it did not pertain primarily to racial discrimination. Although the bill contained a prohibition on insulting people based on race, it was intended more generally to curtail offensive, extremist remarks made by supporters of fascism, national socialism, communism and radical socialism. In government documents, no evidence can be found of a strong vision opposing even a hint of racial discimination. Indeed, in discussing the bill in Parliament, the then-Minister of Justice, Van Schaik, painstakingly avoided any association with anti-Semitic incidents in Germany and used very carefully chosen and guarded wording.[5] The fact that Article 137c was placed in a chapter on 'crimes against public order' is telling: The minister mainly wanted to prevent turmoil in the streets. The minister sought to ensure that there would be no public disturbances, riots or angry mobs, who would openly (in the minister's words), 'with hate and resentment in their hearts,' demonstrate that others had systematically offended their self-respect as a population group. Although the fear of public disturbances had been preceded by the more moralistic argument that discrimination was 'ethically speaking, simply objectionable', 'at odds with Christian charity' and 'went against the country's oldest traditions,' as well as by the argument derived from the Constitution that everyone in the Kingdom of the Netherlands was entitled to equal protection of 'his/her honour and reputation', it was obvious that the minister was ultimately concerned about maintaining public order. Freedom of expression had to yield to this. While it was clear to everyone during the parliamentary debate that the proposed Article 137c was inconsistent with freedom of speech, it was ignored in the discussion and focus was primarily on other parts of the bill, in particular, making insulting comments towards public authorities. After a relatively brief debate in Parliament, Article 137c was added to the Penal Code. It remained there unchanged for nearly 40 years, and, after a sweeping revision in 1971, remains with us to this day.

The Original Article 137c

The 1934 text of Article 137c prohibited intentionally making insulting comments about a population group publicly, orally, in writing or in pictorial form because of that group's race or beliefs. The fact that beliefs were also included as a discrimination ground without much discussion can easily be explained. The role and significance of the Christian religion

5 Parliamentary Papers II, 1933/34, 237. The Dutch government had a vested interest in good relations with Germany. In particular, if war were to break out again in Europe, the Netherlands wanted to maintain its strict neutrality policy, as in World War I.

in Dutch society was immense around 1934. Religion was therefore clustered without much ado under the right to be free from discrimination. This had the striking effect that the adherents of various religious denominations were considered protected minorities. The political debate at this time was characteristically dominated by the specific wish to protect Catholics (who were clearly much less emancipated then). Moreover, the link between race and religion was not at all strange, because this also came into play with Dutch Jews, with whom the terms 'race' and 'religion' were used interchangeably.

Making insulting comments about a population group (defined in the Penal Code as a population group living in the Netherlands) was made punishable. The new criminal provisions immediately generated several important criminal trials, with convictions based on both anti-Semitism and religious discrimination.[6] But that was it;in the period after the Second World War (until 1971), there were hardly any more cases brought before the Dutch criminal courts.

The New York Convention

In 1971, the text of Article 137c was amended when the New York Convention of 7 March 1966 (on eradicating all forms of racial discrimination) was implemented. Lawmakers replaced the phrase 'population group living in the Netherlands' with the more general term 'a group of people' and (though not required by the convention) included the phrase 'the religion or the foundation of their belief system' as well.[7] The feeling was that, in addition to the prohibition of racial discrimination, the same rights should apply to protection from statements representing gross defamation against persons belonging to certain groups or threatening their fundamental legal interests. Religion was classified as such. The explicit mention of 'religion' during the parliamentary debate did not cause any problems. It was generally assumed that the prohibition of religious discrimination already fell under the old criminal provisions and that the new provisions were an unnecessary addition. Rather, the discussion was focused on the issue of whether, by referring to 'race, religion or foundation of their belief system,' the bill had perhaps restricted the scope too much with the new provisions, for it suggested an exhaustive list. Ultimately, this discussion merely resulted in changing the words 'religion or the foundation of their belief system' into the words 'religion or their personal beliefs.' This embodied the collective self-worth which was not to be undermined or discredited. The inquiry into the degree of malice or

6 Dutch Supreme Court, 19 February 1940, 4 March 1940 and 29 April 1940 (*Nederlandse Jurisprudentie* 1940, 754 and 830-831).

7 People expected there to be an international treaty on eradicating religious intolerance. Such a treaty was not adopted, though.

what the malice was directed against was left to the courts. According to members of the government, the court's judgment about what constituted group defamation might be different, depending on the time period and circumstances.

Not everyone was happy. During the parliamentary debate in 1970, MP Roethof criticized what he viewed as the entirely superfluous articles and their broad phrasing. In an amendment, he proposed (in vain) the deletion of 'religion and personal beliefs.' In 1996, the writer Rosier repeated these words about Article 137, concluding: 'It is a strange article, very vague and broadly phrased.'[8]

In taking a look at the substantive parliamentary debate, one cannot escape the feeling that Parliament so fervently wanted to properly regulate the prohibition on racial discrimination that there was not much room for a basic debate about the scope of the ban on religious discrimination. Consequently, a provision was created which, in Rosier's opinion, should have been omitted: 'Nobody can deny an individual in a democratic society the right to find someone else's beliefs, views, religious rites and dogmas, and so forth ridiculous, reprehensible or crazy and to express that opinion, too.'[9] As will be explained below, criticizing religious matters is permissible, but bringing shame on believers is not. The latter will make the critic liable to prosecution.

The Legislative Amendments of 1992, 2003 and 2005

The scope of Article 137c was expanded again in 1992.[10] Insulting a group of people based on their heterosexual or homosexual orientation was made punishable. This legislative amendment resulted from the Dutch government's stringent anti-discrimination policy and the imperative to treat minorities equally. There is not much to say about the parliamentary debate, except that the original idea was to choose the more general term 'sexual orientation,' but this was deemed too restrictive. It is worth pointing out, however, that gender discrimination was not included in Article 137c. This was regarded as placing too much of a burden on freedom of expression. The political discussion led to two objections: Notions about differences between men and women were in practice based too much on one's personal experience, and women were not considered a 'minority group', so protection under the criminal law was unnecessary.

8 T.E. Rosier, '*Discriminerende belediging*', *Recht en kritiek*, No. 22, 1996, p. 305.

9 T.E. Rosier, *Vrijheid van meningsuiting*, Ars Aequi Libri, Nijmegen, 1997, pp. 35-43.

10 Act of 9 October 1991, Bulletin of Acts and Decrees 1991, 623.

For the sake of completeness, the amendment from 2003 should be mentioned, which introduced a second paragraph, detailing the increased penalties for structural discrimination.[11] This amendment was prompted by the fear of verbal abuse by right-extremist organizations.

The statutory amendment of 2005, which also criminalized group defamation based on physical, psychological or mental disability, can likewise be seen within the context of the anti-discrimination policy.[12] There is not much to specifically be said about this amendment, either, except perhaps that Article 137c, which was once an initiative for a prohibition on anti-Semitism in turbulent times, thereby became a catch-all criminal provision. As a result, trying to uncover the rationale for this provision is quite difficult.

THE RATIONALE UNDERLYING ARTICLE 137C

Article 137c currently reads as follows:

> 'A person who makes intentionally insulting comments publicly, orally, in writing or in pictorial form about a group of people because of their race, their religion, their belief system, their heterosexual or homosexual orientation or their physical, psychological or mental disability shall be punished by imprisonment of no more than a year or a fine of the third category.'

The assumption is that at issue here is an offence which must be stopped to prevent social disruption and to protect society against unrest and disorder. The classic rationale underlying Article 137c is closely associated with the New York Convention. Under the principles of that convention, any form of racial discrimination became impermissible. The problem with the convention was that it only had to do with combatting racial discrimination. The ban on religious discrimination was added by the Dutch legislature. The parliamentary debate around these provisions since 1971 implies that lawmakers envisaged equal protection against insults towards a group of people based on their religion, later expanded to include sexual orientation and disability. The original rationale, protecting the public order, has thus been diluted. The goal now seems rather to be protection from gross defamation aimed at persons belonging to certain groups. Further, the criminal provision seems intended in part to eliminate unjustifiable inequality in Dutch society. Strangely, though, the article likewise offers protection to non-vulnerable majority groups, such as heterosexuals.

11 Act of 20 November 2003, Bulletin of Acts and Decrees 2003, 480.

12 Act of 10 March 2005, Bulletin of Acts and Decrees 2005, 111.

Given the ambiguity which the Dutch legislature has created, it seems prudent to go back to the basis of the offence. The rationale must be to diminish the risk of objectionable statements, made intentionally to hurt a group of people and/or disrupt the public order, in the sense that there is a realistic chance that chaos will erupt. The nature of the concept of 'public order', in my opinion, also suggests that it is up to the government (rather than individual citizens), to assess whether statements may potentially disrupt the public order in a dangerous way.

A Few Components

A few components of the crime 'group defamation' will be discussed below, but only insofar as they have expanded from the original meaning of Article 137c through case law or otherwise notably differ from the legislative intention. The component 'orally, in writing or in pictorial form' will not be examined. This component is not distinctive to Article 137c (it can also be found in various other statutory provisions) and does not cause many problems in practice. The most problematic aspects in court cases involving Article 137c are related to proving the components 'publicly', 'making insulting comments' and 'about a group of people.'

Oddly, few problems arise when the case has to do with the original purpose of fighting racial discrimination, for there is not much to say about 'race'. 'Race,' the Dutch Supreme Court teaches us, must be interpreted in accordance with the convention.[13] Likewise, the 'religion or personal beliefs' component does not lead to any problems. The legislative history shows that legislators were not only thinking about Christianity or Judaism, but about all religions which acknowledge the existence of a god or supernatural being, and even less common religions and religions in which a divinity or supernatural being is less self-evident. If a religion is not involved, there may nonetheless be impermissible comments directed at personal beliefs, that is, basic ideas about life which are not based on a belief in a god.[14] There are no known court decisions yet providing guidance on the substance of the most recent grounds, 'heterosexual or homosexual orientation' and 'disability.'[15]

13 Dutch Supreme Court, 15 June 1976 (*Nederlandse Jurisprudentie* 1976, 551).

14 The convictions of animal activists, ecologists and natural healers do not fall under either 'belief systems' or 'political beliefs'; see, for example, The Hague Court of Appeal, 19 May 2003 (ECLI:NL:GHSGR:2003:AF8921).

15 Except that transsexuality is not included under this, Leeuwarden Court of Appeal, 13 January 1995 (*Nederlandse Jurisprudentie* 1995, 243).

PUBLICLY

The first component which is noteworthy is 'publicly.' Case law and literature indicate that it is necessary for a supposed discriminatory remark to be made *at* a public location or at a public gathering. It is sufficient for this to occur at locations or during gatherings or activities which are open in nature, where there is a public or there are people, and the public character of which the accused should have been aware to a greater or lesser degree. Because of this interpretation, the 'open character' requirement will be satisfied fairly easily, so that comments on websites or in social media will indisputably fall under this component.[16] One example is a situation in which a politician made certain statements during a speech, while he was aware of the press being in the audience. He said that he had not really given this any thought, and *that*, so the Supreme Court held, supported the conclusion that when he recognized several journalists, he deliberately accepted the considerable chance that his comments would be published.[17] Still, even without any journalist present, statements may make their way into the media. Handing out a copy of a speech, for instance, constitutes sufficient proof that the insulting comments were made publicly.[18] In contrast, a letter sent to a limited circle of people does not represent adequate evidence of discrimination 'in public.'[19] What is important then, is bringing the statement to the public's attention. Factors which are relevant here include the scope of the circle of persons to whom the statement was made; the position or capacity of those to whom the statement was made; the lack of any prior involvement between the persons to whom the statement was made and the person making the statement; the degree to which, because of its form or content, the statement could be called confidential; the extent to which the statement lent itself to communicating the content outside the circle of persons to whom the statement was directly targeted; the degree to which the statement, due to the manner in which it was made (orally, by letter, by e-mail, by posting on a website accessible to others, etc.), could be seen by others besides the persons directly addressed; and the chance that the content of the statement would be disclosed to other people besides those to whom the statement was directly targeted.[20]

The public character of a comment is key in proving that one's intention was to insult. This was shown (once again) in a remarkable decision made by the Supreme Court in

16 Regarding group defamation through the Internet, see Amsterdam Court of Appeal, 23 November 2009 (ECLI:NL:GHAMS:2009:BK4139) and Arnhem Court of Appeal, 19 August 2010 (ECLI:NL:GHARN:2010:BN4204).

17 Dutch Supreme Court, 29 May 2001 (ECLI:NL:HR:2001:AB1818).

18 Dutch Supreme Court, 2 April 2002 (ECLI:NL:HR:2002:AD8693).

19 Dutch Supreme Court, 30 October 2001 (ECLI:NL:HR:2001:AB3143); 5 April 2005 (ECLI:NL:HR:2005:AS8465).

20 Dutch Supreme Court, 22 April 2014 (ECLI:NL:HR:2014:952).

2003.[21] During a story about intolerance in an urban neighbourhood, a radio reporter had rung the doorbell at a house which had been designated to a Somalian family who had fled to the Netherlands. Neighbors had harassed the family to such an extent that they left the neighborhood. In response to the reporter's questions, the new resident mentioned that she would take action again if another Somalian family came to live in the neighborhood. She would put up a banner reading: 'Hitler forgot a few folks.' She immediately realized that she had said something stupid and was sorry. She swore that this was not her intention and she did not want her comments to be broadcast – in vain, because the comments were broadcast, and the woman was convicted under Article 137c by the court. In essence, the court ruled that the existence of malice is to be assessed solely based on the time at which the statement was made. According to the lower court, it did not matter that after the incident, but before the broadcast, the woman had indicated that she wanted to correct her statement and did not want it to be publicized in its original form. The court's view, however, was wrong, in the Supreme Court's opinion. The defendant argued that it was not her intention that the remarks in question be made public. This decision is intriguing because it allows for, so to speak, a kind of voluntary recanting of an offence which (in the legislature's vision) it is hard to imagine an 'attempted' version of.

Making Insulting Comments

The Dutch Parliament examined at length why the government did not opt to include the word 'discrimination' in the criminal provisions, but instead stuck with 'making insulting comments.' The New York Convention did not mandate this. The reasoning is not persuasive, but silenced the protests, partly because of the simultaneous introduction of a statutory article which contained a definition of discrimination derived from the New York Convention. The parliamentary debate brought about uniformity in the literature and case law on the meaning of 'making insulting comments.' A group's self-worth must be undermined or the group must be discredited *because* the group is of a certain race or religion. The group must have been insulted, aggrieved or needlessly hurt because of the remarks. 'Making insulting comments' here means making objectionable, discriminatory statements. Criticizing a particular religion is explicitly not punishable. Literature and case law are also in general agreement about this. The criminal action against the controversial Dutch politician Geert Wilders, who publicly and repeatedly made disparaging comments about Islam, makes clear how thin the line is here.[22] Fierce criticism can cause people to feel

21 Dutch Supreme Court, 30 September 2003 (ECLI:NL:HR:2003:AG3813).

22 Amsterdam District Court, 23 June 2011 (ECLI:NL:RBAMS:2011:BQ9001). For an in-depth analysis, see L.C. Groen & M.C. Stronks, *Entangled Rights of Freedom: freedom of speech, freedom of religion and the non-discrimination principle in the Dutch Wilders case*, Eleven International Publishing, The Hague, 2010.

aggrieved, but this is not enough to establish that the 'group' as a whole has been discriminated against. In judging these cases, courts are caught between a rock and a hard place, on the one hand, by closely analyzing the context in which the statements were made and, on the other hand, by holding fast to the requisite intent which the defendant must have to discriminate against a group of people.

About a Group of People

While the protection originally focused on a population group in the Netherlands, after the law was amended in 1971, the insults could also be felt by groups of people located outside the Netherlands. This meant the introduction of a component which was fairly simple to prove: 'About a group of people.' If it can be established that the group can be recognized as a collective, this is sufficient proof. The Supreme Court's decision of 2009 (titled: 'The cancer that is Islam'), relevant in this connection, will be discussed later on.

The inquiry into the size of the group is somewhat academic. Should it consist of, say, more than two people? A numerical answer cannot be given. Above, I argued that discriminatory conduct was made a crime in order to protect the public order. In the case of discrimination against three people who supposedly form a 'group,' it is difficult to maintain that public order in the Netherlands will be shaken to its core. In other words, the group must be big enough that, if the group is offended, public order will be seriously at risk. Nonetheless, although the insulting comments may have specifically been made against a single individual, it might still be clear to everyone that, due to their nature and scope, the comments may have been directed towards an entire group.[23] The parameters of the group are determined further by the grounds of discrimination. It should be noted, though, that lawmakers originally thought of groups of people vulnerable within society and who thus deserved protection. Groups of people who, because of the nature of their group, were sufficiently resilient did not need protection under criminal law. By enacting the prohibition on discrimination against heterosexuals (and not including the ground 'gender'), the legislators chipped away at this guiding principle.

23 Dutch Supreme Court, 26 June 1984 (*Nederlandse Jurisprudentie* 1985, 40).

Case Law

It has already been pointed out that Article 137c hardly generated any case law, at least not until 1972. This situation has not changed significantly since then.[24] The case law which does exist has concentrated on the components discussed above. In this section, some cases will be discussed which, from a legal-historical standpoint, are key.

The first case involves a 1952 decision by the Amsterdam Court of Appeal about the book '*Ik heb altijd gelijk* [*I'm Always Right*]' by the Dutch novelist W.F. Hermans.[25] The book contained an excerpt which caused Hermans to be charged with insulting Catholics. In the novel, there is a character who, during the course of the story, is presented as a 'sleazy, alcoholic psychopath who is demoted in the army because of corruption' and who returns to the Netherlands after the failed military campaigns in the former Dutch colony of Indonesia. As the ship approaches the Dutch coastline, the man cries out:

> 'I spit on all of it, on all of you, on Sukarno, on the Queen, on everything. I don't give a shit about any of it. Catholics! They're the most filthy, stinking, underhanded, fucked-up group in our country! But they keep on screwing like there's no tomorrow! They go on reproducing! Like rabbits, rats, fleas, lice! They don't emigrate! They just stay here with their pimply cheeks and teeth rotted from eating Communion wafers!'

Hermans defended himself in court by asserting that a writer cannot be held accountable for what he makes the characters in his novel say. The public prosecutor pleaded for acquittal, which the court granted, finding:

> 'The incriminating passage was in no way utilized in such a way that a detached reader would have to gain the impression that the writer agreed with its content and adopted as his own the aforementioned insulting comments of the person appearing in the novel fragment.'

This acquittal was affirmed on appeal. And it was the last time that criminal actions based on religious discrimination were brought on.[26]

24 Special issue: '*Uitingsdelicten en discriminatie*', *Strafblad*, No. 5, 2007. See also C. Brants, R.S.B. Kool, A. Ringnalda, *Strafbare discriminatie*, Boom Juridische uitgevers, The Hague, 2008.

25 Amsterdam Court of Appeal, 18 December 1952 (unpublished), discussed by J. de Hullu, *Ars Aequi*, Vol. 33, No. 5, 1984, pp. 754-755.

26 The case law remained silent, but the events in 1987 surrounding the intended production of Fassbinder's play '*Garbage, the City, and Death*' in the Netherlands were anything but quiet. The Jewish community felt that the play was anti-Semitic and were furious. After a private staging of the play, further performance of

This was not the case for prosecutions for racial discrimination. Aside from a few cases in which derogatory texts about the Antillean, Surinamese and Moroccan communities were scrutinized,[27] racial discrimination seems to have primarily affected Dutch Jews. As already pointed out, when it comes to Dutch Jews, the terms 'racial' and 'religious' discrimination have been used interchangeably. This is apparent from cases relating to (in brief) denial of the Holocaust and/or the ridicule of various aspects of it.[28] These cases are not so much about people who are merely adherents of the Jewish faith, but about all Jews. Comments are punishable if a direct and repugnant link is made between Jews and Nazi ideology or Jews are otherwise needlessly offended.[29] A few examples can be given. In 1983, criminal proceedings were filed against '*De Bazuin*.'[30] *De Bazuin* [the Trumpet] was a magazine in which an article appeared by someone named Van Gelder, who, paraphrasing a Jewish publicist, had written that:

> 'A typical characteristic of closed religious communities, of "chosen people", is that the religion is wrapped up in laws and rules and that the community members almost automatically want and perhaps help the outside world to go to hell. Such 'religions' ought to be done away with.'

The Arnhem District Court found that '*De Bazuin* had struck a false note' and maintained that Jews had been insulted by reason of their religion. *De Bazuin* was acquitted on appeal, because the mere fact that the publication had been perceived as hurtful was insufficient in proving that the defendant had intended to insult a group of people on account of their religion or race. The Supreme Court upheld the acquittal, despite there not having been a ruling whether the defendant had been acquitted of discrimination based on race or religion. The synchronous handling of race and religion was bolstered once the defendant claimed that it sought to make a contribution to the public debate about Jews, Palestine, the Holocaust and revisionism and that all of this occurred within the frameworks of

---

it was impossible. In 2000, intense criticism by Islamic circles in the Netherlands caused the opera '*Aisha and the Women of Medina*' to end early. This resulted in questions in Parliament and the announcement of a lawsuit, which was, however, never filed. Fassbinder's play was later staged in the Netherlands in 2002 without incident.

27 For example, 'Europe will always be a continent for whites', 'Ali and Mustapha, go back to Ankara', East Netherlands District Court, 26 February 2013 (ECLI:NL:RBONE:2013:BZ2390); 'Coupon: free trip to Morocco', The Hague Court of Appeal, 11 February 2009 (ECLI:NL:GHSGR:2009:BH2481). Negative remarks about the Roma community were examined in Amsterdam District Court, 23 February 2006 (ECLI:NL:RBAMS:2006:AV2447).

28 See F. Janssens, '*De ontkenning van 'Auschwitz' en de strafwet*', *Delikt en Delinkwent*, Vol. 28, 1998, pp. 565-578.

29 Arnhem Court of Appeal, 4 June 1982 (*Nederlandse Jurisprudentie* 1983, 422); Dutch Supreme Court, 10 September 1985 and 27 October 1985 (*Nederlandse Jurisprudentie* 1986, 164 and 1988, 538).

30 Dutch Supreme Court, 16 December 1986 (*Nederlandse Jurisprudentie* 1987, 534).

Article 10 of the European Convention on Human Rights.[31] Another decision by the Supreme Court represents a variation on this theme. The defence argued that the slogan 'Hamas, Hamas, give the Jews the gas,' which football fans had chanted in public, was part of their culture. Therefore, this should not be looked at as group defamation. The lower court did not deem that assertion plausible, arguing that the frequent use of the slogan did not in itself mean that the slogan was part of the culture. The Supreme Court found that the fact that this slogan was an element of the culture of football fans, who did not intend to insult Jewish people, did not preclude a conviction.[32]

The 2009 Supreme Court decision (sadly referred to as the 'The cancer that is Islam' case) has already been mentioned above.[33] The accused had hung up a poster in a window in his home which read:

> 'Stop the cancer that is Islam. Theo van Gogh died for us; who'll be next? Resist! We won't bow down to Allah!'

The defendant was found guilty of group defamation. The court ruled that, by calling Islam a cancer, the defendant had made needlessly hurtful comments about Islam and, hence, made the connection between Islam and its believers - the group of persons practicing this religion. On appeal, the Supreme Court declared that Article 137c only pertains to insulting groups of people because of their religion, race and so forth. The criminal provision was not based on protection of an individual's intimate religious life. The mere fact that the adherents of a particular religion feel hurt by offensive comments about the religion does not equate to comments insulting this group of people on account of their religion.

Contextual Review

In assessing speech offences, courts tend to look at the context in order to determine whether the comments have been made for the sole purpose of participating in the public debate about a historical and/or social issue, and whether the comments were nevertheless needlessly hurtful. This assessment can be seen in a decision by the Supreme Court in 2001.[34] The case related to statements which a former politician of a Christian party had made in an interview. He had said:

31 For example, Den Bosch District Court, 21 December 2004 (ECLI:NL:RBSHE:2004:AR7891), in which the defendant posted on his website a text titled 'The Holocaust which never happened', including a translation of the book '*Did Six Million Really Die?*' by Richard E. Harwood.

32 Dutch Supreme Court, 15 September 2009 (ECLI:NL:HR:2009:BI4739).

33 Dutch Supreme Court, 10 March 2009 (ECLI:NL:HR:2009:BF0655).

34 Dutch Supreme Court, 9 January 2001 (ECLI:NL:HR:2001:AA9368).

> 'We Christians have developed a really nasty trait: We are wrong to make gradations in God's commandments. As if you can be bad and less bad! Yet why should stealing, for example, nicking benefits from the government, be less bad than sins against the Seventh Commandment? Indeed, why should a practising homosexual be better than a thief?'

The Court of Appeal acquitted the politician, finding that although these statements in themselves were insulting, the insulting character was removed by the context in which and the intention with which they were made, because the politician had simply thereby been illustrating his religious convictions. The acquittal, the Supreme Court reasoned, did not represent an incorrect interpretation of the criminal provisions, as the reference to fraud and theft served to explain the view, rooted in the politician's religious convictions, that the homosexual lifestyle was just as sinful. The Supreme Court delved into the interpretation of Article 137c once again in 2003.[35] In a letter to the editor of a newspaper, a clergyman had described, *inter alia*, homosexuality as a 'sick and loathsome sin,' invoking the Bible as justification for this opinion. The lower court followed the line of case law developed until then. The court concluded that, in itself and apart from the context, the comment was insulting to homosexuals, but that it lost its insulting character when the comment was placed within the framework of the clergyman's profession of his faith and because of his intention, namely, to warn humanity. The clergyman was acquitted. The Supreme Court ruled that Article 137c had not been interpreted incorrectly, since the clergyman's remarks were obviously relevant to the social debate and not needlessly hurtful.[36] Using this template, a lower court rendered a judgment about an Internet columnist who, supposedly as a pastor to a virtual Christian community, had written a column in February 2004 in response to the commotion about the film '*The Passion of the Christ*.' The writer suspected that the filmmaker had deleted an offensive section from the movie at the request of a number of prominent Jewish individuals. Two sentences in the column constituted the crux of the indictment. The first sentence read, 'Yet another group of lawless Jews afraid of being exposed, is what I often think then.' The court felt that, within the context, this sentence had to be regarded as a contribution to the social debate,

35 Dutch Supreme Court, 14 January 2003 (ECLI:NL:HR:2003:AE7632).

36 In a similar case, an imam who had made negative comments about homosexuals in a television program was found not guilty (The Hague Court of Appeal, 18 November 2002, ECLI:NL:GHSGR:2002:AF0667). The same result occurred for a police officer who had written rather crass statements in a newspaper about same-sex marriage (Dutch Supreme Court, 9 January 2001, ECLI:NL:HR:2001:AA9367). In Amsterdam Court of Appeal, 11 March 2013 (ECLI:NL:GHAMS:2013:BZ3787), the court acquitted a politician who had said on local television, 'Amsterdam yearns for a gorgeous heterosexual Adam and Eve couple.' A letter to the editor in which the writer had lashed out at asylum seekers was at issue in Dutch Supreme Court, 15 April 2003 (*Nederlandse Jurisprudentie* 2003, 334). The writer had written the letter in response to the murder of a young woman and to express his dissatisfaction about the fact that the residents of an asylum seekers' centre had not been investigated by the police. The comments were deemed insulting in this context.

so that the insulting nature of the comment disappeared. The court felt differently about the second sentence, which read, 'Yes, my friends, Jews today thus still behave like animals.' Even in the broader context of the social debate, this comparison could not withstand the test of criticism, and the defendant was found guilty.[37] A columnist who had written 'that it hasn't really been cool since the Nazi era to say negative things about Jews, but sometimes I can actually understand why the situation got so bad in 1937,' was acquitted for this statement, because the statement was made in a column, which typically amounts to a brief, relatively superficial and somewhat ironic analysis, in which exaggeration is nothing out of the ordinary.[38] In a subsequent case from 2012, the defendant had published a cartoon on the Internet, which, the lower court held, was in itself insulting to Jews because of their race. The cartoon essentially accused the Jews of exaggerating the Holocaust. The defence argued that, in the cartoons, the defendant had sought to demonstrate the difference between assessing insults against Muslims and insults against Jews. The court found that the context of a comment which is in principle insulting may remove its insulting character, but this context must then be readily apparent to third parties. Moreover, even if the context is clear, one must still determine whether the comment was needlessly hurtful. In the court's view, that was the case here. Hence, the defendant's purely subjective intention is not decisive in evaluating the context; rather, what matters is whether this context is apparent to third parties. The Supreme Court agreed.[39] In another instance of group defamation, a website administrator had posted self-written pieces on the site with passages which were highly insulting to Muslims. The court convicted the writer, because there was no conceivable context whatsoever and the remarks (given their offensive nature) did not further any social debate and did not fall by any stretch of the imagination under an artistic or humoristic exception. The Supreme Court upheld this conviction as well.[40]

A 2001 Supreme Court decision on the liability under criminal law of another writer, the author of the book '*Danslessen* [*Dance Lessons*]' is interesting as well.[41] This book included passages allegedly insulting to Jews. One of the characters in the book had stated, 'But, yeah, what do you expect, with a Jew like that at the top?' Rumour had it that this was an unmistakable reference to the mayor of the Dutch town of Zandvoort. The lower court acquitted the writer, because, in principle, a writer should not be held accountable for statements by a character in the writer's novel. The court thus followed the reasoning of the decision on W. F. Hermans's novel. On appeal, the Supreme Court emphasized that freedom of artistic expression is extremely important, but is limited by the interests of

37 Amsterdam District Court, 25 January 2006 (ECLI:NL:RBAMS:2006:AV2201).
38 Amsterdam Court of Appeal, 17 February 2010 (ECLI:NL:GHAMS:2010:BL4528).
39 Dutch Supreme Court, 27 March 2012 (ECLI:NL:HR:2012:BV5623).
40 Dutch Supreme Court, 26 June 2012 (ECLI:NL:HR:2012:BW9189).
41 Dutch Supreme Court, 9 October 2001 (ECLI:NL:HR:2001:ZD2776).

third parties.[42] The limits depend on the circumstances of the case. Considered in isolation, portions of a book may perhaps be insulting, but they will lose that aspect due to the nature and effect of the book and the character's role in the book making the insulting comments. The Supreme Court itself then examined the content of the book. It rejected the appeal, concluding that the challenged excerpts were related to an uproarious scene, which was indisputably not based on reality, and that, in light of the nature and effect of the novel and its other content, the excerpts were not deemed discriminatory or insulting.

THE VALUE OF CONTEXTUAL REVIEW

In a comment to one of the Supreme Court decisions discussed above, Rotterdam criminal law professor Mevis noted that, under this string of case law, the substantive criminal law falsely promises more protection than it can actually offer. This comment seems to be correct. Although convictions were still frequent in the 1980s and 1990s, more recent cases have pronounced one acquittal after another. How can this be explained? The legal literature does not indicate any change in opinion about the applicability of the criminal provisions about group defamation. It is striking, though, that the decisions discussed above mainly dealt with discrimination based on sexual orientation and not, as in the preceding period, insults based on race (primarily the Jewish race). The explanation cannot lie in race discrimination being considered more worthy of punishment. While that might lead to differences in the punishment imposed, it would not explain the acquittals. What's more, the legislature placed 'race, religion, sexual orientation and disability' on the same footing in Article 137c. The acquitted individuals (the clergyman, imam, politician and religious policeman) notably all had strong religious motivations, however. Still, this is not a convincing argument, because other convicted people had an equally strong religious motivation.[43] The only explanation seems to pertain to the contextual review. Was this contextual review wrong? I do not think so, because such review safeguards against overly broad limitations on freedom of speech.[44] The review prohibits 'thoughtless or haphazard' group defamation. Freedom of speech affords protection, so long as the statement was made in a particular context. In the clergyman case, that context was deemed present, because the

42 Court decisions on freedom of artistic expression for cartoonists seem to have become more unpredictable: Utrecht District Court, 22 April 2010 (ECLI:NL:RBUTR:2010:BM1984); Arnhem Court of Appeal, 19 August 2010 (ECLI:NL:GHARN:2010:BN4204). See E. Dommering, '*De dubbele moraal van het groepsbeledigen in cartoons*', *Nederlands Juristenblad*, 2010, Vol. 35, No.1800, pp. 2264-2268.

43 This was the case involving the evangelical spouses Goeree. See B.P. Vermeulen, '*De Goerees en de kardinaal, ofwel: vrijheid van godsdienst versus discriminatieverbod*', in L. Heyde *et al.* (Ed.), *Begrensde vrijheid*, Tjeenk Willink, Zwolle 1992, pp. 258-278.

44 One drawback to such review is that 'the context' has a diffuse framework and is subject to the character of the times and therefore to public opinion as well. Consequently, it is difficult to predict when a person will enjoy freedom of speech in the one case and be liable to criminal prosecution in another case.

comments 'were obviously related to the expression of his religious convictions,' and because his intention was clearly 'to warn humanity.' The context in the imam's case was that 'the challenged textual fragments served to explain his opinion, rooted in his Islamic religious convictions, about the sinful nature of the homosexual lifestyle.' The policeman had placed his remarks within the framework of the public debate on same-sex marriage and had shown that his remarks had been inspired by the Bible. The columnist's acquittal had to do with the fact that cynicism is rather common in columns. And, with the man who had written a letter to the editor, there was no proper context, apparently because he was just a newspaper reader who wanted to vent his displeasure through the letter sent in for publication.

THE PUBLIC DEBATE

The aforementioned case law shows that courts look at the context and, based on this, determine whether the comments should be considered to have been made within a public debate.[45] As stated above, contextual review is a safeguard against overly broad regulation of freedom of expression. If the protection is found in the participation in public debate, further analysis is required, at least if, for the sake of public interest, it is necessary to draw a clear line in the social debate.[46] After all, determining whether there is a public debate is always tricky, as is the question of who, under which circumstances, should determine the outline of this debate. The reference to public debate seems to come from case law by the European Court of Human Rights.[47] The European Court has instructed that there must be ample room in public debate (sometimes called 'social debate') for robust comments to be made. Everyone can agree on this, provided 'robust' is not automatically synonymous with 'rude.'[48] Where the Court has addressed comments which may 'offend, shock or disturb,' the Court seems to have been thinking more about the content rather than the form or wording. However, this is an assumption, which is supported to some extent in the case law by lower courts. Although no uniform criteria can be derived from this case law about what constitutes (participation in) a public debate, the case law does provide several strong clues. However, it is important to stress the significance of the 'in public' component discussed above. For group insults to be punishable, they must be expressed publicly. There are no distinctions here. The protective scope consequently must arise from the character

45 Special issue: '*Het publieke debat*', *Strafblad*, No. 7, 2009.

46 Amsterdam Court of Appeal, 21 January 2009 (ECLI:NL:GHAMS:2009:BH0496).

47 'Political speech or a debate on questions of public interest', *inter alia* in European Court of Human Rights, 26 April 1979 (*Sunday Times v. UK*, Appl. 6538/74); see also A.J. Nieuwenhuis, '*Godsdienstvrijheid en bijdragen aan het maatschappelijk debat*', *NJCM-bulletin*, Vol. 29, No. 2, 2004, pp. 154 *et seq.*

48 Simply using 'particularly strong terms' does not further a social debate, Amsterdam District Court, 2 June 2008 (ECLI:NL:RBAMS:2008:BD2977).

of the debate. Linguistically speaking, a 'debate' is a public exchange of ideas subject to rules. The dictionary does not indicate specifically what those rules entail. The classic example of a debate, though, is a speech being made, with the speaker giving his/her audience the chance to respond and to engage in a discussion with him/her and/or other people in the audience. 'Debating' is arguing, discussing and exchanging ideas. 'Debate' is not a pejorative term; the purpose of a debate is to elevate the subject to a higher level through counter-argumentation or to introduce nuances into the discussion. With respect to the rules which participants in a social debate need to abide by, criminologist Van Stokkom wrote the following:

> 'Respect and decency must be stressed. The rules developed within the disciplines of classic philosophy and rhetoric may largely be utilized in this regard. Within these traditions, a lot of attention is given to the moral limits of the debate and the internal moral principles binding the advocate and opponent to each other. The parties are mutually dependent on one another, if only to gain the public's confidence; excessive eagerness or exaggeration should be punished.'[49]

Still today, this reasoning is supported in lower-court case law. In each instance, the court's point of departure is that a lot may be freely said in public debate in order to discuss topics.[50] After that, however, there are limits. A debate must involve a substantive discussion, in which socially accepted limits are not violated.[51] The content may not be *more* hurtful than is justified by the debate; the statements must at any rate add to the communication.[52] There will be no added value if the statements are merely successive comments.[53] Simply persisting in and unnecessarily repeating a position taken earlier does not really have much to do with debating, either. A debate is going on once one responds to unjust criticism, or once verbal or other attacks need to be parried.[54]

An appeal to adhere to standards of decency is what resonates most in this brief summary of the case law. If the debater loses sight of this, there is no longer a public debate, only public screaming. The debate should not protect the person screaming the loudest.[55]

49 Van Stokkom & Sackers, 2007, pp. 234-235.

50 For example, Arnhem Court of Appeal, 9 September 2008 (ECLI:NL:GHARN:2008:BF7596).

51 Den Bosch District Court, 19 July 2005 (ECLI:NL:RBSHE:2005:AT0494). See also Amos N. Guiora, *Freedom from religion, the limits of freedom of speech*, University Press, Oxford, 2009.

52 See Advocate General Machielse's Opinion in Dutch Supreme Court, 10 March 2009 (ECLI:NL:PHR:2009:BF0655).

53 Amsterdam Court of Appeal, 17 February 2010 (ECLI:NL:GHAMS:2010:BL4528).

54 Amsterdam Court of Appeal, 20 June 2008 (ECLI:NL:GHAMS:2008.BD7024).

55 Amsterdam Court of Appeal, 21 July 2008 (ECLI:NL:GHAMS:2008:BD9027).

PROFESSIONAL DEBATERS

Professional participants (including politicians) have, on the one hand, more manoeuvring room, but on the other hand, greater responsibility.[56] Like other professional debaters, politicians are subject to a '*Garantenstellung.*'[57] Standards of decency apply to them without any limitation. But is it conceivable that it is the subject matter that determines the nature of a public debate? Earlier, court decisions were discussed in which religious leaders had expressed opinions about same-sex marriage. They were entitled to protection, because they had entered into the debate based on their religious or social views. The same holds true for politicians. They, too, may broach subjects which are part of a public debate from their religious-political perspectives. Same-sex marriage, which was a hot item at the time, was indisputably such a subject. When the politician Wilders released the film '*Fitna*' (which sharply attacked Islam), the issue of integration was a hot topic. The question is whether the reverse holds true as well. Should politicians, based on their political but non-religious ideologies, be allowed to elevate subjects to a 'public debate' outside their representative bodies? In the past (1983), a court made a distinction for politicians between statements made in Parliament and remarks made outside of this, such as in the press or on websites.[58] That distinction has faded.[59] Courts have said that politicians in a free society, especially if the politicians are members of opposition parties, ought to be able to articulate their opinions freely. Courts seem to take the 'public debate' route rather quickly, especially if the accent is on exercising control over government bodies or exposing social wrongs. There seems to be less latitude for politicians concerning matters relating to, in particular, religion. Appearances can be deceiving, however. Comments on religion, even insulting ones, may be expressed in a public debate. These comments are inevitability interwoven with socially relevant issues, and it is difficult for courts to make distinctions here. Religious insults which are hurtful, but which at the same time contribute to the public debate, merit protection. The same applies to statements about sexual orientation, but less so about disability and hardly at all about race. The main problem seems to be with politicians who wish to claim the protection of public debate when employing 'sub-texts'.[60] Nobody can object to a public discussion about immigration policy or integration problems.

---

56 Rick Lawson, '*Wild, wilder, wildst, over de ruimte die het EVRM laat voor de vervolging van kwetsende politici*', *NJCM-Bulletin*, Vol. 33, No. 4, 2008, p. 472 *et. seq.*

57 Derived from German law, the term '*Garantenstellung*' refers to the extra responsibility which may be expected from a professional. A private participant in an Internet forum is not a professional and is not engaging in political speech, Amsterdam Court of Appeal, 23 November 2009 (ECLI:NL:GHAMS:2009:BK4139).

58 Dutch Supreme Court, 24 June 1983 (*Nederlandse Jurisprudentie* 1984, 801).

59 See T. Zwart, '*Wilders, ja toestaan!*', *Nederlands Juristenblad* 2009, 271; E. Prakken, '*Wilders: verbieden of toestaan*', *Nederlands Juristenblad* 2009, 270.

60 Term borrowed from Buruma in his comment in Amsterdam Court of Appeal, 21 January 2009 (*Nederlandse Jurisprudentie* 2009, 191).

Nonetheless, a politician is expected to be aware of the responsibility of making a socially acceptable contribution to the public debate. Obviously, incitement to violence or hatred and needlessly hurtful remarks are socially unacceptable, even when uttered indirectly.[61] The Dutch debating culture needs to be based on a large measure of tolerance for one another's opinions. Religious believers are expected to understand the sentiments prevailing in the Netherlands regarding their beliefs. Debaters are expected to conduct a fair debate – no veiled language, no statements used as a cover for punishable group defamation and no suggestive texts.

CONCLUSION

The history of the Dutch statutory article criminalizing group defamation might be called curious, indeed even a bit odd. The offence arose from the desire to combat anti-Semitism immediately, although this goal was concealed. The historical analysis is odd from a legislative standpoint. Specifically, lawmakers have amended the statute four times, giving the impression with the recent addition of new discrimination grounds that Article 137c has become a catch-all offence. Not only have minority groups who deserve protection been included, but also groups who do not need protection under criminal law. Which new discrimination ground will be next, 'Banking orientation'?[62] Partly because of this, the underlying rationale is doomed to be forgotten. Article 137c is an offence involving the risk of harm, which protects against potential unrest on the streets. Yet Article 137c is odd in terms of the case law, too. Two crucial points become evident from the analysis: The contextual review which, in my opintion, is useful in protecting the freedom of speech and, in connection, the protection regarding participation in the public debate. The latter point similarly threatens to give rise to a 'catch-all' defence. If criminal prosecution is imminent because of group defamation, the accused may escape this by claiming participation in the public debate. What exactly constitutes a 'public debate' is not apparent; the case law is still looking for a criterion. Various court decisions hint that a public debate must involve a substantive discussion. In the case against the politician Wilders, the Amsterdam Court of Appeal held that the public interest necessitates drawing a clear line. That line seems to have been drawn in another Dutch criminal provision, to wit, in the prohibition on incitement to violence, hatred, intolerance and/or needlessly offending people. The European Court allows shocking comments to be made. The Dutch Supreme

61 Dutch Supreme Court, 16 April 1996 (*Nederlandse Jurisprudentie* 1996, 627), 2 May 1995 (*Nederlandse Jurisprudentie* 1995, 621), 18 May 1999 (*Nederlandse Jurisprudentie* 1999, 634) and 23 November 2010 (ECLI:NL:HR:2010:BM9132).

62 In connection with the proposal to criminalize a call for a 'bank run', see W.F. Korthals Altes, '*Ik wist niet dat ik het in me had*', *Nederlands Juristenblad*, 2011, 731.

Court has translated this as 'sharp criticism.' The lower courts seem to interpret this primarily as a duty to avoid disproportionate language in the public debate. The judgment in the Wilders case shows that a statement *right at* the edge is the most which is permissible. Freedom of speech is essential to public debate. The debate is not conducted fairly, however, if there is inappropriate criticism, such as needlessly insulting, indirect, veiled or suggestive group defamation. That is considered crossing the line. To phrase it in football terms, you have to play the ball, not the man. Thus, the context of the public debate should no longer afford protection. It is what the curious and odd, yet fascinating, history of Article 137c of the Dutch Penal Code teaches us.

3 An Indefinable Hatred

Some Comparative Law Remarks about the Dutch Criminal Offence of Incitement to Hatred[1]

Aernout Nieuwenhuis

Introduction

According to Section 137d of the Dutch Criminal Code, public incitement to hatred, discrimination or violence against people because of their race, religion or philosophy of life; gender, hetero- or homosexual orientation; or physical, psychological, or mental disability is a criminal offence.

Background[2]

This section, popularly known as the ban on inciting hatred, was introduced in 1971, together with the ban on group defamation, as laid down in section 137c Criminal Code. By introducing these offences, the Kingdom of the Netherlands fulfilled its obligations under the International Convention on the Elimination of All Forms of Racial Discrimination (ICERD). Religion and philosophy of life were included, just as race, on the assumption – which turned out to be false – that there would come into being a similar Convention regarding discrimination on account of religion and philosophy of life. Moreover, discrimination on account of race and religion might be interrelated. In 1991, gender and hetero- or homosexual orientation were included as an element of the policy against discrimination on account of these characteristics. The same holds true for the inclusion of disability in 2006.

Looking back even further, one may point to the ban on group defamation introduced in 1934 in Section 137a (old) of the Criminal Code. In this offence, no special groups or

---

1 This contribution is an English adaptation of my article Een onbestemde haat. Enkele rechtsvergelijkende opmerkingen over artikel 137d Sr gezien in het licht van de vrijheid van meningsuiting, in: A. Ellian and others (Eds.), *Mag ik dit zeggen? Beschouwingen over de vrijheid van meningsuiting*, The Hague 2011, p. 263-286.

2 More extensively: T. Rosier, *Vrijheid van meningsuiting en discriminatie in Nederland en Amerika*, Amsterdam 1997; A.J. Nieuwenhuis, *Over de Grens van de vrijheid van meningsuiting*, Nijmegen 2011; M. van Noorloos, *Hate speech revisited. A comparative and historical perspective on hate speech law in the Netherlands and England & Wales* (PhD thesis), Antwerp 2011.

grounds of discrimination were indicated. The legislator's explicit aim was to curb the overheated political discussion. At the same time the legislator introduced a ban on defaming public authorities. According to the legislator, therefore, the political climate was not only threatened by ill-will between sections of the population, but also by ill-will between the government and sections of the population. One may emphasize the latter aspect by pointing to the hate speech offences in the former Criminal Code for the Dutch East Indies. These were also meant to prevent ill will between sections of the population, but were applied, among others, to critics of the colonial rule.

Application

Section 137c Criminal Code has been successfully applied to, inter alia, offensive references to the holocaust and the calling of members of an ethnic group criminals and rapists. As far as Section 137d Criminal Code is concerned, one may point, among others, to the conviction of the anti-immigration politician Janmaat.[3] In the 1990s, the court considered his utterance 'we will, if we have the power and the opportunity is there, abolish the multi-cultural society' together with banners which were present at the same time reading 'our own people first.' In light of his party's ideas, this utterance was seen as a call for the deportation of people on account of their ethnic origin. Fifteen years later, Geert Wilders has been acquitted for sweeping utterances mainly focussing on the religion of sections of the population (see later paragraphs).

The application of section 137c and d Criminal Code has always triggered discussion.[4] After the turn of the century, criticism has been growing, however. This criticism may be distinguished in four somewhat interrelated parts. First, it has been argued that incitement should only be punishable by law if there is a clear link between an utterance and violent or criminal acts. Second, it has been argued that political speech should have a special position that leaves little room for interference. Third, it has been argued that the fact that controversial opinions cause outrage is not an adequate reason for banning them as hate speech. Fourth, it has been argued that utterances regarding (adherents of) a religion should not be aligned with utterances regarding race.

The other way around, one might say that there is a certain agreement concerning the ban on incitement to violence and on advocacy of an explicitly racist policy. Disagreement starts, however, while answering the question of whether section 137c and d Criminal Code should also be applied to vehement and offensive criticism on the immigration and

3 Supreme Court 18 May 1998, *NJ* 1999, 634.
4 For example, *Strafblad* 2007, p. 363-409.

presence of certain groups, or on, time and again, the desecration of Islam, for example by a comparison with Nazism.

Research question and comparative law perspective

Disagreement not only exists because the criminal Code provisions themselves are not crystal clear, but also because the importance of freedom of speech is valued differently. Therefore, this contribution will try to answer the following question: How should banning incitement to hatred be understood from a freedom of speech perspective? To shed light on this matter and to bring into the open different points of view, a comparative law approach is chosen. The American First Amendment doctrine, inspiring supporters of an almost limitless freedom of speech, would pull to pieces the Dutch bans on group defamation and incitement to hatred and discrimination. On the other hand, the Criminal Code provisions are more congruent with German law and freedom of speech's meaning within the German fundamental rights concept.

The relevant case law of the European Court of Human Rights will be discussed as well. The Court's judgements, showing what sort of utterances may be banned by the contracting states, also encounter the problem of how the interest of freedom of speech should be balanced with the interest of combating discrimination. In this respect, the difference between the Court's considerations and the dissenting opinion in the Féret case is exemplary.[5] Féret, a member of parliament for the Belgian right-wing party the Front National, had protested in several pamphlets, among other things, the immigration of profiteers, the islamification of Belgium, the troublemaking and violence of refugees, and the ostensibly terrorist 'couscous-clan,' as well as advocating precedence for Belgians. In Belgium, Féret had been convicted on account of incitement to hatred and discrimination and the ECtHR did not find a violation of the right to freedom of speech as laid down in article 10 ECHR.

Structure

The research question will be answered by a separate treatment of the four forms of criticism mentioned above: No clear link between utterance and harmful effect, underestimation of the political debate's position, confusing hatred with outrage, and not distinguishing between race and religion well enough. In all of these sections, some relevant characteristics of American and German law will be sketched; the ECtHR's case law will be discussed as well. This detour will bring us back to the Dutch Criminal code section and the discussions

5 ECtHR 16 July 2009, nr. 15615/07, Féret c. Belgique.

on the application thereof. The contribution's subtitle makes clear that this design does not result in a well-rounded argument about the nature and application of section 137d Criminal Code. The contribution's aim, rather, is to gain some insight into a set of problems with which the legislator and the judge are faced.

SPEECH AND HARMFUL EFFECT

Section 137d of the Criminal Code penalizes *incitement to* discrimination, hatred and violence. This makes it likely that the aim of the penalization is the prevention of possible harmful effects of the speech in question. Discrimination and violent acts are themselves prohibited, after all. As far as hatred includes the inclination toward discrimination or the use of violence, there is also a link between speech and undesirable acts.

The question arises: What connection between utterance and action is required before an interference of freedom of speech is justified. To answer this question, of course, requires an estimation of the risks and dangers, which may play an important part. Hobbes' main oeuvre, for example, presents the idea that conflicting opinions may sow the seeds for armed conflict and civil war.[6] Limitations on public speech are therefore permitted rather soon. On the other side of the spectrum is the premise that there should be room for all opinions, advocacy and incitement included, because opinions are not acts. If people are influenced by the utterances concerned, and that influence results in certain actions, they are themselves responsible for their deeds; the speaker cannot be held responsible

That premise has been baptized the Millian principle.[7] The reference to Mill is not incomprehensible, since Mill draws a line where utterances are likely to instigate harmful acts and there is no room for further discussion: '(...) Even opinions lose their immunity when the circumstances in which they are expressed are such as to constitute their expression a positive instigation to some mischievous act.'[8] An example given by Mill is inciting an already excited mob to set fire to a house in front of them. For the rest, conflicting opinions and controversial ideas contribute to the sharpening of one's intelligence and to the progress of knowledge.

6 T. Hobbes (1651), *Leviathan*, Harmondsworth 1982, Part II, ch. 18.

7 T. Scanlon, A Theory of Freedom of expression, in: R. Dworkin (Ed.), *The Philosophy of Law*, London 1977, p. 161.

8 J.S. Mill (1859), *On Liberty*, Harmondsworth 1988, p. 129.

Clear and Present Danger

In the last century, the USA Supreme Court has elaborated the question, in what cases the government is allowed to ban utterances because of their possible undesirable effects.[9] At the beginning of the century, the Court accepted an interference when the speech in question had a 'bad tendency.'[10] The current doctrine, however, is much stricter in this respect. The government may only interfere in the process of opinion forming in a case of 'incitement to imminent lawless action',[11] for example, in circumstances wherein violent acts actually threaten to happen and the utterance incites violence.[12] Taking action against a publication merely because of its violent aim or tenor, or because of the glorification of the violence it includes, is not allowed. This strong protection of freedom of speech is not only based in a certain trust in social debate's purifying effect, but is nourished by a distrust of the government as well.

The First Amendment's protection, however, is weaker if a threat is addressed to one or more specific persons on the spot. In those circumstances, speech may be banned in order to prevent the 'disruption that the fear engenders.'[13] On the other hand, prevention of ill-will between sections of the population, even where racial hatred is concerned, is not sufficient ground for banning speech. In other words, in this respect, extremist political speech, racist or not, is completely protected by freedom of speech.

Public order, in a broad sense

In many other countries, like Germany, the approach differs. It's not necessary that an utterance incites imminent lawless action before an interference is justifiable. Moreover, the very concept of what qualifies as a breach of the peace is different, as the interpretation of the German Criminal Code provision banning stirring up hatred against sections of the population shows. Formally, this ban protects the public order.[14] An utterance may be punishable, however, even if it is not very plausible that it will result in action breaching the peace. Increasing ill-will between sections of the population may be sufficient for an interference of the right to freedom of expression. In accordance therewith, the utterance in question does not have to show what specific breach of the peace is at issue.

A far as the Jewish minority is concerned, the Criminal Code provision has been interpreted to protect their confidence in the rule of law as well. That confidence may be

9 For a clear review, R. Smolla, *Freedom of Speech in an Open Society*, New York 1992.
10 Schenck v. U.S., 249 U.S. 47 (1919).
11 Brandenburg v. Ohio, 395 U.S. 444 (1969).
12 Hess v. Indiana, 414 U.S. 105 (1973).
13 Virginia v. Black, 538 U.S. 343 (2003).
14 T. Fischer, *Strafgesetzbuch und Nebengesetze*, Beck 2009, p. 965.

at issue even in case of an 'entfernter Gefähr' (distant danger) or in case of an adverse effect on 'das Friedensgefühl' (the confidence that one may live in peace).[15] The very fact that hateful utterances are made could be seen as a sufficient cause to that effect.[16]

Social Climate

The European Court of Human Rights also does not require a 'clear and present danger' for an interference in the right to freedom of speech[17]. Government action is also justified when speech endorses[18] or glorifies[19] the use of violence according to the Court. Moreover, interferences are not only allowed in case of advocacy of violence, but in case of stirring up hatred as well.[20] Still, in these seditious speech cases, concerning utterances attacking the government, the hatred required may be seen as an overture to violence.

In the case of utterances attacking minority groups, the rules seem to be different. In Féret c. Belgique, the Court explicitly rejects the requirement that speech should at least advocate a definite lawless or violent act before an interference is justified.[21] If sections of the population are abused and scoffed at, the authorities may give precedence to protecting human dignity and combating discrimination over freedom of speech. Moreover, social peace and tolerance may be protected in the interest of political stability. Although politicians may recommend painful solutions for problems related to immigration and integration, that does not mean they are free to resort to plainly degrading proposals. Otherwise the public at large, and particularly the less informed sections thereof, may be influenced in a way that is incompatible with 'un climat social serein' (a peaceful social climate).

The dissenting opinion in the Féret case argues that the reasons put forward by the court to justify the interference with freedom of speech are too vague. The dissenters indicate that all effects of the utterances mentioned by the court are, at the most, *possible* effects. The authorities should have made them at least more plausible. The dissenters themselves propose a ban only permitted if stirring up hatred tends toward incitement to violence or at least calls for definite acts. Intolerance as such, according to them, is 'un sentiment sans action ou du moins sans tendance manifeste à l'action' (a feeling and no

15 For example, OLG Hamburg 18 February 1975, *NJW* 1975, p. 1088.
16 The extensive interpretation of 'violation of public order' has been criticized, e.g., R. Poscher, Neue Rechtsgrundlagen gegen rechtsextremistische Versammlungen, *NJW* 2005, S. 1316-1319.
17 Cf. the dissenting opinion of Judge Bonello in ECtHR 8 July 1999, Sürek no. 1 v. Turkey. See as well G. Bonello, Freedom of Expression and incitement to violence, in: *Freedom of Expression. Essays in Honour of N. Bratza*, Oisterwijck 2012, p. 349-362. See as well F. Tulkens, When to say is to do: Freedom of expression and hate speech in the case law of the European Court of Human Rights, in: *Freedom of Expression. Essays in Honour of N. Bratza*, Oisterwijck 2012, p. 279-296.
18 E.g., ECtHR 8 July 1999, nr. 23168/94, Karatas v. Turkey.
19 E.g., ECtHR (GC) 8 July 1999, no. 24735/94, Sürek v. Turkey (No. 3).
20 Inter alia ECtHR (GC) 8 July 1999, nr. 26682/95, Sürek no. 1 v. Turkey.
21 ECtHR 16 July 2009, nr. 15615/07, Féret c. Belgique.

act, or at least a feeling without a clear tendency to an act). Therefore, preaching intolerance should not be punishable.[22]

Sedition and hate speech

The Dutch Criminal Code penalizes seditious speech (Section 131),[23] to be defined, among other things, as incitement to lawless action. There is no requirement that the utterance actually has been followed by punishable acts or that there was at least a substantial risk. On the other hand, the utterance must make concrete the punishable acts it incites to. Incitement to violence against groups (Section 137d) has a clear affinity with seditious speech, and a substantial risk of real violence is not required.[24]

In the original decision of the Public Prosecutor not to prosecute Geert Wilders, the affinity was extended to the whole of Section 137d of the Criminal Code, which penalizes not only incitement to violence against groups, but incitement to discrimination and incitement to hatred as well. On the other hand, the Amsterdam Court of Justice ordering the Public Prosecutor to prosecute Wilders disagreed.[25] According to this Court, incitement to hatred has a broader meaning than inciting to lawless action; creating ill-will between sections of the population may also be qualified as incitement to hatred. In another case, the same Court had used the term 'intrinsically discordant'.[26] The former case law using the term ill will between sections of the population, however, does not solve the problem put forward. The question remains: What is meant by ill will? It may cover displeasure, an intolerant attitude, or the overture to a blazing row.

The District Court of Amsterdam, in its judgment acquitting Wilders, does not use the term 'ill-will between sections of the population.'[27] The District Court's approach is that hatred is a rather strong term. Therefore, just creating negative feelings falls short of being punishable. Incitement to hatred requires a 'krachtversterkend' (reinforcing) element. The Court does not elaborate on this term, but one may suppose that the District Court considers hatred almost as a transitional stage between attitude and action. Because no appeals were made in the Wilders case, opinions of an appellate Court or of the High Court about the requirement of a 'reinforcing element' are still lacking.

---

22 Cf R. Post, Religion and Freedom of Speech: Portraits of Mohammed, *Constellations* 2007, p. 79 ff.

23 For an overview see A.L.K. Janssens & A.J. Nieuwenhuis, *Uitingsdelicten*, Deventer 2011.

24 The judge, however, may assess whether violent effects were possible, Utrecht District Court, 26 April 2010, LJN BM 8138.

25 Court of Appeal Amsterdam 11 October 2010, LJN BO0041.

26 Cf. Supreme Court 2 April 2002, *NJ* 2002, 421, m.nt Mevis; see as well Den Haag District Court 12 May 2005, LJN BQ 4301.

27 District Court Amsterdam 23 June 2011, LJN BQ9001.

Résumé

There is a certain consensus that in case of utterances resulting in punishable acts, interferences may be justified. However, the First Amendment doctrine requires an almost immediate connection between utterance and act. A less strict requirement, for example to be found in the interpretation of the Dutch seditious speech provision, is that an utterance at least shows what punishable acts are deemed desirable by the speaker or writer.

By making the incitement to hatred a punishable offence, the connection between speech and action is bound to become more diffuse. It concerns a call for a certain state of mind or emotion that may or may not, for its part, result in certain punishable acts. If the legislator bans incitement to hatred the question therefore remains what link between utterance and acts is required. If the Criminal Code provisions are meant to protect the social climate or to prevent longer term effects on social harmony, the interpretation will differ from an interpretation based on prevention of actual breaches of the peace. The District Court's requirement of a 'reinforcing element' in the Wilders' case may be seen as an example of the second interpretation.

Democracy and incitement to discrimination

Freedom of speech and democracy are more often than not considered as two sides of the same coin. Under the First Amendment, there is pre-eminently room for a robust public debate.[28] There is a certain presumption that a free discussion will lead to the best results[29] or, at least, that government interference has a detrimental effect. In the German Constitutional Court's case law one may find the same considerations, to a certain extent. Permanent discussion and criticism is seen as the best way to control the government and its policy.[30] Therefore, utterances which are seen as part of public debate will be especially protected.[31]

The starting point of the European Court of Human Rights is not altogether different: 'According to the Strasbourg Court's case law there is little scope under Article 10 § 2 of the Convention for restrictions on political speech or on debate of questions of public interest.'[32] One-sidedness and some exaggeration should be permitted as well. The Dutch Courts have adopted this approach. Therefore, under Dutch law, in some cases, the answer to the question if an utterance is to be seen as a contribution to the public debate will often

28 New York Times v. Sullivan 376 U.S. 254 (1964).

29 Inter alia Gertz v. Welch 418 U.S. 323 (1974).

30 Federal Constitutional Court 17 August 1956, *E* 5, 85.

31 Inter alia Federal Constitutinal Court 26 June 1990, *E* 82, 272; Federal Constitutional Court 13 May 1980, *E* 54, 125.

32 E.g., ECtHR 25 November 1999, 23118/93, Nilsen & Johnsson v. Norway.

be decisive as well.[33] Regarding Section 137c Criminal Code (group libel), the context of the public debate may take away an utterance's offensive character, as far as the utterance is not gratuitously offensive.[34] In this respect, one may point to the Amsterdam District Court's judgement in a civil law case against Wilders. The Court did not find Wilders' utterances against Islam, Mohammed and the Koran unlawful, because they were directly connected with Wilders' political opinions, and the utterances as such played a part in the public debate.[35]

The question may arise what the implications of the relationship between democracy and freedom of speech are in respect to Section 137d of the Criminal Code. This paragraph will focus on the ban on incitement to discrimination and explain that the connection between freedom of speech and democracy has to be elaborated to clarify the actual implications.

Freedom of Speech and Democracy in the United States

The concept of democracy in the United States implies that all citizens should be free to express their (political) opinions, whether they are of a conservative, liberal, racist or egalitarian nature. The indivisibility of the First Amendment is seen as a guarantee for minorities and individuals with strongly dissenting opinions, especially for opponents of the government.

This idea of democracy is grounded in two interrelated notions. First, not the government but every single citizen should be the judge of political opinions: 'At the heart of the First Amendment lies the principle that each person should decide for him or herself the ideas and beliefs deserving of expression, consideration and adherence. Our political system and cultural life rests upon this ideal.'[36] Second, in a democracy everything is a possible subject of political debate, including the core values of democracy itself. Constitutional principles or values therefore cannot draw a line as far as freedom of speech in public debate is concerned.

Of course, there is a clear link with the starting point that only incitement to imminent lawless action is punishable. As long as there are no clear and present dangers of violence or other lawless action, the political discussion should go on. Therefore, political opinions of a racist character, as well as advocacy of rebellion,[37] may be disseminated freely. If one

33 E.g., Supreme Court 17 June 1997, *NJ* 1998, 361.

34 Supreme Court 15 April 2003, *NJ* 2003, 334.

35 President Dsitrict Court The Hague 7 April 2008, LJN BC8732.

36 TBS Inc. V. FCC, 114 SCt 2445 (1994); Cf. under the First Amendment there is no such thing as a false idea. However pernicious an opinion may seem, we depend for its correction not on the conscience of judges and juries but on the competition of other ideas', Gertz v. Welch, 418 U.S. 323 (1974).

37 CP of Indiana v. Whitcomb, 414 U.S. 449 (1974).

allows the government more room to interfere in the public discussion, it will always try to silence persons with strongly dissenting opinions or opponents of the government.

Freedom of Speech and Democracy in Germany

The connection between freedom of speech and democracy in Germany has other implications. Not every political opinion gets equal protection. Section 18 of the Basic Law (abuse of right) shows that persons who use their freedom of speech to undermine the 'freiheitlich demokratische Grundordnung' (free democratic basic structure), may not appeal to the right of freedom of speech. One might say that the right to freedom of speech is situated within the basic law's structure. From the outset, therefore, some political opinions like racism and Nazism have a different position,[38] even though the abuse of rights provision actually will only be applied when these opinions are expressed in a militant and aggressive way.

The fact that some sections of the Constitution are unalterable clearly shows the inviolability of certain constitutional principles. One may point first of all to the inviolability of human dignity, laid down in section 1 of the Basic law, which may be relevant, among other things, in case of racist speech. Other utterances aimed at an essential alteration of the democratic structure may as well have a similar position, even though a ban should counter an actual risk that someone's rights are injured.[39] As has been argued in the last section, however, causing fear may be seen as an actual detrimental effect.

Freedom of speech and democracy under the ECHR

One may think that these are all German particularities. However, under international law, especially the International Convention regarding the Elimination of all Forms of racial Discrimination, racist speech is given a special position as well. One may also point to the ECHR (section 17) and the Fundamental Rights Charter of the EU (section 54) both including an abuse of right provision.

Section 17 of the ECHR states that the Convention shall not be interpreted as giving a person a right to engage in any activity aimed at the destruction of any of the Convention rights or freedoms.[40] That does not mean that one may not strive after an alteration of the form of government, for example: 'It is the essence of a democracy to allow diverse political

38 W. Brugger, Freiheit der Meinung und Organisation der Meinungsfreiheit, *EuGRZ* 1987, p. 194.
39 BVerfG 4 November 2009, *E* 124, 300 (Wunsiedel).
40 For a general overview H. Cannie and D. Voorhoof, The Abuse Clause and Freedom of Expression in the European Human Rights Convention: An Added Value for Democracy and Human Rights Protection?, *NQHR* 2011, p. 54-83.

programs to be proposed and debated, even those that call into question the way the State is currently organised, provided that they do not harm democracy itself.'[41]

Section 17 ECHR has been applied to fascist, communist and racist political opinions.[42] In a broader sense, political utterances may be covered by the abuse of right provision when they 'run counter to the spirit of the Convention.'[43] According to the Court, that may hold true for Islamophobic utterances as well.[44] The Court considered the pinning up, shortly after 9/11, of a poster with a picture of the Twin Towers in flames and the text: 'Islam out of Britain – Protect the British People' as an abuse of right.[45] The Court, like the national courts, interpreted the poster as a 'public expression of attack on all Muslims in the United Kingdom.' Such a general and vehement attack on a religious group is 'incompatible with the values proclaimed and guaranteed by the Convention, notably tolerance, social peace and non-discrimination.'

Hate speech is covered by Section 17 of the ECHR, as far as it is part of an effort 'that runs counter to the Convention.' The vehemence of the words used may play a part as well.[46] In Féret, the Court rejected the application of Section 17 of the ECHR, but subsequently stated that 'tolerance and respect for equal dignity of all human beings constitute the foundation of democratic, pluralistic society; Therefore, generally speaking, in democratic societies it may be seen as necessary to punish or prevent all forms of speech that spread, promote, incite or justify hatred based on intolerance (including religious intolerance).'[47]

According to the Court, the utterances at stake represent the community of Muslim immigrants as ridiculous profiteers with a tendency toward crime. Such speech will rouse feelings of contempt, or even hatred against foreigners, especially as far as the less informed part of the public is concerned.

The dissenting opinion did not consider Féret's utterances to be punishable hate speech. Speech should only be qualified as such if it is aimed at the *destruction* of rights and freedoms protected by the Convention. A possible, longer term connection between endorsing prejudices and punishable acts is not a sufficient reason for a restriction of the political debate. According to them, in a democracy, only the unhindered exchange of ideas may lead to the truth, or will at least allow us to make our own political decisions taking into account the arguments of all other participants.

41 ECtHR 25 May 1998, nr. 21237/93, SP of Turkey v. Turkey.

42 The court has also qualified the denials of the holocaust as abuse of right, because it uses to be linked to an anti-Semitic striving, ECTHR 24 June 2003, no. 65831/01, Garaudy c. France.

43 ECtHR 13 December 2005, no. 7485/02, Witzsch v. Germany (dec.).

44 ECtHR 2 October 2008, no. 36109/03, Leroy c. France

45 ECtHR 19 November 2004, no. 23131/023, Norwood v. U.K. (dec.).

46 ECtHR juli 2008, no. 15948/03, Soulas e.a. c. France.

47 ECtHR 16 July 2009, no. 15615/07, Féret c. Belgique.

After all, the starting point in a democratic society is that all persons are capable of making well informed choices. According to the dissenting opinion, the Court alludes to a social class of nitwits not being able to distinguish between the arguments put forward in the public debate by reason of their irrational feelings. According to the dissenting opinion, this is not in agreement with the starting points of democracy.

Freedom of Speech and Democracy in the Netherlands

Striving toward political aims is not unlawful in the Netherlands. The Dutch Constitution lacks an abuse of rights provision. The government deemed the introduction thereof superfluous, because the Criminal Code, in particular Section 137c and d, would be sufficient as a basis to take action against, for example, a racist political grouping.[48] One may point here to the court's consideration, in a case concerning the ban of a racist political party, that a racist political striving conflicts with the 'generally accepted foundations of our constitution.'[49]

Therefore, Section 137d of the Criminal Code apparently draws a line between on the one hand, lawful political speech aimed at an alteration of the law or the Constitution and, on the other hand, political speech striving for aims contrary to certain constitutional foundations. The conviction of the politician Janmaat in the nineties of the last century matches this starting point. His aim was the abolition of multicultural society, interpreted by the court to include the expulsion of certain ethnic minorities. The fact that the abolition would only have taken place after he would have come into power was no impediment for a conviction.

In contrast, the public prosecutor who initially deciding not to prosecute Wilders stressed the fact that Wilders was almost always asking for government measures rather than just pitting people against each other. Therefore, in his opinion, Section 137d of the Criminal Code, in particular the ban on incitement to discrimination, did not apply. Seen in the light of the ICERD, that pre-eminently points to racist political strivings and, seen in the light of the case law, that is a rather restrictive interpretation of the provision at issue. The Amsterdam Court of Appeal, ordering the prosecution of Wilders, argued an opposing approach. Some of Wilders' utterances should be considered abuse of law under the ECHR, whilst others would at least incite to discriminatory government measures and therefore to discrimination.

48 E.g., Handelingen II, 24 February 2005, 52-3361.

49 District Court Amsterdam 18 November 1998, NJ 1999, 377, banning the political party CP86; that party was convicted several times under Section 137c and d Criminal Code.

The District Court acquitting Wilders, for its part, argued that political speech may only be qualified as incitement to discrimination if it exceeds a certain limit.[50] This requirement is not elaborated by the court. One may speculate, however, that advocating a proposal to stop financing Muslim primary schools, or a proposal to stop further immigration of Muslims does not exceed this limit, but the advocacy of a proposal to expel all Muslims might qualify as punishable incitement to discrimination.

Résumé

In the United States, all political views are strongly protected. Equality means that every citizen's political opinion is equally defended. In Europe, generally speaking, there exists a different approach. Political speech denying equal dignity or rights to others may be treated differently. The best example is the idea of an abuse of rights, for example in Germany, which draws a line between debate of a democratic nature and advocacy of proposals that are contrary to the democratic starting points.[51]

Introducing the term 'hatred' makes the situation more complicated. The ECtHR has not only qualified political speech explicitly aimed at the destruction of rights as an abuse of rights, but seems, under certain circumstances, to also include incitement to intolerance. Moreover, not all forms of punishable hate speech qualify as an abuse of right, according to the Court.

The existence of a rather clear line between debate of a democratic nature and other political speech, in my opinion, is a necessary condition for convicting politicians, trying to win supporters, on account of the substance of their proposals. In the Netherlands, that line is not demonstrated clearly in the Constitution. Therefore, the courts have to draw that line in applying Section 137d of the Criminal Code to utterances that may be qualified as incitement to discrimination. The Wilders' court required utterances to 'exceed a certain limit.' That requirement may be considered to be fulfilled if the substance of political proposals is evidently contrary to the principles of the constitution. To call it a clear line, however, would be a step too far.

Hatred and Outrage

In 2003, immediately after the murder of the Dutch filmmaker and columnist Theo van Gogh by a Muslim-fundamentalist, the Dutch Attorney General suggested that the blas-

50 District Court Amsterdam 23 June 2011, LJN BQ9001.

51 That does not mean that it is a sufficient condition; It may be preferable to fight such opinions in the political debate.

phemy provision in the Criminal Code should be revived. Presumably his line of reasoning was that blasphemous speech may provoke violent reactions or may at least contribute to a social climate that forms a breeding ground for violent acts. His suggestion, however, was not well received, and by now the parliament has approved a Bill lifting the ban on blasphemy. The Bill's explanatory memorandum, though, considers that Section 137d of the Criminal Code may be applied to blasphemous utterances if they contribute to the sowing of hatred.[52]

Hereunder, the relationship between freedom of speech and provoking outrage will be sketched; one of the questions to be answered is whether such provocative utterances may be seen as the sowing of hatred.

Freedom of Speech and Outrage in the United States.

In the United States, banning speech merely because of its outrageous nature does not fit within the First Amendment doctrine. The rather recent Snyder v. Phelps case is an excellent example.[53] Members of a sectarian Christian group had the right to, even in the neighbourhood of fallen soldier's burial, freely express their opinion that 'God hates fags' and that American soldiers are deservedly killed in action.

One of the most famous cases, in this respect, is Cantwell v. Connecticut.[54] A Jehova's witness asked the passers-by on the public road if he might play them a record on his portable gramophone. When they assented to the proposal, they heard an offensive harangue against Catholicism and the Pope. Some passers-by were outraged, to say the least, and Cantwell was eventually convicted for a breach of the peace. The Supreme Court, however, judged the tirade to be protected by the First Amendment. The fact that people present were seriously offended was not a sufficient reason for an interference in the right to freedom of speech. That also holds true in case of a fascist and anti-semitic speech for a larger public, according to the Supreme Court in Terminiello v. New York.[55]

Public inconvenience, annoyance and unrest all definitely fall short of being a good reason for an interference.[56] Otherwise, the hostile audience present or even the public at large would determine the scope of freedom of speech. Individuals with dissenting or controversial opinions would be the first victims. Therefore, only the outrage caused by the rather small category of fighting words, face to face, directed toward a specific person,

52 Kamerstukken II 2009/10. 32202, nr. 3.

53 U.S. S.Ct. 2 March 2011 (9-751).

54 310 U.S. 309 (1940).

55 337 U.S. 3 (1949). Freedom of speech is paramount, even if the whole nation is outraged by the burning of the Union Jack (flag), Texas v. Johnson, 491 U.S. 397 (1989).

56 Feiner v. New York, 340 U.S. 315 (1951).

may be ground for an interference. The same holds true if intimidating utterances are directed toward a specific person.[57] Of old, those categories of speech are, in principle, outside the reach of the First Amendment.

The conclusion is that public racist speech may not be banned because of its offensive or outrageous character, apart from racist speech in special settings, for example on the shop-floor or as a form of intimidation directed against a specific person.

Freedom of Speech and Outrage in Germany

In many European Countries, there is more room for a ban on offensive or outrageous speech. In Germany, in 1969, the ban on blasphemy may have been abolished, but the Criminal Code nowadays includes a provision banning the abuse of religions and philosophies of life as well as the rites and organization of religious or philosophy of life associations (§ 166). The provision does not want to prevent offended feelings in general. Satire as such is allowed, but grossly insulting images may be prohibited.

The ban may only be applied if the public order is violated. The legislator wants to protect the social peace, between sections of the population, with a different conviction. The interest protected, therefore, is comparable to the interest protected by the German hate speech ban. Moreover, in the past, the courts have considered that a violation of the public order may also occur when believers' confidence in their religion being treated respectfully is betrayed.[58] This interpretation agrees with the idea that Section 166 of the German Criminal Code not only protects the public order but the right to freedom of religion as well.[59]

Freedom of Speech and Outrage under the ECHR

The ECtHR's approach is comparable. The Court's case law[60] shows that vehement attacks on what believers deem to be holy may be prohibited, if the attacks are considered gratuitously offensive and therefore not a contribution to the public debate. Sometimes, the reference to public order in a broader sense is encountered as well.[61] In some of these blasphemy cases, the dissenting opinion rejects the protection of believers' feelings as sufficient reason for an interference.[62]

57 Virginia v. Black 538 U.S. 343 (2003).

58 OVG Koblenz 2 December 1996, NJW 1997, p. 1174.

59 Federal Administrative Court 11 December 1997, NJW 1999, 304.

60 See L. Lopez Guerra, Blasphemy and religious insult: offenses to religious feelings or attacks on freedoms? in: *Freedom of Expression. Essays in Honour of N. Bratza*, Oisterwijk 2012.

61 ECtHR 20 September 1994, nr. 13470/87, Otto Preminger Institut v. Austria.

62 ECtHR 13 September 2005, nr. 425712/98 I.A. c. Turquie.

Both outrage and hatred regard, first of all, feelings. Therefore, the question may arise of whether hurting feelings or evoking outrage may be qualified as forms of hate speech. The rather broad definition the Court uses - all forms of expression which spread, incite, promote or justify hatred based on intolerance (religious intolerance included)[63] - does not answer the question whether the intolerance provoked may show itself by the outrage provoked.

The 'social harmony,' mentioned in the Féret case, may not only be disrupted by the vehement feelings of the speaker's or publicist's supporters, but also by the outrage directed *against* the speaker or publicist. This lack of clarity disappears, to a certain extent, in the dissenters' approach, which requires a more obvious link between the utterance and a harmful act.

Freedom of Speech and Outrage in the Netherlands

The introduction of the ban on blasphemy in the thirties of the last century should be understood in light of the turbulent political situation. Notably, communists and anarchists did attack church and religion as cornerstones of bourgeois society. These often facetious utterances evoked vehement reactions from believers, even threatening to teach the blasphemers a lesson. In the criminal offence's phrasing, the public order interest was lacking. Offending religious feelings by abusing God in a vehement manner could be banned.

Recently, however, the blasphemy ban has been abolished. More generally, the interest of freedom of speech implies that public debate should not easily be restricted, even when people take offence. Therefore, the Rotterdam District Court did not consider the following utterance unlawful: 'In the thirties, when the national-socialists were coming up, the establishment looked away; nowadays the same is happening regarding islamization'.[64]

A more specific question is the meaning of outrage as far as Section 137c and d of the Criminal Code are concerned. The Supreme Court has judged that criticism of a religion, religious law and religious figures, in whatever way expressed, does not qualify as defamation of a religious group under Section 137c. Only utterances which evidently regard the group itself may be prohibited under this Section.

One may ask if outrage plays a part regarding Section 137d of the Criminal Code. As far as the ban on incitement to hatred is meant to prevent an 'intrinsically discordant situation',[65] evoking outrage might be included as well. If hatred, however, is seen as an overture

63 ECtHR 6 July 2006, nr. 59405/00, Erbakan c. Turquie. This description is based on the definition given by the Committee of Ministers of the Council of Europe in 1997, R(97)20.

64 District Court Rotterdam 21 November 2006, LJN AZ3031.

65 Supreme Court 2 April 2002, *NJ* 2002, 421.

to discrimination or violence by the speaker's supporters, evoking outrage will be out of the Section's reach. An additional argument may be that minorities may deserve protection from hatred against them, but the same minorities are responsible for their own outrage.[66]

In the Wilders case, the Amsterdam District Court has chosen the second approach. Utterances that attack a religion, religious practices or holy books do not qualify as incitement to hatred. To qualify as incitement to hatred, the utterance - and the hatred - should evidently regard the religious group.

Résumé

A ban on incitement to discrimination or violence will not easily cover utterances which have as their main effects hostile reactions or outrage directed against the speaker or publicist. That is less clear in case of a ban on incitement to hatred, especially if the interest protected is a peaceful social climate. This lack of clarity may be retrieved in the term 'hate speech.' Some definitions may seem to include utterances on account of their outrageousness as well: 'Hate speech is expression that aims to cause extreme offence and to vilify its target audience'.[67] The offensive nature of the speech involved may at least become an indication for the qualification 'incitement to hatred'.

The term 'hate speech' in the ECtHR's case law has a certain equivocality. On the one hand, in sedition cases, hate speech is close to incitement to violence and the glorification of violence. On the other hand, in cases of speech directed against minorities like the Féret case, speech may as well be considered hate speech on account of its effects on the social climate. That does not mean, however, that incitement to hatred in Section 137d of the Dutch Criminal Code should be interpreted as broadly as that.

Religion and Philosophy of Life versus Race

Until now, utterances regarding race and utterances regarding religion have been treated more or less alike. Nevertheless, they cannot be placed entirely on the same footing. First, the Convention regarding the Elimination of all Forms of Racial Discrimination includes an obligation to make incitement to racial hatred and propagation of racial discrimination a criminal offense. There are no conventions with a similar obligation as far as religion is concerned.

Section 20 of the ICCPR may prohibit advocacy of hatred regarding both race and religion, but the obligation is not as far reaching as the CERD obligation. Section 20 of the

66 See for example, J. Searle, *Making the Social World*, Oxford University Press 2010, p. 190-191.
67 N. Warburton, *Free Speech, A very Short Introduction*, Oxford 2009, p. 55.

ICCPR seems to require a stricter link between the utterance and its possible effects, because the advocacy of hatred should at the same time constitute incitement to discrimination, hostility or violence. Moreover, Section 20 of the ICCPR does not include an explicit obligation to penalize those utterances. At least, Section 20 of the ICCPR is not aimed at preventing the expression of the opinion that a certain religion is by far superior and all other religions are serious fallacies. Section 4 of the ICERD is definitely aimed at preventing the expression of the opinion that a certain race is by far superior.

Second, this difference between race and religion is not incomprehensible. Skin colour, for example, can be considered an unchangeable quality. To change one's beliefs is not impossible altogether, even if religion might be seen as a part of one's identity. Therefore, an effort may be made to convert people in the interest of salvation. The same holds true for an effort to convince people that all religions result in misery, so the best thing to do is becoming an agnostic. Such efforts are not conceivable as far as race is concerned.

Third, and maybe even more important, is that many religious convictions include, apart from an unprovable core, certain doctrines and moral rules.[68] These ideas are often disseminated and have possible implications for the law on public morality and family law. They may also regard the ratio and the meaning of public authority. Such ideas play their part in public debates. The same holds true for criticism on these opinions. More generally, cultures may be criticized as well. For utterances regarding race interpreted as an unalterable quality there is no similar argument possible.

Race Religion Distinction Irrelevant

Under the First Amendment doctrine, the distinction between speech regarding race and speech regarding religion is not really relevant, because freedom of speech is paramount in both cases. If racist hate speech normally may not be restricted, hate speech on account of religion will be just as free.

The distinction may also be irrelevant if the protection of the social climate is paramount. Utterances regarding religion may result in as much ill will between sections of the population as utterances regarding race. The European Commission against Racism and Intolerance goes one step further. It considers expressing contempt for a religious group or expressing superiority on account of religion quickly to become a form of racism. Therefore, publicly libelling a group of believers should be penalized.[69] Such an argument almost discards the difference between race and religion.[70]

68 This itself may be seen as a certain opinion. In former ages, particularly in Scholastic times, there existed several 'proofs' of God's existence.

69 ECRI, General Policy Recommendation no.7.

70 One may point as well to the slip of the pen in the arrest and case of Janmaat, who would have propagated the abolishment of the multiracial society (in stead of multicultural).

Race Religion Distinction Relevant

A more balanced approach is called for in other cases. The Strasbourg Court, for example, has distinguished between negative comments on a religion which contribute to the public debate, and gratuitous attacks on a religion's holy figures.[71] As far as race is concerned, the idea that negative comments could be considered part of the public debate, as interpreted by the Court, is less conceivable.

In the Féret case, the Court does not pay much attention to the fact that most utterances did concern religion rather than race. The Court does not consider the utterances, attacking certain communities, as part of the protected public debate. The dissenting opinion, as is to be expected, takes a different approach. The dissenting judges object to the apparent extension of the concept of racial discrimination to incitement to religious and cultural prejudice. This extension, according to them, is too easily grounded in the fact that the last-mentioned speech may as well have detrimental effects on social peace.

Netherlands

In respect to Section 137c of the Criminal Code, the Dutch Supreme Court has acknowledged that utterances attacking religious convictions and morals are to be distinguished from speech about persons.[72] Referring to the legislative process, the Court argued that only speech undeniably about a group of people – contrary to speech about ideas and mores living within a group - may be covered by the group libel section. That distinction may be defended on the basis of freedom of speech, although in certain cases it may be deemed somewhat artificial.[73] Anyhow, such a distinction in case of race – this race is inferior, but not the people – is a lot less convincing. That may explain the decision of the Supreme Court to expressly restrict its interpretation of speech about religion.

At the same time, the Supreme Court stated that the 'undeniably about' criterion cannot simply be transferred to Section 137d of the Criminal Code. That is obvious insofar as Section 137d expressly bans incitement to violence against goods as well. The utterance 'set the Christian churches on fire' may, therefore, be punishable, without referring explicitly to a group.[74]

---

71 For example, the depiction of a religion as a fabrication meant to keep the people ignorant may be a contribution to the public debate, ECtHR 2 May 2006, nr. 50692/99, Tatlav c. Turquie.

72 Supreme Court 10 March 2009, LJN BF0655.

73 For example, it is not obvious to make a difference between the utterance 'Roman-Catholicism is a backward conviction' and the utterance 'Roman Catholics are adherents of a backward religion.' In both cases, in my opinion, the utterance concerns the religion.

74 District Court Utrecht 26 April 2010, LJN BM8138.

The more interesting question is, to what extent does the distinction made between speech against convictions and speech against persons play a part as far as incitement to hatred is concerned. It would be strange, for example, if the legislator, having desired to give room to all kinds of comments on ideas and morals regarding Section 137c of the Criminal Code, would have meant Section 137d of the Criminal Code to be applicable to the same utterances. Moreover, the aversion against certain religious convictions, based on personal experiences or on the opinion about a religion's influence in society, may play an important role in the public debate. The prevention of hatred directed against persons, by contrast, is nearer to the prevention of violence and discrimination against persons.

An incidental argument may be that utterances describing a religion as hateful often rest on a certain explanation thereof. However, a Criminal Court is not an appropriate body, if any body can be, to determine what the right interpretation of a religion is. From this argument, it follows naturally that it would be remarkable if the Criminal Code would cover harsh criticism of religions or philosophies of life as, for example, the Scientology Church.[75]

The distinction between race and religion may also be relevant regarding political proposals of a discriminatory nature. First, international law makes a ban on racist political speech obligatory,[76] even when it cannot be seen as incitement to harmful acts. Second, the borderline in a democratic society between robust political debate, and utterances that exceed a certain limit, may possibly be drawn more clearly regarding race than regarding religion. Although striving for the destruction of the rights of people adhering to a certain religion may be a clear case,[77] what remains unclear is which measures may or may not be propagated in order to take care of the problems in a multicultural society.[78]

Résumé

Concerning incitement to violence, the distinction between race and religion is not that important. However, if utterances are aimed at certain convictions, freedom of speech will carry a relatively great weight. In this light, it is quite conceivable that in applying Section 137d of the Criminal Code the Courts will make a certain distinction between on the one

75 E.g., G. Komrij, *De stankbel aan de Nieuwezijds*, Amsterdam 1979.

76 Article 4 ICERD.

77 The argument that the discriminatory measures propagated will only be introduced after the political party involved will have come to power, is not really relevant under this approach, Supreme Court 14 March 1978, *NJ* 1978, 664..

78 In the Janmaat case, Supreme Court 18 mei 1999, *NJ* 634, the Court of Appeal deduced from the context that Janmaat was not advocating the introduction of a 'Leitkultur' but was aiming at the expulsion of people on account of their ethnic descent.

hand, speech about convictions and customs and on the other hand, speech about a group of persons.

If the prevention of outrage and the protection of the social climate are paramount, however, the distinction between race and religion has less importance. Offensive utterances regarding a Supreme Being, a Prophet or a Holy Book sometimes evoke even more outrage than speech attacking the very members of a religious group.

Conclusion

Speech may incite punishable acts. Therefore, a ban on certain forms of hate speech will often focus on the speech's tenor and the possible effects. In this respect, there is a big difference between the utterance 'the multicultural society should be abolished' and stirring up an excited mob threatening to lynch someone. The same holds true for on the one hand, an utterance characterizing a holy book as the product of an aggressive and megalomaniac imagination, and on the other hand, an utterance advocating the expulsion of all persons of an ethnic group.

The answer to the question 'which of the aforementioned utterances should be penalized,' cannot be answered without bearing in mind the meaning and weight of freedom of speech. If an unhampered public discussion is so important that only a clear and present danger will justify a restriction, only the second utterance (the excited mob) is punishable, at the most. The implication of this 'First Amendment approach' will be that not only vehement criticism on religious ideas and customs, but explicit racist speech, will be free. Only racist speech, directed at a specific individual and to be considered a fighting word or having an intimidating character may be banned. On the other hand, if a restriction may be justified by the prevention of possible ill-will and outrage, all four of the utterances mentioned above may be banned.

Section 137d of the Dutch Criminal Code does not agree with the First Amendment doctrine; that much is obvious. First, although incitement is banned, no incitement to imminent lawless action is required. If there is only a small chance that an utterance will result in action, the provision may be applied as well. The penalization of incitement to hatred, apart from incitement to discrimination and violence, stresses even more the weakness of the link required between utterance and action. After all, to hate is not a punishable act, but, at most, a disposition to act. The German and Strasbourg case laws show that restrictions protecting the social climate also drop a clear connection between an utterance and an act as a requirement.

Second, the First Amendment offers the same protection to every single political opinion. In Germany, and under the ECHR, it's different. Section 18 of the German Basic

Law as well as section 17 of the ECHR cover, for example, explicit racist strivings. The ECtHR, in certain cases, has also qualified the less well defined incitement to religious intolerance and hatred an abuse of right. The Dutch Basic Law does not include an abuse of rights provision. Nevertheless, Section 137d of the Criminal Code not only penalizes incitement to discriminatory acts, prohibited by current law, but also covers the propagation of a discriminatory policy, at least if a certain limit is exceeded, as the Wilders Court considered.

Third, The First Amendment doctrine almost completely rejects outrage as a reason for a restriction of freedom of speech. The approach in Germany and under the ECHR differs, especially when a restriction's aim is the protection of the social climate. To what extent evoking outrage may be qualified as incitement to hatred under Section 137d of the Dutch Criminal Code is not quite clear.

In almost all of the cases mentioned above, the distinction between race and religion may play a certain part. Negative utterances about religious doctrine and religious custom may have another quality than negative speech about people. Hatred against religious tenets and morals may be distinguished from hatred against people. As far as race is concerned, those distinctions are not easily conceivable. Making a distinction on account of race will also be more easily qualified as a form of punishable discrimination than on account of religion or culture.

This article shows that the ECtHR does allow a whole range of restrictions on freedom of speech. Put otherwise: Article 10 of the ECHR does not prevent an extensive interpretation of Section 137d of the Dutch Criminal Code. That does not imply that the Strasbourg case law makes such an interpretation obligatory. In this respect, one may point to the national authorities' margin of appreciation in assessing the necessity of an interference in the debate about immigration and integration. According to the Strasbourg Court, the national authorities have a more profound understanding of the reality in their country, and therefore are in a better position to judge what the appropriate measures are to tackle the problems involved.[79]

Therefore, the interpretation of Section 137d of the Dutch Criminal Code, in particular the interpretation of incitement to hatred, is first of all a Dutch national law issue. While interpreting this provision, the courts come up against a range of problems, which have been addressed in this article. Moreover, the Courts not only have to determine the provision's meaning, but the explanation of the utterance itself. Is an utterance's purpose, for example, the expulsion of all Muslims living in the Netherlands, or is the utterance's purpose

79 ECTHR 10 July 2008, nr. 15948/03, Soulas c. France. See as well, ECTHR 20 April 2010, nr. 18788/09, Le Pen c. France (dec.).

a reduction of the amount of radical Muslims who are not agreeing with democracy under the rule of law.

One last remark: Hatred may be undefinable, but criminal provisions are horses of a different color. A citizen expressing his opinion must have some idea about the risks involved in vehement criticism and other forms of extreme speech. The courts must also be on solid ground when applying the hate speech provisions. The foregoing may be an extra argument for a rather restrictive interpretation. Otherwise, incitement to hatred will become a really undefinable offence. In that case, somebody who is inspired by a holy book and admonishes homosexuals may be considered to be in breach of the law; somebody, in his turn, abusing that holy book may run certain risks, and so on. However, hate speech bans should, in my opinion, not interfere with such a public debate.

4 Freedom of Speech: 'It's Politics all the Way Down'

Gelijn Molier

> 'Pornographers, Holocaust deniers, and cross-burners are not for free speech but for pornography, the denial of the Holocaust, and the intimidation of minorities. And on the other side, the homeless advocates who wish to sleep in federal parks, animal rights activists who heap scorn on fur-clad women, and antigovernment protesters are not for free speech either but for housing for the homeless, humane treatment of animals, and a change in U.S. policies.'[1]

> 'There is no such thing as hate speech if you mean by that designation speech that would be judged hateful by an independent norm. Instead there is speech that is hateful to some persons because it offends the ideals to which they pledge allegiance. To those who produce the speech, however, it is not hateful but needful, and they will hear as hateful (or perverse or dangerous) speech that offends against their ideals.'[2]

There is no such thing as 'free speech'

All of the attention devoted to the Wilders trial, in which, according to the leader of the Party for Freedom (in Dutch: 'Partij voor de Vrijheid', abbreviated to PVV) Wilders himself, nothing less than freedom of speech of 1,6 million Dutchmen was at stake, somewhat overshadowed two other news reports. The first of these was the removal, in response to persistent and grave threats, of a cartoon from the website joop.nl by the Dutch network VARA, which depicted the PVV's proposal to realize 'scum villages'. The cartoon represents Wilders as a camp guard who leads recidivists to the gas chambers. Wilders himself threatened, on the day the cartoon appeared, to boycott all VARA television shows, including the election debate, if the cartoon were not 'immediately' removed from the website. He tweeted to his followers: 'What a despicable and sickening cartoon. The chills are running down my spine.'[3]

---

1 S. Fish, *The Trouble with Principle*, Cambridge (MA): Harvard University Press, 1999, p. 90.

2 Fish, 1999, p. 70.

3 This may be found on the website www.elsevier.nl/web/Nieuws/Nederland/289163/Geert-Wilders-verbolgen-over-cartoon-op-VARAwebsite.htm.

Appealing to the import of freedom of speech by arguing that the cartoon contributed to a social debate, since it interpreted the proposition - initiated by the PVV - to realize the 'scum villages', VARA initially refused to remove the cartoon. After all, those who play at bowls must look out for rubs.[4] About ten days later, the editorial team of VARA were turned, not as a consequence of the boycott by the PVV, but, as was said, because of the persistent and grave threats towards VARA employees which were reported to the police.

The second event was even more striking. On April 22, 2011, it was announced that the Arondéus lecture which Thomas von der Dunk was supposed to deliver in the context of the commemoration of the end of the Second World War was no longer taking place. Having reviewed the lecture, two of the five members of the committee which was responsible for the organization behind the lecture requested the advice of Hero Brinkman, in his capacity as leader of the local PVV council, regarding the passages in the text that might present the PVV in a negative light. Having consulted Brinkman, the committee decided to call off the lecture. Having been asked for his opinion, Brinkman said, in the Dutch newspaper *de Volkskrant*, that he did not limit freedom of speech, having merely given his opinion or advice. He continued by presenting his 'advice': 'I told them that if they should provide a stage for this anti-Semite Von der Dunk to counter the PVV, I will not only take him apart in the debate – it may also have been the final Arondéus lecture.'[5]

What may be gathered from these two events? In the first place it is clear that freedom of speech is not absolute for anyone, but that it must always be considered limited. This confirms Stanley Fish's statement that Wilders and the PVV do not simply promote freedom of speech, but seek to convey, above all else, their political message that Islam is a pernicious religion. It also proves something else, namely, that something that is considered by one group to be the promotion of a political conviction is easily interpreted by another group to constitute the spreading of hatred or insult. Is it not ironic that Geert Wilders, who is known, after all, for his liberal stance on free speech, claimed to be insulted by his host, VARA, and that his followers felt insulted upon their 'prophet' being ridiculed in a cartoon. They showed their true colors all the more by resorting to more draconic measures, once VARA had not proved willing to comply with Wilders's call to remove the cartoon. It would appear that threats of violence and intimidation do not only exclusively accompany insults directed at *religious* persons or symbols. Apparently, names *will* hurt, or, more accurately, words do have consequences.[6]

4 He who is part of a debate and makes proposals that are likely to shock others – as a politician may – 'exposes himself to a strong reaction on the part of journalists and the public.' See *Oberschlick v. Austria*, ECtHR 23 May 1991.

5 This may be found on the website www.volkskrant.nl/vk/nl/2824/Politiek/article/detail/1878867/2011/04/22/PVV-achter-schrappen-lezing-Von-der-Dunk.dhtml.

6 Fish, 1999, p. 94: 'Speech, like lunch costs, (...) if utterance always works to advance some interests as defined by some agenda, its effectiveness will always be achieved at the expense of some other interests as defined by some other agenda. Someone always pays when speech takes. There is no speech that is free of conse-

The same can be said with respect to Von der Dunk's lecture. While Von der Dunk considers his lecture to contribute to a social debate on the issue of whether the PVV's proposals may counter the core values of a constitutional state, since the PVV abuses, in his view, freedom of speech in order to stigmatize and discriminate against the Muslim population, the PVV considers his lecture to constitute hatred against the PVV and its followers. This illustrates – again – Fish's point that

> '[a]n utterance is hate speech so long as someone or group will find it objectionable, and since this is a requirement almost any utterance will meet, hate speech is not a limitable category and can be anything (...), even the Declaration of Independence or the Golden Rule. (...). Hate speech, so called, is always at once someone's rationality and someone else's abomination.'[7]

Just as Wilders thinks, and continually claims, to be telling the truth and to be morally right in criticizing Islam, Von der Dunk considers his position to be the morally right one, maintaining that he himself is telling the truth. In other words, from Wilders's perspective, his remarks on Islam are neither irrational nor causing hatred. By the same token, from Von der Dunk's perspective, his remarks on the PVV are neither irrational nor offensive towards the PVV. From their respective worldviews, which are necessarily partial, both are right. In that sense, the limit put on freedom of speech is by definition arbitrary.

The Dutch legislator has placed certain limits on freedom of speech. Important for the present contribution in particular are articles 137c (group insult) and 137d (incitement to hatred, discrimination and violence) of the Dutch Criminal Code.[8] Accordingly, in The Netherlands it is the judiciary that must decide what the limit on freedom of speech is in concrete terms. Judges will, in each case, have to balance the values that freedom of speech seeks to protect against the values whose protection is the foundation of the provisions that limit the same freedom of speech. It is clear that the decision concerning where the line should be drawn is in every case bound by context and dependent on circumstances, but things are actually somewhat more complicated, for it is characteristic of jurisprudence that it provides criteria or viewpoints which may in turn be applied to similar instances.

In the following, I will critically analyze the way in which the judiciary has concretized what articles 137c and 137d stipulate. In addition, I will answer the question whether it is desirable to cling to these provisions as they stand, while the reason behind freedom of speech will in more general terms be examined. I will conclude that freedom of speech is not a neutral principle, devoid of content, to be examined in isolation, but that it is rather

quences – no speech, that is, whose impact can be confined to the sterilized and weightless atmosphere of a philosophy seminar (...).'

7 Fish, 1999, p. 70.

8 In the remainder of this text, articles without further qualification will refer to the Dutch Criminal Code.

part of a certain political system, namely, the liberal democratic constitutional state. This entails that freedom of speech can never be unrestrained; its contents and limits are given in the abstract in line with the core values that constitute the foundation of that liberal democratic constitutional state, to wit, individual freedom and equal value.

Group Insult

Article 137c, first section, of the Dutch Criminal Code reads:

> 'He who publicly, verbally or in writing or image, deliberately expresses himself in any way insulting of a group of people because of their race, their religion or worldview, their hetero- or homosexual orientation or their physical, psychological or intellectual disability, shall be punished by imprisonment of at the most one year or a fine of the third category.'

The Wilders trial is, for now, the highlight, or low point, in a sequence of trials in which the district attorney prosecuted on the basis of group insult. The reflections on article 137c may be listed in three main categories. First, there are group insults because of heterosexual or homosexual orientation. In this instance, cases were involved in which, respectively, a Christian member of parliament, a reverend, an imam and a police officer made insulting remarks about homosexuals. The second category concerns group insult because of race, pertaining to a number of cases where, respectively, a member of parliament, a film maker and a reverend couple were prosecuted for having insulted a group because of their race. The Wilders case, lastly, deals with insulting a certain group of people because of their religion. The judiciary has, over the years, used a line of reasoning in order to decide whether punishable group insult has taken place. This line of reasoning comprises a sort of three-stage rocket: The judge first inquires into whether the remark itself is insulting, after which the context in which the remark was made is examined; finally, the judge determines whether the remark is, in spite of an exculpatory context, unnecessarily grievous. In the second stage, the context, freedom of religion and the question whether the remark contributes to a social debate (freedom of speech) are important elements. Especially the formulation of the phrase 'contributing to a social debate' seems to leave so much room for interpretation that the judge is hardly left with any criteria to decide the case.

The Concept of 'Insult'

In the opinion of Janssens and Nieuwenhuis, the crimes of insult in the Dutch Criminal Code are intended to safeguard the moral integrity of the persons involved.[9] From a more theoretical perspective, the philosophical principle that provides the foundation of the crimes of insult is the status of a morally or ethically full-fledged member of society that must be conferred to every individual. The idea behind the crimes of insult is that the violation of this moral integrity may not only be incurred by acts or certain behavior, but by words as well. In that light, Janssens and Nieuwenhuis define criminal insult as: 'The intrusion or assault on someone's moral integrity.'[10] In the case of article 137c in particular, a punishment can only be administered if the moral integrity of the group, or its members, is violated.[11] One wonders, though, in what circumstances this demand is met. Since people may easily be offended, there must be an 'outwardly observable' failure to acknowledge someone's moral integrity or human dignity. This means, according to these authors, that affronting the *self-esteem* or *self-respect* (or someone else's *self-confidence*) is not legally protected.[12] The reason they provide for this line of thought is that legal notions which are difficult to manage are involved. The judiciary has not been trained to analyze and interpret such notions. It is remarkable, then, that the legislator deems legal protection against grieving remarks directed at a group relevant if *group* insult is involved. This is clear from the fact that article 137c is included in the section of public order crimes. The purpose of the original article, from 1934, was to prevent the public debate from degenerating into brawls and riots among various groups of people. With the expansion of the provision to group insult on the basis of race, religion and worldview, another consideration was incorporated. On the one hand, the legislator sought to meet the obligations of the International Convention on the Elimination of All Forms of Racial Discrimination (ICERD); on the other hand, the legislator went beyond his duty by not only criminalizing incitement to discrimination and hatred because of race, but also insult on the same basis, as well as insult of groups of people because of their religion or worldview.[13]

Strictly speaking, the ICERD by no means obligated the legislator to adopt such an extensive interpretation of the ICERD's demands with respect to the treaty; only racist political propaganda that might lead to discriminatory legislation should be excluded.[14] The same consideration applies to instances of discriminatory propaganda, since discrimination may ensue from such instances. The primary reason why the Dutch legislator exceeded his duties regarding the treaty in the two respects mentioned above is, accordingly,

9 A.L.J. Janssens & A.J. Nieuwenhuis, *Uitingsdelicten*, Deventer: Kluwer, 2005, p. 32.
10 *Ibid.*
11 Janssens & Nieuwenhuis, 2005, p. 134.
12 Janssens & Nieuwenhuis, 2005, p. 32.
13 Janssens & Nieuwenhuis, 2008, p. 150.
14 *Ibid.*

that the Dutch policies developed to counter discrimination are focused on the *public dimension* of the realization of the fundamental right to equal treatment.[15] This means that the *ratio legis* of this provision is no longer exclusively protecting the public order (preventing uproar, manifested in conflicts between groups of people), but also lies in safeguarding minorities from grievances, as their self-confidence would suffer as a consequence, which might jeopardize their role in society. Moreover, a violation of their reputation as a result of insult might affect their position on the labor market. The general idea here is that minorities are usually disadvantaged vis-à-vis the dominant groups and for that reason, require special protection in order to attain a better role in society.[16] The downside to this development, however, is that it makes it possible that grieving people who are especially sensitive to insult are criminalized *without* there being public order problems. If it is difficult enough for the judiciary to decide whether an *individual's* self-respect or self-esteem is affronted, this is *a fortiori* the case for *groups* of individuals. It is not surprising, in light of the foregoing, to find in the jurisprudence a continual struggle of the judiciary with the application of article 137c, especially in cases where insult of a group of people because of their religion is concerned.

INCITEMENT TO HATRED AND DISCRIMINATION

Article 137d, first section, of the Dutch Criminal Code reads:

> 'He who publicly, verbally or in writing or image, incites hatred against or discriminates against people or violent behavior against person or property of people because of their race, their religion or worldview, their gender, their hetero- or homosexual nature or their physical, psychological or intellectual disabilities, shall be punished by imprisonment of at the most one year or a fine of the third category.'

Although article 137d is the only provision in the Dutch Criminal Code in which the word 'hatred' is an element, while this term is nowhere defined, the word does not, according to Janssens and Nieuwenhuis, raise any significant problems. They agree with the following definition, presented in the German literature: 'intense emotional feelings of hostility.'[17] The authors maintain that this interpretation corresponds with the Dutch jurisprudence: It was ruled that a remark constitutes incitement to hatred if it pits groups against each

15 Janssens & Nieuwenhuis 2008, p. 150.
16 Janssens & Nieuwenhuis 2008, p. 150-151.
17 Janssens & Nieuwenhuis, 2008, p. 158.

other, thus causing an 'intrinsically conflictive division'. The judiciary is simultaneously thought to follow the legislator's intention, whose intention is focused on contravening the (possible) *consequences* of hating or hatred, like discrimination and violence, rather than on hating or hatred itself.[18] 'Discrimination' and 'violence' are, for the reason that they are outwardly clear notions, relatively unproblematic. It would be fairly simple for the judiciary to determine whether actual (incitement to) violence is the case, with the facts at its disposal. 'Discrimination' is a more difficult notion to tackle, but the judiciary may in this case resort to article 90quater, which defines discrimination. It reads:

> 'Discrimination or the act of discrimination is taken to be any form of distinction, any exclusion, limitation or preference which has as its goal or may have as its consequence that the recognition or the exercise, on an equal footing, of human rights and fundamental freedoms in political, economic, social or cultural terms, or in any other field of social life is undone or vitiated.'

A detailed study of the relevant jurisprudence shows that it is, in spite of this definition, in practice not easy to determine whether there is 'incitement to discrimination' in the sense of article 137d, or not. The following section will explore the main aspects from the jurisprudence regarding articles 137c and 137d.

Some Observations with Respect to the Jurisprudence Regarding Group Insult and Incitement to Hatred and Discrimination

On the basis of an analysis of the jurisprudence regarding articles 137c and 137d, the following can be concluded. Both the nature of the formulations of these provisions and the way in which they have been concretized in jurisprudence leave the judge faced with the task of ruling a case with considerable latitude in directing a verdict or an acquittal. It is, of course, characteristic of the law that the judiciary may decide a case either way where vague notions are involved, but in the case of crimes of insult, this is an unwelcome situation. The main danger is the constant accusation of political adjudication.[19] This does not only weaken the legitimacy of a specific ruling, but also affects the judiciary's legitimacy on the whole, which in turn threatens the constitutional state. The combination of vague terms and the political minefield, through which the judiciary must maneuver whenever the district attorney prosecutes a politician because of his opinions, leads to the conclusion that one must resort to prosecution only sparsely, and that it is only to take place in cases

18 Janssens & Nieuwenhuis, 2008, p. 158.

19 Cf. M. Fennema, 'De rechter had Wilders wel moeten veroordelen; schaf de onschendbaarheid van Kamerleden maar af', *NRC Handelsblad*, 4 July 2011.

where it is justifiable to conclude, on the basis of clear criteria, that such a politician has indeed committed the crime of group insult, incitement to hatred or discrimination. Still, one wonders whether this result is actually achievable.

A judicial ruling derives its legitimacy from a sufficiently supportive line of reasoning. Whether the line of reasoning is supportive or compelling is, in turn, determined by the construal of the major premise and the presentation of the facts - both must be compelling in light of the rule. The Dutch Supreme Court uses, for its construal of the rule provided by article 137c, the 'three-stage rocket' mentioned above. This construal affords, in my opinion, only a semblance of legal security, since the criterion of a public or social debate is almost fully interpreted in subjective terms in the case of remarks made on the basis of a religious conviction. Sufficient justification is apparently provided if the remark is meaningful 'for the defendant' in order for a public debate to take place. This makes assessing the content of this criterion virtually impossible, the religious conviction being *de facto* decisive to determine the context.

As for cases of racial remarks in which a religious conviction is *not* decisive, the judiciary appears to find few impediments in concluding with group insult, without assessing in detail whether the criterion of a public debate is met. This, at least, creates the impression that 'sacred opinions' are afforded more protection than 'usual opinions'. A Supreme Court ruling of March 10, 2009 has somewhat corrected this unequal treatment: The Supreme Court distinguishes between, on the one hand, making insulting remarks about a group of people because of their faith and, on the other hand, insulting the behavior of those religious people, or their convictions, or their religion (along with its symbols). In the second case, the judge does not need to heed the context, since the remark no longer meets the criteria of article 137c.

This outcome is desirable from the consideration that 'sacred' and 'non-sacred' (i.e. 'usual') opinions should be equated, but the danger of grey areas looms, the more so since the court in the Wilders Case states that 'in view of the similar nature of the provisions (137c and 137d) and how they have been formulated, there is no reason to leave unconsidered the jurisprudence regarding article 137c in interpreting article 137d.' The same applies vice versa, which would mean that the criterion, 'in light of possible associations' that certain remarks might evoke, also applies to article 137c. In that case, however, the distinction between indirect and direct insult would disappear, the foundation to provide such a distinction being taken away. In addition, it is illogical, from a linguistic point of view, and therefore confusing, that a remark is insulting in itself, but that this no longer applies on the basis of the context, meaning that the remark may once again become insulting because of its unnecessarily grievous nature. It would have been more consistent linguistically to consider a remark solely within the context in which it is made and to skip the first stage of the three-stage rocket, incorporating the third stage into the context.[20] To sum up, the way the court has construed the major premise regarding article 137c provides little legal security.

The same consideration applies to the way in which article 137d is interpreted in jurisprudence. The criteria of 'inherently conflictive divide' and 'in light of possible associations', which the judiciary applies in order to specify whether incitement to hatred and/or discrimination is the case, are so vague that the construal of the rule leads to little to no increase in legal security. The court ruling the Wilders case seems to have realized this, given the fact that these two criteria were hardly relevant in deciding whether Wilders was guilty of incitement to hatred and/or discrimination. It rather referred to the jurisprudence regarding article 137c, and in particular the criterion of 'the context of a public debate'. On that basis, a dichotomy was appealed to between remarks by Wilders that *in themselves* incite to hatred and/or discrimination, on the one hand, and *the public context* that would subsequently take away this characteristic of hatred-incitement and discrimination, on the other; such a dichotomy is equally unfortunate from a linguistic-philosophical perspective. If it is said, then, that it is the consequence of words that the speaker has incited to hatred and/or discrimination in itself, it is difficult to see how the public context might offset such a consequence. So either Wilders' words have consequences, including cases where they are uttered in the context of a debate about multicultural society, or they don't. It does not follow from this that Wilders should be convicted, but it is clear that the ruling failed to be properly substantiated. Does this mean that all those laws should be abolished? This is actually a complex question, as it can only be answered once it is clear to what end freedom of speech exists.

Some Legal Theoretical and Concluding Remarks

Freedom of speech cannot be considered an isolated principle; it is rather part of a certain political system referred to as the liberal democratic constitutional state. This system is based on a liberal political philosophy premised upon individual freedom, peace and order within the state. To this end, political liberalism presumes autonomous and equal individuals who are, as a rule, free to live according to their conception of a Good Life (the principle of self-determination), so long as they do not disadvantage others by doing so. The freedom of one individual ends where he inflicts harm on another. It is up to the state, accordingly, to demarcate the limits within which individuals are to decide, in accordance

20 Cf. W. Veraert, 'Beledigen kan alleen in context', *Nederlands Juristenblad*, 2010, vol. 12, p. 725: '(...) words and symbols derive their meaning in part from the specific context in which they are uttered and used.' The original text reads: '(...) woorden en symbolen ontlenen hun betekenis mede aan de specifieke context waarbinnen ze worden geuit en gebruikt.'

with their own convictions, how to live their lives. Regardless of whether an individual's highest aim is to live according to the commands of God or Allah or the teachings of Buddha, Karl Marx or Adam Smith, the state should not interfere, on the basis of the principle of equal treatment, so long as the individual in question leaves others in peace and does not inflict harm upon them. By elevating individual freedom to the highest value, the state relinquishes a claim to a particular vision of the Good Life.

The idea behind this course of action is that people will never be in agreement on such matters, since individuals necessarily hold differing opinions. This means that people adhering to diverse religions, worldviews and political convictions while living together in freedom *and* peace requires a value-neutral state. In other words, if individual (political) freedom is considered to be the main directive, this implies that the state must respect diversity. There is only one value with respect to which the state is not neutral, namely, the very value that must guarantee that every individual is free to be happy or miserable in his own way and in accordance with his own insights and predilections: freedom of belief, thought and action. The values the liberal state protects are thus *qualitate qua* individual values that are embodied in classic rights such as freedom of speech and conscience, freedom of religion, freedom of association and assembly, the right to bodily integrity and the prohibition of discrimination, in accordance with the principle of equal treatment.[21]

This means that freedom of speech *itself* is not a neutral principle, but rather part of a certain sort of political system, which by definition entails a choice for a certain sort of society.[22] This is based on individual freedom and equality. So once freedom of speech is used to realize a sort of society that subverts these individual values of equality and freedom, it undermines its own foundations. In order to be able to continue to exist as a political-social legal order, then, this legal order must necessarily place limits on freedom of speech at the point where said values are in danger of being corrupted by freedom of speech itself.[23] In that light, freedom of speech *cannot* be a principle devoid of content but must have content. The liberal democratic constitutional state presupposes some form of militant democracy in that sense.[24]

21 See, in relation to this matter, for example J. Habermas, *Recht en politiek in een tijd van globalisering*, Zoetermeer: Klement, 2011, p. 62-79.

22 Cf. J.R. Searle, *Making the Social World. The Structure of Human Civilization*, Oxford: Oxford University Press, 2010, p. 190: 'the justification for human rights cannot be ethically neutral. It involves more than just a biological conception of what sort of beings we are; it also involves a conception of what is valuable, actually or potentially, about our very existence.'

23 Fish, 1999, p. 106: '(...) the right to speak cannot be abstracted from the political conditions in the context of which its exercise is meaningful. If speech is allowed to corrode those conditions, it participates in its own undoing, in its own death, and (...) in order to save speech (and the country), there are times when we must act to restrict it.'

24 This is expressed, for instance, in article 17 ECHR, which states that the rights in the ECHR may not be invoked in order to destroy any of the rights and freedoms (of other (groups of) people) set forth therein.

For freedom of speech, this means, in concrete terms, that the limit must be acknowledged where said freedom is employed to discriminate against (groups of) people on the basis of their race, sexual orientation, physical or mental disability, gender or beliefs, or to call for violence against them. This conflicts, after all, with the core values that provide the foundation of the liberal democratic constitutional state, to wit, individual freedom and equality (in the sense of individual equal value). The paradox of freedom of speech is, accordingly, that in order to ensure the classic rights to freedom and equality, it is sometimes necessary to restrict them. At the same time, this evinces the nature and contents of this limitation: No restrictions are warranted save for those that are necessary to ensure those rights. In penal legal terms this means that calling for discrimination and violence should be criminalized, while group insult and incitement to hatred should not.[25]

In other words, the limits of freedom of speech are a result of the ideology of the liberal democratic constitutional state, the focus being on 'constitutional state'. Should the convictions of the majority contrast with the core values behind the constitutional state, such as freedom and equality, the majority is restrained by the law. In that sense, the liberal democratic constitutional state is based on a substantive conception of democracy. In order to guarantee the continuance of the liberal democratic constitutional state, the sovereignty of the people must, in extreme cases, be restrained by the (criminal) law.

It is clear from a ruling of the Amsterdam court in 1998, regarding the ban of the National People's Party/Centre Party '86, that the Dutch constitutional legal order is based

The ECtHR applied this article in *Refah v. Turkey* (*Refah Partisi (The Welfare Party) and Others v. Turkey*, Judgment, Strasbourg, 13 February 2003). A similar situation applies in Germany; article 18 of the Basic Law reads: 'Whoever abuses the freedom of expression, in particular the freedom of the press (paragraph 1 of Article 5), the freedom of teaching (paragraph 3 of Article 5), the freedom of assembly (Article 8), the freedom of association (Article 9), the privacy of correspondence, posts and telecommunications (Article 10), the rights of property (Article 14), or the right of asylum (Article 16a) in order to combat the free democratic basic order shall forfeit these basic rights. This forfeiture and its extent shall be declared by the Federal Constitutional Court.' The original text reads: 'Wer die Freiheit der Meinungsäußerung, insbesondere die Pressefreiheit (Artikel 5 Abs. 1), die Lehrfreiheit (Artikel 5 Abs. 3), die Versammlungsfreiheit (Artikel 8), die Vereinigungsfreiheit (Artikel 9), das Brief-, Post- und Fernmeldegeheimnis (Artikel 10), das Eigentum (Artikel 14) oder das Asylrecht (Artikel 16a) zum Kampfe gegen die freiheitliche demokratische Grundordnung mißbraucht, verwirkt diese Grundrechte. Die Verwirkung und ihr Ausmaß werden durch das Bundesverfassungsgericht ausgesprochen.' A theoretical discussion of this substantive conception of democracy may be found in Q.L. Hong, *The Legal Inclusion of Extremist Speech* (PhD thesis), Nijmegen: Wolf Legal Publishers, 2005. Vide, for a clear review of this PhD thesis and the problems of militant democracy, A. Soeteman, in: *Rechtsfilosofie & Rechtstheorie*, 2006, vol. 35, p. 178-182. See also Nieuwenhuis, 2010, p. 8; S. Rummens, 'De vrije mening van politici', *Rechtsfilosofie & Rechtstheorie*, 2011, vol. 40, p. 3-5.

25 See, in this regard, also M. Fennema, 'Noot bij de uitspraak van het gerechtshof te Amsterdam van 21 januari 2009 waarin het de strafvervolging van Geert Wilders beveelt', *Strafblad*, 2009, vol. 7, p. 198-209. A. Nieuwenhuis & E. Janssen, 'De onduidelijke verhouding tussen vrijheid van meningsuiting en discriminatie. Een analyse van de groepsbelediging en het haatzaaien', *Mediaforum*, 2011, vol. 4, p. 94-104. Arguments in favor of abolishing group insult on the basis of religion or beliefs may be found, for instance, in *Nederlands Juristenblad*, 2003, no. 16, 'Opinie', p. 828-833. G. Molier, 'Over de vrijheid van meningsuiting en groepsbelediging wegens religie', *Civis Mundi*, 2009, vol. 48, p. 162-163.

on such a substantive conception of democracy. Even though the Dutch Criminal Code does not specify such a conception, as is the case in Germany, where a political party may be declared unconstitutional and thereby annulled on the basis of its program if it conflicts with the values of the democratic constitutional state, the National People's Party/Centre Party '86 was banned on account of its committing:

> 'Acts that infringe upon *generally accepted foundations of our system of justice*, such as unjustified violation of *another's freedom or human dignity*. The condemnable nature of race discrimination has been explicitly deemed as such. This means that repetitively inciting, giving rise to or propagating discrimination certainly qualifies as grounds for banning, even under a very restrictive interpretation of the concept of 'public order.'[26]

Freedom of speech is no neutral principle, then, but presupposes a certain view of society. There are those who will consider this a decent view of society, while others will rather consider the sort of society *they themselves* deem desirable, decent, and may consider indecent, for example, one in which gay marriages are allowed on the basis of their *Weltanschauung*.

The foregoing makes it clear that freedom of speech always serves the fulfillment of one political agenda or another, which means that it is indeed 'politics all the way down.'[27] The same applies to the limits set by the law.[28] The judge who must at some point judge whether freedom of speech must be restrained under certain circumstances cannot escape from taking into consideration his view on a decent society, albeit of course within the room the law leaves him.

His decision is obviously directed by the public climate of the moment and the specific context of the case. This also means that the same limit cannot be set for all circumstances: Different circumstances and a different public context may cause the limit to be set differently. Judicial decisions are in that sense always 'ad hoc' and impossibly 'principal' in the sense of 'transcending the individual case.' This does not constitute an argument not to restrict freedom of speech at all. Unless one maintains that words can do no harm, it is

---

26 Amsterdam court, 18 November 1998, *NJ* 1999, 377, 4.3 (italicization G.M.).

27 Fish, 1999, p. 101: '(...) any program of regulation in the name of a sanitized public discourse will rest on an ideological specification of what that discourse is. Even if you pledged yourself to watch out for it, the part of your mind that was doing the watching would itself still be informed by some "value commitment", some ideology. You can no more watch neutrally than you can speak or deliberate neutrally; it is ideology (and politics) all the way down.'

28 Fish, 1999, p. 94: '(...) for since speech is unimaginable apart from consequences and since consequences of any piece of speech will be friendly to some interests and inimical to some others, the decision to draw a line between protected and regulated speech will always be a decision to advance some interests and discourage others, will always, that is, be a political decision.'

necessary for the continuation of our liberal democratic constitutional state to limit freedom of speech.[29]

29 Fish, 1999, p. 101: '[T]otal toleration of speech makes sense only if speech is regarded as inconsequential and unlikely to bring about a result you would find either heartening or distressing.'

5 Extension of Parliamentary Immunity[1]

Remco Nehmelman and Max Vetzo

Introduction

With the acquittal of Geert Wilders on the 23rd of June, 2011, a long-lasting and controversial legal process came to an end. Wilders was prosecuted for the rather strong political statements he had made outside of the parliamentary arena.[2] It is noteworthy that if Wilders would have made his statements during a parliamentary debate, that is, at a moment when Parliament would be 'officially' in session, he could not have been prosecuted. Article 71 of the Dutch Constitution provides that anyone taking part in parliamentary deliberations cannot be prosecuted or otherwise held liable in law for anything he says during the sessions of the States General or its committees or for anything he submits to them in writing.[3] This provision deals with the doctrine of parliamentary immunity. The Dutch legislator opted for a very limited scheme of immunity compared with other European constitutions. A Member of Parliament does not enjoy immunity for statements expressed outside Parliament, which means that he can be prosecuted for alleged criminal statements made outside the assembly. Thus, the limited constitutional regime of parliamentary immunity in the Netherlands entails that the place of action, namely parliamentary proceedings, is essential for immunity. This system is characterised as the system of 'intraparliamentary immunity'. Moreover, this immunity applies not only to parliamentarians, but also to members of the government and even to any other person who is allowed to take part in parliamentary deliberations, such as civil servants.

The Wilders trial led to a debate about the extension of the immunity of parliamentarians. Some legal scholars argued that the reach of parliamentary immunity should be broadened and should also cover statements made outside Parliament. This change would make it impossible to prosecute members of the States General for their political statements made outside the Assembly. Some, including Geert Wilders himself, proposed to change

---

1 This chapter originally appeared as R. Nehmelman, 'Uitbreiding van de parlementaire immuniteit' *in* A. Ellian, G. Molier and T. Zwart (Eds.), *Mag ik dit zeggen?*, Boom Juridische uitgevers, The Hague, p. 243-262. Max Vetzo is responsible for the extension of section 4 on the European Court of Human Rights and parliamentary immunity. In writing this paper we have gratefully made use of the award-winning master's thesis, *Parlementaire immuniteit in een Europese context [Parliamentary immunity in a European context]*, by P.E. de Morree (supervised by R. Nehmelman), Utrecht, 2009, published at: http://Montesqieu-instituut.nl/9353202/d/prijzen_2010/paulien_demorree.pdf.

2 Amsterdam District Court, 23 June 2011, *LJN*: BQ9001.

3 The States General consists of the House of Representatives and the Senate.

the criminal law to the extent that *everyone* in the Netherlands should have full freedom of (political) expression. In this chapter, the doctrine of parliamentary immunity will be discussed and, in addition, different appearances of parliamentary immunity will be distilled. The structure of this chapter is as follows: First, the history of the Dutch parliamentary immunity will be set out. This will be helpful in understanding the development of the concept of parliamentary immunity in the Netherlands. The current codification of article 71 of the Dutch Constitution is regarded as a (provisional) end point of this development. Subsequently, some foreign systems will be looked at. This will show that there is a great variety in how parliamentary immunity is regulated in different countries. Then, the case law of the European Court of Human Rights (ECtHR) will be examined. Over the last few decades, the Strasbourg Court has handed down a couple of relevant, but also contradictory, judgements on the matter of parliamentary immunity. Furthermore, the views on the concept of parliamentary immunity in legal literature will be set out. Both in recent and older literature, legal scholars have discussed the concept and scope of parliamentary immunity. Thereafter, this chapter will rethink the current scheme of parliamentary immunity in the Netherlands. In this context, we will focus on the temporal scope of parliamentary immunity (when does immunity start and end?) and the question whether statements made outside Parliament should also fall within the scope of parliamentary immunity. This chapter will end with a conclusion.

History of the Doctrine of Parliamentary Immunity

Early Development

The doctrine of parliamentary immunity already existed during the Roman Empire. At that time, it was prohibited to attack the Roman people's representatives or interfere with the exercise of their functions.[4] The motive behind this scheme was to guarantee the representatives of the Roman people freedom in the exercise of their activities.[5] The immunity rules for British Members of Parliament are the oldest rules on parliamentary immunity which are still in force. Article 9 of the Bill of Rights, adopted in 1689, states: 'That the freedom of speech, and debates or proceedings in parliament, ought not to be impeached or questioned in any court or place out of parliament.' In the centuries before 1689, England had grown to become a parliamentary democracy. The influence of the Westminster Par-

4 M. van der Hulst, *The Parliamentary Mandate: A Global Comparative Study*, Inter-Parliamentary Union, Geneva, 2000, p. 63.

5 S. McGee and A. Isaacs, *Rules on Parliamentary Immunity in the European Parliament and the Member States of the European Union* (final draft), European Centre for Parliamentarian Research and Documentation, Brussels, 2001, Introduction section.

liament on legislation and on monitoring the government gradually increased over the centuries. The explicit codification of parliamentary immunity in the Bill of Rights should therefore mainly be seen as a protection clause against the British monarch. Before the codification of parliamentary immunity in the Bill of Rights it occasionally occurred that the King imprisoned a Member of Parliament in response to unwelcome statements. In this context, the apprehension of Richard Strode in 1512 is illustrative. Strode, a Member of Parliament, tried to introduce a bill to improve working conditions in the British tin mines on Dartmoor. However, even before Strode could travel to Westminster, he was arrested and imprisoned for obstruction. The British Parliament rejected this way of acting and passed a bill called Strode's Act, officially entitled the Privilege of Parliament Act 1512. This bill condemned the judgement that convicted Strode and stated that judges had to act differently in similar future cases. Nevertheless, the bill did not seem to help much as British parliamentarians were systematically imprisoned for their political statements by order of the King up to 1689. The dethronement of King James II in 1688 is regarded as a turning point in British history, as Great Britain has been a parliamentary democracy ever since.[6] The absolute supremacy of the British monarch ended at that time. Up until now the codification of the rights of Parliament, including parliamentary immunity, in the Bill of Rights has had a very important constitutional value.

Even though immunity is an important parliamentary privilege, the protection provided for in article 9 of the Bill of Rights is limited to what has been said in Parliament. About one century later, in 1791, another model for the protection of the position of representatives originated in France. During the French Revolution, in which the monarchy was overthrown and replaced by the Republic, there was a strong call to strengthen the position of parliamentarians. The French Constitution of 1791 included an immunity clause under which, unlike the British model, parliamentarians not only enjoyed immunity within Parliament, but were also protected against prosecution for their behavior outside of parliamentary deliberations. However, a majority in Parliament could make prosecution possible by lifting parliamentary immunity.

The two models of parliamentary immunity outlined above have served as a model for other Western parliamentary democracies. On the one hand, there is a very limited model that entails that immunity only exists for what has been said in Parliament (intraparliamentary immunity) and, on the other hand, we can see a model that also covers statements and even behavior outside the sessions of Parliament (extraparliamentary immunity). The current Dutch model is similar to the British scheme. The British model, for that matter, has been applied to a lesser extent than the broader French variant. An important difference between the two models has already been demonstrated. In the British and Dutch models,

6 I. Loveland, *Constitutional Law, Administrative Law and Human Rights: A Critical Introduction*, 4th edition, Oxford University Press, Oxford, 2006, p. 265-266.

parliamentary debates enjoy immunity, while in the French model, it is the Member of Parliament who enjoys immunity. Moreover, in the latter scheme the scope of the immunity may vary from covering all actions both within and outside Parliament (inviolability) and protecting the freedom of expression of a member of parliament.

Development in the Netherlands

The first provisions regarding the doctrine of parliamentary immunity in the Netherlands were laid down in the Constitution of the Batavian People of 1798.[7] Even though there were some forms of protection and freedom of advice before 1798, they only had minor significance.[8] It is no surprise that the provisions on parliamentary immunity in the Constitution of 1798 were strongly influenced by the French Constitution of 1791. Actions by members of parliament, both within and outside Parliament, ought to have been non-prosecutable. In the relationship between Parliament, the government and the courts, the freedom and independence of Parliament had to be ensured.[9] The provisions of the Constitution on parliamentary immunity were rather comprehensive. A separate section of the Constitution, entitled 'Safeguarding members of the Representative Body', ensured that Members of the Representative Body could not be 'hunted down, accused, or condemned' for written or spoken statements in the exercise of 'their Post'.[10] If one wanted a member of parliament to be prosecuted for acts committed outside Parliament, then first, similar to the French model, the Representative Body had to give its consent. The Supreme Court was the competent judicial authority to decide on the question whether a member of parliament should be convicted.[11] In the period between 1798 and 1814, the rules on parliamentary immunity were changed on a couple of occasions. Eventually, little remained of the comprehensive scheme that had been introduced in 1798.[12]

Between 1814 and 1848, the legislator barely paid attention to the doctrine of parliamentary immunity. The Constitutions of 1814, 1815 and 1840 only provided for a limited

---

7 Cf. also P.J. Oud, *Het Constitutioneel Recht van het Koninkrijk der Nederlanden*, Deel I *[Constitutional Law of the Kingdom of the Netherlands, Part I]*, 2th edition, W.E.J. Tjeenk Willink, Zwolle, 1967, p. 596.

8 D.J. Elzinga, 'Parlementaire Onschendbaarheid voor Volksvertegenwoordigers, Verouderd Instituut of Onmisbare Bescherming?' [Parliamentary Immunity for Representatives of the People, Obsolete Institution or Indispensable Protection?], *in*: D.J. Elzinga (Ed.), *De Staat en het Recht: Opstellen over Staatsrecht en Politiek* [*The State and the Law. Essays on Constitutional Law and Politics*], W.E.J. Tjeenk Willink, Zwolle, 1990, p. 119.

9 Oud, 1967, p. 595.

10 Article 71 of the Constitution of the Batavian People of 1798. Cf. also G.W. Bannier, *Grondwetten van Nederland [Constitutions of The Netherlands]*, W.E.J. Tjeenk Willink, Zwolle, 1936, p. 65.

11 Article 119 of the Dutch Constitution provides a scheme for the prosecution and trial of misfeasance. In this system the Supreme Court acts as the so-called *Forum Privilegiatum*. This will be further elaborated upon in section 6.

12 Cf. Bannier, 1936, p. 171-172.

immunity in respect of criminal prosecution. The immunity could be lifted by Parliament itself.[13] In 1848, the legislator established a system of parliamentary immunity in the Dutch Constitution. The ideal of strengthening the position of the Dutch Parliament was one of the main reasons for establishing a new Constitution. Unprecedented revolutionary constitutional reforms took place under the inspiring leadership of J.R. Thorbecke. For example, for the first time in Dutch constitutional history, the Constitution provided for a system in which members of the States General would be elected directly by the people.[14] The codification of the doctrine of parliamentary immunity in the new Constitution seems quite logical in the light of the underpinning ideal to strengthen the position of Parliament. The former Article 92 granted immunity for 'advice given by them (members of parliament) in the assembly'. This provision enabled Members of the States General to say what they considered desirable in the light of the public interest without having to fear prosecution.[15] Consequently, the newly introduced system of parliamentary immunity strengthened the independent position of parliamentarians.[16] Adhering to the British model, the Dutch system of parliamentary immunity was restricted to statements made during debates in the States General. Unfortunately, it is not possible to exactly deduce the reasoning on which this system of limited immunity was based. Extending the immunity to behavior of members of parliament outside of parliamentary deliberations would probably be a step too far in the eyes of the Crown. It is also likely that conservative members of parliament would not have agreed with the implementation of a broader concept of immunity.[17]

After 1848, the codification of parliamentary immunity in the Dutch Constitution has undergone some changes. In the Constitution of 1887, the term 'advice' was removed and the scope was broadened to the extent that it also covered the written or spoken statements of members of parliament in the sessions of the States General or one of its committees. This change meant that the statements made did not have to relate to the subject of the meeting.[18] In 1922, the system of immunity was extended to ministers and other persons participating in the debate. In 1948, State Secretaries were also placed under the protection of the immunity clause. By broadening the scope of the provision, parliamentary immunity developed from a personal privilege for Members of the States General to a privilege for everyone participating in the sessions of the States General. Finally, in 1983 the words 'or otherwise held liable in law' were added to the current article 71 of the Dutch Constitution. The legislator thus expressed that parliamentary immunity includes protection against

13 Elzinga 1990, p. 121.

14 However, the suffrage conferred on the Dutch people has to be considered as a census suffrage.

15 Oud 1967, p. 597.

16 P.P.T. Bovend'Eert and H.R.B.M. Kummeling, *Het Nederlandse Parlement [The Dutch Parliament]*, 10th edition, Kluwer, Deventer, 2004, p. 118.

17 According to Elzinga 1990, p. 121 ff.

18 Elzinga 1990, p. 121.

criminal as well as civil, administrative and disciplinary liability. Ever since then, article 71 of the Constitution reads as follows:

> 'Members of the States General, Ministers, State Secretaries and other persons taking part in deliberations may not be prosecuted or otherwise held liable in law for anything they say during the sessions of the States General or of its committees or for anything they submit to them in writing.'

In 1987, this provision was at the centre of an interesting legal dispute. The District Court of The Hague was faced with the question whether Article 71 of the Constitution refers to the persons mentioned in the article itself or to the office that these persons hold.[19] As to the facts of the case, the plaintiff Harm Drost argued that statements made by both Minister Van den Broek and Minister Korthals Altes during a sitting of the Senate were incorrect and misleading. In the view of Drost, these statements unfavorably influenced the process of decision making in the States General and eventually led to his extradition to Germany. Drost reasoned that if article 71 would be interpreted as applying to the participants in the debate in person, it would mean that the provision did not necessarily apply to the participants in the debate in the performance of their duties as ministers. Then, an action could be brought against them for the statements made in the States General as organs of the State of the Netherlands. As the State is liable for the conduct of its organs, this would ultimately lead to the civil liability of the State of the Netherlands. The Court, however, did not follow this reasoning and stated:

> 'The intention of the provision is apparently that ministers and state secretaries must be able to express themselves without reservation during the ssessions of the States General, i.e. knowing that it is not the competence of the courts to check the lawfulness of their statements. If the plaintiff's reasoning would be followed, the Court, in order to assess the liability of the State, would have to look into what the ministers have said. This reading is contrary to the wording of Article 71.'[20]

SOME FOREIGN SYSTEMS

In the foregoing, we have already briefly paid attention to the British system of parliamentary immunity. The British scheme originated in 1689 and is still considered to be one of the most basic British privileges. As mentioned before, the current Dutch provision corre-

19 The Hague District Court, 26 February 1987 (Harm Dost), *Kort Geding*, 134, 1987.

20 The Hague District Court, 26 February 1987 (Harm Dost) *Kort Geding*, 134, 1987, paragraph 6.2.

sponds to the British regime. As to their approach to the concept of parliamentary immunity, both Britain and the Netherlands hold a unique position. This is because, after all, the immunity in both systems is limited to what is said during the sessions of Parliament. The French system of parliamentary immunity, the so-called extraparliamentary immunity, served as a blueprint for many other Western systems.[21] The current French system of parliamentary immunity is enshrined in article 26 of the French Constitution. This provision ensures that a member of one of the Chambers (the National Assembly and the Senate) is able to speak and write freely during the sessions of Parliament. Article 26 of the French Constitution further provides that criminal offences committed by a representative can be prosecuted if the Presidium of the Assembly lifts the immunity of the Member of Parliament concerned. However, it has to be noted that within the system provided under Article 26 of the French Constitution, even though a Member of the French Parliament can be convicted directly after the immunity has been lifted, any detention can only take place after the convicted parliamentarian is no longer a Member of Parliament. The Belgian system has strong similarities with the French model. The Belgian scheme consists of two constitutional provisions. The first provision (Article 58 of the Belgian Constitution) establishes full immunity for statements of parliamentarians which are made in the exercise of their function. In Belgium this provision is also referred to as 'parliamentary accountability'. In this scheme, the decisive factor is not the place where the statement was made, but whether the statement was made in the exercise of the function of a parliamentarian. In that sense, this immunity goes beyond the Dutch system of immunity. However, statements made during (party) political activities should not be regarded as statements made in the exercise of the function of a parliamentarian. Therefore, interviews, speeches at party meetings and press conferences are strangely enough not covered by this provision. In Belgium, unlike the Dutch system, parliamentary immunity also applies to statements made outside Parliament. So the extension of the protective value of immunity is limited in scope. The second provision establishes a special regime for the criminal prosecution of a Member of Parliament (Article 59 of the Belgian Constitution). In Belgium a Member of one of the Chambers cannot be prosecuted, arrested or otherwise held liable in law before a court or tribunal, except when the Chamber of which he is a Member lifts his immunity. A majority decision of the House of which the parliamentarian is a Member is needed in order to lift this immunity.[22]

In Germany, immunity exists for members of the *Bundestag* (not for members of the *Bundesrat*!). Article 46 of the *Grundgesetz* (GG) provides that a Member of the *Bundestag*

---

21 Cf. also R. Nehmelman, *De Verboden Politieke Meningsuiting als Ambtsmisdrijf* [The Forbidden Political Free Speech as Misfeasance] *in* R. Nehmelman (Ed.), *Parlementaire Immuniteit Vanuit een Europese Context bezien [Parliamentary Immunity viewed from a European Perspective]*, Wolf, Nijmegen, 2010, p. 12 ff. Cf. the comprehensive analysis of the Belgian system in the same publication: S. Sottiaux, p. 49 ff.

22 Cf. also ECtHR 16 July 2009, *Féret t. België*, appl. no. 15615/07, *Mediaforum* Vol. 11, no. 10, 2009.

enjoys immunity for the oral or written comments he makes during parliamentary debates (in both plenary and committee sessions). An exception is made for offensive language. The second paragraph of article 46 of the GG provides that the Members of the *Bundestag* also enjoy immunity for statements made outside of the assembly, although this immunity can be lifted by a majority decision of the *Bundestag*. It is established practice that at the beginning of a session of the *Bundestag* the immunity is collectively lifted by the Members.[23] The underlying reason for this is that individual procedures for lifting immunity attract a great deal of publicity. By collectively lifting the immunity at the start of the session of the *Bundestag*, a possible criminal investigation can take place without the media already having interfered because of the prior lifting of immunity.

The European Court of Human Rights and Parliamentary Immunity

For a proper understanding of the doctrine of parliamentary immunity it is necessary to discuss the case law of the European Court of Human Rights.[24] Over the past few decades, the Strasbourg Court has been faced with questions that lie at the heart of the concept of parliamentary immunity. Many of the cases concern the conviction of a parliamentarian. The main question in these cases is whether a conviction can withstand the test of article 10 of the ECHR (freedom of expression). In some cases, article 6 of the ECHR (the right to a fair trial) plays a central role. The question is then raised of whether the immunity of members of parliament constitutes a breach of article 6, as parliamentary immunity prevents third parties from taking legal action against parliamentarians.

First and foremost, it has to be noted that parliamentary immunity for statements made *during* sessions of Parliament must be regarded as absolute in the sense that parliamentarians cannot be held liable in law for the statements they make during parliamentary deliberations. The high-profile decision in *A v. the United Kingdom* is considered to be the start of this line of argumentation.[25] In this case, during the sitting of the British Parliament, Michael Stern, a British parliamentarian, made some remarks on the antisocial behavior of his neighbors and called them 'neighbors from hell'. After that his neighbors were approached by journalists and television reporters and received hate mail. Therefore, the neighbors decided to take legal action against Stern. Eventually, the case ended up in Strasbourg. The neighbors argued that Stern's parliamentary immunity prevented them from taking legal action in respect of statements made about them in Parliament and this

23 ECtHR 8 July 2008, appl. no. 8917/05, *Kart v. Turkey*, Cf. also the case comment on the case: *European Human Rights Law Review*, No. 6, 2008, pp. 795-797.

24 See the comprehensive study by R. Lawson: 'Wild, wilder, wildst. Over de ruimte die het EVRM laat voor de vervolging van kwetsende politici', *NJCM-Bulletin*, No. 4, 2008, pp. 469-484.

25 ECtHR 17 December 2002, *A. v. United Kingdom*, appl. no. 35373/97, *Nederlands Juristenblad*, 2003, pp. 330-331.

therefore violated their right of access to a court under article 6. The ECtHR held that in this case, the doctrine of parliamentary immunity must be regarded as an inherent restriction on the right of access to a court and stated that: 'In all the circumstances of this case, the application of a rule of absolute parliamentary immunity cannot be said to exceed the margin of appreciation allowed to States in limiting an individual's right of access to a court.'[26] This holds despite the fact that the Court found the allegations 'extremely serious and clearly unnecessary'.[27] In the specific circumstances of this case, parliamentary immunity must be regarded as an absolute right that does not constitute a breach of article 6. So, the application of the concept of parliamentary immunity may have far-reaching consequences.

In *A. v. the United Kingdom*, the Court emphasized that Stern had made his statements during parliamentary deliberations. As immunity for statements within Parliament itself 'is consistent with and reflects generally recognized rules within signatory States', this type of immunity 'cannot in principle be regarded as imposing a disproportionate restriction on the right of access to a court'.[28]

As to the question whether article 6 had been violated, the Court deemed of importance whether a statement was made within the assembly. Therefore, in assessing matters of parliamentary immunity, the Court will first look at the question whether a statement is made 'within the exercise of parliamentary functions in their strict sense'.[29] When this 'strict sense test' is passed, no violation of article 6 will be found. However, regarding the assessment of a possible violation of article 6, when statements are not made within the exercise of parliamentary functions in their strict sense, the Court will look into the question whether there is a clear connection between a specific statement and a parliamentary activity.[30] As the Court held in its *Cordova* judgement, 'the lack of any clear connection with a parliamentary activity requires the Court to adopt a narrow interpretation of the concept of proportionality between the aim sought to be achieved and the means employed.'[31] The approach of the ECtHR to the concept of a 'clear connection' is a narrow one. For example, in the case of *Patrono, Cascini and Stefanelli v Italy*, the Court held that the rather strong (political) comments of members of parliament on the dismissal of three

26 ECtHR *A. v. United Kingdom*, paragraph 87 with reference to ECtHR 21 November 2011, *Al-Adsani v. the United Kingdom*, appl. no. 35763/97, paragraph 47.

27 ECtHR *A. v. United Kingdom*, paragraph 88.

28 *Ibid.*, paragraph 83.

29 ECtHR 30 January 2003, *Cordova v. Italy*, appl. no. 40877/89, paragraph 62. See also ECHR 3 June 2004, *De Jorio v Italy*, appl. no. 73936/01, paragraph 53, ECtHR 6 December 2005, *Ielo v Italy*, appl. no. 23053/02, paragraph 50 and ECtHR 24 February 2009, *Conferatti v. Italy*, appl. no. 46967/07 paragraph 72.

30 See for a more detailed view of the steps the Court takes in assessing a possible violation of article 6, R.J.B. Schutgens, *Parlementaire immuniteit [Parliamentary Immunity]*, preadvies NJV Zomer 2013, Deventer, Kluwer 2013, p. 29 and 30.

31 *Cordova v. Italy*, paragraph 63.

Italian judges had no clear connection with their parliamentary activities.[32] According to Schutgens, there are no cases in which the Court has come to the conclusion that a parliamentarian's behavior outside Parliament constituted a clear connection with its parliamentary activities.[33]

For statements made outside Parliament, the Castells case is an important starting point. Castells, a Spanish senator, was prosecuted for insulting the Spanish government in the media.[34] As a supporter of the independence of the Basque Country, Castells, in a newspaper article, accused the Spanish authorities of laxity in prosecuting the perpetrators of murders contrived by right-wing extremists. He accused the government of complicity in the murders. At the insistance of the Spanish Supreme Court, the Spanish Senate lifted Castells' immunity. Both before the Supreme Court and the Constitutional Court, Castells argued that his statements were part of the political criticism that any member of parliament has to be able to engage in. However, both Courts rejected this contention. Castells lodged an application with the ECtHR and claimed that his freedom of expression had been violated. In its judgement, the ECtHR emphasized the importance of a Member of Parliament's right to freedom of expression. The Strasbourg Court held that freedom of expression constitutes one of the essential foundations of a democratic society and it considered the right of freedom of expression to be especially important for parliamentarians, as they represent and defend the interests of their electorate. The court came to the following conclusion:

> 'While freedom of expression is important for everybody, it is especially so for an elected representative of the people. He represents his electorate, draws attention to their preoccupations and defends their interests. Accordingly, interferences with the freedom of expression of an opposition member of parliament, like the applicant, call for the closest scrutiny on the part of the Court.'[35]

One month after its Castells judgement, the Court, in a 'non-parliamentary' case concerning an Icelandic author who had made allegations that excessive violence was common practice by the Icelandic police force, reiterated its standpoint that 'the freedom of expression as enshrined in Article 10 (...) is subject to a number of exceptions which, however, must be narrowly interpreted and the necessity for any restrictions must be

32 ECtHR 20 April 2006, *Patrono, Cascini and Stefanelli v. Italy*, appl. no.10180/04, paragraph 53. See also ECtHR 16 November 2006, *Tsalkitzis v. Greece*, appl. no. 11801/04, paragraph 49.

33 Schutgens 2013, p. 29.

34 ECtHR 23 April 1992, *Castells v. Spain*, with case note, E.J. Dommering, appl. no. 11798/85, *Nederlandse Jurisprudentie*, No. 102, 1994.

35 *Ibid.*, paragraph 42.

convincingly established.'[36] Furthermore, in the case of *Wingrove v. United Kingdom*, the ECtHR held 'that there is little scope under Article 10 para. 2 of the Convention for restrictions on political speech or on debate of questions of public interest'.[37] In the case *Jerusalem v Austria*, the Court recalled its *Castells* judgement and added that freedom of expression constitutes one of the basic conditions for the progress of democratic society and for individual self-fulfilment.[38] More recently, the ECHR has confirmed that the limits of acceptable criticism are wider with regard to a politician than they are with regard to a private individual.[39] Even provocative, offensive, shocking or disturbing statements are in principle protected under article 10 of the ECHR.[40] In the case of *Otegi Mondragon v. Spain*, the Spanish Supreme Court found Arnaldo Otegi, a member of a left-wing Basque separatist parliamentary group, guilty of a serious insult against the Spanish King and sentenced him to one year's imprisonment. During a visit by the Spanish King to the Basque Country, Otegi had stated that the King 'defends torture and imposes his monarchical regime on our people through torture and violence'. The ECtHR found a breach of article 10 of the ECHR even though it held that Otegi's statements portrayed the King in a very negative light, with a hostile connotation and could be regarded as provocative.[41] The right to make these kinds of statements especially, according to the Court, are the demands of pluralism, tolerance and broadmindedness, without which there would be no democratic society.[42]

It is important to note that the Court does not regard the freedom of speech of parliamentarians, regarding statements made outside the parliamentary debate, to be an absolute right. For instance, in the *Piermont* case, the Court made clear that it does look at the exact wording of the statements that were made and the conditions under which those statements were made.[43]In this case Piermont, a German Member of the European Parliament, criti-

36 ECtHR 25 June 1992, *Thorgeir Thorgeirson v. Iceland*, appl. no. 13778/88, paragraph 63. In *Nilsen & Johnsson v. Norway* the Court, referring to *Thorgeir Thorgeirson*, stated that the strict scrutiny approach is not limited to 'arguable allegations of police misconduct', but 'also applies to speech aimed at countering such allegations since it forms part of the same debate'. See ECtHR 25 November 1999, *Nilsen & Johnsson v. Norway*, appl. no. 23118/93, paragraph 44.

37 ECtHR 25 November 1996, *Wingrove v United Kingdom*, appl. no. 17419/90, paragraph 58. The court confirmed this line of argument in ECtHR *Sürek v. Turkey*, appl. no. 26682/95, paragraph 61 and ECtHR 12 July 2001, *Feldek v. Slovakia*, appl. no. 29032/95, paragraph 74.

38 ECtHR 27 February 2001, *Jerusalem v. Austria*, appl. no.26958/95, paragraph 32.

39 See, for example, ECtHR 6 April 2006, *Malisiewicz-Gasior v. Poland*, appl. no. 43797/98, paragraph 57. Cf. also A.R. Mowbray, *Cases and Materials on the European Convention on Human Rights*, 2th edition, Oxford University Press, Oxford, 2007, p. 396.

40 ECtHR 29 October 1992, *Open Door and Dublin Well Woman v. Ireland*, appl. no. 14234/88 and 14 235/88, paragraph. 71-72.

41 Case ECtHR 15 March 2011, *Otegi Mondragon v. Spain*, appl. no. 2034/07, paragraphs 54, 61 and 62.

42 See ECtHR 29 March 2005, *Sokołowski v. Poland*, appl. no. 75955/01, paragraph 41 and ECtHR 23 September 1994, *Jersild v. Denmark*, appl. no. 15890/89, paragraph 37.

43 ECtHR 27 April 1995, *Piermont v. France*, appl. no. 15773/89 and 15774/89, *Nederlandse Jurisprudentie*, No. 498, 1996.

cized the continuation of nuclear testing by France during a visit to French Polynesia. The French authorities expelled Piermont from the country and imposed an entry ban on her. The Court held that the statements made by Piermont were peaceful and were expressed during a demonstration authorized by the authorities. Thus, the context in which statements are made are an important factor to balance in determining the scope of article 10. According to the Court, the fight against intolerance is an integral part of the protection of human rights. In that sense, it is crucial that politicians, in the exercise of their public duties, avoid making statements that foster intolerance.[44]

The context-based approach of the Strasbourg Court in assessing matters of parliamentary immunity, in our opinion, diametrically opposes the Castells case law in which the Court clearly stated that the limits of the freedom of expression for politicians are wider because of their representative function. In this context-based approach, the Court in particular looks at the impact that certain statements can have. This may mean that a politician in fact has more responsibility in expressing his opinions. The aforementioned approach is expressly brought forward in the *Zana* judgment from 1997. In this case, the Court came to the following conclusion:

> 'The statement cannot, however, be looked at in isolation. It had a special significance in the circumstances of the case, as the applicant must have realised. (...) The interview coincided with murderous attacks carried out by the PKK on civilians in south-east Turkey, where there was extreme tension at the material time. In those circumstances the support given to the PKK -. described as a "national liberation movement" - by the former mayor of Diyarbakyr, the most important city in south-east Turkey, in an interview published in a major national daily newspaper, had to be regarded as likely to exacerbate an already explosive situation in that region.'[45]

In the case of *Erbakan* in 2006, the Court also adopted this approach: Politicians have a greater responsibility than others and should therefore, in some circumstances, refrain from statements that lead to intolerance. For that matter, it has to be noted that article 10 paragraph 2 expressly states that the exercise of the freedom of expression carries with it certain duties and responsibilities. This choice of words is remarkable and for that very reason the ECtHR, in the aforementioned Turkish cases, held that the freedom of expression for politicians is accompanied by certain responsibilities. In addition, the Court had already stated this in the context of the Handyside case.[46]

---

44 Cf. ECtHR 6 July 2006, *Erbakan v. Turkey*, appl. no. 59405/00, paragraph 64.

45 ECtHR 25 November 1997, *Zana v. Turkey*, appl. no. 18954/91, paragraph 59-60.

46 ECtHR 12 December 1976, *Handyside v. United Kingdom*, appl. no. 5493/72, paragraph 49: 'From another standpoint, whoever exercises his freedom of expression undertakes "duties and responsibilities" the scope

In two more recent cases we again find the view that a politician has more responsibility concerning his right to free speech and should therefore be more cautious with his statements. In the *Féret* case, the Walloon politician Daniel Féret who was the leader of the Belgian Front National, a far-right political party in French-speaking Belgium, had to take into account the context and the potential impact of his statements. Féret distributed leaflets that depicted immigrants as criminals and profiteers of the Belgian welfare state. After the Belgian public prosecutor's office received several complaints about the leaflets, it successfully requested the Belgian Chamber of Representatives to lift Féret's parliamentary immunity. According to the Belgian court, Féret's statements were not made in the exercise of his function and furthermore had to be qualified as discriminatory statements. According to the Belgian Court, Féret's offending conduct had not fallen within the exercise of a parliamentary activity and furthermore the leaflets contained passages that represented a clear and deliberate incitement to discrimination, segregation, hatred, and even violence, for reasons of race, colour or national or ethnic origin. The ECtHR in its turn reiterated the *Castells doctrine*: While freedom of expression is important for everybody, it is especially so for an elected representative of the people. Nevertheless, Féret's position as a Member of Parliament could not be considered as a mitigating circumstance because it is crucial for politicians to avoid comments that might foster intolerance when expressing themselves in public.[47] The right to freedom of expression, which encompasses political debate, is not absolute in the view of the Court. The Court even went a little further and concluded that some statements could harm democracy. Recommending solutions to immigration-related problems by advocating racial discrimination, in the view of the Court, is likely to cause social tension and undermines trust in democratic institutions.[48] In the present case there had been a compelling social need to justify a restriction on the freedom of expression and there had been no violation of article 10 of the Convention. Thus, according to the Court, parliamentarians have a special responsibility and should be aware of the social context in which they make their statements. The Court held that there had been no violation of Article 10 by a narrow majority of 4 votes to 3. Judge Sajó firmly rejected the majority decision of the Court in his dissenting opinion. He stated that the rise of a xenophobic mentality among members of society, although being an insidious process, should be combated through a free exchange of views. The conviction of a xenophobic parliamentarian was not the right remedy in his view.[49] In this regard, the *Le Pen* case is of importance. In *Le Pen* the Court ruled that the hate speech of the leader of the French *Front National* was

---

of which depends on his situation and the technical means he uses. The Court cannot overlook such a person's "duties and responsibilities" when it enquires, as in this case, whether "restrictions" or "penalties" were conducive to the "protection of morals" which made them "necessary" in a "democratic society".'

47 ECtHR 16 July 2009, *Féret v. Belgium*, appl. no. 15615/07, paragraph 54.

48 *Ibid.*, paragraph 77.

49 Judges Zagrebelsky and Tsotsoria joined his opinion.

contrary to the fight against racial discrimination and furthermore had put the safety and dignity of the entire French population at risk.[50]

What can one deduce from the case law of the Strasbourg Court? On the one hand, the Court makes clear that article 10 of the ECHR has a broad scope as to views expressed by politicians, because they speak on behalf of their electorate (the *Castells* case law) while, on the other hand, the Court states that parliamentarians have a special responsibility. A responsibility that should dissuade them from making certain intolerant statements. In a previous publication, Nehmelman had already said that he does not agree with this ambiguous case law.[51] The Court has to make a clear choice and has to decide whether the limits of free speech are wider in the case of politicians than they are in the case of private individuals, or it should take the view that article 10 of the ECHR limits the right to freedom of expression of politicians because of them having a special responsibility. The Court cannot take a middle course. In our opinion article 10 of the ECHR should have a broad scope with regard to the statements of politicians. Even though we are aware of the disadvantages this approach entails, in our opinion, it is the right way of dealing with this sensitive topic because far-reaching, even harmful statements should be opposed by free speech itself. This point of view will be further elaborated at the end of this chapter.

Arguments For and Against Broadening the Reach of Parliamentary Immunity in Dutch Legal Literature

Introduction

The doctrine of immunity has always been controversial and raises many questions. Why are the limits to free speech wider regarding politicians than regarding private individuals? Should immunity not only cover statements made during sessions of Parliament but also statements made outside of parliamentary deliberations? Or should the concept of parliamentary immunity be abolished in its entirety? These questions that are nowadays relevant were already asked in the distant past. In this section, possible answers to the abovementioned questions will be briefly discussed. The pros and cons with regard to the extension of parliamentary immunity in the Netherlands will become visible, which will make it

50 ECtHR 20 April 2010, *Le Pen, LJN*: BN0891, *Nederlandse Jurisprudentie* No. 429, 2010, with case note E.J. Dommering.

51 Cf. R. Nehmelman, 'Spreken is Zilver, maar wie bepaalt wanneer Zwijgen Goud is? Over de Vraag of de Parlementaire Immuniteit voor Volksvertegenwoordigers moet worden uitgebreid' ['Speech is Silver, but who decides when Silence is Golden? On the Question Whether Parliamentary Immunity for Parliamentarians should be Extended'], *Ars Aequi*, May 2011, pp. 355-360.

possible to make a well-considered decision regarding the matter of broadening the scope of parliamentary immunity.

Abolishing the Existing System of Parliamentary Immunity

In the first half of the twentieth century, three Dutch State Committees examined the doctrine of parliamentary immunity. All of them were faced with the question whether it should be possible to lift parliamentary immunity if a parliamentarian abuses this immunity by making confidential information available to the public. Between 1910 and 1912, the first Heemskerk State Committee was not able to answer this question unequivocally. In 1934, the Koolen Commission advised that it should be made possible to lift immunity in the context of the problematic situation regarding 'revolutionary representatives'. Similar to the Koolen Commission, the De Wilde Commission advised lifting the immunity of parliamentarians who were found guilty of sedition or making confidential information publicly available. Both proposals were rejected by the States General.[52]

Earlier, a more radical proposal had been made. This proposal entailed the abolition of parliamentary immunity in its entirety. The main underlying argument for this proposal was the thought that the privilege of parliamentary immunity no longer fulfilled any function. This proposal was made by Van Os who was assisted by his tutor Krabbe.[53] In 1910, Van Os explained why, in his opinion, the concept of parliamentary immunity had to be removed from the Dutch Constitution. According to Van Os, there was no objective justification for a different treatment of members of the States General compared to other citizens. He put forward the question why a specific group of Dutch civilians (parliamentarians) had to be exempted from a common legal responsibility of the entire Dutch population. Van Os' criticism was based on the following arguments. Firstly, the historical argument for parliamentary immunity had virtually disappeared. As the Netherlands had developed into a stable constitutional monarchy, a Member of the States General no longer had to be protected against the power of the King. Secondly, Van Os argued that immunity was not necessary to protect minority groups in Parliament against the parliamentary majority. Furthermore, Van Os stated that the judiciary was sufficiently independent and impartial in order to judge cases on political issues such as the freedom of expression of Members of Parliament. Van Os also weakened the argument that parliamentarians should enjoy a certain degree of sovereignty. He asked why sovereignty had to be accompanied by the lack of the possibility of prosecuting a member of the States General. Also according

52 Cf. Elzinga 1990, p. 122.

53 W.A.E. van Os, *De Gerechtelijke Onvervolgbaarheid der Volksvertegenwoordigers [The 'Improsecutability' of Representatives of the People]*, J.B. Wolters, Groningen 1910 (introduction written by H. Krabbe).

to Van Os, the related point of the essence of Parliament as a representative state body could not be a valid reason to grant immunity to its members.

Many years later, in 1990, Elzinga tried to weaken Van Os' arguments and advocated in favor of article 71 of the Dutch Constitution.[54] Although Elzinga admitted that many of the original arguments for maintaining parliamentary immunity were no longer valid, he emphasized the importance of the concept of parliamentary immunity. Moreover, he refuted the argument that parliamentary immunity is a privilege for parliamentarians. Elzinga stated that, even though it is not the judiciary who has been given the authority over what is said during parliamentary deliberations, parliamentarians are not inviolable as regards their statements made in the deliberations. Parliament has its own internal mechanisms for disciplining a member of parliament. The President of each Chamber may admonish any member who violates the Rules of Procedure and then, after offering the Member concerned an opportunity to retract the offending remark, may impose parliamentary sanctions.[55] Therefore, the right to freedom of expression during sessions of Parliament is not absolute. Baron de Vos van Steenwijk already argued this in 1927. He stated the following:

> 'Committing libel is unlawful. Both in and outside Parliament. Only the method of enforcement is different. The power of criminal law is replaced by the power of the Rules of Procedure. Whether one considers the parliamentary sanctions sufficient depends on the final aim one wants to attain with imposing sanctions on parliamentarians. If one wants to make it impossible for parliamentarians to speak in Parliament the system of parliamentary enforcement will not suffice, and neither will the criminal enforcement system. But if the final aim is to have the competent authority impose sanctions on a parliamentarian because of his unlawful conduct the system of parliamentary enforcement will be satisfactory.'[56]

According to Elzinga, the parliamentary sanctions imposed by the Speaker of the House may in some circumstances be regarded as even more severe than sanctions imposed by a criminal court. A second argument for maintaining parliamentary immunity is that, according to Elzinga, the threshold for people to take legal action has become lower in the last few decades. This creates the risk that politicians will have to defend themselves before

54 Elzinga 1990.

55 The Speaker of the House has the power to impose the following sanctions on members of parliament who violate the Rules of Procedure: to issue a warning, to forbid a Member from speaking and to forbid a Member from attending the rest of the sitting or further sessions on the same day. These rules are laid down in articles 58-60 of the Rules of Procedure of The House of Representatives respectively article 94 and 98 of the Rules of Procedure of the Senate.

56 R.H. Baron de Vos van Steenwijk, 'Parlementaire Immuniteit' ['Parliamentary Immunity'] *in* Krabbe (Ed.), *Staatsrechtelijke opstellen deel 2 [Constitutional Essays part 2]*, 1927, p. 122.

a court more frequently. Elzinga comes to the conclusion that Parliament should remain a place where its members can perform their duties, which is exercising their right to free speech on behalf of their electorate. In 1995, despite Elzinga's plea, the former leader of the Dutch Liberal Democratic Party (D66) Thom de Graaf wanted to propose an amendment to remove article 71 of the Dutch Constitution. De Graaf was of the view that the system of sanctioning laid down in the Rules of Procedure would be insufficient in the light of the rise of extreme right-wing parties in the Netherlands. Due to a lack of support, De Graaf eventually decided not to propose the amendment.

Arguments For and Against the Extension of Parliamentary Immunity

As seen above, discussions in the Netherlands on parliamentary immunity in the past were focused on the matter of a possible abolition of parliamentary immunity. Nowadays, the question of an extension of parliamentary immunity takes centre stage in debates about parliamentary immunity. To be more precise, the discussion focuses on the question whether parliamentary immunity should also cover statements by the members of the States General made outside of parliamentary deliberations (the so-called extraparliamentary immunity). Jit Peters, an Emeritus Professor of Constitutional Law at the University of Amsterdam, advocated an extension of immunity in an interview in the daily newspaper *Trouw*. In this interview Peters stated:

> 'Some members of the House of Representatives are not even seen in Parliament any more. Suppose they say something in Parliament but no one picks it up. And they make their statements in a room in some small village and a newspaper writes an article about it. Isn't it strange that they can be prosecuted for these statements because of the mere fact that they were made outside Parliament?'[57]

Peters' view led to a discussion in the *Tijdschrift voor Constitutioneel Recht* between the former politician Eric Jurgens and Peters himself.[58] Jurgens wondered why, in a debate between a citizen and a member of parliament, the citizen should refrain from unlawful statements while the Member of Parliament is allowed to say anything he wants.[59] Public debate, that is, a debate that takes place outside Parliament, has to be a level playing field for all participants. He furthermore saw the choice of the legislator for a system of intra-

57 J. Peters, 'Immuniteit moet Breder: Interview met prof. J. Peters' ['The Reach of Immunity should be Broadened: An Interview with Prof. J. Peters'], *Trouw*, 5 July 2008.

58 E.C.M. Jurgens, 'Een gedurfde stelling' ['A Courageous Thesis'], *Tijdschrift voor Constitutioneel Recht*, Vol. 1, No. 3, pp. 322-326.

59 E.C.M. Jurgens, 'Een gedurfde stelling' ['A Courageous Thesis'], *Tijdschrift voor Constitutioneel Recht*, Vol. 1, No. 3, pp. 322 ff.

parliamentary immunity as an argument for maintaining the current system. Moreover, the development of the concept of parliamentary immunity in the Dutch Constitution shows that not only parliamentarians but also any other person taking part in parliamentary deliberations enjoys immunity within the framework provided for by article 71. Moreover, Jurgens warned against the danger of abuse if the scheme would be extended. In this regard, he mentioned the example of the Italian Senator Ianuzzi who could not be prosecuted after insulting a journalist.

Nieuwenhuis, an Associate Professor of Constitutional Law at the University of Amsterdam, also opposes any extension of the current system of parliamentary immunity.[60] He believes that representatives of the people should not be granted a special position for statements made outside Parliament, because their freedom of expression is not clearly distinguishable from that of non-parliamentarians. Political criticism could also be expressed by other people, not being parliamentarians. His main argument against extending the scope of article 71 of the Constitution is illustrated in the following quote:

> 'The connection between freedom of expression and democracy means that the opinion-forming process of all individuals, all voters, all potential politicians, takes centre stage. References to the justifications of freedom of speech can only reinforce this premise. For that reason the freedom of expression of a member of parliament or a politician in a political discussion does not outweigh the right to free speech of an ordinary citizen participating in a political debate.'[61]

However Peters, sticking to his point, states that the immunity should be broadened. According to him, the current limited, intra-parliamentary immunity does not meet the requirements of modern democracy, since the political arena is no longer limited to the parliamentary assembly.[62]

More recently Joop van den Berg, an Emeritus Professor of parliamentary history at the University of Maastricht, advocated rethinking the scheme of immunity under article 71 of the Dutch Constitution. In an article on the website parlementenpolitiek.nl, Van Den Berg concluded that the main problem that extending the scope of article 71 will cause is a jurisdictional one.[63] Like Baron Vos van Steenwijk and Elzinga, Van den Berg argues that in the current situation, both Speakers of the Houses have the power to impose sanc-

60 A.E. Nieuwenhuis, 'Tussen Grondrechtelijke Vrijheid en Parlementaire Onschendbaarheid' [Between a Fundamental Freedom and Parliamentary Immunity'], *Tijdschrift voor Constitutioneel Recht*, Vol. 1, No. 1, 2010, pp. 21 ff.

61 Nieuwenhuis 2010, p. 22.

62 J.A. Peters, 'Immuniteit ook Buiten het Parlementaire Debat' ['Immunity, also Outside Parliamentary Debate'], *Tijdschrift voor Constitutioneel Recht*, Vol. 1, No. 3, 2010, pp. 327-330.

63 J.Th.J. van den Berg, 'Welke rechter?' ['Which judge?'], essay for the website www.parlementenpolitiek.nl, 3 June 2011.

tions for statements made during sessions of Parliament, while the judiciary is the competent authority concerning statements made outside Parliament. An extension of the scope of article 71 of the Dutch Constitution, in principle, will lead to a situation in which there is no authority with the power to impose sanctions on parliamentarians for statements made outside Parliament. Van den Berg therefore raises the question whether the jurisdiction of the Chamber Presidents should be expanded to statements made outside parliamentary deliberations.

Extending the Scope of Parliamentary Immunity in the Netherlands; Possible Models

Extension of the Parliamentary Immunity of Members of Parliament

It is necessary to consider the aforementioned legal framework before taking a position on this complex constitutional matter. For the sake of clarity, we will express our own view regarding Dutch parliamentary immunity directly. In our opinion, parliamentary immunity should be extended in the sense that politicians should enjoy a certain form of immunity for statements made outside parliamentary deliberations. We advocate a limited variant of extraparliamentary immunity. This requires, at least, that the system of intraparliamentary immunity remains intact. The current scheme in which parliamentary immunity covers statements made during sessions of the States General is of great value, as it serves the 'dual interest' of free speech in Parliament and the separation of powers.[64] Parliament, as the centre of open political debate in which, in principle, an absolute freedom of expression applies to all participants, should be protected. The Speaker of the House must exercise general control over debates and, if necessary, impose sanctions on parliamentarians who violate the Rules of Procedure. Moreover, the argument of the separation of powers is an important reason to maintain parliamentary immunity. The States General as an important body in the legislative procedure should not interfere in judicial decisions. The judiciary, for its part, should not have authority over what members of parliament say in their deliberations. For this very reason we are of the view that parliamentary immunity should also cover statements made by representatives outside parliamentary deliberations. Another reason for advocating such an extension lies in the fact that members of parliament have a special position in taking a (leading) standpoint in the public debate. The Netherlands is an (indirect) representative democracy. In this type of democracy the representatives of the people must be free to say or write whatever they think or feel. In that sense, in our opinion, parliamentarians are not equal to other 'ordinary' civilians.

64 *A. v. The United Kingdom*, para. 66 and 77.

Therefore, we reject the equality argument brought forward by some opponents of the extension of parliamentary immunity. From our point of view, only in a system that enables every citizen to influence the political process directly should all citizens enjoy the same protection as regards their political statements.

Possible Variants of Extraparliamentary Immunity

Our plea for the extension of parliamentary immunity does not mean that the immunity should be unlimited and thus absolute. As set out before, the Speaker of the House to a great extent decide how far a representative can go in expressing his views during debates in Parliament. Therefore, an unlimited right to freedom of expression for parliamentarians outside parliamentary deliberations would create a problematic legal vacuum. Even though the right to free speech may be far-reaching, in our opinion it should not be without limits. The question arises as to what a scheme of far-reaching, though limited, extraparliamentary immunity should look like exactly. Numerous variants are possible, some of which find their origins in foreign legal systems and/or constitutional literature. At this point we would like to briefly discuss some possibly interesting systems. A first model is one in which the Speaker of the House or a special Chamber Committee is given the power to decide whether a parliamentarian has gone too far in expressing his opinion outside Parliament. This scheme, in which Parliament is given its own jurisdiction in deciding the scope of extraparliamentary immunity, is similar to the disciplinary committees for special professions such as lawyers and doctors. It may be necessary to introduce new (parliamentary) sanctioning powers, laid down in the Rules of Procedure, in order for this system to have actual effect. One probable disadvantage of the system is that, in the end, political competitors will judge the statements of a fellow member of parliament. This could possibly lead to a situation in which political competitors do not dare to intervene in the strong political statements of a controversial member of parliament because of possibly negative electoral consequences. One should then think, for example, of a committee consisting of parliamentarians from left-wing parties that has to answer the question whether a (far-) right-wing member of parliament has gone too far in his statements during a television program.

The Speaker of the House or a special Chamber Committee having its own jurisdiction, despite being an interesting thought, should be regarded as unrealistic. With this in mind, Nehmelman, in previous publications, has set out a scheme that derives from both foreign (France and Belgium) and historical (the Batavian Constitution of 1798) systems. In this scheme, before a member of parliament can be prosecuted, the House of Representatives or the Senate must lift his immunity. A problem that emerges within this system is the problem of an abuse of the 'lifting power' by political competitors of the parliamentarian concerned. Therefore, Nehmelman has proposed to lift immunity with a qualified three-fifths majority. This solution constitutes the golden mean between a (slightly unrealistic) two-thirds majority and a too simple ordinary parliamentary majority. Above all, in this qualified majority system neither the coalition nor the opposition will have enough votes to lift immunity on its own. After immunity is lifted for the purposes of criminal proceedings, a special procedure at the Supreme Court will be instituted. In this procedure, the Procurator General (*Procureur-Generaal)* will act as a public prosecutor. The parliamentarian concerned will be convicted when a majority of the Supreme Court determines, in these cases consisting of ten members, that he is guilty. There are a couple of reasons for choosing the Supreme Court as the competent judicial authority. First of all, the Supreme Court already has a special position regarding the trial of misfeasance of present and former members of the States General, Ministers and State Secretaries: The so-called *Forum Privilegiatum* (article 119 of the Dutch Constitution). Secondly, in the cases concerned it is necessary to obtain a judgement quickly. Of course, the possibility to lodge an appeal with the Strasbourg court will remain.

In 2010, Nehmelman already argued that the procedure laid down in article 119 may already apply to the alleged criminal conduct of parliamentarians outside Parliament.[65] However, in the context of this chapter it is not possible to set out this complex argument. Basically, it comes down to the fact that alleged criminal statements by a parliamentarian may be regarded as misfeasance within the meaning of article 44 of the Dutch Criminal Code. As a consequence, article 119 of the Dutch Constitution and the Criminal Ministerial Responsibility Act will apply to these types of cases.

In short, the proposed system entails the following: Thescope of parliamentary immunity for members of the States General will be broadened and will also cover statements made outside Parliament. However, in this scheme the States General has the power to lift the immunity of the representative concerned. Nevertheless, the proposed system is faced with a couple of problems. In our opinion, the most important obstacle has to do with candidates for the House of Representatives who are not yet elected. Those persons cannot (yet) enjoy the protection granted to parliamentarians even though they can play a very important role in political debates. A possible solution for this undesirable situation could be that a candidate Member of the House has to decide himself whether he wants to make (possibly criminal) statements. If he is elected he will enjoy immunity for the statements he made, otherwise he has to be regarded as an ordinary citizen and can thus be prosecuted for his statements. With this solution it will be the electorate that decides whether or not a candidate will be granted immunity.[66]

65 Nehmelman 2010, p. 7 ff.

66 A parallel could be drawn between this proposal and the caution money that new political parties have to pay when they do not receive enough votes to be elected into the House of Representatives. In this system a political party also has to make an educated guess as to its chance of 'success'.

Conclusion

This chapter analyzed the concept of parliamentary immunity. By looking into the history of the doctrine of parliamentary immunity, describing different legal systems, and assessing the case law of the European Court of Human Rights, as well as giving an overview of the views in Dutch constitutional literature, this chapter sought to gain an insight into the complex matter of parliamentary immunity. In this chapter, we advocated the extension of the current limited system of parliamentary immunity as laid down in article 71 of the Dutch Constitution. In our opinion, the freedom of expression is especially important for Members of Parliament in an indirect representative democracy. Therefore, we argued that parliamentarians should also be granted immunity for statements they make outside of parliamentary deliberations. In some cases, the ECtHR has followed this line of argument. However, in our opinion, parliamentary immunity should not be absolute. It is possible for the Chambers to lift immunity with a three-fifths majority. The *Procureur-Generaal* then acts as a public prosecutor and the Supreme Court has to answer the question whether the statements of the parliamentarian concerned were unlawful.

6 Free Speech: A Look Back and a Look Ahead

Amos Guiora[*]

Introduction

> *Congress shall make no law respecting an establishment of religion, or prohibiting the free exercise thereof; or abridging the freedom of speech, or of the press; or the right of the people peaceably to assemble, and to petition the Government for a redress of grievances.*
> — *The First Amendment to the U.S. Constitution*

The First Amendment protects the freedom of speech, press, religion, assembly and petition; it is the great protector of individual rights clearly articulating limits of government power. Despite uniform support for the amorphous term 'free speech,' Americans vigorously dispute both what it actually means and what it is intended to protect.[1] For example, 73% of Americans say the First Amendment does not go too far in protecting free speech,[2] yet 31% say musicians should NOT be allowed to sing songs with lyrics that others might find offensive, while 35% would support an amendment banning the desecration of the American flag as a form of political dissent.[3]

This chapter will be divided as follows: Section one will offer a historical overview of free speech in America; section two will offer an analysis of American free speech jurisprudence; section three examines current issues; section four is a 'final word'.

* The author would like to thank Spencer Hall (J.D. expected, S.J. Quinney College of Law, the University of Utah) for his invaluable assistance in the writing of this chapter.

1 First Amendment Center, *State of the First Amendment 2009* (2009) *available at* http://s111617.gridserver.com/madison/wp-content/uploads/2011/03/SOFA2009.analysis.tables.pdf.

2 *Id.* at 2.

3 *Id.* at 6.

History of free speech

Freedom of speech is much revered as a clear symbol of American democracy; nevertheless as the historical survey below indicates it has had clear 'ups and downs'. US Presidents, the Congress and Courts have struggled to define the boundaries of free speech; arguably, nowhere is this struggle more evident than during wartime. Beginning with the Sedition Act of 1798 and continuing to present day tensions and conflicts, successive presidents have struggled to balance civil liberties with national security; line drawing with respect to free speech has been the subject of robust debate.

Sedition Act of 1798

Shortly after the First Amendment was ratified, Congress enacted the Sedition Act (1798),[4] restricting freedom of speech in response to the possible outbreak of war between the US and France.[5] Acting out of concern that sympathizers to France would 'stir up trouble,' Congress passed the Sedition Act imposing criminal penalties for saying or publishing anything 'false, scandalous, or malicious' against the federal government, Congress or the president.[6] Twenty-five American citizens were arrested under the Act,[7] including a Congressman who was imprisoned for calling President Adams a man who had 'a continual grasp for power.'[8] The Act was particularly controversial; Virginia threatened to secede over this issue.[9]

In one of his first official acts as President, Thomas Jefferson, a bitter political opponent of President Adams and the Sedition Act, pardoned all those convicted under this law.[10] The Act was never challenged before the Supreme Court. Forty years later, however, Congress repaid all of the fines exacted under the Sedition Act, with interest, to the legal representatives of those who had been convicted.[11] The congressional committee report declared that the Sedition Act had been passed under a 'mistaken exercise' of power and was 'null and void.'[12] In 1964, the Supreme Court echoed this sentiment, stating that

4 Sedition Act of 1798, ch. 74, 1 Stat. 596.
5 Constitutional Rights Foundation, A Clear and Present Danger, www.crf-usa.org/america-responds-to-terrorism/a-clear-and-present-danger.html (last visited June 12, 2011).
6 *Id.*
7 *Id.*
8 *Id.*
9 *Id.*
10 Geoffrey R. Stone, *Perilous Times: Free Speech in Wartime*, 73 (W. W. Norton & Co. 2004).
11 *Id.*
12 *Id.*

'although the Sedition Act was never tested in this Court, the attack upon its validity has carried the day in the court of history.'[13]

Civil War – The Arrest of Clement Vallandigham

Upon taking office, President Lincoln was faced with a difficult choice between the lesser of two evils: Permit dissenting voices to exercise their rights and risk losing states like Maryland or suppress dissent in an effort to hold the nation together.

Despite being a strong advocate for civil liberties, President Lincoln was greatly concerned with maintaining the fragile Union. In an effort to suppress pro-secessionist groups in border states like Maryland, Lincoln took several measures, including declaring martial law, suspending the writ of *habeas corpus* and arresting individuals suspected of disloyalty in those areas. Lincoln explained that harsh measures were necessary in the early days of the rebellion because 'every department of the Government [had been] paralyzed by treason.'[14] He analogized that a limb must sometimes be amputated to save a life, but that a life must never be given to save a limb.[15]

In March 1863, Lincoln appointed General Ambrose Burnside the Union commander of the Department of Ohio, a state where substantial protests regarding the war had been held. After discovering that newspapers in Ohio were openly critical of the President and the war efforts, Burnside issued General Order no. 38, which announced (among other things) that 'the habit of declaring sympathies for the enemy will not be allowed in this Department.'[16] Burnside, without Lincoln's knowledge, established himself as the ultimate arbiter of such charges.[17]

In May 1863, Burnside arrested an outspoken critic of the war and congressman from Ohio, Clement Vallandigham. Vallandigham was charged and convicted by a military commission, holding that his speeches 'could but induce in his hearers a distrust of their own government and sympathy for those in arms against it.'[18] Vallandigham argued, to no avail, that his speeches were merely an appeal to the people to change public policy by lawful means.

Vallandigham immediately petitioned for a writ of *habeas corpus* in federal court. In response to his petition, Judge Humphrey Leavitt applied a balancing test between Val-

13 *Id.*

14 Executive Order no. 1, Relating to Political Prisoners, Feb. 14, 1862, in 2:2 *The War of the Rebellion: A Compilation of the Official Records of the Union and Confederate Armies 222* (Government Printing Office 1902).

15 *See* Shelby Foote, *The Civil War: A Narrative* 630 (Random House 1963).

16 Stone, *supra* note 10, at 96.

17 *Id.* at 97.

18 Stone, *supra* note 10, at 101.

landigham's civil liberty interest and the government's national security interest; as discussed below, this test continues to be applied today. Judge Leavitt held that General Burnside had acted reasonably given the circumstances, reasoning that during wartime, self-preservation was 'paramount law,' even rising above the Constitution. Leavitt concluded that is was not the judiciary's place to overrule the Commander in Chief during wartime, as a sufficient check on the President's power already existed in Congress' impeachment power.[19]

In response to pleas for the release of Vallandigham, Lincoln justified the arrest with the following statement:

> 'It is asserted… that Mr. Vallandigham was… seized and tried "for no other reason than world addressed to a public meeting, in criticism of the… Administration, and in condemnation of the Military orders of the General." Now, if there be no mistake about this; if this assertion is the truth and the whole truth; if there was no other reason for the arrest, then I concede that the arrest was wrong…'
>
> 'But the arrest, as I understand, was made for a very different reason… his arrest was made because he was laboring with some effect, to prevent the raising of troops; to encourage desertions from the army; and to leave the Rebellion without an adequate military force to suppress it…'[20]

The case raised the question that is as relevant today as it was then: In times of war, should some civil liberties, otherwise protected under the Constitution, be suspended.

WWI – the Espionage Act of 1917

The Espionage Act of 1917 was the first legislation since the Sedition Act (1798) to limit free speech. Passed on June 15, 1917, shortly after the U.S. entered World War I and against the backdrop of fear and uncertainty, it represents a low point for free speech in American history.

The Wilson Administration was deeply concerned about the effect that disloyalty would have on the war effort. To that end, President Wilson asked Congress to give him authority with respect to individuals that might undermine national unity. The President wanted,

19 *Ex Parte Vallandigham*, 28 F Cases 874, 921-24 (Cir. Ct. Ohio 1863).

20 Letter from Abraham Lincoln to Erastus Corning and Others, June 12, 1863, In Stone, *supra* note 10, at 110-111.

among other things, the power of censorship of the media, but Congress refused.[21] According to the legislation the following acts were subject to criminal prosecution:

> To convey information with intent to interfere with the operation or success of the armed forces of the United States or to promote the success of its enemies. To cause or attempt to cause insubordination, disloyalty, mutiny, refusal of duty, in the military or naval forces of the United States, or to willfully obstruct the recruiting or enlistment service of the United States.[22]

The Act also gave the Postmaster General authority to refuse to mail or to impound publications that he determined to be in violation of its prohibitions.[23]

In *Schenck v. United States*,[24] the Supreme Court considered the constitutionality of the Espionage Act. Charles Schenck, the Secretary of the Socialist Party of America, distributed leaflets that advocated opposition to the draft; Schenck was indicted and subsequently convicted for conspiracy to violate the Espionage Act for having caused and attempting to cause insubordination in the military and to obstruct the recruiting process. The Supreme Court, in a unanimous opinion written by Justice Oliver Wendell Holmes, Jr., ruled Schenck's criminal conviction constitutional.

According to Holmes, the First Amendment did not protect speech encouraging insubordination, since, 'when a nation is at war many things that might be said in time of peace are such a hindrance to its effort that their utterance will not be endured so long as men fight, and that no Court could regard them as protected by any constitutional right.'[25] In other words, the circumstances of wartime permit greater restrictions on free speech than would be allowable during peacetime.

In the opinion's most famous passage, Justice Holmes sets out the "clear and present danger" test:

> 'The most stringent protection of free speech would not protect a man in falsely shouting fire in a theatre and causing a panic… The question in every case is whether the words used are used in such circumstances and are of such a nature as to create a clear and present danger that they will bring about the substantive evils that Congress has a right to prevent.'[26]

21 Stone, *supra* note 10, at 147-49.
22 Espionage Act of 1917, 40 Stat 217, 219.
23 *Id.* at 230-31.
24 *Schenck v. United States*, 249 U.S. 47 (1919).
25 *Id.* at 52.
26 *Id.*

Holmes was quick to grant deference to the government during wartime; his analysis focuses on the government's ability to restrict speech during wartime as apposed to First Amendment protections. Though Holmes used the term 'clear and present danger,' it is unclear whether the circumstances truly satisfied such a burden. Schenck, after all, was printing and distributing anti-draft materials; whether that is akin to 'shouting fire in a crowded theater' is arguable, if not doubtful. The core question is the proximity between the speech and the imminent danger arising from that speech; the facts and circumstances in *Schenck* suggest, from a historical perspective, a greatly removed nexus.

One week after *Schenck*, the Supreme Court decided two additional free speech cases. Jacob Frowherk was a copy editor who helped prepare and publish a series of antiwar articles in the *Missouri Staats Zeitung*, a German-language newspaper. Like Schenck, Frowherk was convicted under the Espionage Act and the Supreme Court, in a unanimous decision, upheld his conviction.[27] Again, Holmes gave short shrift to the First Amendment issue, though interestingly, he makes no reference in *Frowherk* or *Debs*[28] to the clear and present danger test.

Eugene V. Debs was an American labor and political leader and five-time Socialist Party of America candidate for the American Presidency. On June 16, 1918, Debs made an anti-war speech in Canton, Ohio, protesting US involvement in World War I; Debs was subsequently arrested under the Espionage Act, convicted and sentenced to ten years in prison and loss of his citizenship.

The Supreme Court found Debs had shown the 'intention and effect of obstructing the draft and recruitment for the war.'[29] In affirming his conviction, the Court cited Debs' praise for those imprisoned for obstructing the draft.

This period marked a low point regarding free speech in America; the test articulated by Holmes in these three decisions raised great concerns regarding the limits of free speech in the US. However, when the Court reconvened for its next session, Justice Holmes apparently had a change of heart; it has been suggested by some that it was a result of his friendship and correspondence with US District Court Judge Learned Hand.

Hand, much revered for his intellect, would become one of the most prominent voices in American jurisprudence. Hand, in 1917, was considered a likely nominee for the US Court of Appeals; that (temporarily) changed in the aftermath of his opinion in *Masses Publishing Co. v. Patten.*[30]

At issue in *Masses* was a provision in the Espionage Act granting the Postmaster General authority both to refuse to mail or to impound publications he determined to be in violation of the Act. Hand claimed that the New York postmaster's refusal to allow circulation of

27 *Frowherk v. United States*, 249 U.S. 204 (1919).
28 *Debs v. United States*, 249 U.S. 211 (1919).
29 *Id.*
30 *Masses Publishing Co. v. Patten*, 244 F. 535 (S.D.N.Y. 1917).

an antiwar journal violated the First Amendment. In his opinion, if a citizen 'stops short of urging upon others that it is their duty or their interest to resist the law,'[31] then he or she is protected by the First Amendment.

Hand's opinion was reversed by the Court of Appeals; in addition, he was not nominated to the Court of Appeals, which is perhaps a reflection of the tenor of the times. Hand, who would ultimately sit on the Appeals Court, reflected that the case 'cost me something, at least at the time,' but added, 'I have been very happy to do what I believe was some service to temperateness and sanity.'[32]

Hand, according to many observers, had a profound impact on his friend Justice Holmes. In *U.S. v. Abrams*,[33] Holmes joined Justice Brandeis in dissent, taking a strong pro-speech position. In *Abrams*, the defendants were convicted for printing and subsequently throwing from windows of a New York City building two anti-war leaflets. The Supreme Court ruled 7–2 that the Espionage Act did not violate the freedom of speech protected by the First Amendment. In his dissent, Holmes wrote that although the defendant's pamphlet called for a cease in weapons production, it had not violated the act because the defendants did not have the requisite intent to cripple or hinder the United States in the prosecution of the war.[34] Holmes' dissent set the stage for what would ultimately become the modern-day clear and present danger test.

Cold War – Communism

In the aftermath of WWII there was grave concern in the US regarding both the rising influence of the Soviet Union and the penetration of communism and communists in the US. In 1940, Congress passed the Smith Act,[35] which criminalized advocating the overthrow of the U.S. government by force or violence.

In 1950, Senator Joseph McCarthy (R-WI) began a nationwide witch-hunt to root out communist sympathizers; virtually the entire nation was swept up in anti-communist fever, if not panic. Judge Hand, now sitting on the Second Circuit Court of Appeals, was critical of Senator McCarthy's efforts. In a public address, Hand stated that 'risk for risk,' he would rather take chance that some traitors will escape detection than risk spreading across the land 'a spirit of general suspicion and distrust.'[36] Now in 1950, would the great

31 *Masses*, 244 F. at 540.
32 Letter from Learned Hand to Charles Burlingham, Oct. 6, 1917, excerpted in Stone, *supra* note 10, at 170.
33 *United States v. Abrams*, 250 U.S. 616 (1919).
34 *See id.* at 628.
35 Smith Act, 18 U.S.C. § 2385 (1940).
36 Stone, *supra* note 10, at 399.

mind behind the decision in *Masses*[37] stand up for the First Amendment against the tidal wave of fear?

Eugene Dennis, the secretary of the Communist Party of America, was an outspoken advocate of communism. Dennis, along with several others party members, was indicted (July 1948) in accordance with the Smith Act for conspiring and organizing the overthrow and destruction of the United States government by force and violence. Smith and his co-defendants, upon conviction by the trial court, appealed to the Second Circuit.

Though Hand was a strong advocate for free speech, as an Appeals Court Judge he was bound by Supreme Court precedent. In analyzing previous Supreme Court holdings, Hand concluded that the Court had been applying a version of the clear and present danger test. As he eloquently put it, 'In each case [courts] must ask whether the gravity of the "evil," discounted by its improbability, justifies such invasion of free speech as necessary to avoid the danger.'[38]

The question before the court, according to Hand, was one of imminence. How long must the government, having discovered such a conspiracy, wait before acting? When does the conspiracy become a 'present danger?' According to Hand, 'the jury found that the conspirators will "strike as soon as success seems possible".'[39] The government is not required to wait until the actual eve of hostilities; rather, it must act once the danger becomes clear and present.[40] Hand's analysis balances the clear and present danger test with national security concerns; as the level of danger increases, the imminence government must demonstrate before it can act decreases. Essentially, Hand proposed a cost-benefit analysis weighing costs of suppression with the cost of the potential harm, was the speech not restricted.

The Supreme Court adopted Hand's balancing test, holding that the threat of communism justified a broader interpretation of imminence. Regarding the defendants, Judge Hand later stated he would 'never have prosecuted those birds.'[41] In his view, the prosecution would do nothing but 'encourage the faithful and maybe help the Committee on Propaganda.'[42] He added, however, this 'has nothing to do with my job,'[43] which was to faithfully apply the law.

In upholding the convictions, the Supreme Court in *Dennis*[44] appeared to give the 'green light' to government officials to aggressively target communist supporters. Between 1951 and 1957, the government arrested and prosecuted 145 members and leaders of the

37 244 F. 535 (S.D.N.Y. 1917).
38 *United States v. Dennis*, 183 F2d 201, 212 (1950).
39 *Id.* at 212-13.
40 *Id.*
41 Letter from Learned Hand to Irving Dilliard, Apr. 3, 1952, excerpted in Stone, *supra* note 10, at 401.
42 *Id.*
43 *Id.*
44 *Dennis v. United States*, 341 U.S. 494 (1951).

Communist Party; 108 were convicted, 10 were acquitted, and the rest were awaiting trial when *Yates*[45] was decided (June 1957).[46] In none of the prosecutions was evidence presented suggestive of concrete plans to use force or violence to overthrow the government.

Between *Dennis* and *Yates*, however, the political climate in America changed significantly: Stalin, the Soviet leader, passed away; an armistice had been declared in Korea; the Senate had condemned Senator McCarthy; and the public attitude toward the 'red scare' had relaxed. In addition, significant changes occurred on the Supreme Court as Justices Harlan, Brennan, Whittaker, and Chief Justice Warren replaced Justices Vinson, Reed, Minton, and Jackson; this change in the Court's make-up led to a significant shift in the Court's judicial philosophy.

In *Yates*,[47] the Court drew a distinction between actual advocacy to action and mere advocacy in the abstract. Justice Harlan stated that the Smith Act did not prohibit 'advocacy of forcible overthrow of the government as an abstract doctrine' even 'if engaged in with the intent to accomplish overthrow.' Such advocacy was simply 'too remote from concrete action.'[48]

While Harlan did not require that the unlawful action be imminent, he did insist that, to be punishable, the advocacy must include a call for specific, concrete action. Thus, a speaker who teaches the general principles of Marxism, even with the intent to promote a revolution, will not cross the line drawn in *Yates*; the Court recognized that actual 'advocacy to action' circumstances would be 'few and far between.'[49] Indeed, following *Yates*, the government filed no further prosecutions under the Smith Act.

Incitement – Clear and Present Danger Today

In 1964, Clarence Brandenburg, a KKK leader, was charged and convicted for advocating violence under the State of Ohio's criminal syndicalism statute for his participation in a rally and for the speeches he made. In particular, Brandenburg stated at one point: 'Personally, I believe the nigger should be returned to Africa, the Jew returned to Israel.'[50] In an additional speech amongst several Klan members who were carrying firearms, Brandenburg claimed: "We're not a revengent organization, but if our President, our Congress, our Supreme Court, continues to suppress the white, Caucasian race, it's possible that there might have to be some revengeance taken.'[51] Brandenburg appealed his conviction to the

45 *Yates v. United States*, 354 U.S. 298 (1957).
46 Stone, *supra* note 10, at 411.
47 354 U.S. 298 (1957).
48 *Id.* at 318, 321.
49 *Id.* at 327.
50 *Brandenburg v. Ohio*, 395 U. S. 444, 447 (1969).
51 *Id.* at 446.

Supreme Court, claiming the statute violated his First Amendment rights; the Court, in its most speech-protective decision, sided with Brandenburg holding that the statute violated his First Amendment rights.

The *Brandenburg* holding imposes a strict scrutiny test as it places a heavy burden on government; under *Brandenburg*, in order for the government to punish speech which purportedly incites others to illegal activity, the government must prove the following: (1) The speaker intended to incite others to commit illegal activity, (2) the illegal activity must be imminent, and (3) the illegal activity must grave.

Prior Restraint – Pentagon papers

The First Amendment was intended to protect against is prior restraints on speech; Blackstone declared that "the liberty of the press is, indeed, essential to the nature of a free state; but this consists in laying no previous restraints upon publication, and not in freedom from censure for criminal matter when published."[52] A prior restraint prevents speech from occurring, as opposed to punishing it after the fact. It typically takes the form of a license or injunction; it has been said, that although a criminal statute 'chills,' an injunction 'freezes.'[53]

As the Supreme Court held in the Pentagon Papers case, "[a]ny system of prior restraints of expression comes to this Court bearing a heavy presumption against its constitutional validity.'[54] This is because "prior restraints on speech and publication are the most serious and least tolerable infringement on First Amendment rights."[55]

The Supreme Court's initial foray into prior restraint was *Near v. Minnesota;*[56] the Court held prior restraints to be unconstitutional, except in extremely limited circumstances such as national security issues. That was not the case in Near, quite the opposite, in fact, for the ruling was in reaction to a prior restraint order issued against a newspaper (owned by Near) after it published exposés of Minneapolis' elected officials' alleged illicit activities. The Court held that the state had no power to enjoin publication of the paper as this was prior restraint reflective of censorship.

The most famous prior restraint case is known as the Pentagon Papers: In 1967, Secretary of Defense McNamara commissioned the compilation 'History of U.S. Decision-Making Process on Vietnam Policy, 1945–1967, otherwise known as the Pentagon Papers. The

52 William Blackstone, Commentaries, 151-152 (1769).

53 *See* Alexander M. Bickel, *The Morality of Consent* 61 (Yale 1975), referenced in Stone, *supra* note 10, at 506.

54 *New York Times v. United States*, 403 U.S. 713, 714 (1971).

55 *Nebraska Press Association v. Stuart*, 427 U.S. 539, 559 (1976).

56 *Near v Minnesota*, 283 U.S. 697 (1931).

Papers took two years to complete and resulted in over 7000 pages of classified documents; McNamara later commented, '[Y]ou know, they could hang people for what's in there.'[57]

In 1971, Daniel Ellsburg, a one-time consultant and supporter of U.S. policy in Vietnam turned anti-war activist, leaked the papers to the New York Times (NYT). The Justice Department immediately sought an injunction in federal court, claiming both that publication was a violation of the Espionage Act of 1917 and presented a serious threat to national security because the papers contained critical intelligence information relevant to the ongoing war effort. Pending the District Court's decision, Ellsburg released the papers to the Washington Post; the Justice Department similarly sought an injunction against the Post. Judge Gesell of the Federal District Court in Washington, DC ruled that the government failed to present evidence that the Papers posed a serious danger to the nation. Thereafter, Judge Gurfein of the Southern District of New York also denied the government's request for an injunction against the NYT; the government immediately appealed both rulings to the Supreme Court.

The government based its appeal on the "national security" exception discussed in *Near*;[58] however, in a brief *per curiam* decision the Supreme Court agreed with the lower court, holding the government had not met its 'heavy burden' of showing a justification for a prior restraint and ordered the injunction be lifted immediately.[59]

Several of the Justices wrote their own opinions in this critical free speech case. Justice Hugo Black wrote 'every moment's continuance of the injunctions against these newspapers amounts to a flagrant, indefensible, and continuing violation of the First Amendment.'[60] Justice Brennan insisted that even in wartime, a prior restraint on the press could be constitutional *only* if the government proved that 'publication must inevitably, directly, and immediately cause the occurrence of an event kindred to imperiling the safety of a transport already at sea.'[61]

Fighting words

Fighting words, like incitement, are not protected by the First Amendment and can be punishable. The difference between incitement and fighting words is subtle, focusing on the intent of the speaker. Inciting speech is characterized by the speaker's intent to make someone else the instrument of her unlawful will whereas fighting words, by contrast, are intended to cause the hearer to react to the speaker.

57 *See* David Halberstam, *The Best and the Brightest* 663 (Random House 1972).
58 283 U.S. 697 (1931).
59 *New York Times*, 403 U.S. at 714.
60 *Id.* at 715.
61 *Id.* at 726-27.

The Supreme Court first developed the fighting words doctrine in *Chaplinsky*[62] in 1942. Chaplinsky was arrested for disturbing the peace after uttering to the local marshal: 'You are a God damned racketeer' and 'a damned Fascist and the whole government of Rochester are Fascists or agents of Fascists.'[63] The Supreme Court upheld the conviction in a unanimous opinion, stating:

> 'There are certain well-defined and narrowly limited classes of speech, the prevention and punishment of which has never been thought to raise any Constitutional problem. These include..."fighting" words — those, which by their very utterance inflict injury or tend to incite an immediate breach of the peace.'[64]

Since *Chaplinsky*, the Court has continued to uphold the doctrine but also steadily narrowed the grounds on which the fighting words test applies. In *Street v. New York*[65] the court overturned a statute prohibiting flag-burning, holding that mere offensiveness does not qualify as 'fighting words.' Consistent with *Street*, in *Cohen v. California*,[66] the Court held that Cohen's jacket with the words 'fuck the draft' did not constitute fighting words because the words on the jacket were not a "direct personal insult" and no one had reacted violently to the jacket. This ruling established that fighting words should be confined to direct personal insults.

In 1992, in *R.A.V. v. City of St. Paul*,[67] the Supreme Court overturned a city ordinance that made it a crime to burn a cross on public or private property with the intent to arouse anger, alarm or resentment in others based on race, color creed, etc. According to the Court:

> 'The ordinance, even as narrowly construed by the State Supreme Court, is facially unconstitutional, because it imposes special prohibitions on those speakers who express views on the disfavored subjects of "race, color, creed, religion or gender..." Moreover, in its practical operation, the ordinance goes beyond mere content, to actual viewpoint, discrimination... St. Paul's desire to communicate to minority groups that it does not condone the "group hatred" of bias-motivated speech does not justify selectively silencing speech on the basis of its content...'

62 *Chaplinsky v. State of New Hampshire*, 315 U.S. 568 (1942).
63 *Id.* at 569.
64 *Id.* at 571-72.
65 *Street v. New York*, 394 U.S. 576 (1969).
66 *Cohen v. California*, 403 U.S. 15 (1971).
67 *R.A.V. v. City of St. Paul*, 505 U.S. 377 (1992).

In addition, the ordinance's content discrimination is not justified on the ground that the ordinance is narrowly tailored to serve a compelling state interest in ensuring the basic human rights of groups historically discriminated against, since an ordinance not limited to the favored topics would have precisely the same beneficial effect."[68]

True threats

Similar to 'incitement' and 'fighting words,' a 'true threat' is another area of speech that is not protected by the First Amendment. A true threat exists where a speaker directs a threat to a person or group of persons with the *intent* of placing the victim in fear of bodily harm or death. Yet the line between protected expression and an unprotected true threat is often hazy and uncertain, often turning on the determination of intent.

For example, in *Watts v. United States*,[69] Watts, a young African-American man, was arrested for saying the following during an anti-war protest in Washington D.C., 'If they ever make me carry a rifle the first man I want to get in my sights is L.B.J. They are not going to make me kill my black brothers.' In overturning his conviction, the Supreme Court ruled that Watts' statement was political hyperbole rather than a true threat: 'We agree with [Watts] that his only offense here was "a kind of very crude offensive method of stating a political opposition to the President".'[70]

In *Virginia v. Black*[71], the Supreme Court decided a case similar to *R.A.V.*[72] under the true threats doctrine. The Court held that cross burning could constitute a true threat and thereby be proscribed by law, *if* it is done with the intent to intimidate or place the victim in fear of bodily harm or death. It may not, however, be used as *prima facie* evidence of intent to intimidate, because cross burning may serve other intentions, such as a show of solidarity.

Hate speech

Hate speech is a hotly contested area of First Amendment debate. Unlike fighting words or true threats, hate speech is a broad category of speech that encompasses both protected and unprotected speech. To the extent that hate speech constitutes a true threat or fighting words, it is unprotected; to the extent that it does not reach the level of a true threat or fighting words it is protected.

---

68 *Id.* at 393-96.
69 *Watts v. Untied States*, 394 U.S. 705 (1969).
70 *Id.* at 707-08.
71 *Virginia v. Black et al.*, 538 U.S. 343 (2003).
72 505 U.S. 377 (1992).

During the 1980s and early '90s, more than 350 public colleges and universities sought to combat discrimination and harassment on campuses through the use of so-called speech codes.[73] Proponents of the codes contend that existing First Amendment jurisprudence must be changed because the marketplace of ideas does not adequately protect minorities. They argue that hate speech subjugates minority voices and prevents them from exercising their First Amendment rights. Similarly, proponents posit that hate speech is akin to fighting words, a category of expression that should not receive First Amendment protection because, as the Court held in *Chaplinsky*, they 'are no essential part of any exposition of ideas, and are of such slight social value as a step to the truth that any benefit that may be derived from them is clearly outweighed by the social interest in order and morality.'[74]

However, speech codes that have been challenged in court have not fared well; though no case has been brought before the Supreme Court on this question, lower courts have struck these policies down as either overbroad or vague. The District Court for the Eastern District of Wisconsin, in the University of Wisconsin school code case, articulated the reasoning behind the codes' lack of constitutional muster:

> 'This commitment to free expression must be unwavering, because there exist many situations where, in the short run, it appears advantageous to limit speech to solve pressing social problems, such as discriminatory harassment. If a balancing approach is applied, these pressing and tangible short run concerns are likely to outweigh the more amorphous and long run benefits of free speech. However, the suppression of speech, even where the speech's content appears to have little value and great costs, amounts to governmental thought control.'[75]

ANALYSIS OF AMERICAN FREE SPEECH JURISPRUDENCE

While a literal interpretation of the First Amendment forbids *any* law abridging speech in *any* form, the Supreme Court has taken a more nuanced approach recognizing legitimate competing interests that must be considered. For example, while free speech is a guaranteed right according to the First Amendment, the executive branch is similarly charged with protecting the safety and security of the nation's citizens. As Justice Holmes articulated, 'the most stringent protection of free speech would not protect a man in falsely shouting fire in a theater, and causing a panic...'[76]

---

73 David L. Hudson Jr., First Amendment Center, Hate Speech and Campus Speech Codes, Sept. 13, 2002, www.firstamendmentcenter.org/hate-speech-campus-speech-codes, (last visited June 12, 2011).

74 *Chaplinsky*, 315 U.S. at 572.

75 *UWM Post, Inc. v. Board of Regents of University of Wisconsin System*, 774 F.Supp. 1163, 1174 (E.D. Wis. 1991).

76 *Schenck v. United States*, 249 U.S. 47, 52 (1919).

This statement, which has been endorsed by every Court since, reflects an understanding that with free speech—as with other constitutionally guaranteed protections—there is no absolutism. Powerful competing interests must be balanced against other competing interests; the question is whether the balancing reflects a rights minimization or rights maximization paradigm. Free speech jurisdiction has travelled a long road in American jurisprudence, arguably in concert with society, which superficially, at least, is more tolerant of dissent than in the past. The caveat is pertinent because one must never forget the rigid, Puritan roots of the American culture; a casual perusal of public discussion regarding same sex marriage, children of same sex parents and abortion highlights a constant strain of ideological rigidity, largely premised on a literalist interpretation of religious scripture. While the assumption that freedom of speech is 'safer' today than 100 years ago is largely correct—as evidenced by recent Court decisions—to assume it is a 'lock' is, arguably, to wade into dangerous waters.

This, of course, cuts both ways: Should, in the name of free speech, Senator McCarthy have been allowed to run wild, ruining careers and causing extraordinary devastation while the executive branch consistently failed to confront him directly? President Eisenhower's pusillanimous conduct was shameful; in that 'spirit' McCarthy has an extraordinary 'run' unabated by the Court, Congress or the executive. Is that in concert with the free speech protection articulated in the First Amendment?

While some would argue that the 'marketplace of ideas' should take precedence over efforts to limit free speech protections, the reality is, arguably, more complicated. As I have argued elsewhere,[77] the danger posed by religious extremist incitement should give serious pause as incitement occurring in Houses of Worship meets the tests articulated by the Supreme Court discussed in section one above. In that vein, while the Supreme Court begins its analysis of free speech questions with the presumption that *all* speech is protected, unless it falls within one of two exceptions, it is not an absolute right.

The analysis must determine whether the proposed restriction is content-based or content-neutral; the former refers to restrictions that apply to particular viewpoints, in which case the proposed restriction carries a heavy presumption that it violates the First Amendment. In such a paradigm, the Court applies a strict scrutiny standard in evaluating its lawfulness; to survive strict scrutiny, the restriction must be *narrowly tailored* to achieve *an important governmental interest*. That means that it cannot be, among other things, over-inclusive, under-inclusive, or vague. This standard effectively places a heavy burden on the government in defending the restriction.

However, if the restriction is content-neutral, whereby the concern is not with the speech itself but rather pertains to the details surrounding the speech, then the government is allowed to set certain parameters involving time, place, and manner. Content-neutral

77 Amos Guiora, *Freedom from Religion: Rights and National Security* (Oxford 2009).

restrictions on speech are reviewed under intermediate scrutiny rather than strict scrutiny, because the speech is restricted solely in the manner in which the information is communicated rather than content itself.

In *U.S. v. O'Brien,*[78] the Supreme Court established a four-part test to determine whether a content-neutral restriction on speech was constitutional: (1) Is the restriction within the constitutional power of government, (2) Does the restriction further important or substantial governmental interest, (3) Is the governmental interest unrelated to the suppression of free expression, (4) Is the restriction narrowly tailored, i.e., no greater than necessary. Subsequently, a fifth factor was added in *City of Ladue v. Gilleo*[79] inquiring whether the restriction leaves open ample opportunities for communication.

Finally, there is an exception to the content-based rule that requires an analysis of the value of the speech in question. Certain forms of speech, such as political speech, are thought to be at the very core of the First Amendment's protection, and therefore, merit the greatest protection under the law. The freedom to openly challenge the government is essential to a democracy. However, as discussed in this chapter, that principle has been 'fungible'; witness Supreme Court holdings particularly during WWI and somewhat in the aftermath of WWII.

Current issues

The American public has been confronted with a number of significant free speech issues in the past few years. I shall examine four: religious extremism incitement (see previous section); a pastor intent on burning the Qur'an; Christian extremists demonstrating at funerals of US military personnel; an Assistant Attorney General (Michigan) who specifically (ruthlessly) targeted a University of Michigan student who was student body President and a homosexual. In examining these four examples, the core question is whether the test articulated by the Supreme Court in *Brandenburg* sufficiently protects the speaker, his audience, the larger public and the intended target of the speech.

Following the attacks on 9-11, Americans were faced with a new reality; warfare as we know it has fundamentally changed. Rather than having an identifiable enemy, such as the Soviet Union or the Nazis, the current threat carries no banner. Its membership spreads from one corner of the globe to the other, and its unifying link is a shared animosity for the United States.

Pastor Terry Jones of Florida leads a small but vocal congregation. On March 20, 2011, Jones held a Qur'an burning that resulted in anti-American violence in Afghanistan, killing at least 12 people. Jones was urged not to do it by virtually every national leader including

78 *United States v. O'Brien*, 391 U.S. 367 (1968).

79 *City of Ladue v. Gilleo*, 512 U.S. 43 (1994).

President Obama, Secretary of State Clinton and perhaps most importantly, General Petraeus, the commander of U.S. forces in Afghanistan who argued that Pastor Jones' conduct would endanger US military personnel in Afghanistan. While Jones did not go forward with his threat, his possible actions present a significant First Amendment dilemma: Is speech protected even though harm *may* result both domestically and internationally?

In that vein, Jones was arrested for attempting to protest outside a Mosque in Dearborn, Michigan. After a brief trial, a jury upheld the city's injunction, claiming that Jones' protest would disturb the peace; ultimately, Jones was held on $1 bail and then released.[80]

While Jones' conduct is considered, by many, to be reprehensible (at best), numerous constitutional law experts claim the court's action was a gross miscarriage of justice and a violation of Jones' First Amendment rights.

The same concerns are relevant with respect to a pastor who, along with his tiny but vocal community, shouts degrading comments at the family and friends of fallen soldiers as they gather to bury their loved ones who died while serving the U.S. The basis for the pastor's conduct: The soldiers died because God hates the United States for its tolerance of homosexuality, particularly in America's military. The Supreme Court recently addressed this issue in *Snyder v. Phelps*,[81] where members of the small but extremely vocal Westboro Baptist Church protested at the funeral of a U.S. Marine who had been killed in Iraq. The protesters carried signs, as they have done at nearly 600 funerals throughout the country over the past 20 years, displaying placards such as 'America is doomed,' 'You're going to hell,' 'God hates you,' 'Fags doom nations,' and 'Thank God for dead soldiers.'[82]

Dissenting Justice Samuel Alito likened the protests of the Westboro Baptist Church members to fighting words and of a personal character, and thus not protected speech. However, the majority disagreed, stating that the protester's speech was not personal but public, and that local laws, which can shield funeral attendees from protesters, are adequate in the context of protection from emotional distress.

Finally, what about the case of Andrew Shrivell, a former Assistant Attorney General for Michigan who has been sued for stalking Chris Armstrong, the first openly gay University of Michigan student body president. Armstrong claimed that Shrivell had been showing up everywhere he went, including school and home. Shrivell apparently started a blog campaign against Armstrong and his 'radical homosexual agenda.' Shrivell claims that the stalking charges are moot because he has never actually spoken to Armstrong, and that he is simply exercising his First Amendment rights.[83] Should Shrivell be allowed

80 *Pastor Who Planned Mosque Protest Out of Jail*, CBS News, April 22, 2011, *available at* www.cbsnews.com/stories/2011/04/22/national/main20056660.shtml.

81 *Snyder v. Phelps*, 131 S.Ct. 1207 (2011).

82 *Id.* at 1213.

83 David Jesse, *Shirvell Fires Back, Claims He's Victim of Gay Agenda*, Detroit Free Press, May 10, 2011, *available at* www.freep.com/article/20110510/NEWS05/110510041/Shirvell-fires-back-claims-he-s-victim-gay-agenda?odyssey=mod|mostcom.

to exercise his free speech rights in this manner? How does the doctrine of hate speech apply?

FINAL WORD

The First Amendment has travelled an extraordinary journey, from clear limits imposed on free speech to an understanding that protecting free speech is important to a vital and vibrant democracy. Needless to say, the road taken has been full of pitfalls and pratfalls reflective both of the extraordinary importance of this protection and the dangers that free speech, arguably, pose. The rocky road directly reflects this tension; to suggest that the tension has been resolved and that limitations will not be posed in the future would be to misread American history.

After all, American history is replete with 'roll backs' of rights in times of crisis, whether real or imagined. This unfortunate tendency, in the speech context, is compounded by the ever changing nature of speech and the media. Rearticulated: Given the extraordinary power of social media, and the speed with which information can be transmitted, it is not unforeseeable that this will force both government and the Courts to increasingly consider imposing limits on free speech when public safety is arguably endangered.

While the Supreme Court's holding in *Snyder*[84] suggests an expansive articulation of free speech, American history suggests the possibility of a 'roll back,' particularly with regard to national security and public order. Though American society has significantly matured over the past 200 years, the responses when 'under threat' are surprisingly uniform and consistent in accepting a rights minimization paradigm imposed by government and upheld by the Court. A careful reading of American history, executive decision making and judicial holdings suggest this possibility must not be discounted in the free speech discussion.

The question, in a nutshell, is whether national security and public order justify minimizing free speech. In some ways, American history has demonstrated a ready willingness to answer in the affirmative. The costs, as repeatedly demonstrated, are significant both with respect to the principles articulated in the First Amendment and on a human, individual basis. A quick perusal of the WWI and post WWII prosecutions offers ready proof. However, as I suggested in my book *Freedom from Religion: Rights* and *National Security*,[85] disregarding legitimate threats to national security is *also* dangerous. The dilemma, then, is determining how serious is the threat to national security and public order, and whether limiting free speech will mitigate that threat and at what cost to individual liberty.

---

84 *Snyder v. Phelps*, 131 S.Ct. 1207 (2011).

85 Amos Guiora, *Freedom from Religion: Rights and National Security* (Oxford 2009).

In looking forward we must, naturally, look backward, but doing so provides a murky picture. One hundred years ago, the answer was clear, as national security took clear precedence. Fifty years ago, the answer suggested a preference for free speech, which has been largely reaffirmed recently. Nevertheless, the question going forward is whether future decisions will reflect recent holdings or whether the complex threats facing society will result in a rollback of free speech protections recently upheld by the Supreme Court.

Part II
The International Dimension of Freedom of Speech

7 CHANGING COURSE BY STEALTH

How the European Court of Human Rights has been moving the goalposts in the area of political free speech

Tom Zwart

INTRODUCTION

For more than three decades, the European Court of Human Rights has regarded Article 10 of the European Convention on Human Rights as a pillar of robust political debate. Five years ago, it started to move away from this position by assenting to measures taken by States Parties to counter 'hate speech.' Consequently, the Court has become considerably less tolerant towards insulting, blasphemous and spiteful remarks made as part of the political debate.

These recent developments will be discussed in section 4. They will be contrasted with the Court's established case law on political free speech, which is laid out in section 2, as well as the case law of the U.S. Supreme Court, which will be the topic of section 3. After having shadowed its Washington counterpart for decades, it parted company with it in 2009. In section 5, the Court's recent turn will be analyzed from the perspective of the rule of precedent and the Court's proper role. Is a narrowly divided Chamber allowed to bring about such a radical change in the Court's case law? Can it do so by interpreting the same text completely differently? Should such a sea change not be left to the amending process which is carried out by political bodies with and an electoral mandate?

THE COURT'S ESTABLISHED CASE LAW REGARDING FREE SPEECH

A democratic society presupposes robust discussion

According to the Strasbourg Court, the concept of a democratic society is part and parcel of the Convention framework. This concept of a democratic society requires the promotion of free political debate. The Court therefore attaches the highest importance to the freedom of expression in the context of a political debate.[1] There is no democratic society without pluralism, tolerance and broad-mindedness. Therefore, Article 10 is not only applicable to information or ideas that are favorably received, but also to those that offend, shock and disturb.[2]

The Strasbourg Court attaches much value to the context within which these views have been expressed. The speaker may be polemical and even aggressive if he is participating in a lively public discussion on a current topic of general interest, like immigration and integration.[3] Under those circumstances, references to Nazism are not taboo.[4]

The Court has indicated that State authorities are allowed to resort to criminal proceedings to tackle certain expressions, as long as they are appropriate and proportional.[5] However, it has cautioned the States parties to exercise restraint. The rationale for this restraint is the dominant position the State has in society. It is required, therefore, to use other means if they are available.[6] Although restrictions on political speech are allowed in principle, very strong reasons are required to justify them.[7] Furthermore, the exceptions set forth in Article 10 need to be construed strictly.[8]

The Court has acknowledged that while freedom of expression is important for everybody, it is especially so for an elected representative of the people. He represents his electorate, draws attention to their preoccupations and defends their interests. Accordingly, interferences with the freedom of expression of an opposition member of parliament call for the closest scrutiny on the part of the Court.[9] According to the Court, statements made by politicians in writing or as part of a public debate are no less deserving of the protection offered by Article 10 than those made on the floor of the House under the cover of parliamentary privilege.[10]

---

1 *Oberschlick v. Austria (No.1)* App No. 11662/85 (ECHR 23 May 1991) § 58; *Feldek v. Slovakia* App No. 29032/95 (ECHR 12 July 2001) § 83; *Erbakan v. Turkey* App. No. 59405/00 (ECHR 6 July 2006) § 55 (iv).

2 *Handyside v. The United Kingdom* App No. 5493/72 (ECHR 7 December 1976) § 49; *Lingens v. Austria* App No. 9815/82 (ECHR 8 July 1986) § 41.

3 *De Haes and Gijsels v. Belgium* App No. 199983/92 (ECHR 27 January 1997) § 48; *Unabhängige Initiative Informationsvielfalt v. Austria* App No. 28525/95 (ECHR 26 February 2002) § 43; *Gündüz v. Turkey* App No. 35071/97 (ECHR 4 December 2003) § 49.

4 *Castells v. Spain* App No. 11798/85 (ECHR 23 April 1992) § 46.

5 Ibid.

6 Ibid.

7 *Feldek v. Slovakia* supra note 1, § 83.

8 *Thorgeir Thorgeirson v. Iceland* App No. 13778/88 (ECHR 25 June 1992) § 63; *Nilsen and Johnsen v. Norway* App No. 23118/93 (ECHR 25 November 1999) § 43.

9 *Castells v. Spain* App No. 11798/85 (ECHR 23 April 1992) § 42; *Jerusalem v. Austria* App No. 26958/95 (ECHR 27 February 2001) § 36.

10 *Jerusalem v. Austria* App No. 26958/95 (ECHR 27 February 2001) § 40.

Exceptions to the Rule: Incitement and Blasphemous Artistic Expressions

According to the Court, there are two types of expression which are less deserving of the protection of Article 10.

First, the Court believes that Article 10 affords less protection to speech which incites violence. When remarks incite violence against an individual, a public official or a sector of the population, the State authorities enjoy a wider margin of appreciation when examining the need for an interference with freedom of expression.[11] Here as well the Court has adopted a contextual approach. If a remark could spark violence it may be suppressed.

In the *Zana* case, a mayor of a community in south-east Turkey had been convicted for expressing his support for the PKK in an interview in a national newspaper.[12] The Strasbourg Court felt that the conviction was not contrary to Article 10. The publication coincided with a number of attacks which were carried out by the PKK on civilians in south-east Turkey. Since there was extreme tension in the region at the time, the interview could act as the spark which could set off the explosives.

While affording less protection to incitement under Article 10, the Court also steadfastly distinguishes it from advocacy that is deserving of such protection. Consequently, in the *Gündüz* case, the petitioner, the leaders of an Islamic sect, had made a number of very critical remarks about democracy and Kemalism in Turkey during a televised discussion.[13] He created the impression that his aim was to destroy democracy and to replace it with Sharia. For this, he had been convicted for incitement by a Turkish court. The Strasbourg Court, however, found that merely defending Sharia without calling for violence to establish it does not amount to incitement.

Similarly, in the *Erdal Tas v. Turkey* case, the petitioner had been convicted for separatism by a Turkish court for raising the Kurdish question in a publication.[14] The Strasbourg Court came to the conclusion that, since the article did not call for violence, armed resistance or insurrection, it was protected by Article 10. The Court took a similar position in *Faruk Temel v. Turkey*,[15] and *Önal v. Turkey*.[16]

---

11 *Zana v. Turkey* App No. 18954/91 (ECHR 25 November 1997); *Sürek v. Turkey (No.1)* App No. 26682/95 (ECHR 8 July 1999).
12 *Zana v. Turkey* App No. 18954/91 (ECHR 25 November 1997).
13 *Gündüz v. Turkey* App No. 35071/97 (ECHR 4 December 2003) § 51.
14 *Erdal Tas v. Turkey* App No. 77650/01 (ECHR 19 December 2006) § 38.
15 *Faruk Temel v. Turkey* App No. 16853/05 (ECHR 1 February 2011) § 62.
16 *Önal v. Turkey* App Nos. 41445/04 and 41453/04 (ECHR 2 October 2012) § 42.

Secondly, the Court holds that Article 10 affords less protection to artistic expressions which ridicule or insult certain religious beliefs.[17] The forfeiture of a film in which God was portrayed as an idiot, Jesus as a wimp and the Virgin Mary as a harlot was deemed acceptable under Article 10.[18] The Court also approved of the prosecution and conviction of a publisher of a novel in which the Prophet was accused of breaking his fast by having sex and by eating. The Court felt that this statement amounted to an offensive attack on matters regarded as sacred by Muslims.[19] These cases present a clash between the freedom of expression and the freedom of religion. Since the expressions are of an artistic rather than a political nature, they have to give way to the religious beliefs of others.

A comparison with U.S. case law

U.S. case law on political speech

Free speech in the U.S. is protected by the First Amendment to the Constitution. The Amendment states that 'Congress shall make no law ... abridging the freedom of speech.' In the U.S. the Supreme Court traditionally has taken a rather libertarian attitude towards freedom of expression.[20] The freedom of expression is regarded as an essential element of the American system of limited government and therefore requires maximum protection.

Some, like Justice Black, have argued that free speech is absolute and therefore cannot be subjected to any restrictions.[21] This so-called 'absolutist' view is based on a literal interpretation of the text of the First Amendment: 'No law' means no law. As is often the case with absolute statements, escapes are sometimes necessary. Justice Black interpreted freedom of speech in a rather narrow way, not covering, for example, peaceful demonstrations. This allowed him to approve of limitations on these rights. Although the view of Justice Black enjoyed some support, in particular from his colleague Justice Douglas, it never became the mainstream approach towards the First Amendment.

The philosopher Alexander Meiklejohn distinguished between public speech, which is protected by the First Amendment, and private speech, which is based on the Due Process

17 *Otto-Preminger-Institut v. Austria* App No. 13470/87 (ECHR 20 September 1994); *I.A. v. Turkey* App No. 42571/98 (ECHR 13 September 2005).
18 *Otto-Preminger-Institut v. Austria* App No. 13470/87 (ECHR 20 September 1994).
19 *I.A. v. Turkey* App No. 42571/98 (ECHR 13 September 2005).
20 Adam Liptak, 'Justices Reject Ban on Videos of Animal Cruelty', *The New York Times*, 20 April 2010, p. 1.
21 Patrick McBride, 'Mr. Justice Black and his Qualified Absolutes', *Loyola of Los Angeles Law Review*, Vol. 2, 1969, pp. 37-70.

Clauses of the Fifth and the Fourteenth Amendments.[22] Comments made about public policy or public officials are considered public speech. As such they enjoy absolute protection under the First Amendment. Private speech is defined as those discussions that relate to the private concerns of citizens. Since they are covered by the liberty concept of the Fourteenth and Fifth Amendments, they may be subjected to limitations.

Although the Meiklejohn dichotomy never became the compass of the Supreme Court, it did have a major impact in one area of First Amendment Law, *i.e.* libel law, as the *New York Times Co. v. Sullivan* case demonstrates.[23] An advertorial published in the New York Times by supporters of Dr. Martin Luther King claimed that the police of Montgomery, Alabama, had been heavy-handed in dealing with protesters at an Alabama university. The Montgomery Police Commissioner, Sullivan, sued the New York Times for defamation. The text contained incorrect statements and was deemed defamatory by an Alabama jury. The jury awarded Sullivan $500,000 in damages.

Justice Brennan for the Court claimed that discussions on the official conduct of public officials should be robust. Consequently, exaggerations and factual errors are inevitable. According to Justice Brennan, under the First Amendment courts are not allowed to apply a truth test. Awarding huge amounts in damages, as the Alabaman jury did, limits free speech. Therefore, the Court concluded that under the First Amendment, public officials cannot recover damages for a defamatory falsehood relating to their official conduct, unless the statement was made with actual malice or reckless disregard. This rule, which clearly drew inspiration from Meiklejohn's approach, has made it very hard to stifle criticism of public officials.

The third school of thought believes that free speech should enjoy a preferred position, i.e. primacy over all other rights. This concept became the official approach of the Supreme Court when it was embraced by Justice Douglas in his majority opinion in *Murdock v. Pennsylvania*.[24] Although the Court no longer mentions the preferred position doctrine by name, it is still committed to the underlying approach. This strong protection of free speech offered by the Court benefits from the fact that First Amendment restrictions, like other limitations on fundamental rights, are subject to the so-called strict scrutiny test.

22 Alexander Meiklejohn, 'The First Amendment is an Absolute', *The Supreme Court Review*, Vol. 1961, 1961, pp. 245-266.

23 376 U.S. 254 (1964).

24 319 U.S. 105 (1943).

Only a compelling governmental interest may justify a restriction on free speech.[25] Restrictions rarely survive this rigorous test, which is 'strict in theory, but fatal in fact'.

Nonetheless, the Supreme Court has accepted that there are limits to free speech as well. Over time, 'clear and present danger,' offensive speech, fighting words and incitement have all been excluded from the realm of the First Amendment.

The first attempt to describe these limits was the so-called 'clear and present danger' test.

In *Schenck v. U.S.*,[26] petitioner Schenck had been convicted under the Espionage Act for distributing leaflets calling on conscripts to resist serving in the armed forces. The tracts had been handed out just after the U.S. had decided to join the war effort during World War I. The Supreme Court had to decide whether this conviction violated the First Amendment.

Writing for the Court, Justice Holmes indicated that the protection afforded by the First Amendment is contextual, therefore it depends on the circumstances. What is allowed in peace time may not be acceptable in times of war. Justice Holmes clearly stated that the First Amendment does not extend to words which are used in such circumstances and are of such a nature as to create a clear and present danger such that they will bring about the substantive evils that Congress has a right to prevent. The famous example he gave was that of falsely shouting 'fire' in a crowded theatre.

While this so-called 'clear and present danger test' was received favorably initially, it lost much of its appeal and legitimacy when the Court started using it to condone the conviction of members of communist parties in *Whitney v. California*[27] and *Dennis v. U.S.*[28] Although these parties advocated the overthrow of the American government, by violent means if necessary, the individuals concerned had limited themselves to discussing ideas alone.

Secondly, in *Chaplinsky v. State of New Hampshire* the Court indicated that 'offensive words' do not enjoy First Amendment protection.[29] Chaplinsky had been arrested for shouting in a public place that the government of Rochester consisted of 'damned fascists.' Apparently, his remarks created some unrest, although the petitioner argued that the unrest was created by the bystanders. The basis for his arrest was a public order law of the state

25 Stephen A. Siegel, 'The Origin of the Compelling State Interest Test and Strict Scrutiny', *The American Journal Of Legal History*, Vol. 48, No. 4, 2006, pp. 355-407.

26 249 U.S. 47 (1919).

27 274 U.S. 357 (1929).

28 341 U.S. 494 (1951).

29 315 U.S. 568 (1942).

of New Hampshire, which banned calling people offensive names. The Supreme Court upheld his conviction. According to the Court, words like 'damned fascist' are epithets likely to provoke the average person to retaliate and thereby cause a breach of the peace.

Thirdly, the Supreme Court made clear that 'fighting words' are not protected in *Feiner v. New York*.[30] Petitioner Feiner spoke with the help of a sound system on a street corner in Syracuse in the state of New York. He made some derogatory remarks about public officials, including President Truman. He also called on black people, many of whom were in his audience, to rise up in arms and fight for equal rights. The people gathered around the speaker became agitated by what he said. The police tried to persuade him to stop, and when he refused to do so, they arrested him for breach of the peace. The majority of the Court led by Chief Justice Vinson felt that the petitioner had crossed the line of argument and persuasion by undertaking incitement to riot. The police were therefore justified in silencing and arresting him and had not violated his First Amendment rights. In a powerful dissent, Justice Black stressed that if a speaker faces a hostile audience, under the First Amendment the speaker needs to be protected, not silenced.

Fourth, in 1969, in *Brandenburg v. Ohio* the Court made a very clear distinction between incitement, which is not protected by the First Amendment, and advocacy, which is.[31] The petitioner, a member of the Ku Klux Klan, had declared that some revenge might have to be taken if the President, Congress and the Supreme Court continued to suppress the white, Caucasian race. The Klan rally had been attended by a television reporter who aired the remarks as part of a television documentary. Consequently, Brandenburg was convicted for advocacy of violence on the basis of an Ohio statute.

In a unanimous *per curiam* decision shared by all Justices, the Court held that advocacy should be distinguished from incitement to imminent lawless action. While the former is protected by the First Amendment, the latter is not. According to the Court, speech that is intended to incite immediate lawless action, or which is likely to incite or produce such action, should be considered unprotected incitement. Only speech posing an immediate threat of harm falls into this category. The outcome of this case made it clear that the Court does not lightly characterize speech as incitement, due to the finding that the 'revenge' remark made by Brandenburg did not meet this threshold.

30 340 U.S. 315 (1951).
31 395 U.S. 444 (1969).

Parallels in Strasbourg Case Law

There are clear parallels between U.S. free speech law, as developed by the Supreme Court, and the Strasbourg Court's interpretation of Article 10 of the European Convention. Although the Strasbourg Court has not mentioned U.S. cases or concepts by name, it is clear that it has drawn inspiration from these while developing its own case law.

The *Lingens* case is a good example of this.[32] Lingens, a journalist, had been criticising the Austrian Chancellor, Bruno Kreisky, for being too accommodating to politicians with a National-Socialist past. In his article he accused Kreisky of 'blatant opportunism', and called him 'immoral' and 'undignified'. Lingens was convicted of defamation by a Vienna Court. In its judgment, the Strasbourg Court made clear that under Article 10 there is more room to criticize politicians than private individuals. Unlike private individuals, politicians expose themselves to close scrutiny of their words and actions by journalists. This statement was clearly inspired by the *Sullivan* rule.

The strong protection of political free speech by the Strasbourg Court closely resembles the preferred position doctrine developed by its Washington counterpart. According to the Strasbourg Court, the concept of a democratic society, which is the backbone of the Convention framework, requires a robust political debate.[33] This elevated position of political speech is mirrored by the Court's narrow interpretation of incitement.

There are, however, clear signs that the Strasbourg Court is parting company with its counterpart in Washington in the area of political free speech. This is highlighted by the difference in the outcome of two recent cases about homophobic comments, *Snyder v. Phelps*[34] and *Vejdeland and others v. Sweden*,[35] which will be discussed in the next section.

The Court's Recent Deviation from the Path

During the past five years, the Strasbourg Court has started to move away from its position that a democratic society requires a robust political debate.[36] This development has progressed in two stages.

32 *Lingens v. Austria* App No. 9815/82 (ECHR 8 July 1986) § 42.

33 *Oberschlick v. Austria (No.1)* App No. 11662/85 (ECHR 23 May 1991) § 58; *Feldek v. Slovakia* App No. 29032/95 (ECHR 12 July 2001) § 83; *Erbakan v. Turkey* App. No. 59405/00 (ECHR 6 July 2006) § 55 (iv).

34 562 U.S. __ (2011).

35 *Vejdeland and others v. Sweden* App No. 18183/07 (ECHR 9 February 2012).

36 Stephan Sottiaux. "Bad Tendencies' in the ECtHR's 'Hate Speech' Jurisprudence', European Constitutional Law Review, Vol. 7, 2011, pp. 40-63; Ian Cram, 'Coercing Communities or Promoting Civilised Discourse?

The first stage of this change of course began when the Court started to water down its definition of incitement considerably. Thus, in *Soulas*, the Court approved of the prosecution and the conviction of the author of an academic book on integration issues in France. In his book the author claimed that the problems in this area could only be solved through 'an ethnic civil war'.[37] Since there was no call for violence, armed resistance or insurrection, this judgment marked a dramatic and sudden departure from the Court's existing case law.

The Court continued this approach in *Leroy v. France*.[38] In that case, the petitioner had published a cartoon apparently endorsing the destruction of the World Trade Centre in New York on 11 September 2001, two days after the event. The applicant had been convicted by French courts of glorifying terrorism. The Strasbourg Court did not agree with the complainant according to whom the conviction amounted to a violation of Article 10. It emphasized that the cartoon had been published two days after 9/11, when everybody was still in shock about what had occurred. In addition, it had been published in a journal appearing in the Basque Country, a politically sensitive region. Therefore, the Court came to the conclusion that the publication might have caused violent reactions and might have had an impact on public order in the region.

While in *Soulas* and *Leroy*, the Court stretched its definition of incitement to the limits, the Court then became more radical: To be guilty of incitement one does not have to incite. This bold step was taken by the Court in December 2009 in the case of *Féret v. Belgium*.[39] The applicant was the leader of a Belgian political party called the Front National, and had been a member of several representative bodies, including the Belgian Parliament. The party had published several pamphlets in which it argued that Belgians deserved better treatment than immigrants, that immigrants needed to be returned to their country of origin and that the islamization of Belgium needed to be stopped. Féret was stripped of his parliamentary immunity, as well as prosecuted, convicted and sentenced to 250 hours of community service with a suspended sentence of 10 months. More importantly, the Belgian court denied him the right to stand for election for a period of 10 years.

In its judgment, the Court added a new paragraph to the usual statements about the importance of political debate.[40] It emphasized that tolerance and the equal dignity of all

Funeral Protests and Comparative Hate Speech Jurisprudence', Human Rights Law Review, Vol. 12, No. 3, pp. 455-478.

37 *Soulas and others v. France* App No. 15948/03 (ECHR 10 July 2008).

38 *Leroy v. France* App No. 36109/03 (ECHR 2 October 2008).

39 *Féret v. Belgium* App No. 15615/07 (ECHR 16 July 2009).

40 Ibid §64.

human beings constitute the foundation of a democratic and pluralist society. Consequently, state authorities may consider it necessary in democratic societies to either punish or prevent expressions that propagate, incite, encourage or justify hatred based on intolerance.

The next step taken by the Court was to assert that incitement to hatred does not require a call to violence or other criminal acts. Personal attacks which ridicule or insult certain parts of the population and specific groups, or promote discrimination, will suffice. Under these circumstances, state authorities are justified in giving precedence to the battle against racism over irresponsible free speech which violates the dignity or the security of parts of the population.[41] Not surprisingly, the Court felt that Belgium had not violated Article 10 when it restricted Féret's freedom of expression.

The Court adopted a similar approach in its admissibility decision in the *Le Pen* case.[42] The well-known leader of the Front National had stated during an interview with *Le Monde* in 2003 that he expected problems as soon as the Muslim population of France increased from 5 million to 25 million. Then the 'ordinary French' would only be able to walk the streets timidly and with their heads bowed. If they would look the Muslims in the eye, they would run the risk of being threatened or even beaten. For these remarks Le Pen was convicted and charged with a 10,000 Euro fine for provoking discrimination. Since his remarks were liable to evoke a sense of exclusion of and hostility towards the Muslim community, the Strasbourg Court rejected Le Pen's claim that France had violated Article 10 as being manifestly ill-founded.

Since the Court was narrowly divided, its judgment in *Féret* could easily have been dismissed as a one-off deviation by one of its Chambers, which was out of sync with the established case law. However, that scenario proved to be incorrect when the Court confirmed its position in the 2012 *Vejdeland v. Sweden* case.[43] The applicants had put leaflets containing disparaging remarks about gay people into the lockers of pupils at a secondary school. They were sentenced to custodial sentences by the court of first instance, which were later commuted into suspended sentences by the Supreme Court. As in *Féret*, the Court emphasized that inciting hatred does not necessarily entail a call for an act of violence or other criminal acts. State authorities are allowed to combat attacks on persons committed by insulting, holding up to ridicule or slandering specific groups of the population.[44] Accordingly, rather than abandoning *Féret*, the Court confirmed its ruling in that case and even extended it to a new field, that of sexual orientation.

---

41 Ibid §73.

42 *Le Pen v. France* App No. 18788/09 (ECHR 12 May 2010).

43 *Vejdeland and others v. Sweden* App No. 18183/07 (ECHR 9 February 2012).

44 Ibid §§ 54-55.

The outcome of the *Vejdeland v. Sweden* case stands in marked contrast to the judgment in *Snyder v. Phelps*, which was handed down by the U.S. Supreme Court in 2011.[45] The case involved Fred Phelps and his followers at the Westboro Baptist Church, who believe that God punishes the United States for its tolerance of homosexuality, particularly within the military. To demonstrate their beliefs, they picket military funerals. In 2006, they picketed the funeral of Lance Corporal Matthew Snyder, who was killed in the line of duty in Iraq in 2006. Phelps and his followers displayed signs bearing slogans such as 'God Hates the USA/Thank God for 9/11,' 'Thank God for Dead Soldiers,' and 'Don't Pray for the USA.' The father of the deceased, Albert Snyder, sued Phelps and the church claiming, *inter alia*, that their actions caused him severe emotional distress. In his defense, Phelps argued that the comments made by him and the members of the church, as well as the picketing and use of signs, were protected under the First Amendment. The Court sided with Phelps. Chief Justice Roberts for the majority reasoned that speech on public issues is entitled to special protection under the First Amendment because it serves the principle that debate on such issues should be uninhibited, robust, and wide-open.

Although there are important differences between the above cases - Snyder is about picketing, not the publication of leaflets, and it did not involve homophobic slogans - the facts are similar enough to draw comparative conclusions.

Conclusion

A comparison between *Vejdeland v. Sweden* and *Snyder v. Phelps* shows how far the Strasbourg Court has diverged from the jurisprudence of the U.S. Supreme Court and its own established case law. After adopting a staunch libertarian position for decades, the European Court of Human Rights is now moving away from this stance and has become less tolerant towards insulting, blasphemous and spiteful remarks made as part of the political debate.

In his forceful dissent in the *Féret* case, Judge Sajó explains that the judgment entails an important philosophical shift.[46] In a democracy opinions are protected because only an exchange of views will bring us closer to the truth. Underlying this protection is the idea that rational human beings are able to make informed choices. Consequently, it is not the role of the government to develop a catalogue of wrong and unacceptable ideas. By contrast,

45 562 U.S. __ (2011).

46 *Féret v. Belgium* App No. 15615/07 (ECHR 16 July 2009), dissenting opinion of Judge Andràs Sajó, in which Judges Vladimiro Zagrebelsky and Nona Tsotsoria join.

the majority in *Féret* portrays human beings, in particular a social group of 'nitwits', as being incapable of responding to arguments because they are driven by irrational emotions.

One questions whether the Court was authorised to re-interpret the law by attaching a completely new meaning to the words 'democratic society' in paragraph 2 of Article 10. Supporters of the Court's evolutive interpretation of the Convention, which regards the document as a living instrument, will no doubt argue that this is within the ambit of the Court's power. The Court, however, is a judicial body, not an agency, a political organ or an NGO, and from this fact flows certain requirements and responsibilities.

While using its status as an international tribunal and its mixed common law-civil law background as justifications,[47] the Court has never fully embraced the rule of precedent. It has, however, committed itself to a 'lite' version of the doctrine of *stare decisis*: Precedents will be followed unless there are good reasons not to do so.[48] Given that the Court operates under the assumption that the Convention is a 'living instrument', these reasons may stem from policy, particularly the desire to adjust its interpretation of Convention articles in light of present day conditions. The 'living instrument' philosophy therefore makes it very easy for the Court to depart from the established case law, while using developments at the international level, within the domestic legal order of the State Party concerned, or both, as a justification.

Although the Court has accorded itself considerable room to manoeuvre in departing from its own precedents, it has also highlighted the need to follow them as much as possible in the interest of legal certainty and consistency.[49] The Court therefore professes restraint in overturning its own precedents, even though its own rules allow it much room to do so. The Court appears, on the surface, to be true to its word, since the number of cases in which it has expressly overruled its prior decisions are few.[50] However, to this number needs to be added the instances where the Court has overruled prior decisions by implica-

47 Luzius Wildhaber, 'Precedent in the European Court of Human Rights', *in* P. Mahoney, F. Matscher, H. Petzold and L. Wildhaber (Eds.), *Protecting Human Rights: The European Perspective*, Köln, Heymann Verlag, 2000, pp. 1529-1542 at 1531.

48 Fredrik G.E. Sundberg, 'The European Experience of Human Rights Proceedings: The Precedent Value of the European Court's Decisions', *Akron Law Review*, Vol. 20, 1986-1987, pp. 629-647 at 631; Wildhaber 2000 at p. 1530 and p. 1532 ; *Chapman v. the United Kingdom* App No. 27238/95 (ECHR 18 January 2001) §70; *Mamatkulov and Askarov v. Turkey* App No. 46827/99 and 46951/99 (ECHR 4 February 2005) §121; *Vilho Eskelinen and Others v. Finland* App No. 63235/00 (ECHR, 19 April 2007) §56.

49 Wildhaber 2000; Sundberg 1986-1987.

50 Alastair Mowbray, 'An Examination of the European Court of Human Rights' Approach to Overruling its Previous Case Law', *Human Rights Law Review*, Vol. 9, No. 2, 2009, pp. 179-201; see e.g. *Pellegrin v. France* App No. 28541/95 (ECHR 8 December 1999) and *Kudla v. Poland* App No. 30210/96 (ECHR, 26 October 2000).

tion.[51] These implied changes of course demonstrate that, like many other courts, the Court is reluctant to openly admit that it is overruling itself.

The *Féret* case clearly belongs to this category. The decision in this case is presented by the majority as flowing from previous case law. One of the architects of the decision, the Belgian judge Françoise Tulkens, has, since retiring, attempted to fit the judgment into a consistent line of cases.[52] However, as the dissent of judge Sajó shows, it actually presents a steady change. The Court has therefore tried to move the goalposts by stealth. A judicial organ adopting such a radical change may bring its legitimacy into question. To distinguish itself from a political organ that is motivated by expediency rather than principle, a court should be wary not to create the impression that it changes its course at will.[53]

In addition, the decision was taken by a significantly divided Chamber rather than by the Grand Chamber. If the Court is entitled to take decisions of this magnitude at all, those decisions should be taken by the Grand Chamber. This idea finds support in the Brighton Declaration, which suggests that overruling precedents will become the prerogative of the Grand Chamber.[54] Even then, the Court should not act in isolation, but actively involve stakeholders by inviting them to submit *amicus* briefs.

As Judge Tulkens suggests, it is likely that in *Féret*, the Court was informed by concerns about the anti-immigration and anti-Islam rhetoric that has emerged in several European countries.[55] Since the drafting of the Convention shortly after World War II, the demographics of the European population have indeed changed beyond recognition. There may be good reason, therefore, to reconsider whether the robustness of the political debate should be preserved in light of the growing importance of values like harmony and respect. Such a reconsideration should, however, not be conducted by the Court, but as part of the amendment process by the political organs which enjoy an electoral mandate.

51 See e.g. *Huber v. Switzerland* App No. 12794/87 (ECHR, 23 October 1990) and *Scoppola v. Italy (No. 3)* App No. 126/05 (ECHR 22 May 2012).

52 Françoise Tulkens, 'When to Say is to Do, Freedom of Expression and Hate Speech in the Case-law of the European Court of Human Rights', Seminar on Human Rights for European Judicial Trainers, Strasbourg, 9 October 2012, available at: www.ejtn.eu/Documents/About%20EJTN/Independent%20Seminars/TULKENS_Francoise_Presentation_When_to_Say_is_To_Do_Freedom_of_Expression_and_Hate_Speech_in_the_Case_Law_of_the_ECtHR_October_2012.pdf

53 Tom Zwart, 'More Human Rights than Court: Why the Legitimacy of the European Court of Human Rights Is in Need of Repair and how it Can Be Done', *in* Spyridon Flogaitis, Tom Zwart and Julie Fraser (Eds.), *The European Court of Human Rights and its Discontents, Turning Criticism into Strength*, Cheltenham, Edward Elgar, 2013, pp. 71-95.

54 High level Conference on the Future of the European Court of Human Rights, Brighton Declaration, 19-20 April 2012, §23.

55 Tulkens 2012 at p. 11.

8 Hate Speech in the case law of the European Court of Human Rights

Good Intentions make Bad Law?

*Koen Lemmens**

Introduction

Limitations on freedom of speech are an evergreen in writings on fundamental rights. The classic rationales underlying freedom of speech indeed favor robust protection of free speech, thus throwing suspicion on (governmental) interferences in this fundamental right.[1] The strong protection of freedom of speech under the First Amendment of the US Constitution during the last decades[2] has surely contributed to a widely shared support for the largest protection possible. The whole case for unrestricted freedom of speech is often summarized by the famous and platitudinous quote 'I disapprove of what you say, but I will defend to the death your right to say it.'[3]

However, no matter how tolerant we are when it comes to protecting freedom of speech, few of us would be willing to accept speech that directly incites imminent violence. Even one of the most vivid defenders of freedom of speech, John Stuart Mill, explicitly recognized that incitement to violence is an acceptable reason to interfere with freedom of speech.[4] Similarly, utterances that constitute menaces and blackmailing will not be covered by freedom of speech.[5]

---

* The author wants to thank Laura Corrado and Jogchum Vrielink for their valuable comments on an earlier version of this text. The usual disclaimer applies.

1 The literature on this topic is immense, especially in the Anglo-Saxon world. A very insightful overview is given by W. Sadurski, *Freedom of Speech and Its Limits*, Kluwer, Dordrecht, 1999.

2 J. Waldron, *The Harm in Hate Speech*, Harvard University Press, Cambridge (Mass.), 2012, pp. 22-23 reminds us of the fact that First Amendment 'absolutism' is a phenomenon that can be traced back to 1931.

3 A quote that is generally attributed to Voltaire, yet it would appear that Voltaire never pronounced or wrote it. The words would have been expressed by Evelynn Beatrice Hall. See: B. Kinne, 'Voltaire Never Said It!', *Modern Language Notes*, 1943, pp. 534-535.

4 www2.hn.psu.edu/faculty/jmanis/jsmill/liberty.pdf, p. 66.

5 As J. Vrielink, who refers to K. Greenawalt's *Speech, Crime and the Uses of Language* (OUP, Oxford, 1989), observes, many communicative acts can constitute forms of unwanted or even outlawed behavior without detriment to free speech concerns. J. Vrielink, 'Silence is Golden? Charting the Intersections of Speech and Direct Discrimination under EU Law with a Special Focus on Racial and Religious Discrimination in Recruitement' in K. Alidadi, M.-C. Foblets and J. Vrielink (Eds.), *A Test of Faith? Religious Diversity and Accommodation in the European Workplace*, Surray, Ashgate, 2012, pp. 121-122.

More problematic are those forms of expression that may not directly lead to violence, but that could or might lead to hatred. Many developed western democracies have adopted legislation forbidding 'hate speech' (the US being a well-known exception).[6] Based on comparative examples, Jeremy Waldron describes such hate speech regulation as 'regulation (...) prohibiting public statements that incite "hatred against any identifiable group where such incitement is likely to lead to a breach of the peace" (Canada); or statements "by which a group of people are threatened, derided or degraded because of their race, colour of skin, national or ethnic background" (Denmark); or attacks on "the human dignity of others by insulting, maliciously maligning or defaming segments of the population" (Germany); or "threatening, abusive, or insulting...words likely to excite hostility against or bring into contempt any group of persons...on the ground of the colour, race or ethnic or national or ethnic origins of that group of persons" (New Zealand); or the use of "threatening, abusive or insulting words or behaviour," when these are intended "to stir up racial hatred," or when "having regard to all the circumstances racial hatred is likely to be stirred up hereby" (United Kingdom).'[7]

In this contribution I will not discuss the concept of 'hate speech' in detail. I will only explain the rationales behind it and sketch why, from a theoretical point of view, hate speech gives rise to particularly complicated debates (II).[8] An in-depth philosophical discussion of hate speech would clearly go beyond the scope of this article.[9] Yet, I will discuss how the European Court of Human Rights (hereinafter: the "ECtHR" or the "Court") deals with hate speech in its case law from a formal point of view (III). The focus here is on the way of constructing the legal reasoning. Furthermore, I will indicate, from a substantive perspective, the outcome of the reasoning, sketching thereby to which kind of expressions the hate speech approach is relevant (IV). Finally, I will briefly touch upon the specific problem of so-called denialism, viz. the denial of historically established human tragedies such as the Holocaust or other genocides (V).

In this text, I will use the term 'hate speech' in its broad sense, so including the varieties of speech that incite violence and hatred. Although this may be question begging from a conceptual point of view, it is justified since, as Antoine Buyse has observed, the Court in its case law does not seem to distinguish very carefully between those two forms of

6 R. M. O'Neil, 'Hate Speech, Fighting Words and Beyond – Why American Law is Unique', *Alb. L. Rev.*, Vol. 76, 467, 2012-2013, pp. 467-498.

7 J. Waldron 2012, p. 8.

8 Once again, the literature on the topic is virtually unlimited. A very comprehensive overview of the theme can be found in I. Hare and J. Weinstein (Eds.), *Extreme Speech and Democracy*, Oxford University Press, Oxford, 2009.

9 See for a comprehensive discussion for instance: Q. L. Hong, *The Legal Inclusion of Extremist Speech*, Wolf Legal Publishers, Nijmegen, 2005.

expression.[10] I also add that although this article focuses on freedom of speech (and therefore on article 10 of the European Convention on Human Rights, hereinafter: the "Convention"), some of the cases discussed may (rather) concern freedom of reunion and assembly (article 11 of the Convention) as well. This is not a matter of flawed methodology: in practice, most questions regarding hate speech are not confined to mere speech. 'Extremists' often come together and create associations, such as political parties or movements. Hate speech therefore covers the exercise of more than only freedom of speech.

HATE SPEECH AND LIBERAL CONSTITUTIONAL THEORY

Reasons for Outlawing Hate Speech

Whether or not to outlaw hate speech is, according to Wojciech Sadurski, one of the most challenging questions for traditional Western liberalism, especially in light of the philosophical underpinnings of freedom of speech.[11] The author, who adopts a very individualistic focus, distinguishes three sets of arguments that are usually mentioned in justifying hate speech bans.[12]

The first argument relates to the problem of the reaction of the victims. The point here is that the audience, confronted with obnoxious forms of speech, can react in a violent way, thus breaching peace and public order. Although we can understand, *prima facie*, that preventing speech that would cause violent reactions makes sense, it is less straightforward upon closer scrutiny. Of course, there is a US Supreme Court doctrine, known as 'fighting words,' which upholds the claim that speech that is so offensive that it leaves the target of the message literally speechless, so that the only possible reaction is using violence against the speaker (thereby immediately breaching peace), is banned. In the *Chaplinsky* case, the US Supreme Court decided that such a form of speech is not protected by the American Constitution.[13] Now, what seems to be essential to the concept of 'fighting words' is that the interaction takes place in a face-to-face context and that the audience cannot avoid hearing the message.[14] However, consider situations in which the communication is less of a face-to-face nature, for example one speaker who addresses a larger audience. We can easily imagine that such a speaker makes utterances that upset the audience. Would

10 A. Buyse, 'Dangerous expressions: the ECHR, violence and free speech', *International & Comparative Law Quarterly*, Vol. 63, No 2, 2014, 493. Hereinafter: Buyse 2014, a.

11 Sadurski 1999, pp. 217-218.

12 Sardurski 1999, pp. 195-217.

13 Chaplinsky v. New Hampshire, 315 US 568 (1942).

14 J. Weinstein, 'Extreme Speech, Public Order, and Democracy: Lessons from *The Masses*' in I. Hare and J. Weinstein (Eds.), *Extreme Speech and Democracy*, Oxford University Press, Oxford, 2009, p. 53 ; Sadurski 1999, p. 68.

it be acceptable, in order to avoid hostile reactions from the audience, to prevent a speaker from speaking? According to US doctrine the answer would be no, unless the audience cannot escape. This is the so-called "captive audience" theory. In the case law of the European Court of Human Rights, the notion of 'captive audience' has received little attention thus far. Nevertheless, in the *Vona* judgment, the Court referred to it in order to uphold the dissolution in Hungary, by court decision, of an anti-Semitic and anti-Roma association. One of the reasons for the Court not to consider the disbanding a violation of article 11 of the Convention (freedom of assembly and association) was the particularly intimidating effect of the association's paramilitary marches on the Roma population. Even at home, the targeted minority could not escape the demonstrations of racial hatred.[15] Judge Zupancic's concurring opinion in the *Vejdeland* judgement also mentioned the captive audience idea, when he used it to explain why homophobic flyers in the lockers of a secondary school cannot lay claim on article 10 of the Convention.[16]

Needless to stress at this point, the concept of captive audience (like the idea of "fighting words") calls for a very strict interpretation. If not, the captive audience concept would boil down to letting the audience decide what is allowed to be said and what is to be silenced.[17] The episode of the well-known Mohammed cartoons offers a good illustration of the dangers a wide interpretation of the captive audience theory could entail. No one questions the right of (some) Muslims to feel offended by the cartoons; consequently, they are allowed to express their feelings by all legal means, including by bringing cases before the courts. Yet it is more questionable whether they could call for a ban of the cartoons, on account of the riots and breaches of public order the drawings could instigate. Here we indeed see people arguing for a protection against their own violence. This problem is known as the 'heckler's veto.'[18] Well-known in the American context, the heckler's veto is not often invoked in the European Court's case law. In only two cases, the Court refers to it. In the *Vajnai* case, the Court could not accept the interdiction of the display of a red star in Hungary because the victims of communism would find the presence of the symbol disrespectful. This would amount to restricting freedom of speech in order to 'satisfy the dictates of public feeling.'[19] In the *Faber* case, a similar reasoning was followed to argue that a flag, with an extreme-right connotation, could be displayed by a demonstrator at a location that was known in the past as a place where many Jews had been killed.[20]

The second reason used to outlaw hate speech is the harm it causes through the reaction of *third* persons. This is, in other words, the hypothesis of incitement to violence. In this

15 ECtHR, Vona v. Hungary, 9 July 2013, para. 66.
16 ECtHR, Vejdeland and others v. Sweden, 9 February 2012.
17 Sadurski 1999, p. 197.
18 O. Fiss, 'Free Speech and Social Structure', 71 *Iowa Law Review*, 1986, pp. 1416 ff.
19 ECtHR, Vajnai v. Hungary, 8 July 2008, para. 57.
20 ECtHR, Faber v. Hungary, 27 July 2012, para. 57.

case, it is not the victim that violently reacts, nor the speaker who directly causes harm, but someone in the audience who, incited by the words, commits violence. In its most extreme form, this hypothesis is a rewording of Mill's example of the mob that is told, in front of the house of the corn-dealer, that corn-dealers are starving the poor to death.[21] The problem is, of course, that the third agent is an autonomous person who can decide not to follow the incitements. So the question is to what extent the speaker should be held responsible for the (possible) actions of third persons. In addition, an element of time has to be taken into consideration. In the fighting words hypothesis, we noticed that the immediacy of the victim's reaction was a crucial element. In the incitement case, the immediacy of the reaction is fundamental as well, since it may be clear that there is an important difference between someone who reacts almost instantly after having heard inflammatory words, and someone who reacts only after a while. Usually, it is argued that a clear-and-present danger test (or an imminent lawless action test) can offer a way out. Judge Bonello repeated in his concurring and dissenting opinions many times that incitement to violence can only be a reason to restrict freedom of speech if the violence that could result from the speech is immediate and serious.[22] By contrast, Sadurski warns against a too loose combination of two distinct elements. One aspect is the remoteness (or immediacy) of the speech, another aspect is its gravity. More precisely, in Sadurski's view, there is a risk of a trade-off: Dangerous speech can be punished in any event, even if the risk of violence is low.[23] Sadurski does not call for a strict combination of the two criteria, but suggests to apply the principles independently.[24] Interestingly enough, the author does not make a sharp distinction between incitement to violence and the mere diffusion of racist 'beliefs.' Spreading beliefs can be potentially forbidden as well, if there is an imminent danger of violence.[25]

The problems sketched here are the conundrum of the hate speech issue. Whenever hate crimes are committed, people try to establish the link between hate speech and the crimes subsequently committed. But how to prove this link?[26] If interpreted in a lenient way, the result is that unpleasant speech that does not entail immediate violence will nevertheless be prohibited.[27]

21 www2.hn.psu.edu/faculty/jmanis/jsmill/liberty.pdf, p. 66.

22 E.g. Bonello (concurring), ECtHR (GC), Arslan v. Turkey, 8 July 1999; Bonello (partly dissenting), ECtHR (GC), Sürek v. Turkey No. 1, 8 July 1999; Bonello (concurring), ECtHR, Ceylan v. Turkey, 8 July 1999.

23 Sadurski 1999, p. 204.

24 Sadurski 1999, p. 204.

25 Sadurski 1999, p. 205.

26 See also: T. Naegels, 'Wat is dat eigenlijk, een klimaat scheppen?', *De Standaard*, 28 May 2014, p. 38.

27 In her partly dissenting opinion in the Erbakan case, Judge Steiner explicitly states that (religious) hate speech can be dangerous over time. Even if there are no direct, i.e. immediate, negative consequences, the long-term effects may be so detrimental to society that national authorities, by virtue of their margin of appreciation, may decide to ban these form of discourse. The judge therefore does not insist on the direct

Finally, there is a third set of arguments related to what Sadurski has called 'psychic injury.'[28] Here, the argument runs that hate speech causes such a deep psychic harm, including feelings of inferiority, that the vilified group cannot participate in society on an equal footing with the other members of society.[29] In the European context, the argument based on the protection of the group is completed by the idea that society and the democratic institutions as such need to be protected. By banning hate speech, society not only protects the minority group and its individual members, but also indicates that some forms of speech and behavior are considered unacceptable.[30] This idea is very present in the case law of the Strasbourg organs (by which I refer to both the Court and the former Commission). For instance, in the inadmissibility decision concerning *Pavel Ivanov*, the Court held that 'a general and vehement attack on one ethnic group is in contradiction with the Convention's underlying values, notably tolerance, social peace and non-discrimination.'[31]

But are they Convincing?

However convincing the arguments in favor of hate speech regulation may be, we should not forget that there is a flip side of the coin.[32] In the first place, there is of course a major problem related to the rationales of freedom of speech. In a liberal State, the idea is not that authorities impose their view on the good life by banning speech they find morally inappropriate. By banning some utterances and expressions by calling them 'hate speech,' authorities may restrict expressions that are covered by the right to free speech. The result is a distortion of the public debate, and more particularly the political debate.[33]

Second, the problem with hate speech regulation is that, even if we accept the very concept of hate speech, there is a risk of subjectivity/inequality, especially in the field of denialism. Why would we outlaw for instance Holocaust denial, when similar bans pertaining to other genocides do not necessarily exist? This is not to say that there are no good or even compelling reasons to do so, but it is far from being straightforward. As will be discussed later on, the European Court of Human Rights is seriously struggling with denialism.[34]

---

link between the hate discourse and the detrimental effects. Judge Steiner (partly dissenting), ECtHR, Erbakan v. Turkey, 6 July 2006.

28 Sadurski 1999, p. 206.

29 Richard Delgado wrote a seminal article on this argument: R. Delgado, 'Words that Wound: a Tort Action for Racial Insults, Epithets and Name-Calling', 17 Harv. C.R.-C.L. L. Rev. 1982, pp. 133-181.

30 Buyse 2014 a, p. 493.

31 ECtHR, Pavel Ivanov v. Russia, 20 February 2007 (admissibility). Similarly: ECtHR, Norwood v. UK, 16 November 2004 (admissibility).

32 Buyse 2014 a, p. 493.

33 Buyse 2014 a, p. 493.

34 See chapter V and P. Lobba, 'A European Halt to Laws Against Genocide Denial?', *European Criminal Law Review*, Vol. 4, no. 1, 2014, pp. 59-77.

Third, there is also a problem of opportunity related to what is called in media law the 'Barbara Streisand' effect (the actress wanted to stop the publication of a photo of a villa of hers since it would violate her privacy. By starting a lawsuit, she obviously publicized the information, whereas in reality she wanted to hide it).[35] If certain utterances have to be banned because of their detrimental content, it may not seem very wise to give extra attention to the vilifier. Yet, this is precisely what happens when hate speech cases are brought to court. In some cases, the extra media exposure is precisely what the racists, holocaust deniers and other kind of hate preachers are looking for.[36] From a symbolic point of view, this is not a very problematic issue: sometimes legal systems want to stress that some forms of behavior are unacceptable, since they touch upon the core values the system wants to defend. However, based on a cost-benefit calculus – or on the proportionality test – it could be questioned whether the costs of prohibiting some forms of speech do not outweigh the benefits.

The Court's Complex Formal Approach to Freedom of Speech

Whoever digs into the vast case law of the European Court of Human Rights on freedom of expression will be struck by its complexity. What I mean here is not that the cases as such are examples of complex legal reasoning, for in many cases rather the contrary is true,[37] but that it has become extremely difficult to understand the rationale underlying the Court's case law in the field of freedom of speech. Equally, it has become a very hard task to predict the outcome of pending cases concerning article 10 of the Convention. Thus, the foreseeability of the law – one of the basic conditions the Court imposes on national legal systems when it comes to restricting fundamental rights – can be seriously called into question.

In order to understand how the Court tackles the problem of hate speech (B.), it is important to sketch how the Court deals with freedom of speech tout court (A.). The Court's conception of free speech constitutes the general interpretative background of the hate speech issue.

35 See also: http://en.wikipedia.org/wiki/Streisand_effect (last accessed: 22 August 2014).

36 J. Vrielink, 'Van haat gesproken? Een rechtsantropologisch onderzoek naar de bestrijding van rasgerelateerde uitingsdelicten in België', KU Leuven, PhD dissertation, 2009-2010, p. 452 et seq.; Buyse 2014a, p. 493.

37 Even former judges admit that the Court sometimes takes rather 'simplistic' views. See: G. Bonello, 'Freedom of expression and incitement to hatred' in J. Casadevall, E. Myjer, M. O'Boyle and A. Austin (Eds.), *Essays in honour of Nicolas Bratza*, Wolf Legal Publishers, Oisterwijk, 2012, p. 350.

Freedom of Speech: Between Pseudo Absolutism and Restricted Freedom

Unlike the First Amendment of the American Constitution, the European Convention on Human Rights does not affirm that no law can restrict freedom of speech. Article 10 of the Convention clearly accepts the idea of possible restrictions on freedom of speech. However, these restrictions are subjected to three conditions. In order to be justified under the second paragraph of article 10, these restrictions have to be lawful (i.e. there has to be a legal basis), pursue a legitimate aim (i.e an aim mentioned in the second paragraph itself), and be necessary in a democratic society. In the first cases where the Court had to deal with interferences in freedom of speech, it stressed that restrictions ought to be exceptional and that freedom of speech should be the rule. This liberal attitude is expressed in the famous quote from the *Handyside* judgment in which the Court held that '*Freedom of expression constitutes one of the essential foundations of such a society, one of the basic conditions for its progress and for the development of every man. Subject to paragraph 2 of Article 10 (art. 10-2), it is applicable not only to "information" or "ideas" that are favourably received or regarded as inoffensive or as a matter of indifference, but also to those that offend, shock or disturb the State or any sector of the population.*'[38] This quote comes back as a refrain in the case law of the Court. Although it cannot be denied that, as an affirmation of a leading principle, this statement is important, it may create a misleading idea of the Court's case law. Indeed, as we will see, the Court is far less liberal in its judgements than this excerpt suggests. The second paragraph of article 10 explicitly states that the exercise of freedom of speech carries with it duties and responsibilities,[39] and in cases concerning the press, the Court explicitly endorses the idea that even a debate on matters of public interest is not wholly unrestricted.

The Handyside case is important for a second reason. The Court introduces here for the first time the concept of the margin of appreciation. Following this theory, national states may be better placed to assess the need of a restriction of a conventionally protected right than the Court. This will notably be the case when it comes to balancing freedom of expression and protected goals such as public morals or rights of others, which may include value laden issues. The margin of appreciation doctrine introduced the principle of subsidiarity in the Court's case law and proved to be very successful in areas where religious and cultural diversity play a key role. It offers states the possibility to limit the Strasbourg control in order to respect their own cultural and religious taboos. Moreover, the margin of appreciation has emerged implicitly in cases where the protection of freedom of speech is balanced against the protection of rights of others. In those circumstances, the Court

38 ECtHR, Handyside v. UK, 7 December 1976, para. 49.
39 ECtHR, Blaja News v. Poland, 26 November 2013, para. 51.

opts for deferential decision-making: It confines its task to verifying whether the national authorities have struck a fair balance between the interests at stake.[40]

Therefore, despite the very affirmative statements of the Court suggesting an almost unlimited freedom of speech, we can observe that the Court does not recoil from accepting restrictions on freedom of speech. Yet, what the Court asks is that the limitations remain exceptions to the general rule. They must by strictly construed and established in a convincing way.[41] These are the parameters that determine the Court's case law pertaining to freedom of speech. Three elements interact: the ambition to protect freedom of speech as much as possible, the need to restrict, albeit in exceptional circumstances, freedom of expression in order to protect other values, and the national margin of appreciation.

Three Apparent Ways to Deal with Hate Speech

Before analyzing how the Court deals with hate speech in its case law, it is necessary to explain what the Court understands by hate speech. However, the Court has not developed a precise definition of hate speech. It has adopted a rather casuistic approach: on a case-by-case basis, the Court has decided which forms of speech are to be considered as hate speech. However, I would strongly hesitate to affirm that 'parameters have been established' in order to distinguish between hate speech and other forms of expression.[42] If such parameters had been defined by the Court, it would not be too complicated to determine whether utterances have to be considered hate speech or not. In reality, the contrary is true. What happens is that the Court qualifies some discourses as hate speech: on the basis of these cases, we then have to try to find the *Leitmotiv*. It follows that every description of hate speech in the Court's case law is by definition incomplete, since it is only based on results from the past. The predictive force of such a description may turn out to be rather limited. At best, the implicit understanding of hate speech by the Court is inspired by the Committee of Ministers of the Council of Europe: 'All forms of expression which incite racial hatred, xenophobia, anti-Semitism and all forms of intolerance, since they undermine democratic security, cultural cohesion and pluralism.'[43]

---

40 As for instance in ECtHR (GC), Von Hannover no. 2 v. Germany, 7 February 2012, para. 107. ECtHR, Couderc and Hachette Filipacchi v. France, 12 June 2014, para. 48 (see, in particular, the dissenting opinion of Judges Villiger, Zupancic and Lemmens, para. 8). However, Sottiaux and Vrielink observed that the Court is at the same time overactive: in various inadmissibility decisions, it introduced considerations pertaining to the merits of the cases. In doing this, the Court influences 'en passant' national case-law. S. Sottiaux and J. Vrielink, 'Activism at the Admissibility Stage: A Threat to the Subsidiary Role of the ECtHR?', in André Alen, Véronique Joosen, Riet Leysen and Willem Verrijdt (Eds.), *Liber Amicorum Marc Bossuyt - Liberae Cogitationes*, Intersentia Antwerpen/Cambridge, 2013, 659-675.

41 ECtHR, Ojala and Etukeno Oy v. Finland, 14 January 2014, para. 40.

42 ECtHR – Press Unit, Factsheet – Hate Speech, July 2013, p. 1.

43 Committee of Ministers of the Council of Europe, Recommendation R 97 (20), 30 October 1997 to which judges Yudkivska and Villiger refer in their concurring opinion in the Vejdeland and others case.

Having made the preliminary remark, we now have to examine the case law on hate speech in detail. What is immediately striking is that the Court basically has three ways to tackle the problem of hate speech.[44] Yet it remains rather opaque why the Court decides to deal with a case using one approach rather than another.[45]

1 The Guillotine

The most outspoken way to deal with hate speech is by using article 17 of the Convention. This article contains an anti-abuse clause and holds that no conventionally enshrined rights can be used to destroy the rights and freedoms of others. This provision is generally considered to be the legal translation of the famous slogan: 'No freedom for the enemies of freedom' (Saint-Just). Within the context of the European Convention, the article should be understood as the emanation of the concept of 'militant democracy.'[46] What the drafters wanted to avoid was extremist antidemocratic forces using the Convention in order to destroy democracy. Given the totalitarian experiences in the first half of the 20th Century, where both dictatorial ideologies of the extreme left and the extreme right misused fundamental freedoms in order to install totalitarian regimes,[47] the insertion of such a provision in the Convention can hardly be seen as a surprise.[48] The drafters of the Convention did not spend, all in all, much time on article 17, as reveals an analysis of the *travaux préparatoires.*[49] When, in 1951, article 2 of the First Protocol (the right to education) was discussed, P.-H. Teitgen recalled the meaning of article 17:

---

44 A. Buyse, 'Contested Contours' in E. Brems and J. Gerards (Eds.), *Shaping rights in the ECHR*, Cambridge University Press, Cambridge, 2014, p. 192 (hereinafter: Buyse 2014b); Y. Haeck, "Article 17 – Verbod van rechtsmisbruik" in J. Vande Lanotte and Y. Haeck (Eds.), Handboek EVRM. Deel 2. Volume II, Intersentia, Antwerp, 2004, p. 249 and 254.

45 Buyse 2014b, p. 203; S. Van Drooghenbroeck, 'L'article 17 de la Convention européenne des droits de l'homme est-il indispensable?', *Revue trimestrielle des droits de l'homme*, 2001, p. 560.

46 J. Velaers, *De beperkingen van de vrijheid van meningsuiting*, Maklu Uitgevers, Antwerp, 1991, p. 255. The concept of militant democracy was coined by the German scholar (and *émigré*) Karl Loewenstein. Robert Kahn reminds us that Loewenstein conceived it before the outbreak of the Second World War. R. Kahn, 'Why do Europeans Ban Hate Speech? A Debate between Karl Loewenstein and Robert Post', *Hofstra Law Review*, Vol. 41, 2012-2013, pp. 559-560.

47 The inevitable example here is J. Goebbels statement that one of democracy's best jokes is that it gave its enemies the tool to destroy it. Cited in: Van Drooghenbroeck 2001, p. 541.

48 Although, it should not be lost out of sight, that the theory of abuse of fundamental rights is not an invention of the drafters of the Convention, let alone an invention of the 20th Century. Quite rightly, Y. Haeck recalls that already at the time of the French Revolution the idea of abuse of constitutional rights was developed. Haeck 2004, pp. 243-244. Differently: H. Cannie and D. Voorhoof, 'The Abuse Clause and Freedom of Expression in the European Human Rights Convention: an Added Value for Democracy and Human Rights Protection?', *Netherlands Quarterly of Human Rights*, Vol. 29, no. 1, 2011, p. 56 stating that the idea of an abuse clause in international human rights came up shortly after World War II.

49 P. Lemire, 'Article 17' in L.-E. Petitti, E. Decaux and P.-H. Imbert (Eds.), *La Convention européenne des droits de l'homme*, Economica, Paris, 1999, pp. 510-512 ; Cannie and Voorhoof 2011, pp. 56-57.

> ...les libertés que nous garantissons dans nos conventions des Droits de l'homme pour le développement de la personnalité humaine et des institutions démocratiques ne peuvent être utilisées à des fins de destruction des régimes de liberté et que nos gouvernements ont le droit d'organiser pratiquement l'exercice sur leur territoire, des libertés définies par la convention de telle sorte qu'elles ne puissent servir à ceux qui veulent détruire la liberté et les régimes démocratiques.[50]

Yet, it is important to understand that the anti-abuse clause leaves little room for discussion. The provision is drafted in a very black and white way: either applicants are supposed to be enemies of the Convention, and then their claim will be inadmissible, or they are not abusers of the Convention, and then the Court will examine the application according to the established practice and rules. Therefore, article 17 has often been described as the "guillotine provision".[51] Such a clear-cut approach is question begging, especially because it is at odds with the general philosophy of the Convention, which is focused on proportionality. The Court's task is more and more to strike a fair balance between competing rights, taking into account the factual circumstances of the case. At the very least, the court's task is to assess whether national authorities have struck a fair balance. Article 17 does not allow for such a balance. In other words: there is a serious risk that the anti-abuse article is used against groups of people without paying attention to their fundamental rights.[52]

From a legal perspective, article 17 may not be a very subtle instrument, but from a sociological angle it has doubtlessly an added value. Indeed, through the Court's use of the anti-abuse clause, we learn much about the taboos and fears of our time. Who are the 'enemies of democracy'? Who are we afraid of? Which groups are believed to be dangers to democracy? Browsing through the article 17 cases, including those where the article was used as an interpretative tool (see point 3), gives a good impression of how (perceived) threats to democracy have changed over time.

There are rather few inadmissibility decisions where the Court, or before the entry into force of Protocol 11 , the European Commission of Human Rights, directly used article 17 as a guillotine to dismiss an application.[53] The two traditional examples are the Commission's decisions in *German Communist Party v. Germany* and *Glimmerveen and Hagenbeek v. Netherlands.* In the former case, the K.P.D complained about the decision of the (Western) German authorities to dissolve and forbid the (Western) German Com-

50 *Receuil des travaux préparatoires V*, p. 1230.

51 Cannie and Voorhoof 2011, p. 58; Haeck 2004, p. 249.

52 On the dangers of the application of article 17, see: Cannie and Voorhoof 2011, pp. 64-72; Buyse 2014b, pp. 203-208.

53 Haeck 2004, p. 250; Van Drooghenbroeck 2001, p. 551.

munist Party, a decision which would be a violation of article 11 of the Convention. Yet, the Commission dismissed the application, arguing that the goals of the Party, i.e. the establishment of the dictatorship of the proletariat, are not compatible with the Convention. On the basis of article 17, the application was found inadmissible.[54] In the latter, the Commission followed a similar reasoning but this time dismissed an application coming from two Dutch citizens who advocated that all non-white inhabitants of the Netherlands had to be removed from the country.[55]

It seems, then, that the Strasbourg organs abandoned the idea of a direct application of article 17 until a decade ago. In 2003, the Court 'rediscovered' the guillotine provision in the *Garaudy* case.[56] The Court decided that Holocaust denial and the rehabilitation of the National-Socialist regime went against the 'text and spirit of the Convention.'[57] In *W.P. and others v. Poland*, the Court confirmed this approach.[58] It can be argued that this 'rediscovery' of the guillotine was perhaps less surprising than it appeared at first sight.[59] Already in the *Jersild* case, where a journalist had been convicted by the Danish authorities on account of an interview with extreme right Danish youngsters (the Greenjackets), the Court observed that the racist declarations made by the Danish Greenjackets would not have been protected by article 10.[60] However, in this case, the journalist was only reporting on them in order to give evidence regarding the situation of the extreme right in Denmark, and the Court found that sentencing the journalist was a violation of the freedom of the press.[61] In the *Lehideux and Isorni* case, about an advertisement in *Le Monde* concerning the controversial French Marshal Pétain, who headed the French Vichy regime during the Second World War, the Court noted that Nazi-glorification would certainly not be protected by article 10 of the Convention. Yet, in this case, the authors of the advertisement disapproved of the Nazi atrocities, but called for a revision of Pétain's conviction after the Second World War for betrayal. Since the appeal was concentrating on the personality of the Marshal and not on the acts of the Vichy or the Nazi regime, the Court considered it protected by article 10.[62]

Nevertheless, and notwithstanding the recent rediscovery of article 17, the Court also indicated that the abuse clause can only be applied on 'an exceptional basis' and in 'extreme

54 ECommissionHR, German Communist Party v. Germany, 20 July 1957 (application no. 250/57).
55 ECommissionHR, Glimmerveen and Hagenbeek v. The Netherlands, 11 October 1979 (application nos 8348/78 and 8406/78).
56 ECtHR, Garaudy v. France, 24 June 2003 (admissibility). Haeck 2004, p. 256.
57 *Ibid.*
58 ECtHR, W.P. and others v. Poland, 2 September 2004 (admissibility).
59 Buyse 2014b, pp. 195-196.
60 ECtHR (GC), Jersild v. Denmark, 23 September 1994, para. 35.
61 *Ibid.*
62 ECtHR, Lehideux and Isorni v. France, 23 September 1998, para. 53.

cases.'[63] The question remains, however, whether the Court does apply its own principles. After all, what is 'exceptional' and what is 'extreme'?

2 The Regular Way

There is a second way for the Court to deal with hate speech. It follows from the case law of the Court that on numerous occasions, the Court refused to apply article 17 of the Convention. Instead of tackling the problem posed by hate expressions by aiming at the speaker ('playing the man'), the Court analyzes the case from an article 10 perspective (or, as the case may be, from an article 11 perspective). Thus, the Court focuses plainly on the discourse ('playing the ball') and does not directly take into account the specific features of the speaker.

I call this approach "the regular way," since the Court analyzes the issue of hate speech in the same way as it deals with all other forms of speech. The three conditions (legality, legitimacy and proportionality) permitting restrictions of freedom of expression are scrutinized. Following this approach, hate speech issues are seen as particular instances of freedom of speech.[64] In part IV, I will explain what this means in practice and how the Court distinguishes between speech that is protected under article 10 of the Convention and speech that is not.

To be thorough, I also have to mention here, as Buyse suggests, those cases where applications are declared inadmissible without any direct reference to article 17.[65] Those cases still fit within the regular approach, because the Court (and previously the Commission) applied the usual admissibility criteria.[66]

3 The Hesitating Way

The third way for the Court (and previously the Commission) to deal with hate speech is a combination of the previous approaches. What the Court (and the Commission) do is argue along the lines of article 10 of the Convention, but use article 17 as an interpretative device. Article 17 then comes in as an element of the proportionality test. In the literature, this is called the indirect application of article 17.[67] The first case in which this technique has been used is the *Kuhnen* case.[68] In this case, the Commission found a complaint made by a German neo-Nazi writer, who had been convicted in Germany on account of some neo-Nazi publications, manifestly ill-founded. The Commission concluded that article 10

63 ECtHR, Paksas v. Lithuania, 6 January 2011, para. 87.
64 E.g. ECtHR, Féret v. Belgium, 16 July 2009; ECtHR, Leroy v. France, 2 October 2008; ECtHR, Soulas and others v. France, 10 July 2008.
65 A. Buyse 2014b, pp. 202-203.
66 ECtHR, Seurot v. France, 18 May 2004 (admissibility: claim manifestly ill-founded); ECtHR (GC), Refah Partisi and others v. Turkey, 13 February 2003, para. 98-100.
67 Buyse 2014b, p. 198; Haeck 2004, p. 251.
68 ECommissionHR, Kuhnen v. Germany, 12 May 1988 (application no. 12194/86).

had not been violated. Its conclusion relied heavily on the proportionality test and, therefore, on the necessity of the interference in a democratic society. To scrutinize the proportionality, the Commission used article 17 as an interpretative device.

Here again, however, a closer look at the case law of the Court shows a lack of systematic approach.[69] It appears indeed that the Court follows the interpretative way in two distinct situations. The first one pertains to the merits of the case: in such circumstances, the judges consider a case under article 10, but use article 17 to interpret the necessity of interference. Their findings relate to the merits of the case.[70] The second, however, only deals with the admissibility of a case. The Court can then decide that an application is manifestly ill-founded. There is hardly any difference in the reasoning: in both situations, the three-step test of article 10 was followed; in both situations, article 17 had a deep impact on the necessity criterion. Yet, in the first case, the Court concluded that article 10 had not been violated, whereas in the second the Court concluded that the application was inadmissible since it was manifestly ill-founded. Arguably, this distinction is a matter of degree: in some cases, the hate speech factor is so clear that it could only lead to the Court declaring the case inadmissible, stating that the application was ill-founded[71] or incompatible with the Convention *ratione materiae*[72]. One may, however, wonder whether there is an important difference between 'the guillotine' of article 17 and the interpretative use of article 17. In other cases, the hate speech factor is less outspoken, and the Court will examine the case following the three step test of article 10, albeit with article 17, as an interpretative tool, seriously determining the necessity test.

The Court's Substantive Approach to Hate Speech

It follows from the previous section that the Court has several ways to address the question of hate speech. It can apply article 17 directly, indirectly by combining it with article 10 of the Convention, or by considering only article 10 of the Convention. The question now is, from a substantive point of view, what kinds of discourses have been found to run counter to the basic values of the Convention.

Without having any ambition of being exhaustive, we can advance 5 major areas where the hate speech topic is particularly relevant.[73] To be clear: the indicated categories are not mutually exclusive and the distinction between them is not always very sharp. As indicated

69 See as well: Buyse 2014b, pp. 198-202.

70 ECtHR, Lehideux and Isorni v. France, 23 September 1998.

71 ECtHR, Schimanek v. Austria, 1st February 2000 (admissibility); ECommission, Rebhandl v. Austria, 16 January 1996 (application no. 24398/94).

72 ECtHR, Garaudy v. France, 24 June 2003 (admissibility).

73 See, for a slightly different approach: Buyse 2014b, p. 204 and ECtHR – Press Unit, Factsheet – Hate Speech, July 2013.

before, the first cases pertaining to hate speech concerned (1) political hate speech (i.e. the appraisal of totalitarian regimes) and (2) racist hate speech including anti-Semitism and denialism. In recent times, the very concept of hate speech has been enlarged to religion (3) and to sexual orientation (4). It goes without saying that the categories proposed can overlap. Much of the hate discourses involve aspects of "societal questions," religion, origin and so-called race, for instance. Finally, there is case law concerning incitement to violence (5).

1 Political Hate Speech

Precisely because the anti-abuse article was intended to protect democracy, it is not a surprise that those who advocate totalitarian doctrines will not be protected by the Convention. In the past, as was already indicated, this meant that neo-Nazism and National socialism were excluded from protection.[74] In the *German Communist Party* case, this same line of reasoning was applied to the proponents of communism.[75]

Recently, we have seen new totalitarian ideologies try to use the freedoms of the Convention to defend positions that are incompatible with the values of the Convention. There is interesting case law concerning Islamic sects and associations. For instance, in the *Hizb Ut-Tahir* case, the Court found an application coming from an Islamic organisation whose aim was to overthrow democratic, non-Islamic governments and replace them with an Islamic State inadmissible *ratione materiae*. The association, whose activities had been interdicted in Germany, could not claim the violation of articles 9, 10 and 11 of the Convention.[76] In the highly controversial *Refah Partisi* judgment, the Court accepted the dissolution of the Turkish Welfare Party, since it not only advocated the establishment of a Shariah system, supposed to go against the underlying fundamental values of the Convention, but also envisaged the use of force in order to obtain this goal.[77]

However, it would be wrong to infer from these cases that no Islamist propaganda can lay claim to article 10 of the Convention. In the *Gündüz* case, the Court argued that

> 'There is no doubt that, like any other remark directed against the Convention's underlying values, expressions that seek to spread, incite or justify hatred based on intolerance, including religious intolerance, do not enjoy the protection

74 For a comprehensive overview of those first cases: S. Van Drooghenbroeck, 'La repression des délits à caractère raciste et négationniste en Belgique' in P. Lambert (Ed.), *Les partis liberticides et la Convention européenne des droits de l'homme*, Bruylant, Brussels, 2005, pp. 68-69, footnote 87.

75 ECommissionHR, German Communist Party v. Germany, 20 July 1957 (application no. 250/57).

76 ECtHR, Hizb Ut-Tahrir and others v. Germany, 12 June 2012 (admissibility); See as well: ECtHR, Kasymakhunov and Saybatalov v. Russia, 14 March 2013, para. 113-114.

77 ECtHR (GC), Refah Partisi and others v. Turkey, 13 February 2003, para. 132.

> afforded by Article 10 of the Convention. However, the Court considers that the mere fact of defending sharia, without calling for violence to establish it, cannot be regarded as "hate speech".'[78]

2 *Racist Hate Speech*

As Voorhoof and Cannie rightly observe, article 17 has – quite quickly – been "detached" from its original goal, i.e protecting democracy against totalitarian enemies, including acts that run counter to the underlying values of the Convention. The first cases where the Court (and the Commission) extended the scope of article 17 concerned anti-Semitism, Holocaust denial and racism.[79]

The problem here is not primarily in understanding how this extension has taken place. Given both the historical context of and close relation between anti-Semitism and Holocaust denial on the one hand and (neo-)Nazism on the other, it is not hard to imagine that the Strasbourg organs wanted to protect the post-war democracies against the same kind of enemies, who appeared sometimes as overt neo-Nazis and sometimes as anti-Semites.[80]

However, the problem with this approach is that it has become a slippery slope. It is clear that strong reactions against racists force them perhaps not so much to change their ideas, but at least to modify the tone and the form of their utterances. Although 'racists' still want to target the same group of people, they no longer characterize them on the basis of race, origins or ethnicity. Instead, they refer to concepts such as culture or religion. The debate may concern, at first sight, mere ideas, but in reality it is directed against other human beings. The difficulty, accordingly, is to understand when exactly only ideas are at stake and when, in fact, we are dealing with racism in disguise. Sandra Coliver already warned against the risk of racists 'watering down' their message, using perhaps a more subtle or ambiguous language in order to fall outside the scope of anti-racism legislation and to appear less extremist.[81]

Drawing a sharp line between those two situations is not always easy, as transpires from the case law of the Court. The Court clearly struggles with one of the issues that occupy a crucial place in the European public debate: immigration and its challenges. Now, it is beyond the shadow of a doubt a quintessentially political debate, which would therefore be entitled to the highest protection. Yet there is of course a point at which critical discussion about immigration can turn into spreading hatred against immigrants. While the

78 ECtHR, Gündüz v. Turkey, 4 December 2003, para 51.

79 Cannie and Voorhoof 2011, pp. 62-63.

80 Cannie and Voorhoof 2011, p. 63.

81 S. Coliver cited in D. Keane, 'Attacking Hate Speech under Article 17 of the European Convention on Human Rights', *Netherlands Quarterly of Human Rights*, Vol. 25, no. 4, 2007, p. 659. Keane also refers to the 2000 Report of the Three Wise Men (Ahtisaari, Frowein and Oreja) on Austria respecting European Values.

former is part of the legitimate political debate, the latter is hate speech that cannot be tolerated under the Convention. That is the theory, in any event. In practice, it is extremely difficult to draw the line between the two situations, as is shown by some recent cases against France and Belgium.

In the *Soulas* case, a French journalist was sentenced because of the publication of a book on the negative aspects of mass migration. More precisely, the author accused Islam of undertaking a conquest of the continent which would lead to civil war. Furthermore, young Muslims were accused of 'ritual rapes.' Since the book depicted a particularly negative image of Muslims in France and the young Muslim community in the *banlieues* in particular, which could induce a feeling of rejection, the Court found that the French authorities did not violate article 10 of the Convention by convicting the author and the publisher. The statements were, according to the Court, not sufficiently severe to fall within the scope of article 17.[82]

In a case concerning the extreme right politician *Le Pen*, who is known in France for his shocking xenophobic statements – the most well-known probably being that the gas chambers were only a detail in history - the Court declared the politician's application inadmissible. Le Pen had been fined by the national authorities because of some xenophobic statements, and he considered the fine to constitute a violation of article 10 of the Convention. Yet, what is striking here is that, compared to the *Soulas* case, the Court seemed more severe towards Le Pen[83] (his case was inadmissible, whereas in *Soulas* a decision on the merits was taken), although the statements he made were not more outrageous than the ones in *Soulas*. Le Pen had said that once there would be 25 million Muslims instead of 5 million in France, they would rule. The French would walk in the streets, their eyes turned down. When they would look up, they would be asked whether they were looking for a fight and then they would get a good hiding.[84] It cannot be seriously questioned that these statements create a very strong feeling of dispraise of the Muslim community. Yet it is hard to see why these declarations would be more of a problem than the ones made by Soulas.

The difficulties the Court has to face when assessing hate speech are well illustrated by the *Féret* case. Féret is a Belgian extreme right politician and, at the time, president of the (Belgian) Front National. He had published several manifestos in which he heavily criticized immigrants, whom he accused of being criminals, terrorists and abusers of the social system. The politician was condemned in Belgium for incitement to hatred and racism. The Court upheld this condemnation, arguing that:

82 ECtHR, Soulas and others v. France, 10 July 2008, para. 48.

83 Along the same lines: R. Lawson, 'Schuifelend langs de afgrond. Politici en de grenzen van de vrijheid van meningsuiting' in A. Ellian, G. Molier and T. Zwart (Eds.), *Mag ik dit zeggen? Beschouwingen over de vrijheid van meningsuiting*, Boom Juridische uitgevers, The Hague, 2011, p. 195 et seq.

84 ECtHR, Le Pen v. France, 20 April 2010 (admissibility).

> 'l'incitation à la haine ne requiert pas nécessairement l'appel à tel ou tel acte de violence ou à un autre acte délictueux. Les atteintes aux personnes commises en injuriant, en ridiculisant ou en diffamant certaines parties de la population et des groupes spécifiques de celle-ci ou l'incitation à la discrimination, comme cela a été le cas en l'espèce, suffisent pour que les autorités privilégient la lutte contre le discours raciste face à une liberté d'expression irresponsable et portant atteinte à la dignité, voire à la sécurité de ces parties ou de ces groupes de la population. Les discours politiques qui incitent à la haine fondée sur les préjugés religieux, ethniques ou culturels représentent un danger pour la paix sociale et la stabilité politique dans les Etats démocratiques.'[85]

The judgment, delivered by a 4/3 majority, confirmed that no violation of article 10 had been committed and that the manifestos did not fall within the ambit of article 17. The close majority is already an indication of the strong, but very different, views reasonable people (including judges) can have on the need to suppress distasteful, provocative statements, which negatively depict certain groups in society. More illustrative of the difficulty of the Court to define a clear position on hate speech is the dissenting opinion by Judge Sajo (with Judges Zagrebelsky and Tsotsoria joining).[86] The dissenters warn particularly against the slippery slope. In particular, they cannot agree with two very important trends. First, they call for a serious clear and present danger test.[87] Contrary to the majority, the dissenters argue that suppressing hate speech is only allowed if there is a direct link with acts of violence and discrimination. Loosening this link means limiting the protection of political speech. Second, the judges find it very hard to extend the concept of racism, which has a rather precise meaning (even under the Convention on the Elimination of All Forms of Racial Discrimination), to aspects of religion and culture.

It remains unclear why a request for referral of this case to the Grand Chamber has not been accepted. As Lawson observes, this cannot be due to the importance of the principles at stake. More likely indeed is the hypothesis that in refusing the referral, the panel has avoided the revelation of a profound division of the Grand Chamber to the public in such an important field.[88]

The argument that a too broad understanding of "hate speech" immediately and negatively impacts on political speech is not a mere illusion. This is demonstrated in the older

85 ECtHR, Féret v. Belgium, 16 July 2009, para. 73.

86 Sajo (dissenting, Zagrebelsky and Tsotsoria joining), ECtHR, Féret v. Belgium, 16 July 2009.

87 See as well, precisely concerning Le Pen and Féret: S. Sottiaux, "Bad Tendencies' in the ECtHR's 'Hate Speech' Jurisprudence', *European Constitutional Law Review*, Vol. 7, 2011, 40-63.

88 Lawson 2011, p. 199.

case of *Willem against France*,[89] in which the court did not find a violation of article 10. In the case, the major of a small town had been convicted for having defended a boycott of Israeli products on account of the behavior of the Israeli army in the occupied territories, and particularly for their non-compliance with UN-resolutions. It was generally accepted that the applicant was not an anti-Semite. In this respect, the Court pretended that the mayor had not been convicted because of his opinions, but because he incited to discrimination. Judge Jungwiert dissented and indicated that what was lacking in the reasoning of the Court was the 'necessity test.' It transpires from Jungwiert's opinion that he did not find the opinions of the applicant very shocking, since he considered them rather a follow-up of unanimous positions of international organizations in 2002. Moreover, the Judge found the judgment poorly reasoned.

As it stands, it remains to be seen to what extent the Willem case is an authoritative precedent in the case law of the Court. As far as I can see,[90] the Court did not refer to this case anymore. This might be an indication of the fact that the case is an exception, but there is of course no certainty as to this conclusion.

These cases illustrate that the polishing strategy does not always achieve its goal: even the 'soft' form of racism can be punished through hate speech regulations. In these cases, the conflict with freedom of speech is exacerbated and the room for harsh political debate considerably restricted.

3 *Religious Hate Speech*

In more recent times, the concept of religious hate speech has been introduced in the Court's case law. Of course, it could be argued that anti-Semitism is related to religion, but I prefer to consider it not so much a problem of the Jewish religion as of the Jewish people. Therefore, cases pertaining to anti-Semitism should rather be dealt with as a matter of racism, rather than religious hate speech.[91]

Similarly, I do not consider hate speech that is inspired by some religious convictions a matter of *religious* hate speech. What I mean here by religious hate speech is hate speech that points at adherents of a given religion. The *Norwood* case is a prototypical example. In this case, the applicant had displayed a poster reading 'Islam out of Britain – Protect the British People.' The poster contained a picture of the Twin Towers and a symbol of a crescent and star in a prohibition sign. The applicant was fined, in the UK, for hate speech

89 ECtHR, Willem v. France, 16 July 2009.

90 Using the Hudoc search engine ('Strasbourg case law' tab).

91 On the connection between racism and anti-Semitism, see for instance: G. Cousin and R. Fine, 'A Common Cause: Reconnecting the study of racism and anti-Semitism', 14 *European Societies*, 2012, pp. 166-185.

against racial and religious groups. The applicant argued that his conviction was a breach of article 10 of the Convention, yet the Court decided, using article 17, that:

> 'Such a general, vehement attack against a religious group, linking the group as a whole with a grave act of terrorism, is incompatible with the values proclaimed and guaranteed by the Convention, notably tolerance, social peace and non-discrimination.'[92]

The *Norwood* case is a perfect illustration of the perverse effects of anti-discrimination legislation, as I explained before. Most citizens have come to realize that hate speech based on race, colour or origins is unacceptable and falls within the ambit of anti-racism legislation. As a reaction, we see that they try to target the groups they dislike by referring to other, more subtle, features of the group. If Norwood criticizes Islam, it could be possible that in fact he was criticizing not only Muslims but also people living in the UK who are not of British descent. Only, he was not directly mentioning origins, ethnicity or race. The Court tried to reveal the *real object* of the claim as directly aimed at all Muslims in the UK. Religion was used to cover the racial/ethnic dimension of the discourse, given the fact that in the UK Islam is traditionally a religion of immigrants. We see immediately how real the risk is that the Court turns into a kind of thought police that does not so much judge what has been said, but rather what the Court believes was intended by the utterance.

Indeed, it will never be that easy to determine the hidden message of the utterances. What has to be avoided indeed is that it becomes hard, if not impossible, to criticize religions. Notions such as "Islamophobia" or "Christianophobia" are in this respect very confusing. Although, in some circumstances, criticizing religion may indeed be a form of ethnic/racial discrimination, this is not necessarily always the case.[93] We should be careful not to grant rights to religions: people have rights, but religions, political ideologies, firmly held beliefs, worldviews and so on have not. We should maintain the right to freely criticize them. In the words of the French philosopher Bernard-Henri Lévy:

> 'Islamophobia – and it can never be repeated enough – is obviously not racism. Personally, I am not Islamophobic. I am far too concerned with the spiritual and the dialogue among spiritualities to feel any hostility towards one religion or another. But the right to freely criticize them, the right to make fun of their dogmas or beliefs, the right to be a non-believer, the right to blasphemy and

92 ECtHR, Norwood v. UK, 16 November 2004 (admissibility).

93 On this: Keane 2007, p. 662-663. The author also indicates how differently the UN Special Rapporteurs on freedom of religion and on contemporary forms or racism dealt with the relation between racism and criticism on religion in their joint report 'Incitement to Racial and Religious Hatred and Promotion of Tolerance'.

apostasy - all these were acquired at too great a cost for us to allow a sect, terrorists of thought, to nullify them or undermine them.'[94]

I believe that it is unfortunate that the Court uses the ambiguous term "Islamophobia" in its case law.[95] I would rather recommend the use of the concept "muslimophobia" or something of that kind, so as to indicate that strong negative feelings towards religions are part of the legitimate intellectual debate, and can be compared to strong feelings of disapproval regarding political beliefs, secular worldviews, ideologies of all kinds and so on. Similar feelings concerning persons, for example Muslims, Jews or Christians, are obviously quite something different. Still, there is some – contested – case law where the Court accepts restrictions on freedom of speech in order to protect the religious feelings of the population.[96]

4 *Sexual Orientation and Hate Speech*

A remarkable case is *Vejdeland and others v. Sweden*, where the Court had to decide whether a conviction, by the Swedish authorities, of the applicants who had been distributing leaflets against homosexuality in a school amounted to a violation or article 10. The leaflets stated that homosexuality was a 'deviant sexual proclivity' which had a morally destructive effect on society and constituted one of the main causes of HIV/AIDS. The Court argued that article 10 had not been violated. It did so by drawing a parallel between racial hate speech and homophobic speech. Thus, the Court first stressed 'that inciting hatred does not necessarily entail a call for an act of violence, or other criminal acts. Attacks on persons committed by insulting, holding up to ridicule or slandering specific groups of the population can be sufficient for the authorities to favour combating racist speech in the face of freedom of expression exercised in an irresponsible manner.'[97] It then added: "discrimination based on sexual orientation is as serious as discrimination based on "race, origin or colour"".[98]

94 B.-H. Lévy, 'Why I Support a Ban on Burqas' (February 15, 2010) www.huffingtonpost.com/bernardhenri-levy/why-i-support-a-ban-on-bu_b_463192.html. [Accessed, March 23, 2013]. A similar point is made, in a more careful way, by H. Bielefeldt, although he rightly warns against a confusion between critique of Islam and 'racism in disguise'. See C. Rath, 'The Hard Core of Islamophobia Is Racist' (January 8, 2010) en.qantara.de/The-Hard-Core-of-Islamophobia-Is-Racist/8275c162/index.html. [Accessed, March 23, 2013]. Along the same lines: J. Vrielink, 'Islamophobia and the law: Belgian hate speech legislation speech and the wilful destruction of the Koran', *International Journal of discrimination and the law* 2014, vol. 14, nr. 1, pp. 54-65.

95 ECtHR, Perinçek v. Turkey, 17 December 2013, para. 47; ECtHR, Orban and others v. France, 15 January 2009, para 34; ECtHR, Leroy v. France, 2 October 2008, para. 27.

96 *E.g.*: ECtHR, I.A. v. Turkey, 13 September 2005, para. 29-30; ECtHR, Wingrove v. UK, 25 November 1996, particularly para. 60; ECtHR, Otto-Preminger-Institut v. Austria, 20 September 1994, para. 56.

97 ECtHR, Vejdeland and others v. Sweden, 9 February 2012, para. 55.

98 *Ibid.*

Vejdeland is, to our knowledge, the only case where the hate speech doctrine has been used in a debate concerning hate speech based on sexual orientation. Regardless of our position on the outcome of the case, which is undoubtedly influenced by the particular factual circumstances of the case akin to a captive audience situation, two trends have to be underscored. The first is that the Court clearly confirms the base line of the *Féret* judgment: insulting, slandering and ridiculing specific groups can be sufficient a reason not to be protected by freedom of speech, even if it is not clear which specific danger the utterances entail *in concreto*. Nevertheless, in two concurring opinions, the importance of the concrete facts are stressed, especially the school context (to be understood as a captive audience situation).[99] It seems, then, that 3 judges still refrain from adhering to this general claim, hinting at the need for a (minimal) clear and present danger test. The second is that the scope of hate speech can be extended in order to include other issues than the ones that traditionally were taken into account under the hate speech doctrine.

5 *Incitement to Violence*

Lastly, the Court obviously takes a strong position on incitement to violence. This should not come as a surprise. In the first place, as already explained at the outset, incitement to violence is generally accepted as a valid limitation on freedom of expression. Furthermore, we have seen that the Court has given a broad interpretation to the concept of hate speech, even including situations where there is no direct link between the utterances and the violent reactions they might entail. Under such circumstances, it is obvious that the Court is even more willing to accept restrictions in cases where the link with violence is more direct. This is particularly true in cases where there is glorification of or incitement to violence.[100] One of the most illustrative examples here is a Grand Chamber judgment concerning a novel, in which it was stated, amongst other things, that Jean-Marie Le Pen advocated murders committed by fictional characters. The Paris Court of Appeal convicted the author and the publisher for defamation towards the politician and his party. The Grand Chamber could not see a violation of article 10:

> 'The Court nevertheless considers that in the present case the Court of Appeal made a reasonable assessment of the facts in finding that to liken an individual, though he be a politician, to the "chief of a gang of killers", to assert that a murder, even one committed by a fictional character, was "advocated" by him,

99 Spielmann (concurring, Nussberger joining) and Zupancic (concurring), ECtHR, Vejdeland and others v. Sweden, 9 February 2012.

100 ECtHR, Saygili and Falakaoglu v. Turkey (no. 2), 17 February 2009, para. 28; ECtHR, Sürek v. Turkey (no. 1), 8 July 1999, para. 62-65.

> and to describe him as a "vampire who thrives on the bitterness of his electorate, but sometimes also on their blood", oversteps the permissible limits in such matters.'(...)
> 'The Court will further have regard to the nature of the remarks made, in particular to the underlying intention to stigmatise the other side, and to the fact that **their content is such as to stir up violence and hatred,** thus going beyond what is tolerable in political debate, even in respect of a figure who occupies an extremist position in the political spectrum.'[101]

The mere fact that some passages of the book could be interpreted as incitement to violence was sufficient reason for the Court to conclude that freedom of speech did not apply. We are far from the idea of a 'clear and present danger' test. Four dissenters indeed questioned the Court's finding that the novel was an appeal to violence or hatred.[102] The *Lindon and others* case shows that there is a real risk of giving an overbroad interpretation to the idea of incitement to hatred.

Denialism: An Easy Case Becoming Hard?

Previously, it was indicated that article 17 has been used in various circumstances in which statements or behavior ran counter to the basic values of the Convention. However, when it comes to denialism, it can be noted that the Court, in practice, only dealt with one particular form of denialism, namely, Holocaust denial.[103] This form of negationism is punishable in many European States.[104]

The Court (and the Commission) never made any problem of this. Holocaust deniers were not allowed to claim that their statements are protected by freedom of speech. It is important to observe that, yet again, a shift in interpretation has taken place. Whereas denialism in practice was strictly confined to Holocaust denial, Paolo Lobba rightly observes that the Court did indicate that denialism can apply to more than only the Holocaust.[105] In theory, denying 'clearly established historical facts'[106] is conceivable, as well as the denial

101 ECtHR (GC), Lindon, Otchakovsky-Laurens and July v. France, 22 October 2007, para. 57. Emphasis added.
102 Judges Rozakis, Bratza, Tulkens and Sikuta dissenting.
103 Lobba 2014, p. 63; Cannie and Voorhoof 2011, p. 63.
104 In 2009, 14 European States had criminalized the denial of the Holocaust. M. Wine, 'Expanding Holocaust Denial and Legislation Against It' in I. Hare and J. Weinstein (Eds.), *Extreme Speech and Democracy*, Oxford University Press, Oxford, 2009, p. 543. See as well: Council Framework Decision 2008/913/JHA of 28 November 2008 on combating certain forms and expressions of racism and xenophobia by means of criminal law, OJ L 328, 6 December 2008, which requires that Member-States punish, albeit under certain conditions, inter alia Holocaust denial.
105 Lobba 2014, p. 63.
106 ECtHR, Lehideux and Isorni v. France, 23 September 1998, para 47.

of 'crimes against humanity'[107] or the 'glorification of war crimes such as torture or summary executions,'[108] to name but a few examples.

Yet in the recent *Perinçek v. Switzerland* case, which was referred to the Grand Chamber on 2 June 2014, the Court had to deal with a conviction, by the Swiss courts, of a Turkish politician who had, during some conferences in Switzerland, denied the Armenian genocide. It follows from the case that he did not contest the violence, but only refuted the legal qualification of genocide.[109] Nevertheless, the Swiss authorities sentenced him for genocide denial.

The Second Chamber of the Court held that this conviction was a violation of article 10 of the Convention. It follows from the judgement that the majority of the judges based its finding on the idea that the interference in the politician's freedom of speech was not necessary in a democratic society. This position was backed by two main underlying arguments.

First, the Court observed that there was no common general consensus about the exact qualification of the atrocities committed in 1915. Only some 20 States worldwide have recognized the events of 1915 as genocide, which is a legal concept that is strictly defined. Moreover, the Court explicitly doubts whether there can be consensus, let alone a scientific one, pertaining to the facts that took place a century ago. Interestingly enough, the Court uses this statement to distinguish the Armenian 'genocide' from the Holocaust. In the latter case, the denial pertains often to the existence of the facts and not to their legal qualification. Moreover, in the case of the Holocaust, there is a clear legal basis allowing the use of the term "genocide". Finally, an international jurisdiction has confirmed the facts.[110]

Second, the Court was not convinced that there was a pressing social need to sanction the applicant.[111] It used a comparative analysis and noted that the denial of genocide – going beyond the well confined case of the Holocaust – was only punished in a limited number of States (apart from Switzerland, Luxembourg and Spain). Yet, as Lobba observes, in the meantime the situation has considerably changed and many States have now adopted legislation punishing genocide denial.[112]

Moreover, in the Spanish case, the Constitutional Court (*Tribunal Constitucional*) annulled the provision that punished genocide denial. The Constitutional Court stated that academic freedom includes the right, without expressing a value judgment or an opinion on their lawfulness, to question the existence of facts.[113] It added that the mere

107 ECtHR, Garaudy v. France, 24 June 2003 (admissibility).
108 ECtHR, Orban and others v. France, 15 January 2009, para 35.
109 ECtHR, Perinçek v. Switzerland, 17 December 2013, para. 52.
110 ECtHR, Perinçek v. Switzerland, 17 December 2013, para. 114-118.
111 ECtHR, Perinçek v. Switzerland, 17 December 2013, para. 119-126.
112 Lobba 2014, p. 74, footnote 79.
113 Tribunal Constitucional, judgment no. 235 of 7 November 2007, *BOE*, 10 December 2007, p. 51, para. 8.

denial of facts does not necessarily contribute to the creation of a climate of violence (*hostilidad)* towards the victims of the crimes of which the existence is denied.[114] The Constitutional Court accepted though that the justification of genocides is punishable by law.

Equally, the French Constitutional Court (*Conseil constitutionnel*) struck down a law that criminalized the denial of genocides recognized by (French) law.[115] The ECtHR observes in this respect that there is no contradiction in recognizing by law, as the French did in the case of the atrocities of 1915, genocide on the one hand, and the non-criminalization of its denial on the other.[116] Finally, the ECtHR also referred to UN Human Rights Committee's General Comment no. 34, in which it is stressed that freedom of expression, such as protected by the CCPR, does not allow the repression of wrong opinions or erroneous interpretations of past events.[117]

Is there a way to integrate *Perincek*, as it stands, in the vast case law on Holocaust denial? Probably there is: it has been suggested that 'harmfulness' is once again the key word. Holocaust denial should then always be seen as being anti-Semitic and therefore harmful *per se*.[118] Incitement to hatred is therefore presumed in the case of Holocaust denial. In the case of denial of other genocides, the harmfulness has to be proven *in concreto*.[119] Finally, some authors already argued that the special position of Holocaust denial is related to geographic proximity. The argument then goes that the States that have been affected by the Holocaust consider its denial a new threat to their democracy, since the deniers often glorify the Nazi regime and advocate the reintroduction of this totalitarian regime. In other words: Holocaust denial is more a threat to European States and their democratic institutions than denial of genocides that did not involve those States.[120]

Since the case has been referred to the Grand Chamber, it remains to be seen whether the conclusions of the Second Chamber will remain valid. In the perspective of the referral, the partly dissenting opinion of Judges Vucinic and De Albuquerque[121] is of utmost importance. First, they suggest that article 17 should have been applied, as they 'doubt seriously as to the admissibility of the case.' But, more importantly, they do believe that article 10 has not been violated. In substance, they clearly refuse the majority's main arguments. On the one hand, the dissenters argue that there is an international consensus

114 Tribunal Constitucional, judgment no. 235 of 7 November 2007, *BOE*, 10 December 2007, p. 52.

115 Conseil Constitutionnel, decision no. 2012-647 of 28 February 2012, www.conseil-constitutionnel.fr.

116 ECtHR, Perinçek v. Switzerland, 17 December 2013, para. 123.

117 ECtHR, Perinçek v. Switzerland, 17 December 2013, para. 124; UN Human Rights Committee, General Comment no. 34 – Article 19: Freedoms of opinion and expression, 12 September 2011, para. 49.

118 Along those lines: ECtHR, Perinçek v. Switzerland, 17 December 2013, para. 119.

119 Lobba 2014, p. 75.

120 On this: S. Sottiaux and J. Vrielink, "De negationismewet op het hellend vlak", *Tijdschrift voor Mensenrechten*, 2005, nr. 4, pp. 6-13.

121 Vucinic and De Albuquerque (partly dissenting), ECtHR, Perinçek v. Switzerland, 17 December 2013.

on the Armenian genocide. On the other, the judges believe that, within the European system of human rights protection, the criminalization of the denial of genocide is required. In the view of the dissenters, punishing the denial of genocide is the direct consequence of article 1 of the Convention on the Prevention and the Punishment of the Crime of Genocide.

The clash of ideas is spectacular. On the one hand, European and international texts can be used to argue in favor of a robust freedom of expression. On the other hand, other European and international texts can be referred to in order to defend the punishment of genocide denial.

The dissenters' opinion is dense, rich and, as often is the case when Judge De Albuquerque engages in the debate, full of learned references. In paragraph 19 of their opinion, however, the dissenters go too far, in my opinion, in criticizing the Spanish Constitutional Court, which made a distinction between denying genocide (which the Constitutional Court believed to be protected by freedom of speech) and justifying it, which the Constitutional Court did not protect.[122] The dissenters argue that this distinction is unacceptable, since it would make it possible for sophisticated (and perverse) minds to avoid the pitfall of denialism by using a more euphemistic message. They also state that academic freedom and the search for truth cannot justify the distinction, as this would allow those who act in bad faith to spread their intolerant, xenophobic hate messages under the pretense of historical or scientific research, rather than racism. In my view, this is an overstated argument[123] and an illustration of the slippery slope reasoning I already warned about. The idea seems to be that if you start accepting regular scientific research, you end up accepting xenophobic denialism. Accordingly, even in good faith, research should be made impossible. It occurs to me that this is the wrong answer: the whole point is that it all depends on the concrete circumstances of the facts and the intentions of the speakers. Admittedly, this will not be a simple task as the example of Islamophobia already illustrated. It will not always be easy to discern, in good faith, racist and xenophobic arguments in disguise. Restricting historical research and preventing the clash of ideas because of possible abuses, however, runs counter to the very rationales of freedom of speech. Furthermore, I believe the dissenters, however laudable their intentions are from a pure humane point of view, fail to see an important difference between denying genocide and justifying it. The difference is the relation between the intention to cause harm and the facts. He who objects to the legal qualification of genocide in specific circumstances can be acting in good faith, without the intention to cause any harm, if we can imagine that the denial is the result of scien-

122 Vucinic and De Albuquerque (partly dissenting), para 19, ECtHR, Perinçek v. Switzerland, 17 December 2013.

123 To be clear: I am not saying that the dissenters are necessarily wrong in believing that Mr. Perinçek was not engaging in a scientific/historical debate and that, as a matter of fact, he was acting in bad faith. Yet the dissenting declaration goes beyond the individual case of Mr. Perinçek.

tific/historical or legal research. However, whoever justifies a genocide does precisely the opposite: the facts are believed to be established, yet they are approved. Logically, a genocide cannot be approved and denied at the same time.[124] It follows that in this case, specific harm is added to the injuries of the victims.

Conclusion

It is a truism to state that hate speech is a permanent challenge to freedom of speech jurisprudence. A strong protection of free speech, especially of political speech, implies indeed that restrictions on freedom of speech must be strictly scrutinized. The danger of broad interpretations of "hate speech" is that free political debate is seriously menaced. We can understand that incitement to hatred should be punished. However, as indicated, it is not always easy to establish a direct link between the harm and the vilifying speech. Moreover, there is another risk. For historical reasons, there are very compelling arguments to restrict the protected categories of victims. Yet, there is a growing tendency to include more and more groups in the category of hate speech victims. Variations on the slogan "Racism is a crime": not only racism is a crime, but Holocaust denial as well, and anti-Semitism too. And Islamophobia, of course. Some may indicate sexism and so on and so forth.[125] We have to be very careful in general with slippery slope arguments, but in the field of hate speech, the arguments may be valid. Maybe, as a society, we should ask ourselves whether we are not exaggerating and perhaps falling into the trap of the heckler's veto. At a certain point, protecting the sensibilities of a growing number of groups in society can boil down to creating new taboos, whereas the very idea of freedom of speech is to have as few taboos as possible.

These questions are not only theoretical. The case law of the European Court of Human Rights reflects the difficulties raised by hate speech issues. Quite understandably, the Court is criticized for its unpredictable approach to hate speech. However, we should not be too critical of the Court either. Given precisely the fierce debate amongst legal theorists and legal philosophers on the acceptability of hate speech regulation, we should not be surprised that the Court is struggling with the concept as well.

As explained, it is far from clear how the Court will decide a case involving extremist speech. Although, in recent times, there seems to be a clear preference for the 'regular

124 Admittedly, reality can be more complex. For example: some elements of a genocide can be denied, whereas the genocide as such is not denied and even glorified. However, the observation remains valid: those specific elements cannot be both approved and denied.

125 This is not a rhetorical argument, as is evidenced by the Belgian Anti-sexism act: Loi du 22 mai 2014 tendant à lutter contre le sexisme dans l'espace public et modifiant la loi du 10 mai 2007 tendant à lutter contre la discrimination entre les femmes et les hommes afin de pénaliser l'acte de discrimination, *Mon.b.*, 24 July 2014.

way,' where cases are scrutinized from the angle of the relevant provision of the Convention (article 10, sometimes article 11) rather than by using the guillotine of article 17. Arguably, this option is the better one, since it allows for a more precise balancing exercise and thus for a more solid protection of free speech.

This approach is for a second reason more than welcome. We have observed a gradual broadening of the hate speech concept. The most illustrative case in this respect is Vejdeland, where hate speech was extended to homophobic discourse. Under such circumstances, I would think that analyzing restrictions following the three-step test of the second paragraph of article 10 is the wisest approach.

Although it can be discussed whether this trend is the result of deliberate considerations, a well-balanced compromise is coming into view. On the one hand, substantively speaking, the Court is willing to expand the notion of hate speech, going beyond the traditional issues in this field (anti-Semitism, Holocaust denial, racism). On the other hand, the Court seems to prefer the balancing exercise as it follows from the second paragraph of article 10. So more cases are suspected of possibly being incitements to hatred, but they are subjected to a closer scrutiny than the one article 17 imposes.

Be that as it may, the main question remains as to how to draw the line between freedom of speech, including the right to defend ideas that disturb, shock or offend and the protection of the democratic, pluralist and tolerant society against its worse enemies. Moreover, we should also bear in mind the risk of a slippery slope. It is not the case that some utterances are morally unacceptable and should therefore be legally punishable. The *rector magnificus* of Leuven University quite rightly observed that not insulting people is a matter of civilisation and so is not feeling insulted too easily.[126] If we take freedom of speech seriously, we should refrain from interpreting too extensively the concept of hate speech. But we should remember as well that not everything that can be said needs to be said.

126 R. Torfs, 'De kleur van Zwarte Piet', *De Standaard*, 23 October 2013, on www.kuleuven.be/metaforum/page.php?FILE=opiniestuk_pers&PID=91#796 (accessed on 21 July 2014).

9 Extreme Speech in a Religious Context

A Legal Theoretical Perspective on the Case Law of the European Court of Human Rights[1]

Marloes van Noorloos

Introduction

The prosecution of Dutch far right MP Geert Wilders has generated much attention for hate speech *against* religious groups. This contribution delves into a different but related aspect of freedom of expression: Religiously *motivated* hate speech and extreme speech. For instance, the members of the Dutch Hofstadgroep – a group of youngsters that exchanged radical Islamic writings, including Mohammed Bouyeri who was also convicted for killing film maker Theo van Gogh – were convicted for participating in a criminal organization because of these extreme publications.[2] The writings exchanged by the Hofstadgroep set forth, amongst other things, that allegiance is only owed to God and not to the Dutch authorities, and that nonbelievers are the enemy. In England, the notorious preacher Abu Hamza Al-Masri was convicted to seven years' imprisonment for hate speech against Jews and for telling mosque visitors that '[k]illing a Kafir [infidel] for any reason you can say it is OK even if there is no reason for it'. He had furthermore compared life among infidels to living 'inside a toilet,' which led Justice Hughes to tell the jury that '[i]t is not an offence to describe living in England as a toilet (...) You are entitled to your views and in this country you are entitled to express them, but only up to the point where you incite murder or use language calculated to incite racial hatred.'[3]

Extreme speech that directly incites to violence – such as incitement to terrorism – usually does not lead to much controversy as regards restricting freedom of expression. Moreover, in many jurisdictions incitement to hatred against groups of people on the grounds of race or religion is a criminal offence, although the legitimacy of such laws is regularly discussed. Things become more controversial where glorification or justification of violence is concerned. Such expressions have been criminalized in England & Wales in the Terrorism

1 This contribution is based on the PhD thesis *Hate speech revisited* (2011, Intersentia) that the author has defended at Utrecht University.

2 M. van Noorloos, 'De 'Hofstadgroep' voor het Haagse hof: over de vrijheid van radicale uitingen in het publieke debat', *Delikt en Delinkwent* no. 5, 2008, pp. 398-475.

3 BBC News, 'Timeline: Hamza trial', 7 February 2006, news.bbc.co.uk/2/hi/4644030.stm; www.cps.gov.uk/publications/prosecution/violent_extremism.html.

Act 2006; in the Netherlands, a bill to that end was not successful because too many doubts were raised about its compatibility with freedom of expression.[4],[5] Even more controversial are expressions in which there is no direct link to violence or hatred against people, but which denounce the liberal democratic order – for instance, propagating a theocratic system. Such expressions point to the dilemma of whether to protect democracy against antidemocratic forces because if they would become too strong, democracy itself would be undermined.[6]

The European Court of Human Rights (ECtHR) has, on a few occasions, had to deal with the problem of antidemocratic speech in a religious context; sometimes under article 10 of the European Convention on Human Rights (ECHR) on freedom of expression, and sometimes under article 11 ECHR on freedom of association where it concerned extreme political parties. This contribution analyzes which theoretical rationales can be found in the ECtHR's case law on extreme religious speech and political activity. It first gives an overview of some of the most pressing legal theoretical questions around religiously inspired extreme speech: On the basis of which rationale could such expressions be prohibited, and what sorts of ideas about democracy and tolerance underpin this? After that, the ECtHR's case law on extreme religious speech and political parties is analyzed.

Legal Theory

Neutrality and Tolerance

Behind the way states deal with extreme religious speech and political parties is the broader question of how states deal with the fact of pluralism among groups in society: What are the limits of toleration? As a result of the Wars of Religion in the 16th century, the gradual realization that no agreement about what constitutes a good life would likely emerge led to the notion that the state should somehow be neutral towards different 'conceptions of the good' in order to enable different groups to live together in peace.[7] While initially focused on religions, this idea of liberal neutrality was later extended to other conceptions about the meaning and value of human life. Conceptions of the good – or 'comprehensive doctrines,' as Rawls calls them – can include many different things:

4 Section 1 Terrorism Act 2006.

5 Voorstel van Wet tot wijziging van het Wetboek van Strafrecht in verband met de strafbaarstelling van de verheerlijking, vergoelijking, bagatellisering en ontkenning van zeer ernstige misdrijven en ontzetting van de uitoefening van bepaalde beroepen, 12 July 2005.

6 See AIVD, *Van dawa tot jihad*, Ministerie van Binnenlandse Zaken en Koninkrijksrelaties, The Hague, 2004.

7 See C. Larmore, 'Political liberalism', *Political Theory*, vol. 18, no. 3, 1990, pp. 339-360; W. Kymlicka, *Contemporary political philosophy. An introduction*, Oxford University Press, Oxford, 2002 (2nd Ed.).

> We can include under it not only an individual's tastes and life-style but also his religious faith and ethical ideals (...) Any attempt to say what is important and unimportant in a human life counts as a conception of the good life; it does not matter particularly what the source of that view may be.[8]

It can thus include religions, but also other moral beliefs and preferences: '...There are a number of equally reasonable yet mutually incompatible philosophical, moral, and religious doctrines, each of which promotes its own distinctive vision of value, truth, obligation, human nature, and the good life.'[9] This plurality between conceptions of the good is a permanent feature of modern democratic societies.[10] Despite the existence of different ideas about the good life, the liberal state does need a core idea of equal justice, otherwise there cannot be a liberal state. This constitutes a paradox in liberal theory. The state must remain neutral, but cannot be neutral with regard to the basic principles that underpin liberalism: 'Political neutrality cannot be neutral between those sets of values which are consistent with the fundamental ideals which provide the initial justification for neutrality (such as toleration and equal moral agency) and those which are not.'[11] The key question is thus how states can keep up a common idea of justice while accepting that people have different conceptions of the good life.[12] Rawls' influential answer to this paradox has been to distinguish between 'the right' and 'the good': States should enforce the right while remaining neutral towards different conceptions of the good. Larmore admits that liberalism indeed has its basis in a core morality, but that this idea is much less comprehensive than the conceptions of the good with which it aims to deal.[13] It is a limited neutrality which does entail certain ideas about equal respect, but is still the least exclusionary towards different conceptions.[14]

The centrality of tolerance then leads to the question of how to deal with those who impose their conviction upon others, or whose convictions may lead to harm to others. Here, Feinberg – building upon Mill's harm principle – makes an important distinction between harm and offence.[15] *Harm* is a setback of one's interests that is a *wrong*; it violates a person's

8 J. Waldron, *Liberal rights, collected papers 1981-1991*, Cambridge University Press, Cambridge, 1993, pp. 161, 163.

9 R. Talisse, 'Two-faced liberalism: John Gray's pluralist politics and the reinstatement of Enlightenment liberalism', *Critical review*, vol. 14, no. 4, 2000, pp. 441-458, at 443.

10 R.J. Ahdar and I. Leigh, *Religious freedom in the liberal state*, Oxford University Press, Oxford, 2005, p. 43.

11 W. Sadurski, *Moral pluralism and legal neutrality*, Kluwer, Dordrecht, 1990, p. 101 and 198.

12 Larmore 1990, p. 357.

13 Larmore 1990, p. 341.

14 T. Wolff, *Multiculturalisme & neutraliteit*, Vossiuspers, Amsterdam, UvA, 2005, p. 119.

15 J. Feinberg, *The moral limits of the criminal law: Harm to others*, Oxford University Press, New York, 1984-1988(a); J. Feinberg, *The moral limits of the criminal law: Offense to others*, Oxford University Press, New York, 1984-88(b).

rights. *Offence*, on the other hand, does not violate a person's interests: It is an uncomfortable mental state, a temporary experience (caused by the wrongful conduct of others) that is unpleasant, shocking, sometimes disgusting, but it does not *harm* – it does not impede interests.[16] Restrictions of the freedom of expression on the basis of *offence* aim to offer protection against unwanted and unexpected confrontations, thus protecting people against offence to their moral sensibilities. As an example, Feinberg mentions religious profanities such as blasphemous words. The problem with offence is that it is very subjective: Taking offence is 'constituted by a set of judgments which only an individual can make.'[17] Prohibition thus gives individuals or groups (whether minorities or the majority) the right to determine what the rest of the people can see or express on the basis of their own sensibilities. When offence becomes so serious that it does impede interests, it can qualify as harm, particularly if the offended state of mind is a symptom or consequence of prior or concurrent harm, or is the cause of subsequent harm.[18]

The harm principle can be specified by looking at the *risk* of harm occurring as a result of an action: What is the probability that harm will result, and what would be the magnitude of the resulting harm? According to Feinberg, 'In general, the greater the social utility of the act or activity in question, the greater must be the risk of harm for its prohibition to be justified.'[19] It becomes clear that conflicting interests can be involved, and thus harm can occur on both sides: On the one hand, a person can be harmed by an act (such as hate speech), while on the other hand, the *prohibition* of an act can harm those who have an interest in engaging in it. In such cases, the relative importance of both interests must be compared, as well as the question to what extent interests are harmed and whether they are certain to be harmed.[20]

When it comes to offence, Feinberg has argued that a balancing of interests should take place between the seriousness of offence and the reasonableness of the offending party's conduct. However, the law should not take offence as seriously as harm: When less invasive means than criminal law are available, these should be considered first.[21] In the balancing process, the *seriousness of offence* is measured by the 'extent standard' (intensity, durability), the 'reasonable avoidibility standard' and the 'volenti standard' (has one willingly taken the risk of being offended?).[22] It does not automatically follow that the more people are offended, the more compelling the case for prohibition: Some innocent actions cause

16 Feinberg 1984-88(a), p. 47-48.
17 C. McKinnon, *Toleration: a critical introduction*, Routledge, London & New York, 2006, p. 132.
18 Feinberg 1984-88(a), p. 49.
19 Feinberg 1984-88(a), p. 191.
20 Feinberg 1984-88(a), p. 203.
21 Feinberg 1984-88(b), p. 3.
22 Feinberg 1984-1988(b), p. 26.

offence to many people but should still be allowed in a liberal state. Yet some actions cause offence 'only' to minorities but are still very serious. In such cases, the other factors, such as the intensity of offence, are more important and lead to a different outcome of the balancing process. Sometimes people are offended because of mere knowledge of certain activities taking place – for instance the knowledge of a blasphemous film being shown, without having to watch it oneself. It would go too far for the law to protect against such offence. The other side of the balancing process, the reasonableness of the offending party's conduct, depends on the personal importance of the conduct to the offending party, the social utility of the conduct, availability of alternative opportunities and the extent to which purely malicious motives played a role. The criterion of social utility implies that prohibiting offensive public expressions generally requires strict scrutiny.

When offensive speech is not also a wrong to particular individuals, prohibition is problematic from a liberal perspective: Prohibiting an 'impersonal' offence because it is a wrong in itself comes very close to *legal moralism* – and this is a ground for criminalization that liberals do not allow. However, the difference between legal moralism and offence is not always easy to make. Legal moralism in the strict sense means prohibiting conduct on the ground that it is 'inherently immoral,' even though it constitutes neither harm nor offence to the actor or others.[23] For liberals, criminal law should not be concerned with enforcing morality as such, but only with protecting the rights of others, with 'grievance morality'.[24] Prohibiting 'harmless immoralities' because immorality is a wrong in itself, without harm to others, is illiberal. Besides strict legal moralism, Feinberg also identified 'legal moralism in the broad sense': Prohibitions on the grounds that actions constitute or cause evils of other kinds than harm or offence. These grounds include preserving a traditional way of life (moral conservatism) and elevating human character (legal perfectionism).[25] Moral conservatism is a form of legal moralism that aims to prevent drastic social change in a group's way of life. Adherents of this view regard change as an evil in itself, regardless of its effect on personal interests or sensibilities (harm and offence) and independent of the inherent immorality of the conduct.[26] The moral conservative 'insists that deviant conduct changes "his" society in essential ways and makes him an alien in his own community.'[27] Moral conservatism is often linked to a type of majoritarianism: Cultural changes are seen as unfair because they are said to violate the interests of the majority that does not consent to the changes. However, majority rule is only legitimate if minorities are left free to become

23 J. Feinberg, *The moral limits of the criminal law: Harmless wrongdoing*, Oxford University Press, New York, 1990, p. 4.
24 Feinberg 1990, p. 154.
25 Feinberg 1990, p. 3.
26 Feinberg 1990, p. 39.
27 Feinberg 1990, p. 48.

majorities, free to persuade other citizens. Using legal coercion to prevent certain social changes is to make an unfair contest between moral beliefs and ways of life.[28] Legal perfectionism refers to using the criminal law to make citizens 'better people': To improve public virtues, civility and character. This too is an illiberal restriction, though many liberals would allow that the state promotes public virtue and raises excellence through education, subsidies etcetera, they deny that criminal law has a role to play in restricting imperfect ways of life.[29]

Militant Democracy

Democracy implies a particular relationship between majority decisions on the one hand and individual rights and minority interests on the other. Liberal democracy demands not just majority rule but also a certain respect for minority views.[30] This is related to the idea of democracy as encompassing the 'relativity of truth': Decisions taken by a democratic majority are not viewed as absolute truths, but rather as 'provisional truths'. Once a minority succeeds in becoming the majority or part of the majority, the situation may change.[31] Therefore minority views should be given due regard in decision-making, it is thought. As Bonger stated:

> [D]emocracy, in accordance with its liberty principles, is rather geared towards relativism, that is, acknowledging the relativity of one's own opinions – in this regard it is fully in accordance with modern science. Tolerant towards others, a tendency to listen to other arguments, averse of imposing one's opinion upon others, eager to convince others by argument – those are principles of democracy.[32]

The notion of relativity of truth also indicates why free discussion and debate are important in a democracy. However, such relativity does not have to imply complete value relativism: Liberal democracy is not relativistic towards the value of equal liberty itself. This does pose a dilemma for liberal democracies, as history has shown how groups can make use of the freedoms that liberal democracy offers – freedom of expression, freedom of association

28 Feinberg 1990, p. 53.

29 J. Raz, 'Free expression and personal identification', in: Waluchow, W.J. (Ed.), *Free expression: essays in law and philosophy*, Clarendon Press, Oxford, 1994, p. 21.

30 M.C.B. Burkens, H.R.B.M. Kummeling, B.P. Vermeulen, and R.J.G.M. Widdershoven, *Beginselen van de democratische rechtsstaat*, Kluwer, Alphen a/d Rijn, 2006 (6th ed.), p. 196.

31 Burkens, Kummeling, Vermeulen & Widdershoven 2006, p. 27.

32 W.A. Bonger, *Problemen der demokratie: een sociologische en psychologische studie*, Noordhoff, Groningen, 1934, p. 87.

and other liberties – to undermine democracy and those freedoms themselves. To what extent can liberal democracies limit people's liberties for the sake of maintaining democracy and fundamental rights? The paradox is that those rights are in turn essential for a well-functioning democracy. The question thus arises as to whether a democracy can ever withhold its democratic rights without giving up on itself.[33] The answer of many states to this democratic dilemma has been to adopt a militant democracy in their laws and/or Constitution: This gives democratic states the right – or even the duty – to defend themselves against the 'enemies of democracy'. This idea originates from the interwar period, when many states contemplated the necessity of a militant democracy as a response to upcoming totalitarian ideologies. Most present-day liberal democracies have adopted some form of militant democracy, some less strident than others.[34]

The extent to which democracy is militant depends on what is meant by democracy: What should be protected exactly?[35] Some argue that the only thing that needs to be defended is the process of majority formation: That states should only target groups that threaten to do away with democratic procedures as soon as they come into power (that would make it impossible for minorities to become a majority again).[36] At the other end of the spectrum is substantive militant democracy (the term 'militant democracy,' as it is commonly used, mostly refers to this version), which regards democracy as a system that entails certain *values*. As democracy is unthinkable without fundamental rights, the idea is that these rights should be protected. In this model, groups that threaten to do away with fundamental rights can legitimately be restricted in their rights – even if they act in a non-violent manner. The democratic paradox is thus very apparent in this substantive model.

Accepting that a democracy can legitimately restrict the liberties of individuals or groups in order to preserve fundamental rights raises the question of how to identify the 'enemies' of democracy. Militant democracy involves the risk of overreaction: Is there a real risk to democracy or fundamental rights, or do states limit the rights of individuals or groups because they consider their views to be immoral or offensive?[37] Militant democracy arguments can easily be misused by the state to suppress unpopular groups or unconventional ideas. The risk of an overenthusiastic militant democracy is all the more pressing nowadays,

33 For a conceptual discussion about this question, see Q.L. Hong, *The legal inclusion of extremist speech*, Wolf Legal Publishers, Nijmegen, 2005.

34 G.P. Boventer, *Grenzen politischer Freiheit im demokratischen Statt. Das Konzept der streitbaren Demokratie in einem internationalen Vergleich*, Dunckler und Humblot, Berlin, 1985.

35 S. Sottiaux, 'Democratie en grondrechten: de inhoudelijke en procedurele democratiemodellen van Dworkin en Habermas', in: M. Adams and P. Popelier, *Recht en democratie: de democratische verbeelding van het recht*, Intersentia, Antwerpen: 2004, pp. 39-64.

36 Hong 2005, p. 150-155.

37 See C. Mouffe, *On the political*, Routledge, London, 2005, p. 76.

with the threat of religiously inspired terrorism being all too easily confused with fundamentalist religious ideas.

Having identified who democracy's enemies are, this still leaves the question: When and how should democracy be defending against them. Prohibiting radical critique of the democratic order is difficult to justify without a real danger: It is of fundamental importance to democracy that the advocacy of far-reaching legal change remains possible, especially because it is often exactly the political exclusion of such groups that makes them resort to violence. However, speech that goes against the state, its organs, or its core democratic principles also presents a potential danger to public order and to the legitimacy of the state. Since the protection of national security and public order are closely linked to majority interests – often translated into state interests – it is particularly important to construe those restrictions in such a manner that the right to freedom of expression of individuals and/or minorities *against* the state is respected.

One approach is to take the risk of violence as a criterion for limiting the democratic rights of individuals or groups – a 'clear and present danger' test, such as is applied in the United States. Other states, such as Germany, have a more preventive militant democracy: This emanates from the experience of extremist groups entering the democratic system in a non-violent manner, becoming repressive only afterwards.[38] The resistance capability of a country's democratic system can play a role here:[39] If stability is so high that there is no great risk of democracy being overthrown, then harsh measures can be disproportionate. One might argue that this particularly lacks legitimacy where small fringe groups are concerned. However, the opposite can be argued too: The more popular extremists become, the less legitimate it is to suppress them. As soon as there is a risk that antidemocratic powers become a majority, democratic values are apparently no longer shared within society at large.[40] In that case, defending democratic values will become the affair of a minority, which in turn seems undemocratic.

38 Boventer 1985, p. 243-246.

39 AIVD 2004, p. 46.

40 W. van der Woude, *Democratische waarborgen*, Kluwer, Alphen a/d Rijn, 2009, p. 67.

The European Convention on Human Rights

Framework

Under Article 10 of the ECHR (freedom of expression), states are allowed to restrict freedom of expression if such an interference is prescribed by law and is necessary in a democratic society in the interests of one of the aims mentioned (e.g., national security). This implies that there is a 'pressing social need' for interference, the reasons given by the national authorities are 'relevant and sufficient' and the restriction is proportionate to the aim pursued. A similar framework is in place for restrictions of freedom of association (article 11, ECHR).

In judging whether interference is necessary in a democratic society, States Parties have a certain margin of appreciation, because the Court holds that states are, in principle, in a better position to judge the necessity of a restriction. This concept allows for a certain degree of pluralism in the Member States of the Council of Europe. However, this margin of appreciation is not unlimited: The Court has consistently judged that it 'goes hand in hand with European supervision'. The role of the ECtHR in judging hate speech and extreme speech is thus different from that of the national courts: Its subsidiary role makes it more difficult to assess with certainty which rationales the Court bases itself on. Article 10 is applicable

> 'not only to "information" or "ideas" that are favourably received or regarded as inoffensive or as a matter of indifference, but also to those that offend, shock or disturb. Such are the demands of pluralism, tolerance and broadmindedness without which there is no "democratic society".'[41]

Expressions in the context of public debate – that is, political speech and debate on questions of public interest – deserve a high level of protection under article 10.[42]

The ECtHR has dealt with the issue of religiously motivated extreme speech mostly in the specific context of Turkey, where the authorities long championed a strict version of secularism. Already during the conception of the ECHR, the Turkish government proposed to include a special restriction clause in article 9 of the ECHR (freedom of religion and belief) in order to deal with religious fundamentalism: This clause was to enable states to restrict freedom of religion in order to prevent fundamentalists from suppressing the

41 ECtHR Handyside v. United Kingdom, 12 December 1976, par. 49.

42 A.J. Nieuwenhuis, *Over de grens van de vrijheid van meningsuiting*, Ars Aequi Libri, Nijmegen, 2006, p. 292.

freedom of others.[43] In the course of history, according to the Turkish government, many attempts at modernization had been frustrated

> 'by stubborn resistance on the part of certain persons or groups of persons who wished to keep the population in ignorance for their own ends. In its determination to go through with those reforms...Turkey has therefore been obliged to start by abolishing the Moslem orders and their archaic institutions.'[44]

The member states of the Council of Europe, however, decided not to include such a specific restriction clause in the Convention.

Political Groups

With regard to extreme religious political activities, the key ECtHR case is *Refah Partisi v Turkey*.[45] Refah Partisi was the largest political party in the Turkish Parliament, and was about to become even larger in 1997 (according to the forecasts, it could have obtained 67% of the votes in the next elections), when the Turkish Constitutional Court dissolved the party on the grounds that it was a centre of activities contrary to the principles of secularism. It justified the dissolution by pointing to several expressions by leaders and members of Refah, including the proposal that adherents of each religious movement should obey the rules of their own organizations rather than Turkish law, and the advocacy of wearing headscarves in State schools. The Constitutional Court did not rely on the party's statute or actions, but merely on the speeches by its members.

The ECtHR's Grand Chamber found that a political party may propose changes in the law or the legal and constitutional structures of the state, provided that (1) the means used are legal and democratic and (2) the change proposed must itself be compatible with fundamental democratic principles[46] – a passage repeated in later case law.[47] With regard to the religious aspect, the Court held that '[p]rovided that it satisfies the conditions, a political

43 C. Evans, *Freedom of religion under the European Convention on Human Rights*, Oxford University Press, Oxford, 2001, p. 43-44; European Commission of Human Rights, Preparatory work on Article 9, 16 August 1956, DH (56) 14, www.echr.coe.int/Library/DIGDOC/Travaux/ECHRTravaux-ART9-DH(56)14-EN 1338892.pdf, p. 5.

44 European Commission of Human Rights, Preparatory work on Article 9, 16 August 1956, DH (56) 14, www.echr.coe.int/Library/DIGDOC/Travaux/ECHRTravaux-ART9-DH(56)14-EN1338892.pdf, p. 5.

45 See also S. Sottiaux, 'Anti-democratic associations: Content and consequences in Article 11 adjudication', *Netherlands Quarterly of Human Rights*, vol. 22, no. 4, 2004(a), pp. 585-599.

46 ECtHR (Grand Chamber) Refah Partisi and others v. Turkey, 13 February 2003, par. 98.

47 ECtHR Yazar and others v. Turkey, 9 April 2002, par 49; ECtHR Herri Batasuna & Batasuna v. Spain, 30 June 2009, par. 79.

party animated by the moral values imposed by a religion cannot be regarded as intrinsically inimical to the fundamental principles of democracy, as set forth in the Convention.'[48] The Court also elaborated upon the 'militant democracy' aspect in its general considerations:

> 'In view of the very clear link between the Convention and democracy (see paragraphs 86-89 above), no one must be authorised to rely on the Convention's provisions in order to weaken or destroy the ideals and values of a democratic society (...) In that context, the Court considers that it is not at all improbable that totalitarian movements, organised in the form of political parties, might do away with democracy, after prospering under the democratic regime, there being examples of this in modern European history.' (par. 99)

In its overall examination of the case, the Court further elaborated its idea of militant democracy by proposing a three-point-test to assess whether dissolution of a political party – on the grounds that it threatens to undermine democratic principles – meets a 'pressing social need'. In this assessment, one should examine (i) whether the risk to democracy was sufficiently imminent; (ii) whether the acts and speeches of the leaders and members were imputable to the party as a whole; and (iii) whether the acts and speeches 'formed a whole which gave a clear picture of a model of society conceived and advocated by the party which was incompatible with the concept of a "democratic society".'[49] Point (i) refers to the question to what extent a militant democracy can be proactive: At which stage can the state intervene? In this regard the Court noted that, considering Refah's real chances of coming into absolute majority power and being able to establish their own envisaged model of society, the state cannot be criticized for not waiting 'at the risk of putting the political regime and civil peace in jeopardy, for Refah to seize power and swing into action' (par. 110).

Under point (iii), the Court divided the content of Refah's plans into three groups: (a) The alleged intention to set up a plurality of legal systems, leading to discrimination based on religious beliefs; (b) the alleged intention to apply sharia to the internal or external relations of the Muslim community within the context of this plurality of legal systems; and (c) the references allegedly made by Refah members to the possibility of recourse to force as a political method. With regard to the plurality of legal systems (a), the Court held that

> 'Refah's proposal that there should be a plurality of legal systems would introduce into all legal relationships a distinction between individuals grounded on

48 Par. 100.

49 ECtHR (Grand Chamber) Refah Partisi and others v. Turkey, 13 February 2003, par. 104.

> religion, would categorise everyone according to his religious beliefs and would allow him rights and freedoms not as an individual but according to his allegiance to a religious movement. The Court takes the view that such a societal model cannot be considered compatible with the Convention system, for two reasons. Firstly, it would do away with the State's role as the guarantor of individual rights and freedoms and the impartial organiser of the practice of the various beliefs and religions in a democratic society, since it would oblige individuals to obey, not rules laid down by the State in the exercise of its above-mentioned functions, but static rules of law imposed by the religion concerned (...) Secondly, such a system would undeniably infringe the principle of non-discrimination between individuals as regards their enjoyment of public freedoms, which is one of the fundamental principles of democracy.'[50]

Regarding point (b), the Court judged sharia's compatibility with the fundamental principles of democracy rather harshly. The Court's Third Section had held that 'sharia, which faithfully reflects the dogmas and divine rules laid down by religion, is stable and invariable. Principles such as pluralism in the political sphere or the constant evolution of public freedoms have no place in it' (par. 72). Without delving into the content of sharia, the Grand Chamber noted:

> 'When read together, the offending statements, which contain explicit references to the introduction of sharia, are difficult to reconcile with the fundamental principles of democracy, as conceived in the Convention taken as a whole. It is difficult to declare one's respect for democracy and human rights while at the same time supporting a regime based on sharia, which clearly diverges from Convention values, particularly with regard to its criminal law and criminal procedure, its rules on the legal status of women and the way it intervenes in all spheres of private and public life in accordance with religious precepts.'[51]

According to the Court, the remarks by Refah's leaders – taken together – gave a clear picture of a model of society organiZed according to religious rules. The Court considered that the creation of a model of society based on sharia is a real risk:

> 'In the past political movements based on religious fundamentalism have been able to seize political power in certain States and have had the opportunity to set up the model of society which they had in mind. (...) in accordance with

50 ECtHR (Third Section) Refah Partisi and others v. Turkey, 31 July 2001, par. 70-71.
51 ECtHR (Third Section) Refah Partisi and others v. Turkey, 31 July 2001, par. 72.

> the Convention's provisions, each Contracting State may oppose such political movements in the light of its historical experience.'[52]

Finally, under point (c) the Court considered the possibility that Refah might take recourse to force as a political method, as some of its members' speeches referred to 'jihad':

> 'Whatever meaning is ascribed to the term "jihad" used in most of the speeches mentioned above (whose primary meaning is holy war and the struggle to be waged until the total domination of Islam in society is achieved), there was ambiguity in the terminology used to refer to the method to be employed to gain political power. In all of these speeches the possibility was mentioned of resorting "legitimately" to force in order to overcome various obstacles Refah expected to meet in the political route by which it intended to gain and retain power.'[53]

Furthermore, Refah's leaders did not take 'prompt practical steps' to distance themselves from those members' speeches. The Court concluded that Refah's plans were incompatible with the concept of a 'democratic society,' and that Refah's dissolution met a 'pressing social need' so that it did not violate article 11.

In this regard, the Court's case law about the radical Islamist organisation Hizb ut-Tahrir is also relevant, even though it is not a political *party* but rather a worldwide movement which aims to establish a caliphate in the Muslim world.[54] Hizb's official stance is that it rejects recourse to violence, and allegations of the group being implicated in violent activities have never been proved; however, their statements are rather ambiguous in this regard. In Russia, the organization was banned and several of its members were convicted for their membership of the group. When this case reached the ECtHR, the Court reiterated that a political organization may pursue its aims on the conditions that (1) the means used are legal and democratic; and (2) the changes proposed must themselves be compatible with fundamental democratic principles.[55] In a 2012 decision the Court had already dealt with Germany's prohibition of Hizb ut-Tahrir: According to the Court, the organization

52 ECtHR (Grand Chamber) Refah Partisi and others v. Turkey, 13 February 2003, par. 124.

53 ECtHR (Grand Chamber) Refah Partisi and others v. Turkey, 13 February 2003, par. 130.

54 ECtHR Kasymakhunov and Saybatalov v. Russia, 14 March 2013, appl.nos. 26261/05 and 26377/06, par. 105.

55 The Court applied the same test in its decision about the Dutch orthodox Christian political party that refused to allow women to stand for elections (ECtHR *Staatkundig Gereformeerde Partij v. the Netherlands* (dec.), 10 July 2012, appl.no. 58369/10, par. 71): Considering that 'the advancement of the equality of the sexes is today a major goal in the member States of the Council of Europe' (par. 72-73), the Court judged the application manifestly ill-founded.

engaged in activities contrary to the text and spirit of the Convention since it called for the violent destruction of Israel.[56] As such, Hizb ut-Tahrir could not enjoy the protection of the rights to freedom of religion, expression, and association (art. 9, 10 and 11 ECHR): The Court invoked article 17 of the ECHR, which sets forth that no one may abuse the rights in the Convention to engage in activities aimed at the destruction of these rights.

In the abovementioned Russian case against two members of Hizb ut-Tahrir, the Court delved more deeply into the group's ideas about religion, politics and society.[57] According to the Court, the organization's literature contains statements advocating violence against Jews and glorifying a holy war to establish the domination of Islam; moreover, Hizb rejects the possibility of participating in the democratic political process to achieve their aims. As to the second part of the test mentioned above, the Court found that the political changes that the organization aims at are incompatible with the Convention. Hizb ut-Tahrir, according to the Court, 'proposes to establish a regime which rejects political freedoms' such as introducing capital punishment for apostasy from Islam (par. 109). Moreover, as in the Refah case, the group wants to establish a plurality of legal systems – e.g. only Muslims will have the right to vote and to be elected – and they wish to introduce a regime based on sharia (the Court also reiterates its view about sharia as set out in the Refah case). Therefore, 'the dissemination of the political ideas of Hizb ut-Tahrir by the applicants clearly constitutes an activity falling within the scope of Article 17' – an abuse of right, according to the Court (par. 113).

Article 10: Gündüz v. Turkey, Erbakan v. Turkey, Mehmet Cevher Ilhan v. Turkey

In the case *Gündüz v. Turkey* from 2003, the ECtHR dealt specifically with anti-secular speech.[58] Mr. Gündüz, the leader of an Islamic sect, had participated in a television debate about democracy and secularism, during which he advocated the abandonment of democracy and secularism, and the introduction of a regime based on sharia. Among other things, he contended that 'anyone calling himself a democrat or secularist has no religion (...) Democracy in Turkey is despotic, merciless and impious.' The Turkish courts convicted him for hate speech; the Government asserted that '[t]hrough his comments, which ran counter to the moral principles of a very large majority of the population, the applicant had severely jeopardised social stability' (par. 31). The ECtHR noted that Gündüz's comments

56 ECtHR Hizb ut-Tahrir and others v. Germany (dec.), 12 June 2012, appl.no. 31098/08.
57 ECtHR Kasymakhunov and Saybatalov v. Russia, 14 March 2013, appl.nos. 26261/05 and 26377/06.
58 ECtHR Gündüz v. Turkey, 4 December 2003.

> 'demonstrate an intransigent attitude towards and profound dissatisfaction with contemporary institutions in Turkey, such as the principle of secularism and democracy. Seen in their context, however, they cannot be construed as a call to violence or as hate speech based on religious intolerance.' (par. 48)

Moreover, the Court considered that the applicant had used the word piç – which is used as an insult in everyday language – to refer to children born out of a civil marriage:

> 'The Court cannot overlook the fact that the Turkish people, being deeply attached to a secular way of life of which civil marriage is a part, may legitimately feel that they have been attacked in an unwarranted and offensive manner. It points out, however, that the applicant's statements were made orally during a live television broadcast, so that he had no possibility of reformulating, refining or retracting them before they were made public.' (par. 49)

The Court concluded that Turkey had violated article 10 by convicting Gündüz. It stressed the large difference between the present case and the Refah Partisi case on anti-secular political parties:

> 'Admittedly, there is no doubt that, like any other remark directed against the Convention's underlying values, expressions that seek to spread, incite or justify hatred based on intolerance, including religious intolerance, do not enjoy the protection afforded by Article 10 of the Convention. However, the Court considers that the mere fact of defending sharia, without calling for violence to establish it, cannot be regarded as "hate speech".' (par. 51)

If the main difference with the Refah case is in the question whether one calls for violence to establish sharia, this seems to imply that the dissolution of Refah, without their members' speeches about jihad, would not have been 'necessary in a democratic society' purely because they advocated sharia. Or does the difference also have to do with the fact that Gündüz is about an individual person without political ambitions, so that there was no real danger to democracy, as opposed to when such speeches are uttered by members of an influential political party? An important factor in this case was that Mr. Gündüz was invited to participate in this debate to present his nonconformist views about democratic values and Islam. The matter was already much debated in the Turkish media, and the views of Mr. Gündüz were already known to the public; it therefore concerned a matter of general interest for public debate. Moreover, the applicant's views were counterbalanced by those of other participants in a pluralistic debate.

There is an additional reason why the Court's judgment in *Gündüz v. Turkey* is important in the context of religiously motivated speech. Setting out the relevant principles in par. 37, it included the following passage that stems from the ECtHR's case law on blasphemy:

> 'However, as is borne out by the wording itself of Article 10 § 2, whoever exercises the rights and freedoms enshrined in the first paragraph of that Article undertakes "duties and responsibilities". Amongst them – in the context of religious opinions and beliefs – may legitimately be included an obligation to avoid as far as possible expressions that are gratuitously offensive to others and thus an infringement of their rights, and which therefore do not contribute to any form of public debate capable of furthering progress in human affairs.'

The fact that this passage is used here suggests that the obligation to refrain from 'gratuitously offensive' expressions in the context of religious convictions also applies to the defamation of *nonbelievers* by anti-secular speech. Article 9 of the ECHR, after all, also includes the freedom not to adhere to any religion or belief. This also came back in a passage in the Third Chamber's judgment in Refah Partisi, which dealt with the remarks of one of the party's MPs that 'revealed deep hatred for those he considered to be opponents of an Islamist regime.' About these remarks, the Court considered that 'where the offending conduct reaches a high level of insult and comes close to a negation of the freedom of religion of others it loses the right to society's tolerance.'[59] The aforementioned passage from Gündüz about the 'obligation to avoid as far as possible expressions that are gratuitously offensive to others' also came back in a 2006 case on religiously motivated hate speech: *Erbakan v. Turkey*.[60] Mr. Erbakan was, at the time, the president of Refah Partisi and held a public speech during his campaign for the municipal elections. This took place in the South-East of Turkey, where terrorist attacks were frequent. The speech included the following:

> 'Dorénavant, il n'existe plus douze partis politiques dans ce pays. Il y en a deux: [celui du] juste (hak) et [celui de l'] injuste (batıl). Les autres, qui sont les autres? Tous à l'exception du Refah sont injustes… ils sont amoureux de l'infidèle… Ils sont tous des usuriers, tous des exploiteurs, tous des oppresseurs et, en plus, nous allons abandonner le monde islamique, nous serons ensemble avec les chrétiens, et les infidèles feront nos lois et nous gouverneront (…)'

59 ECtHR (Third Section) Refah Partisi and others v. Turkey, 31 July 2001, par. 75.
60 ECtHR Erbakan v. Turkey, 6 July 2006.

The applicant was convicted for incitement to hatred on the grounds of religion for making derogatory remarks about nonbelievers. According to the ECtHR, the author reduced the diversity indispensible to a pluralistic society to the simple distinction between 'believers' and 'non-believers,' and expressed the wish to apply this distinction in the political sphere. According to the Court,

> 'de tels propos – s'ils ont été réellement prononcés – tenus par un homme politique notoire lors d'un rassemblement public révèlent davantage une vision de la société structurée exclusivement autours des valeurs religieuses et paraissent ainsi difficilement conciliables avec le pluralisme qui caractérise les sociétés actuelles où se confrontent les groupes les plus divers.'[61]

This was, according to the ECtHR, particularly problematic because the speech took place in a sensitive region where many people had fallen victim to terrorism. The Court also stressed the particular responsibility of the speaker, as a political leader, to avoid exacerbating intolerance: 'Soulignant que la lutte contre toute forme d'intolérance fait partie intégrante de la protection des droits de l'homme, il est d'une importance cruciale que les hommes politiques, dans leurs discours publics, évitent de diffuser des propos susceptibles de nourrir l'intolérance.'[62] In the end, the Court did conclude that there was a violation of article 10, without, however, delving into the substance of the speech. First, because the authenticity of the speech's registration was contested; and second, because Mr. Erbakan was only prosecuted more than 4 years after he gave his speech, so his expressions could no longer be regarded as posing an actual risk or an imminent danger to society. As such, the Court took into account whether the expressions posed a real danger to public order.

In *Mehmet Cevher İlhan v. Turkey*,[63] the applicant was an author who had written several newspaper articles right after a deadly earthquake in North-East Turkey in 1999 that had caused the death of 10 thousand people. In these articles, he suggested that the earthquake was the result of the anti-religious government measures (such as the prohibition of the headscarf at Turkish universities) and the increasingly secular lifestyle of many Turkish people. The author was convicted to two years' imprisonment. The ECtHR first noted that these expressions are part of a relevant public debate; secondly, the Court set out a distinction between (a) the author's criticism of the government measures and (b) his moral criticism of people's lifestyle. While the articles in category (a) did not justify sanctions, in category (b) the Court found one article that deserved further consideration. In this

61 ECtHR Erbakan v. Turkey, 6 July 2006, par. 62.
62 ECtHR Erbakan v. Turkey, 6 July 2006, par. 64.
63 ECtHR Mehmet Cevher İlhan v. Turkey, 13 January 2009.

piece, 'le requérant, pendant qu'il glorifie une partie de la population féminine, à savoir les femmes qui portent le voile, insuffle une haine fondée sur l'intolérance religieuse contre l'autre partie de cette même population, à savoir les femmes qui ne portent pas le voile et qui, selon lui, « s'exhibent piteusement ».' The Court found that in this context – right after the catastrophe – the article's content and discriminatory connotation could present a threat to the peace. In principle, the Court thus found a pressing social need for interfering with the author's freedom of exprsession. Because his sentence was so disproportionate, however, the Court did find a violation of article 10.

Analysis and Conclusion

The ECtHR's case law raises important questions about the way liberal states can deal with extreme religious speech and activities. In Refah Partisi, the Court considered that 'the State's duty of neutrality and impartiality is incompatible with any power on the State's part to assess the legitimacy of religious beliefs'; however, 'in a democratic society the State may limit the freedom to manifest a religion (...) if the exercise of that freedom clashes with the aim of protecting the rights and freedoms of others, public order and public safety' (par. 91-92). The Court further argued that

> 'the principle of secularism is certainly one of the fundamental principles of the State which are in harmony with the rule of law and respect for human rights and democracy. An attitude which fails to respect that principle will not necessarily be accepted as being covered by the freedom to manifest one's religion and will not enjoy the protection of Article 9 of the Convention.'[64]

The Refah and Hizb ut-Tahrir cases clearly indicate how the Court views militant democracy in the realm of political parties. In the first place, a democratic state is allowed to defend its democratic *procedure* – that is, the system of regular elections as well as the method of resolving conflicts peacefully, which excludes the method of violence. Whether only violent methods or also non-violent illegal methods can engage a militant democracy is not clear. In this respect, the concurring opinion of Judge Ress joined by Judge Rozakis in the Refah case provides some notable considerations: He contemplates whether the legality of means also implies that 'more or less minor illegalities' committed would justify dissolution of an entire party, in the light of the principle of proportionality. Besides procedural militance, the Court's case law on political organizations also makes clear that a democratic state can uphold the *substance*, the basic values that underlie democracy. These

64 Par. 93.

basic values may include the principle of secularism, the Court makes clear. Even if a majority of the people should want to introduce a theocratic regime or a regime based on sharia, the state can take measures to prevent this. The fact that a political program is incompatible with the current *principles and structures* of a state does not make it as such incompatible with the rules of democracy. In *Socialist Party and others v. Turkey*, the Court held that '[i]t is of the essence of democracy to allow diverse political programs to be proposed and debated, even those that call into question the way a State is currently organised, provided that they do not harm democracy itself.'[65]

In the Refah case, the Court indicated that whether the rights of a political party can be infringed with the purpose of upholding democratic values depends on the imminence of the risk they pose. If there is a real risk for democratic principles, a state does not have to wait until the risk actually emerges: The Court does allow for proactive measures. The question remains:

> 'How the "imminent risk to democracy" requirement relates to the "incitement to violence" standard central to the Court's article 10 jurisprudence, and endorsed by both the Third Section and the Grand Chamber in the context of article 11. Does a political party qualify for dissolution because its program or statements by its leaders incite to violent conduct, even where that party does not pose and imminent threat to democracy?'[66]

In the Hizb ut-Tahrir cases, however, the concrete risk that the group posed to a democratic society did not play a role at all. The Court did not consider the actual strength of the group in Germany or Russia, issues that are arguably very relevant in considering whether to limit rights and freedoms with the aim of upholding democracy. On the one hand, prohibiting powerful political groups is particularly antidemocratic and thus requires strict scrutiny. On the other hand, prohibiting extreme viewpoints in the context of a political party at risk of coming to power is arguably more proportionate than in the context of smaller groups, just as prohibiting extreme speech by an influential politician is arguably more proportionate – but also more antidemocratic – than prohibiting extreme speech by less influential individuals.

Another open question, which stems particularly from the Refah case, is to what extent the precise content and interpretation of fundamental rights can be challenged: The speeches of Refah's leaders, after all, were not by definition *against* the concept of human rights per

65 ECtHR (Grand Chamber) Socialist Party and others v. Turkey, 25 May 1998, par. 47.
66 Sottiaux 2004(a), p. 596-597.

se. In their view, the principle of non-discrimination was compromised by the strong secularism advanced by the Turkish government – they thus proposed a different interpretation of this principle.

The Court accepts that states defend a large set of 'core values' of a democratic society against powers that might undermine these values. For the Court, neutrality as regards different 'conceptions of the good' means that movements that are too extreme can rightly be kept out of the democratic process in order to protect neutrality and tolerance – at least, when a party has a large electoral potential. When there is a risk that a party becomes very powerful, the state may intervene proactively to prevent the danger that fundamental rights will be undermined.

The Court's case law about Article 11 and religious-political organizations actually expresses a kind of 'anti-pluralism for the sake of pluralism.' In order to safeguard a democracy that accepts a plurality of ways of life, the Court had to limit the pluralism of political parties.

Yet outside the context of political parties, in the case of *Gündüz v. Turkey*, the Court did not find it necessary to restrict pluralism – after all, the speech of one sole individual did not pose a real risk to democracy. The Court held that states should tolerate expressions of fundamentalist religious conceptions that go against the principle of secularism – at least, as long as they do not constitute hate speech or incitement to violence (though other case law suggests that in practice, public order considerations can rather easily provide a reason to restrict article 10). The fact that such expressions are considered within the general framework of article 10 and not as particularly *religious* expressions under article 9, means that the Court does not have to delve into the interpretation of religion and the extent to which speech emanates from religious convictions.

However, the Court's case law also shows that such cases about extreme speech in the context of secularism involve the same risk of 'majoritarianism' that was seen in blasphemy cases: In states where secular majorities exist, there can be a tendency to restrict the right to free speech of religious minorities. In this regard, the dissenting opinion of Judge Türmen in the Gündüz case is exemplary:

> 'In the present case, it is not the religious feelings of believers but the feelings of a great majority of the Turkish population who choose to lead a secular life that were attacked. I am concerned that the present judgment may be interpreted by the outside world to mean that the Court does not grant the same degree of protection to secular values as it does to religious values. Such a distinction, intentional or unintentional, is contrary to the letter and spirit of the Conven-

> tion. As Judge Pettiti rightly pointed out in his concurring opinion in Wingrove, "the rights of others" as mentioned in paragraph 2 of Article 10 cannot be restricted solely to the rights of religious believers. The rights of secular people are also included in this expression.'

However, in the same manner as it is questionable whether blasphemy really infringes upon the rights of believers, it is doubtful whether the mere propagation of sharia and anti-secularism infringes upon the rights of nonbelievers. In *Gündüz and Erbakan*, the Court seemed well aware of the risk of majoritarianism: It proved sensitive to the context and circumstances surrounding the expressions, although the case of Erbakan leaves one wondering what the Court would have decided had Erbakan been prosecuted directly after his speech and had there been evidence of his authentic speech. In *Mehmet Cevher İlhan*, the Court did lean towards majoritarianism – with a questionable reasoning based on public order arguments ('threat to the peace' immediately after the earthquake). The Court does place the case in the context of public order, but it is not completely clear what danger these expressions pose for public order. Preventing offence seems to play an even more important role here, as the case is merely about criticizing a lifestyle and reasoning that an earthquake is 'God's punishment'. Offence, however, does not seem sufficient reason to prohibit speech in the Gündüz case (in line with the Court's general reasoning that expressions may offend, shock or disturb).

The Court's ruling in *Erbakan v. Turkey* also brings up questions about the space for extreme ideas in political discourse. The Court found it very serious that Erbakan's speeches, by making a sharp distinction between believers and nonbelievers ('we/they'), led to religious intolerance. Yet one may ask whether inciting to such antagonism is not inevitable in politics, certainly in a context where secularism is such an important discussion point. Where is the line between criticizing the powers that be – one of the most important functions of freedom of expression – and inciting political violence? The external context (is there a history of violence in a certain region?) seems to play a large role here.

The Court thus struggles with how much militant democracy it is willing to take on. Though the outcomes of such cases vary - depending on whether they concern (membership of) a political organization or the speech of a lone individual, and the potential connection to public order problems – many of the ECtHR's *arguments* in dealing with religiously motivated speech and political parties incline towards a militant democracy conception which aims to protect, but at the same time restricts, democracy and fundamental rights against anti-secular powers.

10 Restricting Free Speech in Times of Terror: An ECHR Perspective

Jan-Peter Loof

Introduction

A particular relation exists between terrorism and the right to freedom of expression, the right to impart information and ideas. Among specialists in the field of terrorism theories it is not uncommon to see terrorist violence as acts of communication: 'Terrorism is theatre'. Terrorist victims serve as instruments to convey a message to the target. The terrorist act is designed to intimidate or otherwise influence the intended recipient of the communication.[1] The ease by which audio and video messages can be spread to a worldwide audience of literally billions of people through the use of internet and social media makes this theatrical aspect of terrorism all the more prominent.

Also, from the perspective of the prevention of terrorism and counterterrorism strategies, the mass communication of extreme messages and pictures of terrorist acts on the internet has provoked much debate. A number of studies and several government agencies conclude that extremist (video) messages on the internet, and posts on social media or web fora, can contribute to radicalization.[2] Online information or propaganda may inspire radicals into extremist acts or create a climate in which terrorism becomes a possibility.[3] Banning such messages is technically difficult: The internet offers ample options to secure anonymity or avoid interception and tracing of communications. Furthermore, the internet 'broadcast yourself' era makes censorship of extremist messages – in the sense of measures to prevent the broadcast of such information – almost an impossibility. Nevertheless, calls for the criminalization of extremist speech and the glorification of terrorism are regularly heard. Such calls often come from politicians and ordinary citizens who are not only shocked by pictures of the beheadings of Europeans or Americans by ISIL terrorists in Syria or Iraq, but by the fact that some members of their own society *anno* 2014 digitally

1 See Alex P. Schmidt and Janny de Graaf, *Violence as Communication. Insurgent Terrorism and the Western News Media*, London: Sage Publications 1982, p. 176.

2 *Inter alia* T. Stevens and P.R. Neumann, *Countering online radicalisation: a strategy for action*, London: International Center for the Study of Radicalisation and Political Violence 2009, p. 12-13; Nationaal Coördinator Terrorismebestrijding (NCTb), *Jihadisten en het internet – Update 2009*, The Hague April 2010.

3 C.J. De Poot *et al.*, *Jihadistisch terrorisme in Nederland. Een beschrijving op basis van afgesloten opsporingsonderzoeken*, The Hague: WODC 2009, p. 131.

express support for these horrifying acts.[4] Already Article 5 of the Council of Europe Convention on the Prevention of Terrorism, signed in Warsaw on 16 May, 2005, required the State Parties to adopt 'such measures as may be necessary to establish public provocation to commit terrorism as a criminal offence under their domestic laws'.[5] A similar clause on 'provocation to commit a terrorist offence' was adopted in a European Union instrument: The Framework Decision of 9 December, 2008, amending Framework Decision 2002/475/JHA on combating terrorism.[6]

On the other hand, there is the fundamental importance to democracy of the freedom of speech. In the context of effective political democracy and respect for human rights, freedom of expression is not only important in its own right, but also it plays a central part in the protection of other individual rights. Furthermore, without a broad guarantee of the right to freedom of expression (protected by independent and impartial courts), there is no free country, and no democracy.[7] This freedom requires that even the advocacy of far-reaching legal or societal change should remain possible, keeping in mind that it is often the political exclusion of radicals that makes them resort to violence. Belgian scholar Stefan Sottiaux even dares to raise the question whether terrorist acts, given their communicative aims, deserve protection as expressive conduct.[8] He points at several court decisions in Europe and the US in which it was recognized that freedom of expression may cover non-verbal expressive conduct such as flag-burning, the boycotting of certain shops, walking in the line of fire of hunters to protest against a grouse shoot and blockading a public road.[9] However, his inevitable conclusion is that there cannot be any legal right to engage in violent terrorist activity, whatever its expressive dimension may be. Actions that are liable to provoke violence, and even non-violent acts of sabotage that constitute forms of coercion into abandoning a lawful activity (such as hunting, whale fishing, producing nuclear energy), do not enjoy the same privileged protection as political speech, debate on questions of public interest, or the peaceful demonstration of opinions on such matters.[10] And, of

4 E.g., in August 2014 the leader of the Dutch Christian-Democratic Party in parliament suggested that glorification of terrorist acts should be criminalized. An author stressing the need for limits to the freedom of expression in order to prevent acts of terrorism is Amos Guiora, see Amos N. Guiora, *Tolerating Intolerance: The Price of Protecting Extremism*, Oxford University Press 2013.

5 ETS No. 196; entry into force 1 June 2007.

6 OJ L 330/21.

7 Jochen Abr. Frowein, Freedom of expression under the European Convention on Human Rights, in: *Freedom of expression and restrictions included in the penal code and other legal texts*, CM/Monitor (97) Inf, Strasbourg: Council of Europe 1998, p. 7-17.

8 Stefan Sottiaux, *Terrorism and the Limitation of Rights. The ECHR and the US Constitution*, Oxford-Portland (Oregon): Hart Publishing 2008, p. 74-81.

9 Ibidem.

10 See, e.g.: ECtHR 23 September 1998, appl.no. 24838/94, *Steel and Others v. UK*; ECtHR 4 May 2000, appl.no. 33698/96, *Drieman and Others v. Norway.*

course, one could also argue that extreme speech should be viewed as antidemocratic. Advocacy of radical change should remain possible, but only if it presupposes peaceful change, obedience to the law, change within the constitutional structure, change with respect for the fundamental rights and freedoms of others, or change of this constitutional structure by means that stay within the law. The use of violence to achieve one's political goals is at odds with democracy, which is based on the principle that conflicts shall be resolved peacefully through dialogue.[11]

As far as extremist expressions are concerned, there is the paradox of tolerance: An absolute tolerance may lead to the tolerance of the ideas promoting intolerance, and the latter could then destroy tolerance. At this point I would like to quote Dutch hate speech expert Marloes van Noorloos who writes:

> 'Political violence endangers the lives of innocent civilians as well as the public order and security on which a democracy depends for its survival. Accordingly, the most compelling reason for restricting extreme speech is the harm to individuals and society that results from it if words would turn into deeds. It is therefore important to critically examine the proximity between various forms of extreme speech and their potential consequences.'[12]

It is against this background that this article endeavours to analyze the standards of the European Convention in Human Rights (ECHR) and the case-law of the European Court of Human Rights (ECtHR) with respect to permissible restrictions on the freedom of expression, on account of public order, national security or other grounds, in cases relating to terrorism. What room do they leave for the criminalization of – or restriction of – terrorism-related extremist speech?

In order to do so, a brief introduction to the protection offered to freedom of expression by the ECHR, and to the general features of its limitation system, is first given (para. 2). Following on from that, several situations concerning measures restricting the freedom of expression in the context of national security or terrorism-related issues are then discussed in more detail. The ECtHR's judgments concerning various forms of terrorism-related speech or subversive and violent expression are then reviewed (para. 3). We will see that a series of Turkish cases in the second part of the 1990s have set the tone for the Court's approach. The conclusions that can be drawn from these Turkish cases, and some

11 See, e.g., ECtHR 8 July 1999 (Grand Chamber), appl.no. 23168/94, *Karatas v. Turkey*, § 50.

12 L.A. van Noorloos, Criminalizing speech in the context of terrorism: human rights and state responsibilities, in: M.F.H. Hirsch Ballin *et al.* (Eds.), *Shifting Responsibilities in Criminal Justice*, The Hague: Eleven International Publishing 2012, p. 129. *See also*: L.A. van Noorloos, *Hate Speech Revisited. A Comparative and Historical Perspective on Hate Speech Law in the Netherlands and England & Wales* (PhD thesis Utrecht), Antwerp: Intersentia 2011.

later cases against other states, are also presented (para. 4). After that, the analysis continues in order to discover whether the approach of the Court may have changed in the post-9/11 era, influenced by some apparent new dimensions in both terrorist activities and terrorism-related speech (para. 5). This analysis cannot do without some discussion on the effectiveness of and the legal difficulties in prohibiting or criminalizing terrorism-related expressions, based on the experience in some European countries (para. 6). The concluding paragraph 7 sums up the significant developments in the ECtHR's case-law, in combination with the discussion on the effectiveness of free speech restrictions, in an attempt to indicate the potential room for restrictions on the freedom of expression, in the context of terrorism, from the perspective of the ECHR.

Freedom of Expression and its Limits: The ECHR Framework

The right to freedom of expression is guaranteed by Article 10 of the ECHR. The first paragraph of this Article indicates that 'this right shall include freedom to hold opinions and to receive and impart information and ideas without interference by public authority and regardless of frontiers'. The second paragraph of the Article contains the limitation clause:

> 'The exercise of these freedoms, since it carries with it duties and responsibilities, may be subject to such formalities, conditions, restrictions or penalties as are prescribed by law and are necessary in a democratic society, in the interests of national security, territorial integrity or public safety, for the prevention of disorder or crime, for the protection of health or morals, for the protection of the reputation or the rights of others, for preventing the disclosure of information received in confidence, or for maintaining the authority and impartiality of the judiciary.'

Thus, the second paragraph allows for free speech restrictions that are deemed necessary in the interests of national security, public safety, the prevention of disorder or crime, the protection of health or morals and the protection of the rights and freedoms of others. The list of the possible grounds for restricting the freedom of expression is exhaustive. Domestic authorities may not legitimately rely on any other ground falling outside the list provided in paragraph 2. Therefore, when called to enforce a legal provision which would in any way interfere with the freedom of expression, the national courts – and ultimately the ECtHR – must identify the value or interest protected by the respective provision and check if that interest or value is one of those enumerated in paragraph 2. Only if the answer is affirmative may the courts apply that provision to the individual concerned.However, the ECHR also offers another approach to exclude certain extremist expressions from free speech protection, in particular by applying Article 17 (prohibition of abuse of rights) of the Convention. Both approaches will be studied in more detail below. First, some remarks regarding the contents of the freedoms guaranteed by Article 10.

The freedom to hold opinions is a prior condition to the other freedoms guaranteed by Article 10, and it almost enjoys an absolute protection in the sense that the possible restrictions set forth in paragraph 2 are inapplicable. Macovei explains:

> 'States must not try to indoctrinate their citizens and should not be allowed to operate distinctions between individuals holding one opinion or another. Moreover, the promotion of one-sided information by the State may constitute a serious and unacceptable obstacle to the freedom to hold opinions.
> Under the freedom to hold opinions, individuals are also protected against possible negative consequences in cases where particular opinions are attributed to them following previous public expressions.'[13]

The ECtHR has repeatedly stated that freedom of expression constitutes one of the essential foundations of a democratic society, one of the basic conditions for its progress and for each individual's self-fulfilment. The Court has added that the exercise of the freedom to impart information and ideas allows for a free criticism of the government, which is the main indicator of a free and democratic government. It has stressed the role of the press in imparting such information and ideas and has underlined the right of the public to receive them.[14] Moreover, the ECtHR has considered that value judgments, in particular those expressed in the political field, enjoy a special protection as a requirement of the pluralism of opinions, crucial for a democratic society.[15] However, such value judgments should be supported by a sufficient factual basis.[16]

The freedom to receive information includes the right to gather information and to seek information through all possible lawful sources. The 'expression' protected under Article 10 is not limited to words, written or spoken, but extends to pictures, images and

13 Monica Macovei, *Freedom of expression. A guide to the implementation of Article 10 of the European Convention on Human Rights* (Human rights handbooks, No. 2), Strasbourg: Council of Europe 2004, p. 8.

14 E.g., ECtHR 8 July 1986, appl.no. 9815/82, *Lingens v. Austria*; ECtHR 25 June 1992, appl.no. 13778/88, *Thorgeir Thorgeirson v. Iceland*; ECtHR 18 July 2000, appl.no. 26680/95, *Sener v. Turkey*; ECtHR 29 March 2001, appl.no. 38432/97, *Thoma v. Luxembourg*; ECtHR 19 April 2001, appl.no. 32686/96, *Maronek v. Slovakia*; ECtHR 26 February 2002, appl.no. 29271/95, *Dichand and Others v. Austria*; ECtHR 15 December 2009, appl.no. 821/03, *Financial Times Ltd. and Others v. the United Kingdom*, para. § 59.

15 E.g., ECtHR 29 September 1999, appl.no. 28114/95, *Dalban v. Romania*.

16 ECtHR 27 Fenbruary 2001, appl.no. 26958/95, *Jerusalem v. Austria*; ECtHR 26 February 2002, appl.no. 29271/95, *Dichand and Others v. Austria*.

other actions intended to express an idea or to present information. Moreover, Article 10 protects not only the substance of the information and ideas but also the form in which they are expressed. Therefore, printed documents, radio broadcasts, paintings, films or electronic information systems and other means for the production and communication, transmission or distribution of information and ideas are covered by Article 10 and protected under this article.[17]

Another prominent aspect of the ECtHR's case-law on Article 10 is the protection it offers to expression which carries a risk of damaging, or actually damages, the interests of others. Macovei correctly states:

> 'Usually, the opinions shared by the majority or by large groups do not run the risk of interference by the states. This is why the protection afforded by Article 10 also covers information and opinions expressed by small groups or one individual even where such expression shocks the majority.'[18]

Perhaps one of the best-known and most-cited phrases from the ECtHR's case-law deals with exactly this aspect:

> 'Article 10 protects not only the information or ideas that are favourably received or regarded as inoffensive or as a matter of indifference, but also those that *offend, shock or disturb*; such are the demands of that pluralism, tolerance and broad-mindedness without which there is no democratic society (*emphasis added – JPL*).'[19]

As far as the limitation clause in the second paragraph of Article 10 is concerned, it is important to see that it contains three requirements: An interference with the right to freedom of expression is justified if (1) it is prescribed by law, (2) it has one or more of the legitimate aims referred to and (3) it is necessary in a democratic society for achieving such an aim or aims.

The list of legitimate aims in Article 10 (2) has already been discussed above. The 'prescribed by law' requirement was explained by the ECtHR in the famous *Sunday Times v. the United Kingdom* judgment from 1979.[20] For an interference to be prescribed by law,

---

17 Macovei 2004 (*supra* note 13), p. 15 gives a list of the relevant ECtHR judgments.

18 Macovei 2004 (*supra* note 13), p. 15.

19 See, among many other authorities, ECtHR 7 December 1976, appl.no. 5493/72, *Handyside v. the United Kingdom*, para. 49; ECtHR 26 April 1979, appl.no. 6538/74, *Sunday Times v. the United Kingdom*, para. 65; ECtHR 8 July 1986, appl.no. 9815/82, *Lingens v. Austria*, para. 41; ECtHR 18 May 2004, appl.no. 58148/00, *Editions Plon v. France*, para. 42; ECtHR 7 February 2012, appl.no. 39954/08, *Axel Springer AG v. Germany*. para. 78.

20 ECtHR 26 April 1979, appl.no. 6538/74, *Sunday Times v. the United Kingdom*.

the domestic law that provides a legal basis for the interference must satisfy the criteria of 'accessibility' and 'foreseeability'.[21] Accessibility requires that an individual must have an indication that is adequate in the circumstances of the legal rules applicable to a given case:[22] The law must be in the public domain in some form or another. Foreseeability means that this law must be formulated with sufficient precision to enable the citizen to regulate his conduct: 'He must be able – if need be with appropriate advice – to foresee, to a degree that is reasonable in the circumstances, the consequences which a given action may entail.'[23] The ECtHR has repeatedly stated in this respect that, in drafting regulations, it is impossible to be completely accurate at all times. Many laws inevitably allow for a certain discretion on the side of the executive. However, the law must indicate the scope of any such discretion conferred on the competent authorities and the manner of its exercise with sufficient clarity, having regard to the legitimate aim of the measure in question, to give the individual adequate protection against arbitrary interference.[24] These safeguards need not, however, always be provided in the text of the relevant legal regulations themselves: The required clarity and accuracy of the regulations can also be provided by the explanatory notes to the legal regulations, or by a further interpretation given in published court rulings.[25] Protection of the individual from arbitrariness on the part of the government does, however, require that the law is sufficiently 'clear in its terms' for the people to understand – if necessary with the aid of appropriate advice – under which circumstances the government may exercise a certain power which violates a fundamental right and which conditions are attached to the exercising of this power.[26] In addition, the requirement for sufficient safeguards against arbitrariness means that the legal system must provide for the existence of legal procedures in order to contest any alleged arbitrary violations of fundamental rights.[27]

The ECtHR's settled interpretation of the 'necessary in a democratic society' test in the context of Article 10 (2) of the ECHR can be summarized as follows. In the first place, the interference must fulfil a 'pressing social need.'[28] According to the ECtHR, the term 'nec-

21 *Idem*, para. 49.

22 *Ibid. See also* ECtHR 25 March 1983, appl.no. 5947/72, *Silver and Others v. the United Kingdom*, para. 86-87 and ECtHR 26 March 1987, appl.no. 9248/81, *Leander v. Sweden*, para. 50.

23 ECtHR 26 April 1979, appl.no. 6538/74, *Sunday Times v. the United Kingdom*, para. 49.

24 *Idem.*, para. 67. See also, eg, ECtHR 22 November 2012, appl.no. 39315/06, *Telegraaf Media Nederland Landelijke Media B.V. and Others v. the Netherlands*, para. 90

25 *Idem.*, paras. 88-89 and ECtHR 4 June 2002, appl.no. 33129/96, *Olivieira v. the Netherlands*, paras. 50-59.

26 See, eg, ECtHR 2 August 1984, appl.no. 8691/79, *Malone v. the United Kingdom*, paras. 67-68; ECtHR 24 April 1990, appl.no. 11801/85, *Kruslin v. France*, para. 30.

27 See, eg, ECtHR 2 August 1984, appl.no. 8691/79, *Malone v. the United Kingdom*, paras. 67-68 and ECtHR 26 March 1987, appl.no. 9248/81, *Leander v. Sweden*, para. 51.

28 E.g., ECtHR 7 December 1976, appl.no. 5493/72, *Handyside v. the United Kingdom*, para. 48; ECtHR 26 April 1979, appl.no. 6538/74, *Sunday Times v. the United Kingdom*, paras. 59-62; ECtHR 26 November 1991, appl.no. 13585/88, *Observer and Guardian v. the United Kingdom*, para. 59.

essary' is, on the one hand, not to be interpreted as 'narrowly' as the terms 'indispensable,' 'absolutely necessary' or 'strictly necessary' but, on the other hand, not as 'broadly' or 'flexibly' as the terms 'admissible,' 'ordinary,' 'useful' 'reasonable' or 'desirable' (all of which also occur in the ECHR).[29] In the second place, the interference should be proportionate to the legitimate aim pursued. This element of proportionality contains some further sub-principles: (1) *Relevance and suitability* (the limiting measure must be capable of achieving the legitimate aim pursued and the justification put forward by the authorities must be 'relevant and sufficient');[30] (2) *subsidiarity* (the limiting measure must be the least restrictive means to achieve the relevant aim); (3) *proportionality in the narrow sense* (a reasonable relationship must exist between the limiting measure and the legitimate aim pursued and the interference with the right may not be such that the essence of the right is eroded).[31]

In assessing the necessity and proportionality of a limiting measure – so in deciding whether such a 'need' exists and what measures should be adopted to deal with it, the national authorities are left a certain margin of appreciation. However, in the standard phrasing of the Court, 'this power of appreciation is not (...) unlimited but goes hand in hand with European supervision by the Court, whose task it is to give a final ruling on whether a restriction is reconcilable with freedom of expression as protected by Article 10.'[32] In connection with this, the ECtHR sometimes also investigates how a similar problem is solved in other European states (the so-called 'common ground' method), in which respect the fact that many other countries take similar measures may not necessarily be decisive but will certainly play an important role in the positive assessment of the proportionality of the violation.[33] The non-existence of a 'European consensus' at least influences the width of the margin of appreciation the Court leaves to the Contracting States.

After this brief sketch of some relevant general aspects of the ECHR framework concerning the protection of freedom of expression, let us now turn to the ECtHR's case-law on some specific free speech issues relating to national security, prevention of disorder or crime and terrorism in order to explore which restrictions are permitted.

---

29 ECtHR 7 December 1976, appl.no. 5493/72, *Handyside v. the United Kingdom*, para. 48.

30 *Idem.*, paras. 48-50. Also ECtHR 25 November 1997, appl.no. 18954/91, *Zana v. Turkey*.

31 For an analysis of the principle of proportionality in the ECtHR case law: Marc-Andre Eissen, The Priniciple of Proportionality in the Case-Law of the European Court of Human Rights, in: R.St.J. MacDonald *et al.* (Eds.), *The European System for the Protection of Human Rights*, Leiden/Boston: Martinus Nijhoff 1993, p. 125-146; Yutaka Arai-Takanashi, *The Margin of Appreciation Doctrine and the Principle of Proportionality in the Jurisprudence of the ECHR*, Antwerp: Intersentia 2002.

32 See, among many other authorities, ECtHR 17 December 2004 [GC], appl.no. 33348/96, *Cumpănă and Mazăre v. Romania*, para. 88; ECtHR 22 November 2007, appl.no. 64752/01, *Voskuil v. The Netherlands*, para. 63; ECtHR 11 December 2008, appl.no. 21132/05, *TV Vest AS and Rogaland Pensjonistparti v. Norway*, para. 58.

33 Arai-Takanashi 2002 (*supra* note 31), p. 207-210.

Prohibition and Punishment of Expressions of Support for Separatism and Terrorism: The Turkish Cases

In the past two decades, the ECtHR has been faced several times with cases concerning government action against (alleged) terrorist or separatist manifestations. A first stream of cases started in the mid-1990s. These cases were mainly against Turkey and concerned manifestations which the Turkish government regarded as support to the Kurdish Workers' Party (PKK) or which were otherwise regarded as instigating or inciting terrorism or separatism. In this stream of cases, the ECtHR developed a 'full scale doctrine to assess interferences with expressions that are potentially harmful to national security.'[34] However, in some earlier cases the Strasbourg organs already dealt with situations in which the contracting states had relied on national security interests to justify interferences with the freedom of expression. These earlier cases mostly concerned the protection of state and military secrets,[35] as well as limitations to the free speech of members of the military or the public in order to maintain discipline.[36]

Furthermore, the Turkish cases were preceded by an admissibility decision of the former European Commission of Human Rights (ECommHR) which related to a complaint of various British reporters about a decree issued by the UK government in 1988. This decree – referred to as the *Broadcasting Ban* – prohibited the British broadcasting corporations from broadcasting 'any words spoken, whether in the course of an interview or discussion or otherwise' by representatives of terrorist organizations of Northern Ireland, political parties associated with those organizations (such as *Sinn Fein*) or other persons who supported these organisations.[37] In a further explanation of the decree, the government had clarified that the orders applied only to direct statements and not to reported speech, which

34 Sottiaux 2008 (supra note 8), p. 88.

35 ECommHR 13 December 1984 (adm. dec.), appl.no. 100078/82, *M v. France* (concerning a suspected spy who was caught while in possession of a system with which he could communicate in code by computer); ECtHR 26 November 1991, appl.no. 13585/88, *Observer and Guardian v. the United Kingdom* and ECtHR 26 November 1991, appl.no. 13166/87, *Sunday Times v. the United Kingdom* (No. 2) (both concerning an injunction against the publication of the book *Spycatcher*, which in the eyes of the UK government contained sensitive information on some past operations of the security services); ECtHR 16 December 1992, appl.no. 12945/87, *Hadjianastassiou v. Greece* (concerning the disclosure of military secrets about a missile guidance system to a private company).

36 ECtHR 8 June 1976, appl.no. 5100/71, *Engel and Others v. the Netherlands*; ECommHR 20 January 1987 (adm.dec.), appl.no. 11603/85, *Council of Civil Service Unions and Others v. the United Kingdom*; ECommHR 6 July 1987 (adm.dec.), appl.nos. 11567/85 and 11568/85, *O. Le Court Grand-Maison and L. Fritz v. France*; ECtHR 19 December 1994, appl.no. 15153/89, *VDSÖ and Gubi v. Austria*; ECtHR 26 September 1995, appl.no. 17851/91, *Vogt v. Germany*; ECtHR 25 November 1997, appl.no. 24348/94, *Grigoriades v. Greece*.

37 ECieRM 9 mei 1994 (adm.dec.), appl.no. 18714/91, *Brind and others v. UK*. Further comments on this broadcasting ban en similar measures in other countries can be found in Sandra Coliver, Commentary on the Johannesburg Principles of National Security, Freedom of Expression and Access to Information, in: Sandra Coliver *et al.* (Eds.), *Secrecy and Liberty: National Security, Freedom of Expression and Access to Information*, Leiden/Boston: Martinus Nijhoff 1999, p. 51-53.

had led to a practice of using pictures of video images of speakers accompanied by a voice over account of the statement. Although the ECommHR considered the decree to be an interference with the freedom of the press as guaranteed by Article 10 of the ECHR, it only considered it to be a limited one, whereas the prohibition included in the decree did not have any consequences for 'the words that can be spoken or the images that can be shown on television or the radio.' The ECommHR understood that it was impracticable for reporters to have to use the voice of an actor when broadcasting certain interviews, and also questioned the usefulness of the prohibition, since it had hardly any consequences for the contents of the information available to the public. The very absence of such consequences, however, gave the ECommHR cause to consider the violation of the right to freedom of the press to be in reasonable proportion to the aim of the decree, namely the combating of terrorism.[38]

And now the Turkish cases. The *Zana* case in 1997 concerned statements made by Mr Zana, the former mayor of Diyarbakir (the capital of the province of Anatolia in south-east Turkey; the region where serious disturbances occurred since 1985 because of armed conflict between the PKK and Turkish security troops). In August 1987, while detained in the military prison of Diyarbakir for various convictions, he was interviewed by the national Turkish newspaper *Cumhuriyet* and stated, among other things: 'I support the PKK national liberation movement; on the other hand, I am not in favour of massacres. Anyone can make mistakes, and the PKK kill women and children by mistake ...'.[39] Zana was prosecuted for expressing support for an armed separatist movement which, according to the Turkish criminal statutes, constitutes the offence of 'praising or defending serious crimes in public and thus threatening public security.' A special national security court sentenced Zana to twelve months' imprisonment.[40] The ECtHR had to review whether this interference with the right to freedom of expression pursued a legitimate aim and, after some consideration, replied affirmatively to this question:

> 'The Court notes that in the interview he gave the journalists the applicant indicated that he supported "the PKK national liberation movement" (...) and, as the Commission noted, the applicant's statement coincided with the murders of civilians by PKK militants.
> That being so, it considers that at a time when serious disturbances were raging in south-east Turkey (...) such a statement – coming from a political figure well known in the region – could have an impact such as to justify the national

38 ECommHR 9 May 1994 (adm.dec.), appl.no. 18714/91, *Brind and others v. UK*. A similar conclusion was reached in ECommHR 9 May 1994 (adm.dec.), appl.no. 18759/91, *McLaughlin v. the United Kingdom*.

39 ECtHR 25 November 1997, appl.no. 18954/91, *Zana v. Turkey*, para. 12.

40 *Idem.*, paras. 17 and 26.

> authorities' taking a measure designed to maintain national security and public safety. The interference complained of therefore pursued legitimate aims under Article 10 § 2.'[41]

The Court also considered the interference necessary and proportionate, in particular taking into account the inherent contradictory nature of Zana's statements (on the one hand expressing support for a terrorist organization which used brute force to achieve its objectives, and on the other hand rejecting the use of violence and mass murders while setting aside the mass murder of women and children as 'mistakes' which 'anyone can make')[42] and the specific circumstances in south-east Turkey at the time of Zana's statements:

> 'The statement cannot, however, be looked at in isolation. It had a special significance in the circumstances of the case, as the applicant must have realised. As the Court noted earlier (...), the interview coincided with murderous attacks carried out by the PKK on civilians in south-east Turkey, where there was extreme tension at the material time. (...)
> In those circumstances the support given to the PKK – described as a "national liberation movement" – by the former mayor of Diyarbakır, the most important city in south-east Turkey, in an interview published in a major national daily newspaper, had to be regarded as likely to exacerbate an already explosive situation in that region. (...)
> Having regard to all these factors and to the margin of appreciation which national authorities have in such a case, the Court considers that the interference in issue was proportionate to the legitimate aims pursued. There has consequently been no breach of Article 10 of the Convention.'[43]

Some seven months later, the *Zana* case was followed by the case of *Incal v. Turkey*.[44] This case concerned the confiscation of a communist leaflet criticizing measures taken by the local authorities of the City of Izmir against squatters' camps. The pamphlet refered to 'state terror against Turkish and Kurdish proletarians,' and called on 'all democratic patriots' to oppose the 'special war being waged against the proletarian people' *inter alia* by forming 'neighbourhood committees.'[45] Here, the ECtHR found a violation of Article 10:

---

41 *Idem.*, paras. 50.
42 *Idem.*, para. 58. The ECtHR does not hesitate to label the PKK as a terrorist movement.
43 *Idem*, paras. 59-60 and 62.
44 ECtHR 9 June 1998, appl.no. 22678/93, *Incal v. Turkey*.
45 *Idem.*, para. 10.

> 'The Court certainly sees in these phrases appeals to, among others, the population of Kurdish origin, urging them to band together to raise certain political demands. Although the reference to "neighbourhood committees" appears unclear, those appeals cannot, however, if read in context, be taken as incitement to the use of violence, hostility or hatred between citizens.
> (...) Admittedly (...), it cannot be ruled out that such a text may conceal objectives and intentions different from the ones it proclaims. However, as there is no evidence of any concrete action which might belie the sincerity of the aim declared by the leaflet's authors, the Court sees no reason to doubt it.'[46]

In finding a violation the Court also took into account the radical nature of the interference in question: Preventive confiscation before distribution of the leaflet. This preventive aspect alone raises extra problems under Article 10.[47]

After *Zana* and *Incal*, the ECtHR in June, 1999 judged a series of other cases concerning criminal prosecution for expressing or distributing messages which the Turkish authorities regarded as a threat to the national unity and territorial integrity of the state, and in which the Turkish government invoked (*inter alia*) 'national security' as a ground for restriction. I have singled out a few of these cases:

- The *Arslan* case, concerning the conviction of the author of a book in which Turkish action against the Kurds was criticized, the Turks were portrayed as culturally inferior oppressors and part of Turkish territory was referred to as the 'country of Kurdistan;'[48]
- The *Gerger* case, concerning the reading out of a letter, praising 'the Kurdish guerrilla warfare' against 'Turkish imperialism' and pleading for the liberation of the Kurdish workers, at a memorial ceremony for two Marxist student leaders who had been sentenced to death in 1972;[49]
- The *Sürek and Özdemir* case, concerning the conviction of the publisher and editor-in-chief of a Marxist-oriented weekly magazine for publishing in that magazine (a) an interview with two PKK leaders in which it was pronounced that 'the war against the Turkish oppression' would be fought to the bitter end, and in which the formation of an independent Kurdish state was advocated and announced and (b) a joint appeal by several banned political groups to the Turkish parliament to cease exercising power over Kurdistan and to give the Kurds the opportunity of forming their own independent state;[50]

46 Idem., paras. 50-51.
47 Idem., para. 56.
48 ECtHR 8 July 1999, appl.no. 23462/94, *Arslan v. Turkey*, paras. 8-21.
49 ECtHR 8 July 1999, appl.no. 24919/94, *Gerger v. Turkey*, paras. 9-17.
50 ECtHR 8 July 1999, appl.nos. 23927/94 and 24277/94, *Sürek and Özdemir v. Turkey*, paras. 9-20.

- The *Çetin and Others* case, concerning the prohibition issued by the governor on the importing and distributing in the region, in which a state of emergency had been proclaimed (south-east Turkey), of the newspaper "Ülkede Gündem" and various other papers and magazines, as they were regarded as posing a threat – not specified further – to state security.[51]

In all of these cases, the ECtHR, in reviewing the legitimate aim of the interferences with the right to freedom of expression, reverts to its ruling in the *Zana* case:

> 'The Court considers that, having regard to the sensitivity of the security situation in south-east Turkey (see the Zana v. Turkey judgment of 25 November 1997, *Reports* 1997-VII, p. 2539, § 10) and to the need for the authorities to be alert to acts capable of fuelling additional violence, the measures taken against the applicants can be said to have been in furtherance of certain of the aims mentioned by the Government, namely the protection of national security and territorial integrity and the prevention of disorder and crime. This is certainly true where, as with the situation in south-east Turkey at the time of the circumstances of this case, the separatist movement had recourse to methods which rely on the use of violence.'[52]

The Court thus, in light of the armed conflict in south-east Turkey, considered the actions of the Turkish authorities as being in the interest of (*inter alia*) national security and territorial integrity. With regard to the necessity and proportionality of the actions of the Turkish authorities restricting freedom of expression, however, the Court in all four cases arrived at a different conclusion than in the *Zana* case.

In the *Arslan* case, the Court was of the opinion that it ensues from the fact that the criticism was expressed by a single individual and not published through mass media but in a literary document, that the threat of this criticism to national security, public order and territorial integrity was only limited. The fact that Arslan's book (in its second edition) was published near the end of the first Gulf War in 1991, when many Iraqi Kurds were concentrated near the Iraqi-Turkish border, creating an even more tense situation, did not affect this. The Court furthermore notes that, although in some places the tone of the book is very negative and hostile towards the Turkish population, it does not incite violence, armed resistance or insurrection. Partly due to the severity of the punishment imposed

51 ECtHR 13 February 2003, appl.nos. 40153/98 and 40160/98, *Çetin and Others v. Turkey*, paras. 9-12.

52 ECtHR 8 July 1999, appl.nos. 23927/94 and 24277/94, *Sürek and Özdemir v. Turkey*, para. 51; EHRM 8 July 1999, appl.no. 24919/94, *Gerger v. Turkey*, para. 41 and ECtHR 8 July 1999, appl.no. 23462/94, *Arslan v. Turkey*, para. 40. ECtHR 13 February 2003, appl.nos. 40153/98 and 40160/98, *Çetin and Others v. Turkey*, para. 47 has a more concise wording (no reference to the Zana case), but follows the same line of reasoning.

on Arslan, the Court considered the interference with the right to freedom of expression to be disproportionate and concluded that Article 10 of the ECHR had been violated.[53]

In the *Gerger* case, the Court reached a similar analysis: The message of Gerger was read out to a limited audience during a memorial ceremony and the threat to national security and territorial integrity was thus also limited. Although Gerger wrote about conflict, resistance and liberation, he did not incite violence or armed resistance against the Turkish authorities. The interference with Gerger's right to freedom of expression was therefore considered to be disproportionate.[54]

In the *Sürek and Özdemir* case, the same line was followed. The Court first of all stated that:

> 'The limits of permissible criticism are wider with regard to the government than in relation to a private citizen or even a politician. In a democratic system the actions or omissions of the government must be subject to the close scrutiny not only of the legislative and judicial authorities but also of public opinion.'[55]

The Court subsequently considered that the fact that the contested statements were expressed by (leaders of) banned organizations was insufficient reason for punishing the publication of those statements. And even if the statements by interviewed PPK leaders were evidence of a non-conciliatory attitude towards the Turkish authorities and a one-sided view of the violence in south-east Turkey, the Court reasons that it was part of the role of the press to draw the attention of the public to such a view and that the publication did not incite hatred or violence. The Court therefore concluded that the interference with the right to freedom of expression was disproportionate.[56]

In *Çetin and Others*, like earlier in *Aydin*, the preventive nature of the restricting measure is of importance. In this case, the Court rules that the preventive seizure of a magazine or a prohibition to distribute it could in itself be reasonable, given the existence

---

53 ECtHR 8 July 1999, appl.no. 23462/94, *Arslan v. Turkey*, paras. 47-50. Comparable judgments are: ECtHR 8 July 1999, appl.no. 23556/94, *Ceylan v. Turkey*; ECtHR 8 July 1999, appl.nos. 23536/94 and 24408/94, *Başkaya and Okçuoğlu v. Turkey*; ECtHR 8 July 1999, appl.no. 23500/94, *Polat v. Turkey*; ECtHR 8 July 1999, appl.nos. 25067/94 and 25068/94, *Erdoğdu and İnce v. Turkey*; ECtHR 18 July 2000, appl.no. 26680/95, *Şener v. Turkey*.

54 *Compare* ECtHR 8 July 1999, appl.no. 24246/94, *Okçuoğlu v. Turkey*. This case concerned a publication in magazine that was only marginally distributed. Therefore the ECtHR considered the risk for national security to be limited (see para. 48 of the judgment). In ECtHR 28 September 1999, appl.no. 22479/93, *Özturk v. Turkey*, the Court, besides the fact that the words used in a biography of a Maoist activist did not incite to violence or hatred, also took into account that the book had been on open sale since 1991, apparently without aggravating the separatist threat feared by the government.

55 ECtHR 8 July 1999, appl.nos. 23927/94 and 24277/94, *Sürek and Özdemir v. Turkey*, para. 30.

56 *Idem.*, paras. 61-64. The analysis of the ECtHR's majority that the published interview with the PKK-leadership did not incite violence or armed battle is heavily disputed. See the joint *dissenting opinion* of judges Wildhaber, Kūris, Strážnická, Baka and Traja and the *dissenting opinion* of the Turkish judge Gölcüklü.

of a state of emergency, However, the laws regulating such a state of emergency should contain sufficient safeguards against arbitrariness to protect the freedom of expression, which in this case they did not.[57]

Amidst this series of Turkish cases where the ECtHR finds a violation of Article 10, two cases go in the other direction. In *Sürek (No. 1)* and *Sürek (No. 3)* the Court upheld the restrictions to the freedom of expression.[58] In *Sürek (No. 1)* the disputed publications were two readers' letters in a weekly review, both strongly condemning the military action in south-east Turkey and the suppression of the Kurdish people. The Court maintained that the words and phrases used in the published letters indicated 'a clear intention to stigmatise the other side to the conflict by the use of labels such as "the fascist Turkish army," "the TC murder gang," and "the hired killers of imperialism" alongside references to "massacres," "brutalities" and "slaughter."' According to the court, the letters 'amount to an appeal to bloody revenge by stirring up base emotions and hardening already embedded prejudices which have manifested themselves in deadly violence.'[59] Moreover, one of the letters 'identified persons by name, stirred up hatred for them and exposed them to the possible risk of physical violence.'[60] Therefore, the criminal conviction of the editor of the review, because of the publication of both letters, was justified.[61]

In *Sürek (no. 3)*, the same editor had been convicted for the publication of a news comment which *inter alia* called for 'a total liberation struggle' for Turkish Kurdistan.[62] The ECtHR considered it 'clear that the impugned article associated itself with the PKK and expressed a call for the use of armed force as a means to achieve national independence of Kurdistan' and contained the message that 'recourse to violence is a necessary and justified measure of self-defence in the face of the aggressor.'[63] Bearing in mind that the article was published in the context of the security situation in south-east Turkey, the Court came to the conclusion that the content of the article must be seen as capable of inciting further violence in the region, thus justifying the conviction of the editor.

57 ECtHR 13 February 2003, appl.nos. 40153/98 and 40160/98, *Çetin and Others v. Turkey*, paras. 59 and 63-66.

58 ECtHR 8 July 1999, appl.no. 26682/95, *Sürek v. Turkey (No. 1)*; ECtHR 8 July 1999, appl.no. 24735/94, *Sürek v. Turkey (No. 3)*. Compare ECtHR 20 January 2000 (adm.dec.), appl.no. 35402/97, *Hogefeld v. Germany*.

59 ECtHR 8 July 1999, appl.no. 26682/95, *Sürek v. Turkey (No. 1)*, para. 62.

60 *Idem.*, para. 63.

61 *Idem.*, paras. 64-65.

62 ECtHR 8 July 1999, appl.no. 24735/94, *Sürek v. Turkey (No. 3)*, para. 40.

63 *Ibid.*

Some Conclusions Based on the Turkish Cases

The series of Turkish cases analyzed above suggests that the ECtHR considers the (possible) use of violence or incitement to violence an essential point.[64] The ECtHR's rulings show that publications or other forms of expression that incite violence against individual government officials, against the government machinery as a whole or against other citizens, have consequences for the *margin of appreciation* to which a state is entitled in reviewing the necessity and proportionality of any interference with the right to freedom of expression. When an inciting statement identifies persons by name, stirs up hatred for them and exposes them to the possible risk of physical violence, the suppression of such speech will easily satisfy the democratic necessity test. The *margin of appreciation*, which is usually already wide in the case of state action in the interest of national security, is even wider when incitement to violence is concerned, and drastic measures (often pertaining to criminal law) are consequently more readily considered to be justified. The same is true if an expression has a clear intention to stigmatize the other side in a conflict. Such expressions are more likely to be considered as incitement to terrorism.[65] The ECtHR is also prepared to consider the possibility that an impugned text may conceal objectives and intentions different from the ones it proclaims.[66] This is, however, compensated by the fact that the Court, apart from possible concealed intentions, also requires 'evidence of any concrete action' before characterizing an expression as incitement to terrorism or violence. If there was nothing in a publication's content suggesting incitement to violence or separatism, the ECtHR will hold that the interference with the applicant's freedom of expression was not 'necessary in a democratic society.'[67]

However, it is not only the words or phrases used that count.[68] The *Çetin and Others* case shows that, in the case of preventive intervention in the freedom of expression, adequate national possibilities for reviewing the lawfulness of this intervention must be provided. In addition, preventive restrictive measures relating to press publications will be not be as easily acceptable as those relating to television and radio broadcasts, as the latter

---

64 See also some later ECtHR judgments: ECtHR 15 June 2000, appl.no. 25723/94, *Erdoğdu v. Turkey*, para. 50; ECtHR 16 March 2001, appl.no. 23144/93, *Özgür Gündem v. Turkey*. In this last case, the ECtHR not only concluded to a violation of Article 10 because of the disproportionate actions by the Turkish authorities (a police raid on the offices of a newspaper and the arrest of all journalists on suspicion of illegal support for the PKK), but also because the Turkish authorities fell short of their positive obligation to protect the journalists against threats and bomb attacks by unknown individuals.

65 See also ECtHR 10 October 2006, appl.no. 4119/02, *Halis Dogan v. Turkey (No. 3)*.

66 ECtHR 28 September 1999, appl.no. 22479/93, *Özturk v. Turkey*, para. 68.

67 See also ECtHR 17 July 2001, appl.no. 30882/96, *Association Ekin v. France*.

68 A separate point, not further discussed here, is that the disproportionate nature of a conviction or punishment for an allegedly inciting publication in itself may lead to the ECtHRs conclusion of a violation of Art. 10. See, eg, 27 November 2012, appl.no. 37569/06, *Bayar and Gürbüz v. Turkey*; ECtHR 13 July 2013, appl.no. 1544/07, *Belek and Özkurt v. Turkey*.

have a far more direct and far-reaching impact. This is why this case, which concerned the prohibition on a newspaper's distribution, according to the Court differs from the case concerning the UK *Broadcasting Ban* discussed above.[69]

Furthermore, as Sottiaux has excellently analyzed, the ECtHR's 'interpretation of the content of an expression depends very much on its assessment of the contextual setting.'[70] The contextual evaluation by the Court is also aimed at assessing the probable impact of the expression: '[I]n deciding whether there is incitement, the Court considers such factors as the authority of the speaker (e.g. a private individual as opposed to a public figure), the means used to convey the message, and the security situation prevailing at the time.'[71] Expressions which, taken literally, do not invite the audience to resort to violence may, depending on the circumstances, nevertheless be interpreted as incitement in the context of a serious terrorist campaign.[72] On the other hand, the use of phrases that conventionally indicate that the author is advocating certain conduct, may, given the context, not be considered as incitement. Inciting phrases in an artistic expression such as a poem, or in other formats that are distributed to only a limited amount of readers, listeners or viewers, may receive protection under Article 10.[73] Broadcasters traditionally receive a more reduced protection, because of the potentially greater impact of the broadcasting media.

As far as the personal stature of the author of an expression is relevant, the *Zana* case suggests that a public figure should be more cautious in his or her expressions. Adding up to this is the ECtHR's admissibility decision in the case of *Hogefeld v. Germany*. The applicant in this case was the former member of the German left-wing terrorist movement Red Army Faction (RAF), who served a lifetime prison sentence for her involvement in several terrorist attacks. She challenged the German authorities' decision not to allow her to be interviewed by press and radio journalists. In declaring Hogefeld's complaint inadmissible, the Court weighed that although during her trial she had distanced herself from terrorist attacks and had not incited further violence, she had continued to claim that the fight for a different world had to be conducted as a confrontation. And since she was one of the main representatives of the RAF, her words could possibly be interpreted by her

69 See more recently ECtHR 15 June 2010, appl.nos. 8306/08, 8340/08 and 8366/08, *Turgay and Others v. Turkey*, concerning the suspension of the publication of several newspapers in the Kurdish region in the for one or more months.

70 Sottiaux 2008 (*supra* note 8), p. 98.

71 *Ibid.*

72 See ECtHR 25 November 1997, appl.no. 18954/91, *Zana v. Turkey*; ECtHR 16 March 2001, appl.no. 23144/93, *Özgür Gündem v. Turkey*.

73 In ECtHR 11 January 2005, appl.no. 30007/96, *Halis v. Turkey*, the Court concluded to a violation of Art. 10 *inter alia* because the impugned article was actually never published, since the whole edition of the newspaper was seized. In ECtHR 7 February 2002, appl.no. 28496/95, *E.K. v. Turkey*, the Court considered certain phrases could be interpreted as a praise of armed struggle but nevertheless offered protection under Art. 10 because the phrases were part of an article in a conference book on the Kurdish question.

supporters as an appeal to continue the activities of the RAF.[74] Some of the Turkish cases, on the other hand, show that the mere fact that an interview is given by a leading member of a terrorist organization cannot, in itself, justify an interference with the freedom of expression by criminally convicting the journalist involved in printing the interview. The public has a legitimate interest in gaining 'insight into the psychology of those who are the driving force behind the opposition (…) and to assess the stakes in the conflict.'[75]

New Dimensions in the Post-9/11 era: The Transnational Nature of Terrorism and Religious Extremism

What now remains to be seen is whether the 'full scale doctrine' of the ECtHR built on the Turkish cases concerning expressions related to Kurdish separatist terrorism (and a few later cases, some against other countries), still stands *anno* 2014. In my view, two factors have given the ECtHR's approach to terrorism-related expressions a somewhat new dimension. The first factor – obviously – is the changing nature of terrorism as shown by the 9/11 Al-Qaeda attacks and the subsequent attacks in Madrid, London, Djakarta, Bali and several other places around the world. The threat of terrorism has gained a transnational dimension, which makes it all the more difficult to ascertain at what point the security situation in a certain county reaches the level where one might argue that restrictive measures towards certain expression might be justified because of the inflammable situation. Also, the post-9/11 era has shown a growing interconnectedness between terrorism and religious extremism, in particular – but not exclusively – Muslim extremism.

Religious Intolerance and Extremism

There are some cases that might contain indications of the way in which the Court reacts to these new dimensions. A first case to discuss is *Gündüz v. Turkey*.[76] The applicant in this case was a self-proclaimed member of an Islamist sect. During a televized debate broadcast late in the evening, he spoke very critically of democracy, describing contemporary secular institutions as 'impious,' fiercely criticizing secular and democratic principles and openly calling for the introduction of sharia law. He was convicted of openly inciting hatred and hostility on the basis of a distinction founded on membership of a religion or denomination. The applicant alleged a violation of his right to freedom of expression. The Court noted that the applicant, who had represented the extremist ideas of his sect, with

74 ECtHR 20 January 2000 (adm.dec.), appl.no. 35402/97, *Hogefeld v. Germany*.
75 ECtHR 8 July 1999, appl.nos. 23927/94 and 24277/94, *Sürek and Özdemir v. Turkey*, para. 61.
76 ECtHR 4 December 2003, appl.no. 35071/97, *Gündüz v. Turkey*.

which the public was already familiar, had been taking an active part in an animated public discussion. That pluralist debate had sought to present the sect and its unorthodox views, including the notion that democratic values were incompatible with its conception of Islam. The topic had been the subject of widespread debate in the Turkish media and concerned a problem of general interest. The Court considered that the applicant's remarks could not be regarded as a call to violence or as 'hate speech' based on religious intolerance. As regards the relationship between democracy and sharia, the Court reiterated its note, from the famous *Refah Partisi (the Welfare Party) and Others v. Turkey* judgment, that it was difficult to declare one's respect for democracy and human rights while at the same time supporting a regime based on sharia.[77] It considered that sharia, which faithfully reflected the dogmas and divine rules laid down by religion, was stable and invariable and clearly diverged from Convention values, particularly with regard to its criminal law and criminal procedure, its rules on the legal status of women and the way it intervened in all spheres of private and public life in accordance with religious precepts. However, the Court pointed out that the *Refah Partisi* case concerned the dissolution of a political party whose actions seemed to be aimed at introducing sharia in a State party to the Convention and which, at the time of its dissolution, had the real potential to seize political power.[78] Since that situation was hardly comparable with the one in issue in the *Gündüz* case, it held that there had been a violation of Article 10.

In the *Erbakan v. Turkey* case of 2006, the ECtHR reiterated that restrictions on the freedom of expression of intolerant persons are permitted in case of forms of expression which spread, incite, promote or justify hatred based on intolerance:

> 'La Cour souligne que la tolérance et le respect de l'égale dignité de tous les êtres humains constituent le fondement d'une société démocratique et pluraliste. Il en résulte qu'en principe on peut juger nécessaire, dans les sociétés démocratiques, de sanctionner voire de prévenir toutes les formes d'expression qui propagent, incitent à, promeuvent ou justifient la haine fondée sur l'intolérance (y compris l'intolérance religieuse)'[79]

This case concerned a politician of the Welfare Party – in fact, he was a former prime minister of Turkey – who had openly incited hatred and hostility in the population based on religious, racial and regional distinctions during a speech at a rally in the mid-1990s (before the Welfare Party was abolished in Turkey). In light of the earlier *Refah Partisi* judgment, one would have expected that the criminal conviction of Erbakan, given the

77 ECtHR 13 February 2003 [GC], nos. 41340/98, 41342/98, 41343/98 and 41344/98, *Refah Partisi (the Welfare Party) and Others v. Turkey*, para. 123.

78 *Idem.*, para. 108.

79 ECtHR 6 July 2006, appl.no. 59405/00, *Erbakan v. Turkey*, para. 56.

nature of his speech and his expressed fierce support for the establishment of sharia in Turkey, would not violate Article 10. The Court judged differently. However, the main reasons for this conclusion of the Court laid in the peculiar circumstances of the case. The Court noted in particular that the authorities had not sought to establish the content of the speech in question until five years after the rally, and had done so purely on the basis of a video recording whose authenticity was disputed. Furthermore, it had not been established that at the time of his prosecution the speech in question had given rise to, or been likely to give rise to, a 'present risk' and an 'imminent danger.'[80] Lastly, the Court took into account the extremely severe sentence imposed.[81] Given these peculiar circumstances, the outcome of the *Erbakan* case might be labelled as 'one of a kind.'

Unprotected Speech under Article 17 of the ECHR

Although somewhat outside the field of terrorist-related expressions, it is noteworthy that, as a rule, the ECtHR will declare inadmissible, on grounds of incompatibility with the values of the Convention (by applying Article 17 of the ECHR), applications which are inspired by totalitarian doctrine or which express ideas that represent a threat to the democratic order and are liable to lead to the restoration of a totalitarian regime.[82] Expressions containing a general, vehement attack against a religious group, for instance by linking the group as a whole with a grave act of terrorism, or by denying it its existence as a nation, are also considered incompatible with the values proclaimed and guaranteed by the ECHR, notably tolerance, social peace and non-discrimination.[83] The same is true for expressions that contain any form of holocaust denial or negationism.[84] In *Orban and Others v. France*, the ECtHR noted that statements pursuing the unequivocal aim of justi-

80 *Idem.*, para. 68.

81 *Compare*, eg, ECtHR 8 June 2010, appl.no. 4870/02, *Gül and Others v. Turkey*, para. 43.

82 See, e.g. ECommHR 20 July 1957, appl.no. 250/57, *Communist Party of Germany v. the Federal Republic of Germany*; ECommHR 12 October 1989, appl.no. 12774/87, *B.H; M.W; H.P; G.K. v. Austria*; ECtHR 14 November 2006 (adm.dec.), appl.no. 32842/02, *Medya FM Reha Radyo ve Iletişim Hizmetleri A. Ş. v. Turkey*.

83 ECtHR 16 November 2004, appl.no. 23131/03, *Norwood v. the United Kingdom*. The applicant had displayed in his window a poster supplied by the British National Party, of which he was a member, representing the Twin Towers in flames. The picture was accompanied by the words 'Islam out of Britain – Protect the British People'. As a result, he was convicted of aggravated hostility towards a religious group. See also ECtHR 20 February 2007 (adm.dec.), appl.no. 35222/04, *Pavel Ivanov v. Russia* (concerning anti-semitism).

84 E.g., ECtHR 24 June 2003, appl.no. 65831/01, *Garaudy v. France*; ECtHR 2 September 2004, appl.no. 42264/98, *W.P. and Others v. Poland*; ECommHR 18 October 1995, appl.no. 25062/94, *Honsik v. Austria*; ECommHR 24 June 1996, appl.no. 31159/96, *Marais v. France*; ECtHR 13 December 2005 (adm. dec.), appl.no. 7485/03, *Witzsch v. Germany*. Denial of the Jewish holocaust seems to obtain a special status in the ECtHR's case law, since in the recent *Perinçek v. Switzerland* judgment (17 December 2013, appl.no. 27510/08), the Court found the criminal conviction of a Turkish man for disputing the genocidal character of the mass killings of Armenians by the Ottoman empire in violation of Art. 10.

fying war crimes such as torture or summary executions likewise amounted to deflecting Article 10 from its real purpose.[85]

The case of *Hizb Ut-Tahrir and Others v. Germany*[86] brings together both the aspect of transnational terrorism and religious extremism. It concerns the prohibition in Germany of the activities of an Islamic association, which advocated the overthrow of non-Islamic governments and the establishment of an Islamic Caliphate throughout the Muslim world. In particular, at least in the view of the German authorities, several publications and speeches of members of the association do deny the State of Israel's right to exist, and call for the violent destruction of this State and for the banishment and killing of its inhabitants. The German government *inter alia* argued that the ban was necessary in a democratic society in the interest of public security and public order, since 'public security within the meaning of the Convention (...) according to which human rights and fundamental freedoms constitute the basis of world peace, also include(s) international security and world peace' and '[p]ublic order in Germany also include(s) the special relationship with Israel.'[87] The government refers to its special commitment to the security of the State of Israel.[88] It would have been interesting to see how the Court would respond to this line of reasoning. The Court's decision, however, circumvents the need for this by declaring the application inadmissible as a form of abuse of rights under Article 17. Basically, the Court agrees with the German court's analysis of the texts published by the association and some of its prominent members, and concludes that the association 'attempts to deflect Article 11 of the Convention from its real purpose by employing this right for ends which are clearly contrary to the values of the Convention, notably the commitment to the peaceful settlement of international conflicts and to the sanctity of human life.'[89]

One should be cautious about translating these considerations to the context of the freedom of expression. After all, *Hizb Ut-Tahrir and Others* contains no indication that the association's members were prosecuted for any of the published texts or statements. However, it is difficult to understand that an organisation could be banned on the basis of the nature of its publications, without these publications themselves being illegal and not deserving the protection of Article 10.

Actually, the more recent judgment of the ECtHR in the case of *Kasymakhunov and Saybatalov v. Russia* gives a solid basis for this line of thought.[90] This case concerns Articles 7, 9 and 11, as well as Article 10. The applicants were two members of Hizb ut-Tahrir, who were arrested as members of an illegal organization, after the Supreme Court of the Russian

85 ECtHR 15 January 2005, appl.no. 20985/05, *Orban and Others v. France*, para. 35.
86 ECtHR 19 June 2012 (adm.dec.), appl.no. 36109/03, *Hizb Ut-Tahrir and Others v. Germany*.
87 *Idem.*, para. 64.
88 *Ibid.*
89 *Idem.*, para. 74.
90 ECtHR 14 March 2013, appl.nos. 26261/05 and 26377/06, *Kasymakhunov and Saybatalov v. Russia*.

Federation, on 13 February, 2013, found fifteen organisations, including Hizb ut-Tahrir, to be terrorist organizations and prohibited their activity in the territory of Russia. The applicants challenged their criminal convictions as a violation of the above indicated ECHR provisions.

The Court noted that both applicants were members of Hizb ut-Tahrir and were engaged in spreading its ideology by distributing its literature and recruiting new members. The court recalled that Hizb ut-Tahrir's aims were clearly contrary to the values of the Convention and considered the fact that, during the meetings held by the local section of Hizb ut-Tahrir, one of the applicants made statements calling for violence against Jews, while the other applicant urged new recruited members to fight the unfaithful with weapons.[91] Moreover, the Court refered to the findings of several experts who examined the leaflets and brochures distributed by the applicants. These experts were unanimous in finding that they contained statements calling for violence. Thus, the experts noted that Hizb ut-Tahrir's literature advocated and glorified warfare in the form of jihad, a term which was mainly used in its meaning of 'holy war,' to establish Islamic domination. Some of the documents in question also stated that it was permissible to kill any citizen of enemy States, among which were named, besides Israel, the United States of America, the United Kingdom, France and Russia.[92] Furthermore, the Court considered it significant that the experts also noted that, although Hizb ut-Tahrir clearly aspired to gain political power in order to overthrow non-Muslim governments and impose Islamic rule worldwide, it rejected any possibility of participating in the democratic political process:

> 'The terminology used in Hizb ut-Tahrir's literature to refer to the methods to be employed to gain political power was so ambiguous as to give cause to believe that recourse to violent methods was envisaged (...). It follows from the above that the means which Hizb ut-Tahrir plans to use in order to gain power and to promote a change in the legal and constitutional structures of the States where it is active cannot be regarded as legal and democratic.'[93]

Also, the Court observed that the changes in the legal and constitutional structures of the State proposed by Hizb ut-Tahrir were as such incompatible with the fundamental democratic principles underlying the Convention. Hizb ut-Tahrir proposed the establishment of a regime which rejects political freedoms, in particular freedom of religion, expression and association, declaring that they are contrary to Islam. They intended to

91 *Idem.*, para. 107.
92 *Ibid.*
93 *Idem.*, para. 108.

introduce capital punishment for apostasy from Islam and to ban all political parties which were not based on Islam. And this is not all:

> 'Furthermore, in its literature Hizb ut-Tahrir clearly states its intention to introduce a plurality of legal systems, that is, a distinction between individuals in all fields of private and public law, with different rights and freedoms afforded depending on religion. Thus, according to Hizb ut-Tahrir's Draft Constitution (…), only Muslims will have the right to vote and to be elected, to become State officials or to acquire membership of political parties. Different tax rules and family laws will be applicable to Muslims and to adherents of other religions. The Court has already found that such a system cannot be considered to be compatible with the Convention system because it undeniably infringes the principle of non-discrimination on the ground of religion (…). Similarly, some provisions of the Draft Constitution promote differences in treatment based on sex, for example providing that women cannot take up high-ranking official positions. These provisions are hard to reconcile with the principle of gender equality, which has been recognised by the Court as one of the key principles underlying the Convention and a goal to be achieved by member States of the Council of Europe. (…)
> [T]he Court observes that the regime that Hizb ut-Tahrir intends to set up will be based on sharia. However, it has previously found a regime based on sharia to be incompatible with the fundamental principles of democracy, particularly with regard to its criminal law and criminal procedure, its rules on the legal status of women and the way it intervenes in all spheres of private and public life in accordance with religious precepts. An organisation whose actions seem to be aimed at introducing sharia in a State Party to the Convention can hardly be regarded as complying with the democratic ideal that underlies the whole of the Convention.'[94]

Finally, the Court underlined that the activities of Hizb ut-Tahrir were not limited to promoting religious worship and observance, in accordance with the requirements of Islam, in the private sphere: 'They extend outside the sphere of individual conscience and concern the organization and functioning of society as a whole. Hizb ut-Tahrir clearly seeks to impose on everyone its religious symbols and conception of a society founded on religious precepts.' The conclusion of the Court was that the dissemination of the political ideas of Hizb ut-Tahrir by the applicants clearly constitutes an activity falling within the scope of Article 17 of the Convention:

94 *Idem.*, paras. 110-111.

> 'The applicants are essentially seeking to use Articles 9, 10 and 11 to provide a basis under the Convention for a right to engage in activities contrary to the text and spirit of the Convention. That right, if granted, would contribute to the destruction of the rights and freedoms set forth in the Convention and referred to above.'[95]

Glorification of Violence and Terrorism

The free speech judgment of the ECtHR that is most directly related to the 9/11 attacks is the case of *Leroy v. France*.[96] The applicant in this case was a cartoonist. One of his drawings representing the attack on the World Trade Centre was published in a Basque weekly newspaper on 13 September, 2011, with a caption which read: 'We have all dreamt of it... Hamas did it.'[97] Having been sentenced to payment of a fine for 'condoning terrorism,' the applicant argued that his freedom of expression had been infringed. The Court held that there had been no violation of Article 10. It argued that, through his work, the applicant glorified the violent destruction of American imperialism, expressed moral support for the perpetrators of the attacks, commented approvingly on the violence perpetrated against thousands of civilians, and diminished the dignity of the victims. Despite the newspaper's limited circulation, the Court observed that the drawing's publication had provoked a certain public reaction, capable of stirring up violence and of having a demonstrable impact on public order in the Basque Country.[98]

In *Leroy v. France* the ECtHR seemed to pay less attention to the fact that the expression had a kind of artistic-satirical form and was not circulated among a huge number of viewers or readers. As far as the legitimate aim for the prosecution of Leroy – and as such for the restriction of his freedom of expression – is concerned, the ECtHR still seeks the direct link between the publication and the disturbance of public order in the country concerned: The already tense situation in the Basque Country is a relevant element of the publication's context (although, on a critical note, I find it hard to see how a cartoon on a terrible but completely unrelated event in the US could re-inflame the violent strife for independence in the Basque region).

To my knowledge, only in one other case has the ECtHR labelled an expression as 'condoning terrorism' or an 'apology for terrorism.' This was the case of *Resul Tasdemir v. Turkey*, when the following slogan was shouted during a demonstration in Ankara: 'HPG (the armed wing of the PKK) to the front line in retaliation!'[99] Cases on this issue,

95 *Idem.*, para. 113.
96 ECtHR 2 October 2008, appl.no. 36109/03, *Leroy v. France*.
97 *Idem.*, para. 6.
98 *Idem.*, paras. 43-45.
99 ECtHR 23 February 2010, appl.no. 38841/07, *Resul Tasdemir v. Turkey*.

also in recent years, continue to be the result of the tense situation between the Turkish authorities and the PKK.[100]

The Imminence of Violence and the Potential to Seize Political Power

As far as free speech restricting measures are concerned – for those expressions that do not fall outside the scope of Article 10 protection because of their abusive nature in the sense of Article 17 – the ECtHR's case-law does not seem to differ much from the doctrine built on the Turkish cases at the end of the 1990's. That is, incitement to actual violence in the context of a region that suffers from an ongoing conflict or a politically tense situation remains the main justification for restrictions on the freedom of expression. With regard to advocating the establishment of a legal system based on religious norms that are not compatible with the ideals that underlie the whole of the ECHR, *Hizb Ut-Tahrir and Others* and *Kasymakhunov and Saybatalov v. Russia* indicate that such expression will not receive protection under the Convention. *Refah Partisi* and *Gündüz* seem to suggest, in this respect, that the potential to seize political power is a factor that influences the ECtHR's proportionality test. Regarding this aspect, a closer look at the recent *Vona v. Hungary* judgment is relevant. This judgment concerns the dissolution of an association and movement which was rallying against the Roma population in Hungary.[101] Therefore, the main ECHR Article at stake was Article 11 (freedom of association and assembly). However, the ECtHR acknowledged the close links to freedom of expression.[102] In this case, the Court recalls that a State does not have to wait until a political movement has had recourse to violence before intervening. Even if that political movement has not made an attempt to seize power, and the danger of its policy is not sufficiently imminent, a State is entitled to take preventive measures to protect democracy, as long as it is established that such a movement has started to take concrete steps in public life to implement a policy incompatible with the standards of the ECHR.[103] As it happened, the movement's activists had marched in villages wearing military-looking uniforms in a military-like formation, together with salutes and commands. Although the ECtHR admitted that 'ideas or conduct cannot be excluded from the protection provided by the Convention merely because they are capable of creating a feeling of uneasiness in groups of citizens or because some may perceive them as disrespectful,'[104] it nevertheless concluded that, in this case, the organizers

100 ECtHR 29 November 2011, appl.no. 43807/07, *Kılıç and Eren v. Turkey*; ECtHR 2 February 2012, appl.no 13304/03, *Savgin v. Turkey*, para. 45; ECtHR 17 December 2013, appl.no. 12606/11, *Yavuz et Yaylalı v. Turkey*, paras. 50-52. Compare ECtHR 22 April 2010, appl.no. 40984/07, *Fatullayev v. Azerbaijan*.

101 ECtHR 9 July 2013, appl.no. 35943/10, *Vona v. Hungary*.

102 *Idem.*, para. 53 and 63.

103 *Idem.*, para. 57.

104 *Idem.*, para. 63.

of the rallies had conveyed the message that they had the intention of using, and the resources to orchestrate, militarized force in order to achieve their aims.[105] Furthermore, the paramilitary formation had been reminiscent of the Hungarian Nazi movement (Arrow Cross), responsible for the mass extermination of Roma in Hungary. In the eyes of the ECtHR, the reliance of an association on paramilitary demonstrations expressing racial division and implicitly calling for race-based action must have had an intimidating effect on members of a racial minority, therefore exceeding the scope of protection under the Convention for freedom of expression or of assembly.[106]

Interestingly, the use of the paramilitary features and Nazi reminiscent symbols by the Hungarian movement did not cause the ECtHR to apply Article 17 in *Vona*. The Court notes:

> '[I]t has not been argued by the Government that the applicant expressed contempt for the victims of a totalitarian regime (…) or belonged to a group with totalitarian ambitions. Nor does the information contained in the case file support such a conclusion. The applicant was, at the material time, the chairman of a registered association. He complains about the dissolution of that association together with that of a movement which, in the domestic courts' view, constituted an entity within that association, essentially on account of a demonstration which had not been declared unlawful at the domestic level and did not lead to any act of violence. In these circumstances, the Court cannot conclude that the Association's activities were intended to justify or propagate an ideology of oppression serving "totalitarian groups".'[107]

The Court also pointed out that, since the main issue of the case concerned the freedom of association of Article 11, one should not simply copy the Article 17 standards developed in free speech cases and apply these outside this area.[108] In the earlier judgment of *Vajnai v. Hungary*, which was decided under Article 10, the Court already indicated that the use of old communist symbols by a left-wing association should not be seen as a form of contempt for the victims of the former communist regime or as a form of racist expression justifying the application of Article 17.[109]

105 *Idem.*, para. 65.
106 *Idem.*, paras. 66-70.
107 *Idem.*, para. 37.
108 *Ibid.*
109 ECtHR 8 July 2008, appl.no. 33629/06, *Vajnai v. Hungary*, paras. 24-26.

Legal Clarity, Foreseeability and Effectiveness: Legislative Struggles on the Issue of Criminalizing Terrorism-Related Speech

In paragraph 1, mention was made of the Council of Europe and European Union initiatives in the field of extreme speech and terrorism. I will focus here on Article 5 of the Council of Europe Convention on the Prevention of Terrorism,[110] which requires that the contracting parties adopt such measures as may be necessary to establish 'public provocation to commit terrorism' as a criminal offence under their domestic laws. According to Article 5, this phrase means:

> 'The distribution, or otherwise making available, of a message to the public, with the intent to incite the commission of a terrorist offence, where such conduct, whether or not directly advocating terrorist offences, causes a danger that one or more such offences may be committed.'

The main aim of the Convention was exactly to make this *indirect provocation* a criminal offence, thus remedying the existing lacunae in international law on this issue.[111] The explanatory report to the Convention states that states have a certain discretion in the formulation and implementation of the offence: 'For instance, presenting a terrorist offence as necessary and justified may constitute the offence of indirect incitement.'[112] However, the report describes some factors limiting the scope of this indirect incitement: (1) There has to be a specific intent to incite the commission of a terrorist offence; (2) the provocation shall be committed unlawfully and intentionally; (3) it shall cause a danger that such an offence might be committed.[113] Furthermore, the report also refers to the ECtHR:

> 'When considering whether such danger is caused, the nature of the author and of the addressee of the message, as well as the context in which the offence is committed shall be taken into account in the sense established by the case-law of the European Court of Human Rights. The significance and the credible nature of the danger should be considered when applying this provision in accordance with the requirements of domestic law.'[114]

110 *See* Van Noorloos 2012 (*supra* note 12), p. 133-135 for some important comments on the 2008 amendments to the EU Framework Decision on Combating Terrorism.
111 Council of Europe Convention on the Prevention of Terrorism – Explanatory Report, para. 10, 18 and 97.
112 *Idem.*, para. 98.
113 *Idem.*, paras. 99-100.
114 Idem., 100.

Several authors have criticized the nevertheless wide scope of Article 5.[115]

In the United Kingdom, Article 5 of the Council of Europe Convention was implemented by several provisions in the Terrorism Act 2006. Section 1(1) of this Act creates the offence of 'direct or indirect encouragement or other inducement (...) to the commission, preparation or instigation of acts of terrorism.' In order to commit this offence, one does not need to have a specific intent to direct or indirect encouragement, recklessness as to whether members of the public will be directly or indirectly encouraged or otherwise does suffice.[116] Also, statements that 'are likely to be understood by members of the public as indirectly encouraging the commission or preparation of acts of terrorism' include every statement which 'glorifies the commission or preparation (whether in the past, in the future or generally) of such acts or offences.'[117] Section 20 of the Act explains that glorification includes 'any form of praise or celebration.'

In the passage through Parliament, the glorification of terrorism offence was one of the most contentious clauses of the Terrorism Act 2006. Taking as a standard the ECHR requirements of legal clarity and foreseeability (see paragraph 2), the Joint Committee on Human Rights argued 'terms such as glorification, praise and celebration are too vague to form part of a criminal offence.'[118] One critical commentator expressly focused on foreseeability-type difficulties concerning expressions on the Internet:

> 'In particular, clause 1 does not specify which "members of the public" would be "likely to understand" the statement as incitement. If a statement were published to 1 million people, therefore, it would be an offence within the meaning of clause 1(1)(b) if the publisher were aware that one or two mentally unstable readers might regard it as "direct or indirect encouragement" to terrorism.
>
> If a statement were published on the Internet, it would conceivably be available to anyone in the world with a computer. In such circumstances, it would therefore become a criminal offence under clause 1 for a person to publish even the most innocent statement so long as he or she reasonably believes or "has reasonable grounds to believe" that anyone in the world, no matter how unreasonable their interpretation, may regard it as incitement. (...) [S]omeone in the UK (...) would be liable for prosecution to the extent that statements which they make on the Internet (whether through their home pages or posting

115 J.P. Loof, 'Terrorismebestrijding, de Raad van Europa en het EVRM', in: E. van Dongen e.a. (Eds.), *Terrorismebestrijding met mensenrechten*, Leiden: NJCM-Boekerij 2005, p. 51-73; A. Hunt, 'The Council of Europe Convention on the Prevention of Terrorism', *European Public Law* 2006, vol. 12, no. 4, p. 603-628, at p. 622; Van Noorloos 2012 (*supra* note 12), p. 132.

116 Section 1(2) Terrorism Act 2006.

117 Section 1(3) Terrorism Act 2006.

118 Session 2005-2006, HL 75-I HC 561-I at p. 27-28.

> to message boards) might be thought to encourage any person in any country with access to the Internet to commit an act of terrorism> Someone making a comment on the Internet in the UK would therefore be liable for the effect of their remarks on readers reasonable and unreasonable alike in such places as Afghanistan, Chechnya, Iraq or the West Bank.'[119]

Many other commentators argued that the requirement to show intent would be an essential safeguard against the manifest injustice of punishing a person for what others unreasonably understood him to mean.[120]

The above may serve as an indication of the definition problems the legislature faces when it comes to criminalizing terrorism-related expressions. Another issue under the limitation clause of Article 10 of the ECHR might be the effectiveness of the interference with freedom of expression. Can a restricting measure that is ineffective in achieving the legitimate aim fulfil the proportionality requirement? Basically, the aim of legal measures like the prohibition of glorification of terrorism is to prevent the creation of an environment in which people with radical ideas might come to believe that terrorist acts are acceptable. Do these kind of measures help in securing this aim?

Several experts in the field of counterterrorism argue that banning radical speech that does not go accompanied by violent inclinations is not productive: The repression as a result of the legislation might become a source of radicalization or allow detainees to be seen as heroes or martyrs to their cause.[121] There is even a real danger that criminalizing the expression of support for terrorism will drive such beliefs underground. Saul states, 'rather than exposing them to public debate – which allows erroneous or misconceived ideas to be corrected and ventilates their poison – criminalizing risks aggravating the grievances often underlying terrorism, and thus increasing, not reducing, its likelihood.'[122] Censorship of radical speech may also be counterproductive in that it adds to stigmatization

119 I. Awan, 'The Problem with Defining Terrorism and the Impact on Civil Liberties – Britain is Beginning to Create a Monster with Large Claws, Sharp Teeth and a Fierce Temper?', *CCSE Journal of Politics and Law*, Vol. 1, No 2, June 2008, p. 8.

120 E.g., Article 19, *The Impact of UK Anti-Terror Laws on Freedom of Expression. Submission to ICJ Panel of Eminent Jurists on Terrorism, Counter-Terrorism and Human Rights*, London, April 2006, p. 7-8.

121 International Peace Institute, *Combating Incitement of Terrorism and Promoting Intercultural Dialogue*, Expert Meeting Report of October 2010, p. 2.

122 Ben Saul, 'Speaking of terror: Criminalising incitement to violence', *UNSW Law Journal*, Volume 28 (3), pp. 868-886, at p. 885. *Compare*, S. Moskalenko & C. McCauley, 'Measuring political mobilization: the distinction between activism and radicalism', *Terrorism and political violence* 2009, vol. 21, no. 2, p. 257. Bibi van Ginkel, *Incitement to Terrorism: A Matter of Prevention or Repression?*, ICCT Research Paper, August 2011, www.icct.nl/download/file/ICCT-Van-Ginkel-Incitement-To-Terrorism-August-2011.pdf, contains a load of references to further literature on this issue.

of the groups concerned, which may cause increasing tension between parts of the population.[123]

Given these doubts as to the effectiveness of broad restrictions on freedom of expression as a type of counterterrorist measure, one might argue that they do not seem to meet the 'relevant and sufficient' requirement and the proportionality test under the second paragraph of Article 10 of the ECHR.

CONCLUSIONS

It is established ECtHR case-law that freedom of expression constitutes one of the essential foundations of a democratic society and one of the basic conditions for its progress and for each individual's self-fulfillment. The freedom of expression does not only protect 'information' or 'ideas' that are favorably received or regarded as inoffensive or as a matter of indifference, but also to those that 'offend, shock or disturb' because – in the words of the Court – '[s]uch are the demands of pluralism, tolerance and broadmindedness without which there is no 'democratic society.' Any interference with this freedom must be construed strictly, and the need for any restrictions must be established convincingly. Furthermore, interferences should be prescribed by law (in accessible and foreseeable legislation), pursue a legitimate aim and be necessary (in order to counter a pressing social need). The Contracting States have a certain margin of appreciation in assessing whether such a need exists, but it goes hand in hand with European supervision, embracing both the legislation and the decisions applying it, even those given by an independent court. In exercising its supervisory jurisdiction, the Court looks at the interference in the light of the case as a whole, including the content of the impugned work and the context in which it was published. In particular, it must determine whether the measure in issue was 'proportionate to the legitimate aims pursued' and whether the reasons adduced by the national authorities to justify it were 'relevant and sufficient.' In doing so, the Court has to satisfy itself that the national authorities applied standards which were in conformity with the principles embodied in Article 10 and, moreover, that they based themselves on an acceptable assessment of the relevant facts. However, as far as the necessity and proportionality of a speech restricting measure is concerned, the state parties do have a wide margin of appreciation.

There is little scope under Article 10(2) to restrict political speech or debate on matters of public interest. Nevertheless, the Court has accepted the restriction of expressions that can be characterized as hate speech or (direct or indirect) incitement to violence. Expressions that incite violence against individual government officials, against the government

123 T. Choudhury, 'The Terrorism Act 2006: Discouraging terrorism', in: I. Hare & J. Weinstein, *Extreme speech and democracy*, New York: Oxford University Press 2009, p. 463-487.

machinery as a whole or against other citizens, have consequences for the *margin of appreciation* to which a state is entitled in reviewing the necessity and proportionality of any interference with the right to freedom of expression. When an inciting statement identifies persons by name, stirs up hatred for them and exposes them to the possible risk of physical violence, or stigmatizes the other side of a certain conflict, the suppression of such speech will easily satisfy the democratic necessity test. On the other hand, the ECtHR requires 'evidence of any concrete action' before characterizing an expression as incitement to terrorism or violence. Besides the words or images used in an expression, some contextual factors are important: The personal stature of the author (public figure or not), the size of the audience (mass media or not), the form of the expression (artistic or not) and, last but not least, the sensitive security situation in a certain region (since this makes actual violence a more likely consequence of extremist speech). Another relevant factor is whether or not the measures have a preventive character: Prior censorship is not lightly judged as justified. This may, however, depend on the form of publication. Restrictive measures relating to press publications will be not be as easily accepted as those relating to television and radio broadcasts.

The ECtHR does not consider prosecution for the offence of glorification of (or apology of) terrorism incompatible with Article 10 of the ECHR, although the cases so far each time concerned publications in politically tense regions, where actual terrorist attacks were not uncommon. The link between the publication and the potential consequences, however, does not need to be a strong or direct one, nor does the author have to show a clear intent to incite. The Court's approach to glorification of terrorism does not take away from the fact that drafting legislation on such an offence is a strenuous job, given the requirements of legal certainty and foreseeability. Furthermore, the effectiveness of such a restrictive measures in achieving the aim of preventing further radicalization of certain individuals, and establishing a climate in which terrorist acts become a possibility, is highly disputed among counterterrorism experts.

The most difficult element in the analysis of the ECtHR's case-law on terrorism-related speech is the issue of religious extremism. The 2004 *Gündüz* case seems to indicate that expressions denying the value of democracy and fierce calls for the establishment of sharia law can receive protection under Article 10 as long as these expressions are coming from a single individual without the potential to seize political power (i.e. *Refah Partisi*). In some more recent cases, the ECtHR seems to have made somewhat of a shift on this issue. *Vona* suggests that earlier interventions against a (political) movement are allowed, even if no attempt to seize power has been made, as long as it is established that such a movement has started to take concrete steps in public life to implement a policy incompatible with the standards of the ECHR. And *Hizb Ut-Tahrir and Others* and *Kasymakhunov and Saybatalov v. Russia* contain even stronger indications that advocating the establishment of a legal system based on religious norms that are not compatible with the ideals that underlie the whole of the ECHR will not receive protection under the ECHR. The distinguishing features between the *Gündüz* case on the one hand and *Hizb Ut-Tahrir and Others* and *Kasymakhunov and Saybatalov v. Russia* on the other might be that in the latter two cases, the expressions were used by persons representing an organization that had some kind of plan to gain political power, and did not only advocate a legal system incompatible with the ECHR ideals, but also contained calls for the violent destruction of Israel and for a 'holy war' against some other states. So after all, the element of incitement to violence seems to be the one triggering the application of Article 17 in order to exclude protection under article 10.

Does this mean that the dimension of religious extremism has not caused a major shift in the ECtHR's approach to terrorism-related speech in the past decade? I indeed think that the recent case-law ultimately does not show a very different approach than the doctrine which was built on the earlier Turkish cases. The only difference that the aspect of religious extremism seems to cause is that the ECtHR is not inclined to do the balancing test under Article 10(2). It rather declines ECHR protection altogether, thus making room for restricting measures by states against this type of expression somewhat bigger.

11 The Civilizational Limitation of Freedom of Speech

Ambrogino G. Awesta

Introduction

In 1993, Samuel P. Huntington introduced 'The Clash of Civilizations' thesis. According to this thesis, the fundamental source of conflict that would dominate this new epoch, as the latest phase in the evolution of conflict in the modern world (i.e. the post-Cold War era) would be primarily cultural rather than economic or ideological. In this regard, he explains that 'civilizations are differentiated from each other by history, language, culture, tradition and, most important, religion.'[1] Furthermore, he contends that this clash of civilizations would take place at two different levels: The *micro*-level and the *macro*-level. The focus of his theory is, however, on the macro-level, at which '[...] states from different civilizations compete for relative military and economic power, struggle over the control of international institutions and third parties, and competitively promote their particular political and religious values.'[2] However, what remains unanswered is the question concerning the consequence of this development on, for instance, fundamental rights and freedoms. It must be granted, however, that he does briefly touch upon this issue by stating that the 'Western efforts to propagate such ideas [like fundamental rights] produce instead a reaction against "human rights imperialism" and a reaffirmation of indigenous values, as can be seen in the support for religious fundamentalism by the younger generation in non-Western cultures.'[3]

Accordingly, the present article aims to conduct a case study regarding the macro-level at which the clash of civilizations – with religion at its core – has imperiled fundamental rights and freedoms. However, for the sake of surveyability, the scope of this study has been narrowed down to the fundamental right to freedom of speech, which is, more than any other right, existentially endangered and constrained by the civilizational clashes. Henceforth, an attempt will be made to determine the extent of this perilous limitation that is imposed on this fundamental right.

1 Samuel P Huntington and others, *The Clash of Civilizations? The Debate* (Foreign Affairs, New York 1996) 4.
2 Ibid 7.
3 Ibid 17.

Legal Limits of the Freedom of Speech at the International Level

The foregoing takes away nothing from the fact that the existentially imperiled right of freedom of speech is not of an absolute nature, which means that it can be confined by means of limitations that are prescribed by law and are considered to be necessary for the realization of legitimate aims. One of the prime means that can constrain this right is the principle of non-discrimination, which can be based on various grounds. One of the grounds on the basis of which discrimination is prohibited is 'religion' in the broadest sense of the term, which, however, is not independently codified in a distinct legal instrument. This ground is merely formulated as a right among other rights that, in the case of collision with the right to freedom of expression, can impose a limitation on this latter right. The provisions on the right to freedom of religion protect the individual as the sole bearer of this right in both its internal and external dimension, which may be respectively designated as '*forum internum*' and '*forum externum*.'[4] This means that protection is provided to the religious person and not to religion as such.

Nevertheless, as we will elaborate further, in recent years, and by means of defamation laws, an attempt has been made to extend the scope of protection beyond the bearer of this right so that protection would also be provided to the objects and symbols of religion. This extension may be said to come down to the broadening of the ambit of the external dimension of religion, for not only the mere expression of religious conviction is covered, but also the means through which such a conviction is manifested. Such a manifestation can adopt the following forms: '(a) To worship or assemble in connection with a religion or belief, and to establish and maintain places for these purposes; (b) To establish and maintain appropriate charitable or humanitarian institutions; (c) To make, acquire and use to an adequate extent the necessary articles and materials related to the rites or customs of a religion or belief; (d) To write, issue and disseminate relevant publications in these areas; (e) To teach a religion or belief in places suitable for these purposes; (f) To solicit and receive voluntary financial and other contributions from individuals and institutions; (g) To train, appoint, elect or designate by succession appropriate leaders called for by the requirements and standards of any religion or belief; (h) To observe days of rest and to celebrate holidays and ceremonies in accordance with the precepts of one's religion or belief; (i) To establish and maintain communications with individuals and communities

4 The freedom of religion as contained in Article 18 of the ICCPR is, in principle, a non-derogable right, even in time of public emergency, as it is prescribed in Article 4(2) of the ICCPR and re-emphasized in the General Comment No.22 and 29. The permissibility of restrictions is, however, independent from the issue of derogability and must be justified on the basis of paragraph 3 of Article 18 ICCPR. It is imperative to note that only the *manifestation* of a religion or belief may be subjected to limitations since, according to Article 20 of the ICCPR and General Comment 11, 19, and 22, no manifestation of religion or belief may amount to, among others, discrimination, violence or hostility. Thus, not the '*forum internum*' of religion may be limited, but only its '*forum externum*'.

in matters of religion and belief at the national and international levels.' It goes without saying that the endeavor to extend this scope will have the consequence that not only the individual as the bearer of this right will be protected but also 'religion' as such – encompassing doctrines and symbols of veneration – will gain protection, with possible implication(s) for other fundamental rights in general and the right to freedom of expression in particular.[5]

As regards the limitations on fundamental rights and freedoms, particularly the right to freedom of expression, it can be observed that the competence for practicing this right has always been negatively defined. This negative formulation implies that the enjoyment of rights can take place only when governmental interference is minimized and the government is forced to refrain from any (arbitrary) involvement in the exercise of fundamental rights by its citizens. On the contrary, fundamental rights have also been conceived as containing a positive obligation which encompasses not only the active involvement of the government in respecting, protecting and fostering such rights in the conduct of its own functions, it '[...] also requires States parties to ensure that persons are protected from any acts by private persons or entities that would impair the enjoyment of [such rights, particularly] the freedoms of opinion and expression to the extent that these Covenant rights are amenable to application between private persons or entities.'[6] The latter is especially interesting in light of contemporary developments, whereby the fundamental right to freedom of expression is jeopardized not only by the state itself, but also by other actors, which Paul Cliteur rightly brings to attention by stating that 'since 1989 the world has become acquainted with a new situation concerning the notion of the freedom of speech. Prior to that time, the most important restriction of this freedom was formed by the *legislation* of the nation-states. After that time, there have also been organized and unorganized *violent networks and individuals* that constrain an effective exercise of the freedom of speech.'[7]

Notwithstanding this development regarding the extrajudicial confinement of this fundamental right, the official parties involved put the emphasis on the classical limitations imposed by the state, which is also seen in the legal history of this provision.[8] Accordingly,

5 Article 6 of the Declaration on the Elimination of All Forms of Intolerance and of Discrimination Based on Religion or Belief.

6 ICCPR General Comment No. 34, and 31; See also *Gauthier v Canada*, Communication No. 633/1995.

7 Afshin Ellian, Gelijn Molier and Tom Zwart (Eds.), *Mag Ik Dit Zeggen? Beschouwingen over de Vrijheid van Meningsuiting* (Boom Juridische uitgevers, The Hague 2011) 67 [own translation].

8 "The first drafts of the article contained [already] a clause to the effect that every person should have the right to freedom of opinion and expression without interference by governmental action. [...] As originally proposed, the phrase 'without interference' was followed by the phrase 'by governmental action'. There were [however] two views regarding this point. One was that the article was intended to protect the individual only against governmental interference [...]. The other view was that the article should protect the individual against all kinds of interference [...]." in Marc J Bossuyt, *Guide to the "travaux préparatoires" of the International Covenant on Civil and Political Rights* (Martinus Nijhoff Publishers, Dordrecht 1987) 378-379.

the Special Rapporteur on this fundamental right '[...] notes that the question of non-State actors has been traditionally defined as relating to the duty of States to exercise due diligence and to ensure that individuals and collective private entities respect the law and do not abuse or infringe upon the rights of others. The Special Rapporteur accepts that primary attention must continue to be focused on the commissions and omissions of governments which lead to violations of fundamental rights. At the same time, however, he cannot remain indifferent to the fact that, with regard to the rights that are the subject of this mandate, an increasing number of actions by non-State individuals and entities have a marked and severely negative impact on the enjoyment of those rights by others.'[9] This reasoning makes clear that, whereas the existence of menace stemming from non-state actors is undeniable, nonetheless, no serious attention is paid to this perilous phenomenon while, for example, Article 5(1) of the ICCPR explicitly emphasizes that 'nothing in the present Covenant may be interpreted as implying for any State [but also] group or person any right to engage in any activity or perform any act aimed at the destruction of any of the rights and freedoms recognized herein or at their limitation to a greater extent than is provided for in the present Covenant.'[10]

Still, the current extrajudicial curtailment of this fundamental right takes place because certain individuals and groups in society tend to be offended by utterances about their religion, whereas the right to freedom of expression encompasses also expressions that may be regarded as deeply offensive,[11]as long as the exercise of this right meets the legal conditions enumerated in Article 19(3) and the limitations elucidated in Article 20[12] of the ICCPR; notwithstanding, the exercise of this right carries with it 'special duties and responsibilities.' This implies that while expressions may be offensive, robust and critical vis-à-vis religious doctrines and practice, even in a harsh manner,[13] they need, nevertheless, not amount to advocacy of hatred that would constitute incitement to discrimination, hostility or violence.[14] As long as this is not the case, as Principle 12(3) of the Camden

9 UNCHR 'Civil and Political Rights, Including the Question of Freedom of Expression: Report of the Special Rapporteur on the promotion and protection of the right to freedom of opinion and expression' (13 February 2001) UN Doc E/CN.4/2001/64.

10 ICCPR General Comment No. 34, *Velichkin v Belarus*, Communication No. 1022/2001. The same is reiterated in Article 5 of the ICESCR [emphasis added].

11 *Ross v Canada* Communication No.736/1997 rendered on 18 October 2000.

12 Article 20 ICCPR reads as follows: "*1. Any propaganda for war shall be prohibited by law. 2. Any advocacy of national, racial or religious hatred that constitutes incitement to discrimination, hostility or violence shall be prohibited by law*". ICCPR General Comment No. 11.

13 UNCHR 'Report of the Special Rapporteur on the Promotion and protection of the right to freedom of opinion and expression' (2012) UN Doc A/67/357.

14 As the Camden Principles on Freedom of Expression and Equality defines in Principle 12: "The term 'hatred' and 'hostility' refer to intense and irrational emotions of opprobrium, enmity and detestation towards the target group. The term 'advocacy' is to be understood as requiring an intention to promote hatred publicly towards the target group. The term 'incitement' refers to statements about national, racial or religious groups

Principles on Freedom of Expression and Equality provides, 'states should not prohibit criticism directed at, or debate about, particular ideas, beliefs or ideologies, or religions or religious institutions.'

Freedom of Speech versus Defamation of Religion

That being said, since 1999, the concept of 'defamation of religion' has been pushed forward within the UN framework by mainly, if not solely, the Organization of the Islamic Conference.[15] Later that year, the Economic and Social Council applauded its addressal within the context of 'the United Nations Year of Dialogue among Civilizations.'[16] With this concept, an attempt is made to effectively combat defamation of religions and cultures as a means of promoting human rights, social harmony, religious and cultural diversity[17] – considered to be a cherished asset for the advancement and welfare of humanity at large[18] – in order to improve, among other things, awareness and understanding of the common values shared by all humankind,[19] and to use 'religious and cultural diversity in a globalized

---

which create an imminent risk of discrimination, hostility or violence against persons belonging to those groups". UNCHR Res 23 (1999) UN Doc E/CN.4/1999/167.

15 This idea was, for the first time, fostered by the Organization of the Islamic Conference by means of a draft resolution submitted by Pakistan to the UN Commission on Human Rights in 1999; UNCHR 'Racism, Racial Discrimination, Xenophobia and all Forms of Discrimination' (20 April 1999) UN Doc E/CN.4/1999/L.40. For further information see Austin Dacey, *The Future of Blasphemy: Speaking of the sacred in an age of human rights* (Continuum, London 2012).

16 UNCHR Res 23 (1999) UN Doc E/CN.4/1999/167, UNCHR Res 84 (2000) UN Doc E/CN.4/RES/2000/84. UNCHR Res 4 (2001) UN Doc E/CN.4/RES/2001/4, UNCHR Res 9 (2002) UN Doc E/CN.4/RES/2002/9, The purpose of this is formulated as follows: "that religious and cultural diversity in the globalizing world needs to be used as a vehicle for complementary creativity and dynamism and not as a rationale for a new ideological and political confrontation" in UNCHR Res 4 (2003) UN Doc E/CN.4/RES/2003/4, UNCHR Res 6 (2004) UN Doc E/CN.4/RES/2004/6, UNCHR Res 3 (2005) UN Doc E/CN.4/RES/2005/3, UNGA Res 60/150 (20 January 2006) UN Doc A/RES/60/150, UNGA Res 64/156 (8 March 2010) UN Doc A/RES/64/156.

17 UNCHR Res 4 (2001) UN Doc E/CN.4/RES/2001/4, UNCHR Res 9 (2002) UN Doc E/CN.4/RES/2002/9, UNCHR Res 4 (2003) UN Doc E/CN.4/RES/2003/4, UNGA Res 60/150 (20 January 2006) UN Doc A/RES/60/150. Later on, also ethnic and linguistic diversity is added to this list. See UNGA Res 63/171 (24 March 2009) UN Doc A/RES/63/171, Human Rights Council Res 10/22, 'Combating defamation of religions' (26 March 2009) UN Doc A/HRC/RES/10/22, UNGA Res 64/156 (8 March 2010) UN Doc A/RES/64/156.

18 UNGA Res 60/150 (20 January 2006) UN Doc A/RES/60/150.

19 UNCHR Res 9 (2002) UN Doc E/CN.4/RES/2002/9, UNCHR Res 4 (2003) UN Doc E/CN.4/RES/2003/4, UNCHR Res 3 (2005) UN Doc E/CN.4/RES/2005/3, UNGA Res 61/164 (21 February 2007) UN Doc A/RES/61/164, Human Rights Council Res 4/9, 'Combating defamation of religions' (30 March 2007) UN Doc A/HRC/RES/4/9, UNGA Res 62/154 (6 March 2008) UN Doc A/RES/62/154, Human Rights Council Res 7/19, 'Combating defamation of religions' (27 March 2008) UN Doc A/HRC/RES/7/19, UNGA Res 63/171 (24 March 2009) UN Doc A/RES/63/171, Human Rights Council Res 10/22, 'Combating defamation of religions' (26 March 2009) UN Doc A/HRC/RES/10/22, UNGA Res 64/156 (8 March 2010) UN Doc A/RES/64/156. The question remains as to what these common values, that are held to be shared by all humankind, amount to.

world as a vehicle for complementary creativity and dynamism, and not as a rationale for a new ideological and political confrontation.'[20] This discourse on the defamation of religion started with the recognition that hatred, intolerance, acts of (psychological and physical) violence and discrimination *against human beings* on the grounds of religion or belief constitute an affront and offense to human dignity, a disavowal of the principles of the Charter of the United Nations,[21] and a violation and illicit restriction of human rights and fundamental freedoms.[22] In this regard, states had been summoned to counter intolerance and related violence based on religion or belief[23] by taking the necessary measures, since it had been considered imperative to create conditions for fostering and encouraging greater harmony, peace, social justice, and tolerance within and among societies – through, among other things, interreligious and intercultural dialogue.[24] The aim of this is to promote mutual understanding and appreciation of religious and cultural diversity and values,[25] to ensure *tolerance of and [universal] respect for religion and belief* and their value systems, and, in the same context, to combat attacks on *religious places, [sites, shrines, symbols, and venerated personalities]*.[26] Henceforth, we see the shift in protection from persons to ide-

20 UNCHR Res 6 (2004) UN Doc E/CN.4/RES/2004/6, UNCHR Res 3 (2005) UN Doc E/CN.4/RES/2005/3.

21 UNCHR Res 23 (1999) UN Doc E/CN.4/1999/167, UNCHR Res 84 (2000) UN Doc E/CN.4/RES/2000/84, UNCHR Res 9 (2002) UN Doc E/CN.4/RES/2002/9, UNCHR Res 4 (2003) UN Doc E/CN.4/RES/2003/4, UNCHR Res 6 (2004) UN Doc E/CN.4/RES/2004/6, UNCHR Res 3 (2005) UN Doc E/CN.4/RES/2005/3, UNGA Res 60/150 (20 January 2006) UN Doc A/RES/60/150, Human Rights Council Dec 1/107, 'Incitement to racial and religious hatred and the promotion of tolerance', (30 June 2006) UN Doc A/HRC/DEC/1/107, UNGA Res 61/164 (21 February 2007) UN Doc A/RES/61/164, UNGA Res 62/154 (6 March 2008) UN Doc A/RES/62/154, Human Rights Council Res 7/19, 'Combating defamation of religions' (27 March 2008) UN Doc A/HRC/RES/7/19, UNGA Res 63/171 (24 March 2009) UN Doc A/RES/63/171, Human Rights Council Res 10/22, 'Combating defamation of religions' (26 March 2009) UN Doc A/HRC/RES/10/22, UNGA Res 64/156 (8 March 2010) UN Doc A/RES/64/156.

22 UNCHR Res 4 (2001) UN Doc E/CN.4/RES/2001/4, UNGA Res 63/171 (24 March 2009) UN Doc A/RES/63/171 [emphasis added].

23 UNCHR Res 23 (1999) UN Doc E/CN.4/1999/167.

24 Human Rights Council Res 4/9, 'Combating defamation of religions' (30 March 2007) UN Doc A/HRC/RES/4/9, Human Rights Council Res 7/19, 'Combating defamation of religions' (27 March 2008) UN Doc A/HRC/RES/7/19.

25 UNCHR Res 4 (2001) UN Doc E/CN.4/RES/2001/4, UNCHR Res 9 (2002) UN Doc E/CN.4/RES/2002/9, UNCHR Res 4 (2003) UN Doc E/CN.4/RES/2003/4, UNCHR Res 6 (2004) UN Doc E/CN.4/RES/2004/6, UNCHR Res 3 (2005) UN Doc E/CN.4/RES/2005/3, UNGA Res 61/164 (21 February 2007) UN Doc A/RES/61/164, Human Rights Council Res 4/9, 'Combating defamation of religions' (30 March 2007) UN Doc A/HRC/RES/4/9, UNGA Res 62/154 (6 March 2008) UN Doc A/RES/62/154, Human Rights Council Res 7/19, 'Combating defamation of religions' (27 March 2008) UN Doc A/HRC/RES/7/19, UNGA Res 63/171 (24 March 2009) UN Doc A/RES/63/171, UNGA Res 64/156 (8 March 2010) UN Doc A/RES/64/156.

26 UNCHR Res 23 (1999) UN Doc E/CN.4/1999/167, UNCHR Res 84 (2000) UN Doc E/CN.4/RES/2000/84, UNCHR Res 4 (2001) UN Doc E/CN.4/RES/2001/4, UNCHR Res 9 (2002) UN Doc E/CN.4/RES/2002/9, UNCHR Res 4 (2003) UN Doc E/CN.4/RES/2003/4, UNCHR Res 6 (2004) UN Doc E/CN.4/RES/2004/6, UNCHR Res 3 (2005) UN Doc E/CN.4/RES/2005/3, UNGA Res 61/164 (21 February 2007) UN Doc A/RES/61/164. Later, also sites, shrines and symbols are added to this list which have to be both respected and protected, especially when they are vulnerable to desecration or destruction. See UNGA Res 63/171 (24 March 2009) UN Doc A/RES/63/171. In addition, in the following resolution also 'venerated personalities'

ologies in the broadest sense of the term, which is still contradictory to the very essence of human rights. Yet, in this endeavor, deep concern is expressed regarding the negative stereotyping of religions and the intensification of the campaign to defame religions[27], particularly Islam, by arguing that Islam[28] is frequently and wrongly associated with violence, human rights infringements and terrorism,[29] particularly by political parties and associations that incite acts of violence, cultural prejudice,[30] xenophobia (Islamophobia) or related intolerance and discrimination towards Islam and any other religion,[31] or proclaim and promote ideological superiority and racist ideologies.[32] It thus goes without saying that this shift in approach from protection of the human person to the protection of ideology in the broadest sense of the term has led to the fact that instead of persons, ideologies (including their value systems and institutions) are now being protected. This idea of 'defamation of religion requires the state [and finally the judiciary] to determine which ideas are acceptable, as opposed to which facts are true. A fundamental rule of law problem presents itself in the notion of 'defamation of religion,' inasmuch as belief cannot be empirically proven true'[33] which makes the arbitrary usage of such laws by the state more probable, while our contemporary multicivilizational world affair, which is being enhanced by globalization, is prone to impose further limitations on the freedom of

are included: Human Rights Council Res 10/22, 'Combating defamation of religions' (26 March 2009) UN Doc A/HRC/RES/10/22, UNGA Res 64/156 (8 March 2010) UN Doc A/RES/64/156.

27 UNCHR Res 4 (2003) UN Doc E/CN.4/RES/2003/4.

28 UNCHR Res 4 (2003) UN Doc E/CN.4/RES/2003/4, UNGA Res 62/154 (6 March 2008) UN Doc A/RES/62/154, Human Rights Council Res 10/22, 'Combating defamation of religions' (26 March 2009) UN Doc A/HRC/RES/10/22.

29 The fact that emphasis is merely put on Islam is apparent from the following example whereby the Commission on Human Rights "*alarmed* at the impact of the events of 11 September 2001 on Muslim minorities and communities in some non-Muslim countries and the negative projection of Islam, Muslim values and traditions by the media, as well as at the introduction and enforcement of laws that specifically discriminate against and target Muslims" in UNCHR Res 9 (2002) UN Doc E/CN.4/RES/2002/9, UNCHR Res 4 (2003) UN Doc E/CN.4/RES/2003/4, UNCHR Res 6 (2004) UN Doc E/CN.4/RES/2004/6, UNCHR Res 3 (2005) UN Doc E/CN.4/RES/2005/3, UNGA Res 60/150 (20 January 2006) UN Doc A/RES/60/150, Human Rights Council Res 4/9, 'Combating defamation of religions' (30 March 2007) UN Doc A/HRC/RES/4/9, UNGA Res 62/154 (6 March 2008) UN Doc A/RES/62/154, Human Rights Council Res 7/19, 'Combating defamation of religions' (27 March 2008) UN Doc A/HRC/RES/7/19. It is asserted that terrorism is not to be associated with any religion, nationality, civilization or ethnic group. See UNGA Res 63/171 (24 March 2009) UN Doc A/RES/63/171, Human Rights Council Res 10/22, 'Combating defamation of religions' (26 March 2009) UN Doc A/HRC/RES/10/22, UNGA Res 64/156 (8 March 2010) UN Doc A/RES/64/156, UNGA Res 65/224 (11 April 2011) UN Doc A/RES/65/224.

30 UNGA Res 63/171 (24 March 2009) UN Doc A/RES/63/171.

31 UNCHR Res 23 (1999) UN Doc E/CN.4/1999/167, UNCHR Res 84 (2000) UN Doc E/CN.4/RES/2000/84, UNCHR Res 4 (2001) UN Doc E/CN.4/RES/2001/4, Human Rights Council Res 4/9, 'Combating defamation of religions' (30 March 2007) UN Doc A/HRC/RES/4/9, UNGA Res 62/154 (6 March 2008) UN Doc A/RES/62/154, Human Rights Council Res 7/19, 'Combating defamation of religions' (27 March 2008) UN Doc A/HRC/RES/7/19.

32 UNGA Res 63/171 (24 March 2009) UN Doc A/RES/63/171, UNGA Res 64/156 (8 March 2010) UN Doc A/RES/64/156.

33 Allen D Hertzke (Ed.), *The Future of Religious Freedom: Global Challenges* (OUP, Oxford 2013) 70.

expression. For it seems that not only aggrieving utterances about the human person are now liable to limitation, but also expressions about ideologies in the broadest sense of the term.

From Protection of Religion to Protection of the Individual against Discrimination Based on Religion

Nevertheless, in recent years, we can observe a reversal of this development[34] – albeit marginal – for it is acknowledged that, as the Special Rapporteur on the promotion and protection of the right to freedom of opinion and expression asserts, 'the right to freedom of religion or belief, as enshrined in relevant international legal standards, does not include the right to have a religion or belief that is free from criticism or ridicule. Indeed, the right to freedom of expression includes the right to scrutinize, debate openly, make statements that offend, shock and disturb, and criticize belief systems, opinions and institutions, including religious ones, provided that they do not advocate hatred that incites hostility, discrimination or violence. At the international level, the Special Rapporteur welcomes the shift from the notion of "defamation of religions" to the protection of individuals against incitement to religious hatred. The Human Rights Council [...] has adopted by consensus a resolution on combating intolerance, negative stereotyping and stigmatization of, and discrimination, incitement to violence and violence against, persons based on religion or belief (resolution 19/25) [under a variety of pretexts relating to security and irregular immigration]. In that resolution, the Council condemns any advocacy of religious hatred that constitutes incitement to discrimination, hostility or violence, whether it involves the use of print, audiovisual or electronic media or any other means. It also recognizes that [in this clash of civilizations] open [constructive and respectful] public debate of ideas, as well as interfaith and intercultural dialogue, at the local, national and international levels can be among the best protections against religious intolerance and can play a positive role in strengthening democracy and combating religious hatred, convinced that a continuing dialogue on these issues can help overcome existing perceptions.'[35]

This reversal of approach is also evident from, for example, General Comment No. 34, wherein it is stated that 'prohibitions of displays of lack of respect for a religion or other belief system, including blasphemy laws, are incompatible with the Covenant, except in the specific circumstances envisaged in article 20, paragraph 2, of the Covenant. Such

34 This reversal is also observable from the names of the documents which were changed from 'combating defamation of religions' into 'combating intolerance, negative stereotyping and stigmatization of, and discrimination, incitement to violence and violence against, persons based on religion or belief'; UNGA Res 16/18 (12 April 2011) UN Doc A/HRC/RES/16/18.

35 UNCHR 'Report of the Special Rapporteur on the Promotion and protection of the right to freedom of opinion and expression' (2012) UN Doc A/67/357.

prohibitions must also comply with the strict requirements of article 19, paragraph 3, as well as such articles as 2, 5, 17, 18 and 26. Accordingly, for instance, it would be impermissible for any such laws to discriminate in favor of or against one or certain religions or belief systems, or their adherents over another, or religious believers over non-believers. Nor would it be permissible for such prohibitions to be used to prevent or punish criticism of religious leaders or commentary on religious doctrine and tenets of faith.'[36] Accordingly, the previous attempt to criminalize blasphemy is reversed and laws restricting blasphemy as such are considered to be incompatible with universal human rights standards.[37] In this way, the endeavor to protect religion as such is overruled by the original intention of the law, namely, the protection of the human person. The return to the original intention of the law is thus, as stated in the course of the present study, evident from the United Nations documents in the latter years whereby the protection from, among other things, intolerance, discrimination and acts of violence directed towards persons belonging to religious minorities has regained the attention it deserves.[38]

For instance, great concern is often expressed about '[...] serious instances of intolerance, discrimination and acts of violence based on religion or belief, intimidation and coercion motivated by extremism, religious or otherwise, occurring in many parts of the world, including cases motivated by Islamophobia, Judeophobia and Christianophobia, in addition to the negative projection of certain religions in the media and the introduction and enforcement of laws and administrative measures that *specifically discriminate against and target persons* with certain ethnic and religious backgrounds, particularly Muslim minorities, and that threaten to impede their full enjoyment of human rights and fundamental freedoms.'[39] As has become evident in the course of this discourse on blasphemy, great importance has been attached to the situation of Muslims but with one main difference. Before the aforementioned reversal of approach and return to the original intention of the law, special emphasis had been put on the psychological and physical assaults and attacks against places of worship, cultural centers, businesses and properties as well as

36 ICCPR General Comment No. 34. Concluding observations on the United Kingdom of Great Britain and Northern Ireland-the Crown Dependencies of Jersey, Guernsey and the Isle of Man (CCPR/C/79/Add.119), 2011.

37 Austin Dacey, 'United Nations Affirms the Human Right to Blaspheme', *Religion Dispatches Magazine* (11 August 2011) www.religiondispatches.org/archive/politics/4985/united_nations_affirms_the_human_right_to_blaspheme_%7c_politics_%7c_/ accessed 3 December 2013.

38 See for instance UNGA Res 16/18 (12 April 2011) UN Doc A/HRC/RES/16/18, UNGA, Nineteenth session 'Racism, racial discrimination, xenophobia and related form of intolerance, follow-up and implementation of the Durban Declaration and Programme of Action' (16 March 2012) UN Doc A/HRC/19/L.7, UNGA, Twenty-second session 'Racism, racial discrimination, xenophobia and related form of intolerance, follow-up and implementation of the Durban Declaration and Programme of Action' (18 March 2013) UN Doc A/HRC/22/L.40.

39 UNGA Res 65/224 (11 April 2011) UN Doc A/RES/65/224 [emphasis added].

religious symbols of Muslims.[40] However, with the reversal of approach, vilification is considered to be a serious affront not to religion but to human dignity, which can lead to the illicit restriction of the freedom of religion of the *adherents* and incitement to religious hatred and violence. Thus, discrimination on the basis of religion or belief is considered to constitute a violation of human rights that can lead to social disharmony, due to which states are requested to combat this burgeoning trend and the resulting discriminatory practices against *adherents* of all religions.[41]

Freedom of Speech versus Hate Speech Related to Religion

Yet, as we can observe, defamation of religion[42] as such is prone to the defamation of the adherents of that religion as well, a result of which being that the borderline between hate speech and freedom of expression is very thin and perilous, and must be attentively guarded against abuse. The former consists in the prohibition of advocating hatred or inciting hostility, discrimination or violence, while the latter may appear by offending, shocking, disturbing and criticizing belief systems, opinions and institutions, including religious ones. This becomes more pressing when the resurgence of hate speech and the lightning speed of its circulation through the mass media and Internet in this globalized world are borne in mind. Other relevant issues include the rising immigration flows and population movements, the declining domestic economies and the emergence of terrorism, which have all fostered a growing tendency to stigmatize specific groups and communities.[43]

However, the acceleration of multicivilizationalism which underpins this discourse ought not to lead to a premature acceptance of bans on hate speech, since it has already

40 UNCHR Res 9 (2002) UN Doc E/CN.4/RES/2002/9, UNCHR Res 6 (2004) UN Doc E/CN.4/RES/2004/6, UNCHR Res 3 (2005) UN Doc E/CN.4/RES/2005/3, UNGA Res 60/150 (20 January 2006) UN Doc A/RES/60/150, UNGA Res 61/164 (21 February 2007) UN Doc A/RES/61/164, Human Rights Council Res 4/9, 'Combating defamation of religions' (30 March 2007) UN Doc A/HRC/RES/4/9, UNGA Res 62/154 (6 March 2008) UN Doc A/RES/62/154, Human Rights Council Res 7/19, 'Combating defamation of religions' (27 March 2008) UN Doc A/HRC/RES/7/19, UNGA Res 63/171 (24 March 2009) UN Doc A/RES/63/171, Human Rights Council Res 10/22, 'Combating defamation of religions' (26 March 2009) UN Doc A/HRC/RES/10/22, UNGA Res 64/156 (8 March 2010) UN Doc A/RES/64/156 [emphasis added]. This wording is generalized in the later documents wherein, instead of Muslims, reference is made to the adherents of religions in general; See for instance UNGA Res 65/224 (11 April 2011) UN Doc A/RES/65/224 and UNGA Res 16/18 (12 April 2011) UN Doc A/HRC/RES/16/18.

41 UNGA Res 65/224 (11 April 2011) UN Doc A/RES/65/224.

42 This is evident from, e.g., UNGA Res 65/224 (11 April 2011) UN Doc A/RES/65/224 whereby the states are urged "to take all possible measures to promote tolerance and respect for all religions and beliefs and the understanding of their value systems and to complement legal systems with intellectual and moral strategies to combat religious hatred and intolerance" but also when one "underlines the need to combat vilification of religions, and incitement to religious hatred in general, by strategizing and harmonizing actions at the local" national, regional and international levels through education and awareness-raising.

43 UNCHR 'Report of the Special Rapporteur on the Promotion and protection of the right to freedom of opinion and expression' (2012) UN Doc A/67/357.

been determined, during the debate on the question of additional restriction, that the confinement of the freedom of expression should contain as few restrictions as possible.[44] Even in the case of hate speech, it is crucial to keep in mind that 'with regard to the prohibition of any advocacy of national, racial or religious hatred that constitutes incitement to discrimination, hostility or violence established under article 20(2) of the Covenant, it is important to establish a clearer understanding of the terms to prevent any misapplication of the law. This formulation includes three key elements: First, only advocacy of hatred is covered; second, hatred must amount to advocacy which constitutes incitement, rather than incitement alone; and third, such incitement must lead to one of the listed results, namely discrimination, hostility or violence. As such, advocacy of hatred on the basis of national, racial or religious grounds is not an offence in itself. Such advocacy becomes an offence only when it also constitutes incitement to discrimination, hostility or violence, or when the speaker seeks to provoke reactions on the part of the audience.'[45] What is more, '(a) Hate speech laws should, at a minimum, conform to the following: (i) No one should be penalized for statements which are true; (ii) No one should be penalized for the dissemination of hate speech unless it has been shown that the perpetrator had the intention to incite discrimination, hostility or violence.'[46] Thus, against this background, it is possible to state that the acceptance of bans on hate speech has to be accompanied by the necessary circumspection and reticence.

CONCLUSION

The foregoing inquiry leads us to the conclusion that the acceleration of multicivilizationalism is bound to impose limits on the fundamental rights and freedoms in general and on the fundamental right to freedom of expression in particular. As Huntington rightly contends, at the center of this menace stands the notion of religion that certain parties deploy for promoting, among others, their political and religious values. This has been done through, for instance, the 'dialogue among civilizations' and the 'defamation of religions' campaigns. The fundamental right to freedom of expression is of course not an absolute right, but it should not be forgotten that this right may be limited only through the prescribed legal conditions and not through extrajudicial and political means. Yet, the

44 Marc J Bossuyt, *Guide to the "travaux préparatoires" of the International Covenant on Civil and Political Rights* (Martinus Nijhoff Publishers, Dordrecht 1987) 398. This is especially crucial in the case of incitement to commit genocide as it comes to the fore in Article III (c) of the Convention on the Prevention and Punishment of the Crime of Genocide.

45 UNCHR 'Report of the Special Rapporteur on the Promotion and protection of the right to freedom of opinion and expression' (2012) UN Doc A/67/357.

46 UNGA, Second session 'World Conference Against Racism, Racial Discrimination, Xenophobia and Related Intolerance, Preparatory Committee' (22 March 2001) UN Doc A/CONF.189/PC.2/24.

aforementioned campaigns have caused a shift in approach even within the law, whereby not only aggrieving utterances about the human person seem to be subject to limitations but also expressions about ideologies in the broadest sense of the term. All this while, the original intention of the law is to confer rights on the human person as the sole bearer of them and not to protect ideologies and objects of veneration. The aforementioned developments show, however, that various attempts have been made to further confine this fundamental right in a way that would go beyond the contemporary legal limitations, so that protection is not only provided to the human person but also to religion and all its venerated features.

Nevertheless, we have seen, in recent years, that a reverse development has taken place whereby, once again, more importance is attached to the fundamental right to freedom of expression by not accepting the limitations imposed upon it by, among others, the discourse on defamation of religion. Thus, despite the aforementioned assaults on this fundamental right, we can observe a reversal of approach whereby it is acknowledged that the right to freedom of religion or belief does not include the right to have a religion or belief that is free from criticism. For the right to freedom of speech includes the right to scrutinize, debate openly, make statements that offend, shock and disturb, and criticize belief systems, opinions and institutions, including religious ones, provided that they do not advocate hatred that incites hostility, discrimination or violence. Henceforth, with this reversal of approach the endeavor to protect religion as such is overruled by the original intention of the law, namely, the protection of the human person. Yet, it has to be remembered that the defamation of a religion is also likely to defame that religion's adherents, and as a result, the borderline between hate speech and freedom of speech is very thin and perilous, and should therefore be attentively guarded against abuse. This becomes more pressing with the current acceleration of multicivilizationalism.

Part III
The Legal-Philosophical Dimension of Freedom of Speech

12 Exploring the Limits of Freedom: Heresy in a Free Society

Afshin Ellian

Etymologically, heresy derives from 'hairein,' a Greek word meaning 'to choose.' A 'heretic,' then, is one who chooses, one who therefore exemplifies freedom of individual thought, and by implication, who does not accept at least some of the doctrines of the corporate Church. If, on the one hand, the heretic is one who chooses, then the heretic exists by affirmation – but, on the other hand, in the context of an organized Church, the heretic is also one who may refuse. It is in this sense, more than any other, that the heretic can be termed a dualist – for as soon as the representatives of an institutionalized Church insist on a particular set of doctrines and no others, those who choose are placed between two worlds or spheres. The institutionalization of the historicist Church in turn creates the possibility of the heretical.
Arthur Versluis[1]

The raison d' être of politics is freedom, and its field of experience is action.
Hannah Arendt[2]

The Dutch Struggle with Freedom of Expression

Every religion or ideology that is not limited by the principle of freedom demands that its own sacred dogmas be protected by the state. Multiculturalism, considered as a semi-religious organized ideology, has its own heretics. The multicultural church counts few rooms. Is a liberal state obligated to safeguard a church's sacred dogmas, by means of the criminal code? History shows that penal legislation may indeed contribute, to a modest extent, to the settling of political and ideological conflicts. Since the September 11 attacks in New York and Washington, the world has become a battlefield of ideas. This struggle cannot be resolved by merely resorting to repression or bombings. Oppressive measures do not extirpate ill ideas. They can at most restrain ill-willed people from committing criminal acts.

---

1 Arthur Versluis, *The New Inquisitions. Heretic-Hunting and the Intellectual Origins of Modern Totalitarianism*, Oxford: Oxford University Press 2006, p. 3.

2 Hannah Arendt, What is Freedom?, In: *Between Past and Future. Eight exercises in political thought*, New York: Penguin Books 1968, p. 146.

Ever more words are the combatants in the arena of law and politics. Every battle, including battles that are fought by means of words, involve some risk. Two people have by now been murdered: Pim Fortuyn (1948-2002) and Theo van Gogh (1957-2004). This is a sad state of affairs. The Dutch legal order appears to be strong and deeply embedded, and cannot, as such, be destabilized by two assaults. Still, each assault leaves its marks on a nation's collective memory. With respect to his battle in particular, which is still overshadowed by the terrorist threat posed by political Islam, it is necessary, according to Paul Cliteur, to develop strategies in the field of 'Cultural CounterTerrorism.'[3] It is to Cliteur's merit that the issue surrounding the religious nature of terrorism and the intellectual strategies to realize deradicalization has reached the center of the present European intellectual debate.[4] This debate would not be possible without freedom of expression being acknowledged in the first place. That freedom applies to everyone, including those who defend Islamic fundamentalism. The penal legal limit that may not be crossed is (the threat of) violence.

I will briefly discuss a number of important, relevant processes and events with respect to freedom of expression in The Netherlands. For decades, freedom of expression was not intensely discussed here. The last time a politician was convicted irrevocably was in 1999, when the Dutch Supreme Court affirmed the conviction of parliamentarian Hans Janmaat, the former leader for the Centre Democrats in the House of Representatives, who had participated in a demonstration where extreme-right views were expressed in the town of Zwolle. Such demonstrations were attended by few people and, in addition, took place in remote places. Janmaat made a speech during this extreme-right demonstration, saying: 'As soon as we have the opportunity and the power to do so, we will abolish the multicultural society.' The bystanders shouted 'our own people comes first,' 'full is full' and 'The Netherlands is for the Dutch.' Janmaat was prosecuted for these exclamations and convicted in three instances. The court of appeals stated that Janmaat's fellow citizens are protected, on the basis of article 137e of the Dutch Criminal Code, against rabble-rousing that may impair their human dignity. The Supreme Court upheld the verdict of the lower instances, maintaining that public (oral) incitement to discrimination had taken place.[5] After that, the issue of freedom of expression did not stir much excitement, at least in legal terms. This calm state of affairs would, however, not last.

---

3 Paul Cliteur, Cultural Counter-Terrorism, In: *Terrorism: Ideology, Law and Policy*, Dordrecht: Republic of Letters Publishing 2011, pp. 457-490.

4 Paul Cliteur, *The Secular Outlook. In defence of moral and political secularism*, Oxford: Wiley-Blackwell 2010.

5 Supreme Court May 18, 1999, *NJ* 1999, 634.

On September 11, the Western world changed. The attacks in New York, Washington and Pennsylvania claimed nearly 3000 lives. These attacks were committed by a number of radical Muslims, in the name of Islam. The political climate changed globally. Under these circumstances, Pim Fortuyn entered the political arena. The public uproar reached its climax with the arrival of Fortuyn. He took a stand against the excesses of the multicultural society and targeted Islam in particular. To him, Islam was a 'retarded religion', unwilling and unable to respect the basic values of Western civilization.[6] Several complaints were filed against Fortuyn. Before the district attorney had the opportunity to complete his inquiry, however, Fortuyn was murdered by Volkert van der G., on May 6, 2002, on site at the Media Park.

The struggle of political Islam did not end with the September 11 attacks: In Iraq alone, tens of thousands of citizens died in terrorists assaults. Europe, too, was struck hard: Madrid suffered many losses in 2004, and London faced the same faith in 2005. The murder of Van Gogh on November 2, 2004, introduced Islamic terrorism in The Netherlands. The freedom of expression debate was once more the focus of attention. This time, Ayaan Hirsi Ali, a politician associated with the People's Party for Freedom and Democracy, played an important role. A short film, called 'Submission' that Hirsi Ali had made together with Theo van Gogh in 2004, which dealt with the emancipation of Muslim women, led Mohammed Bouyeri to kill Van Gogh. In addition, the circle to which Bouyeri belonged threatened to kill a number of politicians and opinion formers. This circle – the Hofstad Network – was caught soon after the murder of Van Gogh. The court convicted most of its members of participation of a terrorist organization. In addition, they were convicted of incitement to hatred of those of other persuasions.[7] Geert Wilders, parliamentarian for the Party for Freedom, is heavily guarded against the continual international threat directed at him in person.

Under these upheaving circumstances, taking place around November 7, 2004, a few days after the murder of Van Gogh, someone in Valkenswaard put up a provocative poster of A3 size at his window, facing the street, reading 'End the tumor called Islam. Theo died for us; who will be next? Fight this NOW. National Alliance, we will not bend to Allah. Become a member. N.A., P.O. Box [001], [city], www.nationalealliantie.com.' The accused was prosecuted for breaking article 137c of the Criminal Code: Intentionally insulting a group of people because of their religion. Is the sentence 'End the tumor called Islam' a punishable expression? The Supreme Court concluded, in consideration 2.5.1: 'Only

6 P. Fortuyn, *De islamisering van onze cultuur. Nederlandse identiteit als fundament*, Uithoorn: Karakter 2002, pp. 15-48.

7 Supreme Court February 2, 2010, *LJN* BK5193, *RvdW* 2010, 276.

needlessly offensively expressing oneself with respect to a group of people on account of their adhering to a religion is punishable. Insulting a group of people because of their religion is only punishable on the basis of article 137c of the Criminal Code – according to the legislative history – if one insults the people who belong to the group collectively with respect to what is characteristic of them in that capacity, namely, their religion, and insults them precisely because they adhere to that religion. Every criticism of opinions shared by the group, even severe criticism, falls outside the scope of article 137c of the Criminal Code.'[8] According to the Supreme Court, not only Islam but the behavior of the group in connection with the faith in question – so in this case the behavior of Muslims – may be criticized.

Is it allowed to call Islam a tumor? The Supreme Court is perfectly clear in consideration 2.5.2: 'The mere given that offensive expressions pertaining to a religion also aggrieve the adherents to that religion is not sufficient to equate those expressions with expressions about those adherents, so about a group of people because of their religion in the sense of article 137c of the Criminal Code.' The Supreme Court acknowledges, as a matter of fact, the distinction between Islam and Muslims.[9] Shortly after September 11, I also appealed for a distinction between Islam, political Islam and Muslims in The Netherlands and internationally. I made an attempt to explain the differences between those three categories in appearances in the media and at scientific conferences. I will return to this below.

The Supreme Court's ruling on 'End the tumor called Islam' immediately aroused attention, since the district attorney decided at the same not to prosecute Wilders. The Advocate General Machielse addressed the Wilders case in his conclusion to that ruling. How did the case start? A number of people had filed a complaint against Wilders for incitement to discrimination, hatred and the punishable insult of groups of people. In other words, the well-known crimes of expression were concerned. The complaints against Wilders were based on the following statements by Wilders: 'At the core of the problem lies the fascist Islam, the sick ideology of Allah and Mohammed as laid down in the Islamic *Mein Kampf*: The Qur'an'; 'The Qur'an is the *Mein Kampf* of a religion that seeks to eliminate others [...]'; 'I have had enough of Islam in The Netherlands: No more Muslim immigrants. [...] I have had enough of Qur'an in The Netherlands: Ban that fascist book'; 'If Muslims want to stay here, they will have to tear half the pages from the Qur'an and throw them away'; 'The borders must be closed, no more Muslims should be accepted into The Netherlands, many Muslims should leave The Netherlands, Islamic criminals must be

8 Supreme Court March 10, 2009, *LJN* BF0655, *NJ* 2010, 19, with an annotation by P.A.M. Mevis.

9 H. Sackers, De opmerkelijke geschiedenis van art. 137c Sr, in: A. Ellian, G. Molier & T. Zwart (Eds.), *Mag ik dit zeggen? Beschouwingen over de vrijheid van meningsuiting*, The Hague: Boom Juridische uitgevers 2011, pp. 309-329.

denaturalized'; and 'Islam is a violent religion. If Mohammed were alive today and resided here, I would suggest driving him out of the country in tar and feathers, as the extremist he would be.'

The short film Fitna (of March 27, 2008), made by Wilders himself in order to indicate a number of violent aspects of Islam and was part of the complaint against Wilders. The district attorney did not want to prosecute Wilders as his expressions were thought not to be punishable. Subsequently, the plaintiffs requested the Amsterdam court of appeals in 2010 to prosecute him, pursuant to article 12 of the Dutch Code of Criminal Procedure, which affords anyone whose interest is involved to make such a request. The court of appeals decided, in accordance with the plaintiffs' wish, that Wilders should be prosecuted, greatly elaborating on its reasons.[10] The district attorney acted in accordance with this decision, but pleaded that Wilders be acquitted of all charges. This outcome was understandable, given the fact that the district attorney had initially argued in detail why Wilders did not express himself punishably. It would in fact be strange if the district attorney were to deviate from its own stance. The situation would have been different if the court of appeal's decision had referred to the evidence, but that was not the case. The case would eventually turn out to be a peculiar one with a number of lows, such as the recusal of the Judges and the interrogation of the Judge Tom Schalken.

I will discuss a number of details from these trials below. Subsequently, I will provide a legal theoretical reflection on the penal legal conflict with regard to freedom of expression that has come to the forefront over the last years. The Wilders case features prominently here. This issue raises a number of questions. Why are artists and commentators granted more freedom than politicians and representatives? Has a new hierarchy come to pass? Is the aesthetic domain the most important one? Does it have a godlike status, meriting a virtually unlimited form of freedom? The political domain has been classified under the aesthetic one. Is this classification not an apolitical and in a certain sense nihilistic one? Man has succeeded in creating works of art under the direst of circumstances. Even in a prison or on Devil's Island, a creative mind can produce works of art. A poem can be written anywhere. Freedom and art are not necessarily intertwined. True, art can blossom more easily in freedom than under a tyrannical rule, but the principle of freedom and politics (and thus politicians, as its practitioners) are interrelated concepts. The political domain is a necessary condition for freedom to exist, while freedom is an ultimate goal for the political domain. That which unnecessarily restricts the freedom of a people and its representatives is apolitical. What are the consequences of the 'aestheticizing' of the public order for politics and ethics? There may be freedom forgetfulness. A vivid love of

10 Court of appeals Amsterdam, January 21, 2009, *LJN* BH0496, *NJ* 2009, 191, with an annotation by Y. Buruma.

art should not lead to cynicism and an enfeeblement of politics. The Wilders trial provides the opportunity to question the obviousness of the aesthetic predominance. In order to comprehend this process, we also need to review previous penal rulings with regard to crimes of expression. We also need to confront fundamental legal theoretical issues and dilemmas surrounding freedom. This article has the semblance of an annotation, more specifically, the Donkey trial[11] of our generation: The Wilders trial.

Haec Libertatis Ergo vs. Haec Religionis Ergo

'Spain is not all there is: Praise God, if you will, that you were born a Dutchman.' Those are the magic words by Gerard Kornelis van het Reve, trusted to the paper and thereby to us, along with his own Donkey trial. The portrayal of God as a donkey was the basis of the criminal charge: 'If God is to let himself be captured once again in the Living Dust, he will return as a Donkey, unable to produce a few syllables, undervalued, reviled and thrashed, but I will understand him and go to bed with him at once, placing bandages on his little hoofs, so as to make sure I will not be scratched too much by his contortions as he climaxes.'[12] Reve had blasphemed, but he was acquitted, article 147 of the Criminal Code not being applied. If we replace 'God' with 'Allah,' however, a serious problem arises. The Minister of Foreign Affairs and the National Coordinator for Security and Counterterrorism would be busy dealing with some Muslim diplomats and Muslim terrorists. Neither of these groups are supporters of freedom of expression. I displayed a passage from Reve's work during a lecture and asked the students what their thoughts were. A Dutch student of Moroccan origin told me that after reading the passage he no longer understood what the commotion with respect to offending Islam was about. What happened during the Donkey trial? What is the penal essence of a trial with respect to a crime of expression? Is it a discussion, or a dialogue, with the judge?

Reve expressed himself during his trial. Parliamentarian Wilders kept quite. Judge Jan Moors, who would later be recused as the president of the Amsterdam court in the Wilders trial, was deeply disappointed in Wilders, as the defendant used his right to silence. He uttered the following words, which have now become widespread and led to his recusal: 'The court has read the case file, but also reads newspapers and at present also watches television. Others tend to reproach you for presenting an issue while evading the debate

11 This concerns the prosecution of the Dutch author Gerard Kornelis van het Reve (1923-2006) in 1966 on the count of blasphemy of which he was ultimately acquitted. After this trial, no one would be accused of blasphemy, making the law on which the crime was based a dead latter law. The law was recently rescinded.

12 Jan Fekkes, *De God van je tante ofwel het Ezel-proces van Gerard Kornelis van het Reve. Een documentaire, samengesteld door Jan Fekkes*, Amsterdam: Arbeiderspers 1968, p. 32.

that ensues from it. It seems that you repeat this course of action today.'[13] Apparently, the judges had been prepared for an interesting and feisty debate with Wilders; what is possible in the media can be accomplished here, too, the judges had thought. Wilders is not allowed to evade the debate, the judges seemed to suggest. Has a trial become a place for debate? Or is its purpose to determine the truth of the matter? Wilders remained silent. He did speak on occasion, but not at the incitement of the court. The judges, who were after a debate with Wilders, were disappointed; their disappointment was clear to all. I presume that these judges were familiar with the Donkey trial, where the defendant and his witnesses did interact with the judges. Those judges were not disappointed at Reve's eloquence:

- The court president: 'Do you admit to having published this piece in this way in the magazine *Dialoog*?'
- Reve: 'I do, your Honor.'
- The court president: 'What ideas do you propagate?'
- Reve: 'I write; I do not propagate anything. And when I imagine the incarnation of God, this appears in the form of the most enchanting being I know. That does not have to be a human being. It could be a lamb, but I adore a donkey even more. The intimacy with the deity every human being seeks has a clearly sexual character for me.'
- Judge: 'Do you not think the act you describe is perverse?'
- Reve: 'If the animal is God, it is not for me to judge. There are various opinions regarding what is perverse; if the animal appreciates the act, would it be reproachable?'[14]

Wilders did not blaspheme the Christian God, but Islam. In a nearly identical way, the defendant Wilders questions the definition of the crime of incitement to hatred and insult. After all, opinions vary on the meaning of 'insulting a group of people' and 'incitement to hatred.' To us, as lawyers, it is easier to take sides with the defendant Reve than with the defendant Wilders. Reve is an artist. Should we regard these cases unencumbered by various considerations emerging from the principles of democracy and freedom, it appears that the artist and the opinion-former are raised above all other participants in society. From a legal historical point of view, this is a misconception. Again: Some hold that freedom of expression in a broad sense should only exist for artists, academics and reporters. This constitutes a reversal of values: Freedom of expression was first and foremost realized for representatives, meaning politicians. In due course, this right was afforded to other cate-

13 www.trouw.nl/tr/nl/4324/Nieuws/article/detail/1814817/2010/10/05/Wrakingsverzoek-Wilders-afgewezen.dhtml.

14 Jan Fekkes, *op. cit.*, p. 34.

gories of people. The freedom an artist enjoys is a derivative of political freedom in general. Nevertheless, there are still lawyers who think that the freedom of expression which was granted to Reve, should not be granted to Wilders. In the age of the internet, this position can no longer be held, unless one seeks to be tyrannical. Why should artists be granted more leeway to say and claim what they want than politicians?

FREEDOM AS A POLITICAL CATEGORY

Freedom of expression was and is in the first place one of the fundamental rights of politicians. Ever since the democratic changes in the modern era, freedom of expression is a necessary component of parliamentarianism as the beating heart of a democratic system, either with or without a president as the head of state. Where does the concept of freedom find its origin? Was it invented by artists? Incidentally, artists seldom prove a paragon of freedom. Was the concept of freedom invented by religious people? In Christianity, truth is the main issue, while justice in the guise of an absolute submission to the will of Allah – and thereby to his laws – is characteristic of Islam. Classical Arabic does not even include a word for freedom in the sense in which it is used in Western thought. *Hurriyya*, or freedom, is derived in Arabic from the word *hurr*, which indicates the legal status of a person. *Hurr* refers to a free person, a person who is not a slave. The concept of freedom as a political category was unknown to Islam and the Islamic legal order. In the wake of the French revolution, the Turks and Arabs attempted to introduce *liberté* as Hurriyya in Islamic culture and the Islamic legal order, in the guise of a political category. The young Ottomans and Persians were the ones to make this attempt.[15] Freedom is not a given.

Because of Christianity's dominion, freedom (which was inherited from Roman political thought) disappeared from the forefront. Freedom thus gained the appearance of a mirage. Hannah Arendt concludes from this state of affairs: 'There is no preoccupation with freedom in the whole history of great philosophy form the pre-Socratics up to Plotinus, the last ancient philosopher. And when freedom made its first appearance in our philosophical tradition, it was the experience of religious conversion – of Paul first and then of Augustine – which gave rise to it.'[16] It was only in modern times, after the religious wars had ended, that freedom once again became an important political category. Inner freedom, being free to think, is a natural given that no one can take away from a human being. An inner sense without an external manifestation could not and cannot be denied to slaves and prisoners. It is because of this given that this inner sense without external signs is, by defi-

15 Bernard Lewis, *Islam in History. Ideas, People, and Events in the Middle East*, Chicago and La Salle, Illinois: Open Court Publishing Company 2001, pp. 323-336.

16 Hannah Arendt, *op. cit.*, pp. 145-146.

nition, politically irrelevant, according to Arendt. Without a political order, including a legal order, freedom in word and deed is inconceivable. Freedom founds the political in the sense of polis (in modern times, too): 'If, then, we understand the political in the sense of the polis, its end or *raison d' être* would be to establish and keep in existence a space where freedom as virtuosity can appear. This is the realm where freedom is a worldly reality, tangible in words which can be heard, in deeds which can be seen, and in events which are talked about, remembered, and turned into stories before they are finally incorporated into the great storybook of human history.'[17] Ever since the Enlightenment, freedom has become characteristic of legal orders. In 'Beantwortung der Frage: Was ist Aufklärung?' Kant maintains: 'For enlightenment of this kind, all that is needed is freedom.' What is freedom in that sense? It is the most innocuous form of all freedom: '[...] freedom to make public use of one's reason in all matters. [...] The public use of man's reason must always be free, and it alone can bring about enlightenment among men.'[18] Freedom is a public matter, a political category. Freedom receives its sense and meaning only in the public realm.

Freedom and anarchy are irreconcilable. The public realm that is demarcated by laws is a necessary condition for freedom to exist. What is freedom in that sense? It refers to freedom to act, freedom of speech, freedom to write and publish. Acting and speaking (including the written word) are the ways in which politics is manifested in a democratic legal order. The thinkers that are inclined to despotism do not uphold freedom of expression that is largely concerned with 'talking' rather than with 'physically acting.' Still, that 'talking' is essential to democracy. A democratic state with a representative organ functions and develops itself through a clash of ideas. For whom, then, is freedom of expression intended? For kindred spirits? Kindred spirits, comrades, brothers and sisters of the same faith – with the same interpretation of that faith – are, of course, always free. Freedom of expression was not conceived for kindred spirits. Friends are, after all, always allowed to be free. Freedom of expression was conceived for the opponent, the recalcitrant, the heretic, the witch, the reprehensible, the other-minded and the apostate. Whoever enjoys the privilege of being born and raised in the luxury of freedom does not grasp the severity of the absence of freedom, and is in danger of perishing because of freedom forgetfulness. The principle of freedom, an inalienable foundation of the democratic legal order, is formulated superbly by the European Court of Human Rights in the *Handyside* case.[19] In that famous case, the Court defined the minimal limits of freedom of expression in a public discussion: 'Freedom of expression constitutes one of the essential foundations of such a society, one of the basic

17 Hannah Arendt, *op. cit.*, pp. 154-155.

18 Immanuel Kant, An Answer to the Question: 'What is Enlightenment?', In: *Kant Political Writings*, edited by H.S. Reiss, Cambridge: Cambridge University Press 2010, p. 55.

19 Handyside v United Kingdom (1976).

conditions for its progress and for the development of every man. Subject to paragraph 2 of Article 10 (art. 10-2), it is applicable not only to "information" or "ideas" that are favourably received or regarded as inoffensive or as a matter of indifference, but also to those that offend, shock or disturb the State or any sector of the population. Such are the demands of that pluralism, tolerance and broadmindedness without which there is no "democratic society". This means, amongst other things, that every "formality", "condition", "restriction" or "penalty" imposed in this sphere must be proportionate to the legitimate aim pursued.' Nevertheless, it appeared necessary to prosecute Wilders.

Prosecution is Purifying: The Discussion Should Continue and Improve, but Without the Heretic

Egbert Dommering, attorney at law, wrote an interesting article in the newspaper *NRC-Handelsblad* of January 28, 2009, and the editorial board selected a telling title: 'Prosecution has a purifying effect.' He upheld the decision of the Amsterdam court regarding Wilders' prosecution, zealously arguing in its defense. Dommering also expressed his wish that the judge had convicted Wilders: 'The court's decision may contribute to the quality of the public discussion regarding integration, which has suffered considerable damage recently.' Could the judge really improve the quality of a heated public discussion? What does a judge know about such a debate? What does he know about the debate regarding integration? Is Dommering confusing the judge with God? The origins of the power, competence and knowledge Dommering attributes to a judge are surely to be located on the other side of being. A political discussion arises when the majority is not certain what the case is. Someone who knowingly and willingly involves a judge risks the deterioration of the judicial authority. In addition, is it the judge's task to improve the quality of public discussions? The judge looks for the truth in the legal sense in an individual case, the value of his judgment not being decided by a public discussion or a political viewpoint. What about crimes of expression?

I call crimes of expression crimes of opinion, for opinions that are expressed are decisive here. Opinions are subjected to a criminal investigation. The legitimacy of articles 137c, 137d and 137e of the Criminal Code has been the subject of discussion for some time now. The penal clauses regarding crimes of expression were realized in the 1930s in order to enable 'penal legal actions against antiSemitic expressions from national-socialist and fascist factions, as well as against certain forms of antireligious propaganda.'[20] These clauses

20 Memorie van Toelichting met betrekking tot uitvoering van het ICERD van 7 maart 1966 inzake de uitbanning van elke vorm van rassendiscriminatie. Kamerstukken zitting 1967-1968, no. 9724 and Kamerzitting 1969-1970, no. 9724.

were changed in 1971, in order to implement the International Convention on the Elimination of All Forms of Racial Discrimination of March 6, 1966 (the ICERD). Racial discrimination is defined there as 'any distinction, exclusion, restriction or preference based on race, colour, descent, or national or ethnic origin which has the purpose or effect of nullifying or impairing the recognition, enjoyment or exercise, on an equal footing, of human rights and fundamental freedoms in the political, economic, social, cultural or any other field of public life.' In particular, the treaty demands from the countries that have ratified it that they penalize disseminating ideas on racial superiority, racial hatred or incitement to racial discrimination. We should not lose sight of the fact that this treaty was agreed to at a time that was characterized by a struggle against apartheid[21] in South Africa and decolonization. The memory of the Second World War was the reason behind the ICERD. The Soviet Union and its satellite states supported this treaty, which is not surprising, given their opposition to freedom of expression, which is restricted by the treaty. The United States' stance was more balanced: It agreed with the treaty's intent, but did not want to ratify it as it would contravene the American Constitution, notably, the right to free speech.

In The Netherlands, too, some skeptical voices were raised regarding these clauses. Legal scholar Van Bemmelen even considered articles 137c and 137d of the Criminal Code, as well as their previous versions, to be very vague and broad.[22] Other prominent scholars, such as A.H.J. Swart, did not prove enthusiastic about implementing the ICERD. In his article *Rassendiskriminatie en de Nederlandse strafwet*, Swart stated: 'Considering all these things, it is not surprising that the House of Representatives, in discussing the law, showed little enthusiasm to realize the three new articles. This was also the position of the government itself.'[23] Swart thought that the new clauses would, in practice, hardly be used, much like the original ones. The United Kingdom, too, was worried. Swart quotes the opinion of the British delegation in preparing the treaty. It provides an interesting contribution against the background of the current discussion about the penal limits of freedom of expression: 'A clear criterion was formulated by the British delegation that cooperated to the preparation of the treaty; penalization would be fitting where the use of the constitutionally guaranteed right is misused, with demonstrable and concrete damage in its wake, leading to punishable facts. The draft law is more far-reaching.'[24] Swart thought it necessary, appealing to the British delegation, to limit the usage of broad notions such as 'insulting a group of people' or 'incitement to hatred' to two criteria: Demonstrable damage and

21 The International Convention on the Suppression and Punishment of the Crime of Apartheid (1973) is relevant here.

22 J. M. Van Bemmelen, Belediging en vrijheid van meningsuiting, In: *Nederlands Juristenblad 1969*, p. 441.

23 A.H.J. Swart, Rassendiskriminatie en de Nederlandse Strafwet, In: *Delikt en Delinkwent* vol 1, 1970, p. 65 ff.

24 A.H.J. Swart, *op. cit.*, p. 74.

punishable facts. Unfortunately, neither of these criteria were taken seriously thereafter in the legal discourse on crimes of expression.

Dutch parliament, too, was very concerned about these clauses. The government sought to take away the concern surrounding these clauses by means of an example: 'We are unable to grasp why various doubtful cases would remain with the text as it has now been proposed. They remark that offending 'migrant workers' is not covered by the proposed clause.'[25] This optimistic stance has not, unfortunately, been confirmed. It was feared that these broad clauses would restrict freedom of expression needlessly, making opinions more easily punishable. These articles are part of the political crimes of our Criminal Law, and their application is necessarily subject to a political deliberation. In its Memorandum of response, the legislator[26] attempted to relativize the application of these penal clauses. It was necessary to be careful with respect to penalizing insulting groups of people: 'Several reasons may be adduced for this outcome. In the first place, penal stipulations are drafted with the goal of protecting groups of people so as to mitigate societal conflicts. Penal law can only provide a slight contribution to resolving societal tensions. Its application may even lead to aggravating conflicts. In addition, freedom of expression is at issue. Every needless restriction is undesirable. It must be reminded that many groups of people don't need protection from penal law. In any event, the need to provide such protection corresponds with the degree to which a group is vulnerable, taking into consideration its means of self-defense. The extent to which possible assault directed at the group may disturb society and to which it is to be expected that society itself will act must also be taken into consideration. These considerations have led us to suffice with the minimal measures to protect groups from insult.'[27] The Dutch legislator says, unambiguously and clearly, that these penal stipulations make a modest contribution to eliminating unwelcome opinions.

In contrast to Dommering, the legislator knew that applying penal law would have no purifying effect. Intentionally inflicting sorrow or, more generally, imposing punishments usually does not change the opinion of someone guilty of a crime of expression. Crimes of expression and the trials that follow them have only produced saints and political criminals, such as Socrates, Jesus, Nelson Mandela, Joseph Stalin and Ayatollah Khomeini. Dommering *cum suis* should study up on the history of freedom and tyranny as well as the foundations of democracy. Can such intolerable ignorance be remedied? Can a parliamentarian democracy function without freedom of expression? Can freedom of expression of parliamentarians, in the era of mass communication, including social media, be limited

25 Memorie van Antwoord, 1969-1970, no. 9724, p. 3.

26 In The Netherlands, the government and parliament together constitute the legislator.

27 Memorie van Antwoord, Zitting 1969-1970, no. 9724, p. 3.

to the parliament building? In the age of Facebook, even Egypt's president Mubarak, with all his intelligence services and means of oppression, could not contain the people, who converged on Tahrir Square in Cairo in 2011. Has Dommering ever seen the images from Tahrir Square?

Artists are free, which is a very comforting thought, but what about politicians? Should they all become artists in order to be able to make known the same opinions outside the protection of parliament? A representative might quote himself outside parliament. Applied hypothetically to Wilders: 'I, Wilders, would hereby quote parliamentarian Wilders, who just said in parliament that there are too many mosques.' Acts of parliament can still be quoted freely. In addition, people can still watch live broadcasts that show parliamentary debates on the Internet and television. What Wilders did in my hypothetical case is called the *art of speech*. Poets in Egypt under the regime of Mubarak excelled in it. Islamic thinkers used the tactics in the Middle Ages called the *art of writing* in philosophy.[28] Don't we want to have the possibility for anyone to quote the acts of parliament wherever he wants? In that case, democracy and freedom would cease to exist. That is certainly an option: Most people on earth do not live under a rule of freedom and democracy!

Again: Freedom is a political principle. The artist who enjoys his freedom because of parliamentary democracy is allowed to say more than a politician. This is a peculiar state of affairs. All political freedoms in a liberal constitutional state are derived from the principle of freedom as a constitutive principle that provides the people with the opportunity to let itself be represented. Prior to and during this representation there will be an intense struggle for doctrines and dogmas. This nonviolent struggle is the 'fuel' on which democracy runs. The opinions (*doxai*) collide. A political truth is founded in evident facts and opinions. In spite of that, some lawyers, moralists and politicians seek to determine a supra-legal limit of responsibility for representatives. In that light, Dommering wrote, in the article quoted above: 'The norm is that a parliamentarian is free to participate in a public discussion, but has a special responsibility as a parliamentarian. He is then to use freedom of expression, one of the basic rights of democracy, properly.' What does that special responsibility mean? What does the constitution say about it? Article 50 of the Constitution must be studied anew before implementing supra-legal responsibilities for parliamentarians: The States General (constituting together the House of Representatives and the Senate) represent the entire Dutch population. The principle of sovereignty for the people, expressed in this article, is diminished in article 67, section 3 in favor of individual parliamentarians so as to protect – in addition to the generality of the representation (article 50) – the individuality of the mandate of representation of a parliamentarian: The members of parliament

28 Leo Strauss, *Persecution and the art of writing*, Chicago, Chicago University Press, 1980.

vote without burden. Legal moralists should not think up a special, undefinable and rather subjective burden for representatives. True, parliamentarians have a special responsibility with which nonelected institutions and persons in the constitutional state are not burdened, this responsibility consisting of the fact that they represent those who have cast their vote on them in realizing legislation, in controlling the government and in conducting debates. This may entail that they need to express themselves fiercely, pugnaciously and at times derogatorily. Should they transgress the limits of decency, others will have to address them in- and outside parliament. Not only Islam or immigration are concerned here. Economic matters, social benefits, health care and foreign relations, too, often lead to heated and sometimes offensive discussions.

'Responsibility' is in this case a political notion. What is a justified action to some may be very unjustified to another. Consensus with regard to the question of whether a certain action may be qualified as a justified one may only be reached in retrospect, after several years have passed. Again, the issue is not especially Wilders but rather the constitutional principles of a liberal democratic state. Wilders is a fleeting phenomenon, but the principles will last. The fight against a heretic should never lead to the abolishment of the basic principles of democracy. Democracy is a conflictual society and legal order. The French philosopher Claude Lefort rightly indicated that a democratic order institutionalizes conflicts.[29] He who seeks to uphold the constitutional state, and considers Wilders to be a danger to the constitutional state, may not abolish the constitutional principle of freedom in the case of Wilders in order to protect Islam or Muslims. Wilders must, in turn, also realize that the principle of equality is indissolubly linked to democracy.

The court is no place for debate, and the judge is no television host who coordinates a debate. The judge may not be involved in theological or political debates. Ideas and words are free, while outward actions are punishable. Words cannot be prosecuted or judged. Words[30] that lead to criminal acts must be inquired in the course of a judicial procedure. This gives rise to the question of whether the jurisprudence distinguishes between sacred and normal opinions.

29 Claude Lefort, Politics and Human Rights, In: *The Political Forms of Modern Society. Bureaucracy, Democracy, Totalitarianism*, Cambridge: Polity Press, 1986, pp. 239-272.

30 I do not refer here to libel, slander or insult. These are not qualified as opinions.

SACRED BOOKS AND UNHOLY OPINIONS: THE HERETIC SHOULD BE ON THE FUNERAL PYRE

I made it clear as early as 2003 that discrimination is taking place between normal and sacred opinions.[31] I will limit myself here to three examples of unequal treatment. Parliamentarian Leen van Dijke was prosecuted for violating articles 137c and 137e of the Criminal Code, having said in an interview with the magazine *De Nieuwe Revu* of June 24, 1996, that 'we Christians have developed a very pernicious quality: we unjustifiably see degrees in God's commandments. As if things can be considered wicked and less wicked! By contrast, why would stealing, for example illegally taking social benefits from the government, be less wicked than sinning against the seventh commandment? Indeed, why would a practicing homosexual be any better than a thief?' The court of appeals acquitted the defendant. The Supreme Court, subsequently, on January 9, 2001, confirmed the court of appeal's ruling, stating that these expressions were directly related to the expression of the suspect's religious conviction and are consequently significant to him in the public discussion. Advocate General Machielse attached special importance to the context of the expressions and concluded, appealing to Vermeulen, that 'proclamation of belief by its nature often brings with it that adherents of other beliefs or nonbelievers are offended.'[32] The Advocate General subsequently argued that proclamation of belief is – considering the legislative history – a basic right: 'The plaintiff has not proclaimed, for instance, that all practicing homosexual are criminals, just as thieves are.' This reasoning is clearly illogical, since the defendant compared homosexuals with thieves and benefit frauds, the latter two groups of people being criminals, who stand to be punished. Why were the crimes of expression introduced? Did the legislator not set out to punish precisely those who incited to hatred or have called for violence against a group of people? It is correctly observed, by the way, that the defendant had abandoned the Biblical terminology in his statements and had expressed himself in the context of present-day penal concepts such as stealing benefits from the government.

A Rotterdam Imam caused a lot of commotion in the course of an interview in the current affairs program 'Nova' of May 3, 2001. He stated that man is not allowed deviate from his true nature, given to him by Allah. This is, of course, a central dogma in Islamic and other monotheistic faiths. What should happen to someone who conducts his life in an unnatural way? The imam knows what must be done: 'Should he deviate, he needs to receive treatment.

31 Afshin Ellian, Van Janmaat tot El Moumni. De discriminatie tussen gewone en heilige meningen, In: 'Vloeken, schelden en schimpen', *Justitiële Verkenningen* 3.03 (WODC) The Hague: Boom Juridische uitgevers 2003, pp. 26-36.

32 B.P. Vermeulen, Artikel 6, In: Akkermans en Koekoek, *De Grondwet; een artikelsgewijs commentaar*, second edition, p. 124.

Islam commands that this symptom of homosexuality must be eradicated thus.' El-Moumni thinks that 'homosexuality is not confined to those who are inflicted with this disease; it can spread. If it is contained within a group, we may treat that group and educate the individuals so that they don't despair but will find their way to the path of righteousness.' After that, he observes: 'We may not kill such a person. It is not up to the individual to punish. The judge is the proper authority to apply the laws of the Qur'an. Islam does not accept anarchy.' This is a defendant with a clear worldview. The court[33] acquitted the defendant on the basis of freedom of religion. This is a very peculiar ruling – the defendant, being a spiritual leader, spoke in terms of 'education,' 'disease' and 'deviation' – that may be considered incitement to hatred in light of the context, viz., the Islamic culture, in which gay people may be put to death on account of their sexual orientation. Should these expressions be considered in isolation from their context, being based on Sharia? The expressions are understandable against the background of Sharia. According to a number of Sharia scholars, gay people should be executed.[34] Is this to be understood as folklore from previous times? The policy is at present actually applied in countries where Sharia is the norm, such as Iran and Saudi Arabia. This is the real religious context in light of which endangering aspects of these rulings are to be judged. It is also generally known that homosexuality is a dangerous taboo in Islamic cultures. On that account, gay people are often subjected to inhumane treatment in those cultures, while those who carry a sacred book with them will be protected. Proclamation of belief is an important basic right, the Advocate General maintained.

Religious opinions are apparently attributed a special status. What about 'normal' opinions? The late Hans Janmaat (1934-2002), former leader of the Centre Democrats, expressed himself rather harshly about immigrants, to whom he consistently referred to as foreigners. His appearance was also anything but sympathetic; nor were his rhetorical talents exceptional, and he was considered repugnant by many. At the same time, his party was rightly characterized as extreme right. The Centre Democrats also consorted with other extreme right groups, such as (quasi) Neo-Nazi movements. The party's presentation was, in short, not fortunate. Still, a trial is not the appropriate venue to judge a politician. People are not prosecuted and convicted of being unsympathetic or for spewing unwelcome opinions without observing the rules of rhetoric. Janmaat participated, in his capacity as the leader of the Centre Democrats, in a demonstration in Zwolle that had been organized by the Centre Democrats and Centre Party '86. At this demonstration, Janmaat addressed those present and uttered the words cited above: 'As soon as we have the opportunity and the

33 El Moumni: Court of appeals November 18, 2002, *NJ* 2003, 24.

34 Ahmad ibn Naqib al-Misri, *Reliance of the Traveller. A classic Manual of Islamic Sacred Law*, Beltsville: Amana Publications 1994, pp. 610-611.

power to do so, we will abolish the multicultural society.' The court of appeals judged that fellow citizens' human dignity should be protected, which led to the conviction of Janmaat for incitement to discrimination of people on account of their race. The court of appeals, on December 29, 1997, qualified what Janmaat had remarked as a 'discriminatory expression with regard to groups of ethnic minorities residing in The Netherlands, since these remarks cannot be considered to have another objective than the expulsion from Dutch society of those who belong to ethnic minorities.'[35] The court of appeals also stated that Janmaat participated in a demonstration focused partly on removing those belonging to ethnic minorities from Dutch society, in contrast to the politicians who limit themselves to pointing out the problems with policies focused on integrating ethnic minorities in Dutch society. The demonstration was attended by very few people, the number of reporters exceeding that of the number of participants, just as in all other demonstrations organized by extreme right factions. Who were the politicians that were allowed, according to the court of appeals, to vent their criticism of the immigration policies? The leader of the People's Party for Freedom and Democracy, Frits Bolkestein, whose party was at that time part of the government, was referred to. Were Janmaat's remarks intent on excluding ethnic groups from Dutch society?

The Supreme Court[36] affirms the court of appeal's ruling and concludes that public verbal incitement to discrimination of people on account of their race has occurred. This is a peculiar ruling, for it does not really say anything. The Supreme Court simply does not provide a judgment concerning the contents. Yet this highest court did not consider the court of appeal's ruling incomprehensible. Advocate General Fokkens did, however, try to provide a substantial contribution in examining Janmaat's remarks. Fokkens insisted that Janmaat's remark, 'As soon as we have the opportunity and the power to do so, we will abolish the multicultural society,' could not in itself be considered to be aimed at removing ethnic minorities from Dutch society. What was chanted by the bystanders is what made Janmaat's remarks punishable: 'Our own people comes first,' 'full is full' and 'The Netherlands is for the Dutch.' Those slogans provided a context to Janmaat's remarks; they *were* focused on removing ethnic minorities from Dutch society – or were they?

Some years later, in 2001, Pim Fortuyn entered the political arena. He, too, uttered the forbidden slogan: 'Full is full.' Having been criticized for it, he changed it to 'it is too crowded in The Netherlands.' From 'full' to 'crowded'! After that, People's Party for Freedom and Democracy leader Gerrit Zalm stated, during an election debate in 2002, broadcasted by television network RTL 4, that The Netherlands is full; 'full is full'. Applying

35 Court of appeals Arnhem December 29, 1997.
36 Supreme Court May 18, 1999, No. 634.

the logic of Fokkens and the Supreme Court we cannot but conclude that Fortuyn's and Zalm's remarks were intent on removing ethnic minorities from Dutch society. They sought to close the Dutch borders to new immigrants. In less than 2 years the Supreme Court's ruling had apparently lost its legitimacy. A penal legal reasoning should last at least several decades, which was not the case here. This is a troubling outcome. The ruling was simply mistaken, illogical and barely supported by arguments, a mistake which should certainly not be repeated. A Supreme Court ruling should draw boundaries between right and wrong and between politics and law, and be able to distinguish between the political climate on the one hand and legal wisdom on the other. That is what may be expected from the highest court. The Supreme Court, just like the Public Prosecution Service, had come under the pressure of political correctness. That pressure has now dissipated. Christian Democratic Appeal leader and vice prime minister Verhagen wrote in the Dutch newspaper *de Volkskrant* of June 29, 2011, about the discontent of the Dutch population: 'Populists usually think that the government meddles with too many things, that taxes are too high, that mass immigration poses a problem and that Islam is often rather uncivilized. You may disagree with those points of view, but one would be indolent if one were to dismiss them as being unreasonable.' We now live in other times.

Leiden professor 't Hart provided an annotation to this ruling. He pointed out that elsewhere in Europe, fierce debates were also taking place concerning the desirability of a multicultural society. Hart was very critical of the apparent lack of support for the ruling. The concept of 'multicultural society' had been equated with that of 'multi ethnic,' while it remains unclear what a multicultural society actually is.

The Supreme Court makes it appear as if multiculturalism[37] is a religious conviction of the state, which must be enforced by the state by means of violence and compulsion. The multicultural church effectively produced its own heretics. To be sure, not all heretics are equally pleasing and charming. Some are more mediagenic than others, while there may be differences in the power they wield. But what is a multicultural society when one has managed to exalt multiculturalism? Our constitution does not mention such a form of society. A democratic legal order is an indeterminate one. The identity of this legal order is not noted down in a constitution for eternity. That is precisely what distinguished totalitarianism from democracy. A democratic society cannot be substantivelyspecified

37 I refer to a small number of critical studies of the multicultural society of some renowned scholars: P.B. Cliteur, *Moderne Papoea's. Dilemma's van een multiculturele samenleving*, Amsterdam: Arbeiderspers 2002; Gerrit Manenschijn, *Levenslang mores leren. De uitdaging van multiculturele samenleving*, Kampen: Uitgeverij Ten Have Baarn 2003; Bassam Tibi, *Europa zonder identiteit? De crisis van de multiculturele samenleving*, Antwerp: Deltas 2003.

by the state and its organs as a catholic, protestant, socialist, Islamic, racial or multicultural society.

In *La question de la démocratie*, Claude Lefort reaches the conclusion that democracy is the historic society par excellence; it is a society that includes the undetermined and safeguards it. Totalitarianism resists this indeterminacy.[38] The indeterminacy of the democratic state safeguards the indeterminacy of a democratic society in which citizens can find a way to the future in freedom. A democratic legal order is a vital part of a dynamic society that is literally realized through continually speaking and acting. In that respect, the democratic society is open to what will happen. That is why the constitution does not correspond with the desire of some who describe society ideologically with an eternal point of reference. According to Lefort, we should not confuse this indeterminacy with empirical facts. Multiculturalism is a factual state of affairs from which other facts may ensue. Pleasant and less pleasant facts can emerge from a pluralistic society. It may be that in 100 years, there will no longer be a multicultural society but a mono-cultural one: The intermingling of various cultures might bring to pass a new unity, nobody knows. What nobody knows cannot be protected or penalized by penal law. The concept of 'multiculturalism' is a sociological description of present-day communities, which should not be confused with concepts such as 'race' or 'religion.' Heretics at times say absurd things. How could Janmaat abolish the multicultural society? How could he bring to an end the situation in the largest Dutch cities, in which almost half the people come from abroad? In order to remedy these absurdities, democracy uses a clear mechanism: The public discussion. The highest court should have referred Janmaat and the district attorney to that discussion.

The defendant regularly made remarks that are reprehensible from a political and ethical perspective, but we must be reminded that an individual, however reprehensible he may be, is only tried and convicted on the basis of the indictment. As a consequence, a defendant may never be prosecuted for everything he does, including his political misdeeds. Janmaat was convicted on the basis of his faulty biography, apparently appealing to a less solidified constitutional right, namely, freedom of expression. Why were his expressions not interpreted in the context of a public discussion? Was he not, after all, a politician, just like his colleague Van Dijke, and was it not his task to participate in public discussions both within and outside parliament? Meindert Fennema analyzes the Janmaat case ruthlessly: 'The prosecution policy regarding racism was initiated by the minister for justice. The Attorneys general had, at the initiative of the minister for justice, circulated a directive instructing district attorneys to inquire into every possible application of article 137d of

38 Claude Lefort, *Democracy and Political Theory*, translated by David Macey, Cambridge: Polity Press 1988, pp. 9-21.

the Dutch Criminal Code and to prosecute whenever possible. The Public Prosecution Service was to report its findings to the House of Representatives. [...] The separation of powers, to which politicians presently appeal whenever they are asked to comment on Hans Janmaat's conviction, was never respected in precisely the respect of the application of article 137d.'[39] The official creed had to be protected and the heretics had to be prosecuted.

It may be objected at this point that Nazism came to power utilizing democratic means. The Weimar republic is a true nightmare for every parliamentarian democracy. In the final democratic elections (of November 1932), the National Socialist German Workers' Party obtained 33.1 percent of the votes; within four months, this party had lost almost two million votes. The Nazis could not realize a majority vote through free elections.[40] The explosive increase of the relatively large support was not only the result of the economic circumstances but was also related to the Weimar republic itself, in which pressure groups played a decisive part in destructing democracy. In 1931, Hitler called Ernst Röhm back to lead the Sturmabteilung. 260,000 violent Nazis acted as animals against the communists, social democrats, liberals, Jews, Catholics, conservatives and others who had another orientation.[41] When the Nuremberg Laws were passed in 1935, democracy was already dead and buried. Hitler had at that time been in power for two years. A decision to adopt the laws was made, of course, but it was not a majority decision taken in the course of a democratic decision process. By suppressing the freedom of expression of others, Hitler managed to realize a regime comprised of lies and propaganda. Freedom of expression for those with diverging opinions was factually removed by the violence of militia. In order to safeguard democracy, then, freedom of expression should not be restricted but, by contrast, be protected both legally and *de facto*. Where freedom is absent, politics and the legal order result in tyranny. The problem of the Weimar republic was that the state was not up to the task of combatting the violent militia and activists in the streets. The state monopoly of violence had been violated. Freedom disappeared in the emerging tyranny. Hitler rose to power *inter alia* because of the use of violence, the economic crisis and the demise of the Weimar republic. Hitler was no heretic, but evil itself and the founder of the diabolical church.

39 Meindert Fennema, Schrap het haatzaaiartikel uit het Wetboek van Strafrecht, In: *Vrij Nederland*, March 23, 2003.

40 Ian Kershaw, *Hitler. 1889-1936: Hubris*, London: Penguin Press, 1998, p. 461.

41 Ian Kershaw, *op. cit.*, p. 416.

The Final Stage, the Judge: The Heretic on the Line

The judge has spoken. Wilders has been acquitted on all counts. In contrast to the court of appeals, the court took into consideration the precise context in which Wilders made his remarks. Those remarks had to be interpreted in order to infer their meaning. That is why the court judged several remarks by means of the phrases 'as such' and 'the coherence with the rest of the interview or article in which the remark was made.' The court reached the conclusion that Wilders mainly focused, as a politician, on pernicious aspects of Islam and the Qur'an: 'Considering that the defendant, in his expressions, attacks the religion rather than individuals (Muslims), it cannot be proved legally and compellingly that through these expressions he incites hatred against and/or discrimination of Muslims, as he has been charged with.' Some of Wilders' remarks did have a discriminatory nature, but these were, according to the court, political propositions he made in the course of a public discussion, and which he suggested in his capacity as representative. The judge also pointed to the nature and extent of the discussion: 'The court establishes that in the period in which the remarks were made the multicultural society and immigration featured prominently in the public discussion. As this discussion intensifies, freedom of expression is awarded more room. As was said, even then, remarks may not offend, shock and disturb.' The judge seemed to say that many people, including those who oppose Wilders, took part in the discussion, and matters became intense. Not just Wilders' position, with respect to Islam and multiculturalism, was fierce; the same qualification applies to some other politicians (such as Ayaan Hirsi Ali and Frits Bolkestein) and intellectuals. For that reason, the judge did not want to punish just one participant in this discussion, which would effectively mean eliminating him legally. The judge took into consideration justice, democracy and the legitimacy of his ruling. With regard to the expression 'If you walk on the street, you will see to what it leads. You can sense that you are no longer in your own country. [...] There is a struggle going on and we must defend ourselves,' the judge cautions Wilders: 'The defendant ventures on the limit of what is legally allowed by expressing himself in this way. In the interview, the defendant claims not to have a problem with Muslims but rather with Islam. The court rules that the expression, in light of the rest of the interview, does not incite the extreme emotion of a deep resentment and hostility that constitutes hatred.'

Wilders is on the threshold. Violence (as well as calling to committing crimes), as an inherent element of hatred, is of crucial importance here to be able to speak of incitement to hatred. The court has ruled thus, and the case has come to a final conclusion. The circus has broken up. International media followed this trial, many wondering why Islam and Muslims merit a separate protection? Islam does not merit a special protection in any event. Islamic feelings do not even merit an added protection, as the Supreme Court ruling on the poster 'stop the tumor that is called Islam'[42] shows. Similarly, Muslims do not merit any more protection than do other citizens in The Netherlands. After all, no vulnerable minority is concerned here. Muslims participate very intensely to politics, public administration, science and other sectors of society, to which may be added that their country of origin offers protection to Muslims. Moreover, it is precisely because of fierce debates that a change in the position of Muslims has come to fruition. According to the National Coordinator for Security and Counterterrorism, fewer Muslims radicalize at present than a few years ago. Even the showing of the movie Fitna (March 2008) has not led to unruly behavior. Dutch Muslims have not resorted to vandalism, for which even Wilders complimented them. The court maintained the same distinction on which the Supreme Court had previously insisted, between Muslims and Islam. Is this distinction justifiable?

Since 2001, I have discussed, both nationally and internationally, the distinction between three phenomena: Islam, Political Islam and Muslims.[43] At conferences, and in articles, I have argued time and again why these categories should not be confused. Wilders has acted in accordance with said categories. One must ponder whether Islam can coincide with Muslims, and what the implications of their being indistinguishable concepts would be. John Locke (1632-1704) already distinguished, in his works on tolerance, between Catholicism and Catholics.[44] If all Catholics were to live strictly by the rules of Catholicism, they would never be able to be citizens of a country not ruled by Catholics, since they must abide by the rules that contravene any sort of free and tolerant society. There are, of course, various sorts of Catholics. The same line of reasoning applies to Muslims. If Muslims coincide with Islam, Muslims can only live under an Islamic regime. This presupposes that Muslims are precisely aware of what Islam means, and that Muslims should voluntarily conduct their lives according to the norms of Islam.

A survey of Muslims living in different countries makes it clear that these presumptions are not verified for the majority of Muslims. The majority seldom visit a mosque; if not, countries such as Turkey (with a population of 80 million people) and Egypt (the same number of people) should have to erect tens of thousands of additional mosques. Someone who considers Muslims and Islam as interchangeable categories view all Muslims in the world as one entity. In reality, there are many sorts of Muslims: Those who drink whisky,

42 Supreme Court March 10, 2009, LJN: BF0655.

43 A. Ellian, The legal order of political religion: A comparative study of political Islam and political Christendom, In: *Terrorism: ideology, law and policy*, edited by Gelijn Molier, Afshin Ellian and David Suurland, Dordrecht: Republic of Letters 2011, pp. 187-236.

44 John Locke, An Essay on Toleration, In: *Locke, Political Essays*, edited by Mark Goldie, Cambridge: Cambridge University Press 1999, p 145 ff.

those who are believers (in many varieties), those who don't believe, atheist Muslims, whoremongers, mobsters, Sufi Muslims, terrorist Muslims etc.

Do all these categories form an indestructible unity with Islam? And is Islam conceivable without Muslims? There are no Greeks who believe in Apollo, and yet Apollo still exists. Islam, as an essential part of history, will always be there. Islam is no longer dependent on Muslims: It is a historic concept. What is a Muslim? If one of your parents is a Muslim, then so are you. If you do not want to be one, you will be an apostate, with all the consequences that follow from it. If 'Islam' and 'Muslims' were to refer to the same phenomenon, all the defects of Islam would have to be attributed to Muslims, which is incorrect and unwarranted. First of all, the proposition is untrue. Most Muslims don't even know what Islam means exactly. Second, with some exceptions, a single Muslim cannot represent the entire Islam. Islam is not, from a theological point of view, the result of activities from Muslims. Islam is the will of Allah. If no distinction remained between Islam and Muslims, there would be a permanent expression of Allah's will in every newborn Muslim. This is, from an Islamic theological point of view, not only absurd but also a sign of blasphemy. That is why imams worldwide state that the shortcomings of Muslims are not to be attributed to Islam. Why is that? Because Islam is, from the perspective of Muslims and the Islamic tradition, the one perfect religion, which is also the eternal expression of the will of the Supreme Being, while a Muslim, being a human being, may be seduced to sin and commit crimes. Some may not like this, but Wilders has acted in accordance with Islamic thought. Islam itself makes the distinction between Islam and Muslims. I, too, follow the line of thought that once one lets Islam and Muslim coincide, one should be willing to attribute all the violent aspects of Islam to Muslims. This would mean the end of any possibility of peace with Muslims.

The trial has concluded in favor of freedom of expression and democracy. In the end, Wilders has acknowledged, not in court but elsewhere, that some of his expressions are crude and demeaning. The heretic has lost his status as a heretic. He may offend, criticize and mock the multicultural church, since there are apparently no official dogmas with regard to multiculturalism and Islam that must be defended by means of state violence. The heretic is free. The multicultural church has inflicted some damage. The generation that succeeds us will still discuss the trial that ended heresy by acquitting the heretic. *Hairein*, heresy, is choosing. Lawyers who uphold a liberal constitutional state are often the true heretics of this world. They, too, will have to choose. Freedom is nothing other than a continual repetition of an eternal heresy. Thus the adventure began of man as an eternally vulnerable beginner, a heretic.

13 Making the World Safe for Democracy

Freedom of Speech and Modern Democracy

Arie-Jan Kwak

Introduction

One hundred years ago, the Great War started with Austria's declaration of war against Serbia after the assassination of Franz Ferdinand in Sarajevo. Soon, almost every European nation was involved, and while the conflict escalated, it spread to other continents as members of the British Commonwealth and English, German and French colonies in Africa and Asia got involved. Woodrow Wilson had promised the American electorate to keep the United States out of the war, but in April, 1917, he decided that it was no longer possible to remain neutral and declared war on Germany, Austria and their allies. By the spring of 1918, four million American soldiers were mobilized and in the last months of the war the US army effort proved to be decisive. Wilson persuaded many Congress-men and those in the American public who were still against entering the war with these well-known words:

> 'The world must be made safe for democracy. Its peace must be planted upon the tested foundations of political liberty. We have no selfish ends to serve. We desire no conquest, no dominion. We seek no indemnities for ourselves, no material compensation for the sacrifices we shall freely make. We are but one of the champions of the rights of mankind. We shall be satisfied when those rights have been made as secure as the faith and the freedom of nations can make them.'[1]

'The first casualty when war comes is truth,' US Senator Hiram Warren Johnson reportedly said when he pleaded against Wilson's intention to lead American into war.[2] Johnson probably referred to the fact that governments of nations that are at war almost always censure critical opinions and thereby curtail the freedom of speech of its citizens. The Bush doctrine, devised after 9/11 to justify the invasion of Afghanistan and Iraq in

1 President Woodrow Wilson's address before a joint session of Congress on April 2, 1917, to seek a Declaration of War against Germany.

2 There is, however, no record of this.

order to fight Al Qaida, also appealed to freedom and democracy, and Bush repeatedly said that he hoped that the military interventions might tip off a process of democratization in the Middle East. At home, however, many Americans felt that the need to stand united in this war against terrorism was so important that they allowed the Bush administration to seriously restrict their hard-won freedoms (and especially their right to privacy) without much protest. In the war that makes the world safe for democracy, democracy is generally just so much lumber; democratic war is a contradiction in terms.

Carl Schmitt famously presented the distinction between friend and enemy as characteristic of the political domain. Schmitt thought of politics in terms of what later came to be known as *identity politics*; the kind of politics involved when identity defining characteristics such as race, ethnicity, or religion are at stake.[3] In the first part of this essay, I will explore the logic of such politics of recognition and the implications for a basic democratic value such as the right to freedom of speech. In the second part of this article, I will contrast this with the egalitarian culture that seems intrinsic to democracy. With Ronald Dworkin I will argue that this egalitarianism comes with the *moral* obligation to respect the equal dignity of fellow citizens and human beings in general.

In the Netherlands, this moral obligation has been made into a *legal* obligation as the Dutch criminal code qualifies hate speech, incitement to violence and, especially, incitement to discrimination against individuals and groups as punishable by law. Criminal law, however, seems to be a rather poor instrument for this purpose; the use of force by the state might destroy the democratic culture that it sets out to defend. Teaching subjects a lesson in equality by means of criminal law seems as contradictory as the idea of a democratic war.

THE POLITICS OF RECOGNITION

We are presently at war, and have been for the past 1400 years. According to the Dutch politician Geert Wilders, the moment Mohammed founded the Islamic faith, this dangerous ideology declared war on us infidels:

> 'Islam is above all a political ideology; a totalitarian doctrine aimed on domination, violence and oppression (...) Islam is striving for world power. Jihad is the duty of every Muslim. The Koran prescribes behavior that is in contradiction with our legal order such as anti-Semitism, discrimination of women, killing infidels and holy wars until Islam will dominate the world.'[4]

3 Not to mention gender and sexual orientation.

4 Election program PVV (Party for freedom) 2010-2015. "Het is oorlog, Vz, het vrije Westen is de oorlog verklaard. Onze vrijheid, onze cultuur, de toekomst van ons land en onze kinderen staat op het spel. We

But there is not just a war going on between Islam and those Islam purportedly tries to subjugate to its laws and customs, there is also a 'total war' going on between the reigning (leftist) political elite in the Western world and the common people Wilders represents. Thus, we are also involved in a class war and, in the war against Islam, the reigning 'multicultural elite' have taken sides with our enemy. This elite try to hide the ugly truth about Islam from all of us by silencing its critics:

> 'Everywhere in Europe, not only in the Netherlands, the multicultural élite is fighting a total war against their population, the issue of which is the continuation of mass-immigration and Islamizing, which will result eventually in an Islamic Europe – a Europe without freedom: Eurabia.'[5]

Wilders uses very strong language here, he frames his political objectives in terms of a 'total war' and 'a violent struggle for world domination.' According to Carl Schmitt, this is not only typical of Wilders, but of politics in general: 'The specific political distinction to which political actions and motives can be reduced is that between friend and enemy,' he wrote in 1932.[6] This German jurist and political philosopher famously characterized politics as a struggle for domination between friends and enemies, thereby arguing that *partiality* is the typical ethos of the political sphere.

In short, *politics is war by other means*, to paraphrase the famous quote by another German who wrote a classic on the subject of war.[7] In their strife for power, politicians inadvertently divide the world into camps: Those who are with us and those who are against us. Politics demands building and continuously maintaining a network of political allies that functions as your power base in the struggle against your political enemies. This is indeed how Wilders presents his political mission to us.

The ultimate implication of this concept of the political is that there is no neutral ground from which a third party can evaluate and reconcile the political ideologies that compete for prominence. Schmitt argues that the political battle is ultimately an *existential* battle between 'us' and 'them.' If we want to protect our collective identity – the values, standards and habits that we identify with and that make us into a community – it is necessary to confront the other, the stranger:

---

moeten keihard terugslaan, zowel in Nederland en de rest van het bedreigde Westen als in Irak en Syrië." Geert Wilders tijdens het parlementaire debat over de militaire interventie in Irak, 2 oktober 2014.

5 'De totale oorlog van de elite tegen het volk', *De Pers*, 11 February 2011; cp. H. de Bruijn, *Geert Wilders in debat, over de framing en reframing van een politieke boodschap*, Boom Lemma uitgevers, The Hague 2010, p. 38-41.

6 Schmitt, C., *The Concept of the Political*, The University of Chicago Press, Chicago 1996, p. 26.

7 "Der Krieg ist eine bloße Fortsetzung der Politik mit anderen Mitteln": War is merely the continuation of politics (or policy) by other means. Von Clausewitz, *On War*, Princeton University Press, Princeton NJ 1984 (1832), p. 87.

> 'And it is sufficient for his nature that he is, in a specially intense way, existentially something different and alien, so that in the extreme case conflicts with him are possible. These can neither be decided by a previously determined general norm nor by the judgment of a disinterested and therefore neutral third party.'[8]

Schmitt argues that it is up to the parties themselves to find out, in real circumstances, to what extent this strange 'other' is a threat to their own identity and way of life – 'die eigene, seinsmäßige Art von Leben.' In such a struggle there is no neutral ground, no 'independent norm' from which we can judge and reconcile the claims and slogans of the conflicting parties. We can see this particularly well when we try to decide whether the words used in political struggles are to be protected under the right to the freedom of speech or to be outlawed as an example of hate speech. With regard to the freedom of speech, there is no politically neutral ground; *it's politics all the way down*, Stanley Fish writes:

> 'There is no such thing as hate speech if you mean by that designation speech that would be judged hateful by an independent norm. Instead there is speech that is hateful to some persons because it offends the ideals to which they pledge allegiance. To those who produce the speech, however, it is not hateful but needful, and they will hear as hateful (or perverse or dangerous) speech that offends against their ideals.'[9]

Obviously, the striving parties think of their ideas, their customs and their beliefs (whether of a religious nature or not) as superior to those of their political enemies. They think of these beliefs are generally *true*, and the political strife therefore is all about protecting the truth against the lies and deceit of those who try to submit us to their 'truth.' Indeed, Wilders often frames his political struggle as a conflict to protect the truth from those who try to deceive us with their lies: 'Facts, facts, facts and only facts' Wilders said about the statements about Islam for which he was criminally prosecuted in 2011. And surely, 'telling the truth cannot be a crime.'[10]

Wilders' Freedom Party (PVV) recently called the Moroccan culture inferior to Western civilization.[11] During a recent election gathering, the PVV-members demanded less Moroccans in the Netherlands and Geert Wilders promised them that this was going to

8 Schmitt 1996, p. 27.
9 Fish, S., *The Trouble with Principle*, Harvard University Press, Cambridge Mass. 1999, p. 70.
10 'Wat waar is, kan niet strafbaar zijn', *Dagblad de Limburger*, 20 January 2010.
11 'PVV: Marokkaanse cultuur minderwaardig', *Telegraaf*, 13 May 2014.

be arranged.[12] PVV sympathizers undoubtedly think that the fact that Morocco is an Islamic country is part of the problem. The PVV and its sympathizers generally associate Islam with anti-Semitism, homophobia, discrimination of women, and violence against apostates; there must be some sort of relation between Islam and the high criminality rate of young Moroccan men. Islamic values are therefore a threat to our liberal constitution and identity, they argue; we need to take a stand and fight the influence of Islam before it is too late.

On the other hand, surely many people in the Islamic world think of the West as inferior. The modern Western culture is thought to be materialistic, individualistic, sexually and morally degenerate, imperialistic and hypocritical. By contrast, Islam is considered to be spiritual, communitarian, morally pure and high minded. When Islam is part of your identity, it becomes part of your sense of self-worth, or *dignity*, just like the Westerners take personal pride in the achievements of Western civilization. From Schmitt's point of view, however, this is all part of the political game. *Of course* 'die eigene, seinsmäßige Art von Leben' is superior to the 'others' culture and way of life. This civic pride is actually indispensable for a political community to flourish, as it is a source of public-spiritedness, courage, and self-sacrifice – in one word, civic pride is a source of public *morale*.

Indeed, according to Francis Fukuyama such *megalothymia*, this sense of superiority, is characteristic of the struggle of recognition that politics often entails. Francis Fukuyama echoes Schmitt's analysis when he says that 'the desire for recognition is the most specifically political part of the human personality because it is what drives men to want to assert themselves over other men.'[13] This may come as a surprise to some. Fukuyama realizes that in the Western world we often do not think of politics in such terms. According to Fukuyama, 'to the extent we generalize about politics, we are much more likely to view it as a competition for power between economic interests, a struggle to divide up wealth and the other good things in life.'[14]

Seeing politics as merely 'a competition for power between economic interests' may indeed have its merits. A struggle for recognition leads to high-minded and uncompromising identity politics. Depicting the political realm as a kind of marketplace, however, changes its character for the better. The advantage of thinking in terms of interests – as opposed to existential, identity-defining values – is that interests make compromises possible and that politics becomes much more pragmatic and business-like.[15] We can think of politics as a marketplace for ideas, and this market will facilitate the free expression,

12 The Dutch prosecution office investigated this "Less Moroccans-speech" and has decided to prosecute Wilders as it constituted a criminal act under provisions 137c, and 137d of the Dutch Criminal code. 'Wilders wacht vervolging', *NRC Handelsblad*, 9 October 2014.

13 Fukuyama, F., *The End of History and the Last Man*, Hamish Hamilton, London 1992, p. 163.

14 Fukuyama 1992, p. 162.

15 Cp. Posner, R.A., *Law, Pragmatism, and Democracy*, Harvard University Press, Cambridge Mass. 2003, p. 166; cp. Schumpeter, J.A., *Capitalism, Socialism and Democracy*, Boston: George Allen & Unwin, 1976, p. 269-302.

discussion and evaluation of these ideas such that 'politics is more likely to discover truth and eliminate error, or to produce good rather than bad policies.'[16]

The marketplace is the home of the *homo economicus*, the individual who maximizes his individual satisfactions, preferences, and self-interest.[17] Many feel that to describe politics in such terms makes a caricature of our political practices and institutions; some may even feel that this image totally perverts politics. In the Islamic world especially, some probably think of this as typical for Western 'civilization.' Schmitt does not think of politics as a marketplace at all, he thinks of is as an *arena* that is characterized by a struggle for recognition that ultimately allows for no compromise. In the political arena, *the winner takes all*; in the end, mediation is not an option because there is no neutral, middle ground.

Is politics about (economical) interest or is it about identity? Probably about both. It is clear, however, that interest-based politics does not provoke as much passion and emotion in people as identity-politics. If it does not directly concern his or her own purse, the reeling and dealing of interest-politics leaves the average citizen cold. This is perhaps the most important *selling point* of such a political culture: 'The interaction on the marketplace is deliciously superficial,' Richard Posner writes. When the ideological feathers have been shaken off, the relationships between the parties will be down-to-earth and pragmatic:

> 'Competition for wealth and other private goods is intense. But it is less tense, less emotional, and less dangerous than the struggle for power, which is to say for the means of physical coercion. As Samuel Johnson said, men are rarely so innocently engaged as when they are trying to make money. Commercial rivalry is, in a sense, deliciously superficial, lacking the threat of "psychic annihilation" that is latent in political conflict even when it does not lead to violence, because political beliefs are often deeply rooted in people's sense of identity.'[18]

The strength of such a businesslike and pragmatic political culture is, however, simultaneously its weakness. Marketplace-politics is not very mediagenic, and the public is generally not very interested in it. It pays much more for politicians to frame their political struggle as a *clash of civilizations* rather than as merely a matter of ordinary horse trading to get the best political deal. Appealing to people's self-interest is therefore not always a very good political strategy. Georg Lakoff writes:

> 'People do not necessarily vote in their self-interest. They vote their identity. They vote their values. They vote for who they identify with. They may identify

16 Dworkin, R., *Freedom's Law*, The Moral Reading of the American Constitution, Harvard University Press, Cambridge Mass. 1996, p. 200.

17 Posner, R.A., *The Problems of Jurisprudence*, Harvard University Press, Cambridge Mass. 1990, p. 353.

18 Posner, 2003, p. 173, 174.

> with their self-interest. That can happen. It is not that people never care about their self-interest. But they vote their identity. And if their identity fits their self-interest, they will vote for that.'[19]

The far-reaching consequence of voting your identity is that, ultimately, politics has indeed the character of an irresolvable, existential battle between 'us' and this strange 'other'; a battle that, as described by Schmitt, always threatens to degenerate into violence. And as there is ultimately no neutral ground, Schmitt argues that law is subordinated to politics and not the other way around. In the end, violence has the last word.[20]

In short, it is either us or them; politics is ultimately about identity and in identity-politics, there is no impartial third party who can intervene and mediate. Thus, this battle will, if necessary, ultimately end in war. As Fukuyama states: 'It is [therefore] not surprising that so many political philosophers have seen the central problem of politics as one of taming or harnessing the desire for recognition in a way that would serve the political community as a whole.'[21] How is political order possible in a world full of people ready and willing to sacrifice their self-interest, their goods, and even their life, for recognition in a modern culturally diverse and pluralistic society?

THE EGALITARIAN PLATEAU

In his book *The End of History and the Last Man* published in 1992, Francis Fukuyama famously claimed that mankind has actually once and for all solved this political problem. The history (of political thought) has come to an end and the last man in the title of the book is the modern (liberal egalitarian) democrat. In the Western world, the political morality has already been thoroughly transformed and, according to Fukuyama, the rest of the world is sure to follow. Pivotal to this solution is the total ban on *megalothymia*, the desire to be recognized as superior. Indeed, 'megalothymia has been ethically vanquished from the moral world,' Fukuyama writes, and has been replaced by two things:'The first is a blossoming of the desiring part of the soul, which manifests itself as a thorough-going *economization* of life.' This 'thorough-going economization' refers to the unleashing of economic man; indeed, in the Western world we do not see this materialistic individualist as a threat to the moral fabric of the community anymore, we nowadays see the *homo economicus* as instrumental for the wealth and thereby political stability of modern society

19 G. Lakoff, *Don't Think of an Elephant! Know Your Values and Frame the Debate*, Chelsea Green, White River Junction 2004, p. 19; cp. G. Lakoff, *Moral Politics, How Liberals and Conservatives Think*, University of Chicago Press, Chicago 2002.

20 Schmitt 1996, p. 26.

21 Fukuyama 1992, p. 163.

as a whole.[22] We already saw how refocusing on (economic) interests can change the attitudes of those involved in the dispute, and Fukuyama argues that this attitude replaced the boastful pride of aristocratic man.

'The second thing that remains in place of *megalothymia* is an all-pervasive iso-thymia, that is, the desire to be recognized as the equal of other people.'[23] *Isothymia* is the second best option when superiority cannot be (permanently) secured. And indeed, hardly any member of a modern democracy ever states a claim to superiority over other human beings in society; both moral and legal claims are nearly always framed in terms of a right to *equality*. Fukuyama:

> 'The *megalothymia* of the few would have to give way to the *isothymia* of the many. Men would not cease to have chests, but their chests would no longer inflate with such overbearing pride. Those whom the old, pre-democratic world failed to satisfy were the vast majority of mankind; those left unsatisfied in the modern world of universal recognition are many fewer in number. Hence the remarkable stability and strength of democracy in the contemporary world.'[24]

Ronald Dworkin argues that 'the abstract egalitarian principle' that Fukuyama refers to here is indeed generally accepted by now.[25] We all think that modern government has to respect the egalitarian standard, the legitimacy of modern government largely depends on the fact that each and every citizen under its authority feels he or she *matters*, and matters *equally*. The modern state competed with the authority of other authorities and institutions in society, of which the church was preeminent, and in this competition it gradually conquered the hearts and minds of the members of the population by guaranteeing equal respect for their liberty and equal concern for their vested interests.

The Canadian political philosopher Will Kymlicka referred to Dworkin's *Taking Rights Seriously* when he argued that, indeed, every plausible political theory nowadays has equality as its ultimate value. A modern political theory that argues from the axiomatic superiority of one group of human beings over others (like the racist national-socialist political theories for example) have no standing whatsoever in contemporary political philosophy. Kymlicka refers to this as the 'egalitarian plateau' which implies that 'the fundamental argument is not whether to accept equality, but how to best interpret it.'[26]

---

22 The classical references here are (of course): Smith, A., *The Wealth of Nations*, and Mandeville, *The Fable of the Bees*, cp. Posner 1990, p. 382.

23 Fukuyama 1992, p. 190.

24 Fukuyama 1992, p. 334.

25 Dworkin, R., *Sovereign Virtue*, Harvard University Press, Cambridge Mass. 2000, p. 128.

26 Kymlicka, W., *Contemporary Political Philosophy*, Oxford University Press, Oxford UK, 1990, p. 4, 5; cp Dworkin, R., *Taking Rights Seriously*, Harvard University Press, Cambridge Mass. 1977, Nagel, T., *Mortal Questions*, Cambridge University Press, Cambridge UK 1979, p. 111.

The social and cultural development of an egalitarian democratic society might partly be the result of the 'horizontalization' of a standard that was originally only meant to address the vertical relation between the state and its subjects. Modern democratic government is not allowed to arbitrarily discriminate between citizens, but this norm spread throughout society and is now thought to address the (more or less) horizontal relationships among the citizens themselves as well. Of course, we do not owe others the level of concern that we owe to those we hold dear as friends and relatives. We do not expect people to become saints and sacrifice their lives, goods and interests, and especially not the lives, goods and interests of their friends and families, to the benefit of total strangers.[27]

Although we cannot and do not expect total strangers to show us the level of concern they show their friends and families, Dworkin argues that, in important matters, we do expect others to act with *integrity*: 'That is, according to convictions that inform and shape their lives as a whole, rather than capriciously and whimsically.' Moreover, Dworkin goes on to say that:

> 'We assume [...] that we can recognize other people's acts as expressing a conception of fairness or justice or decency even when we do not endorse that conception ourselves. This ability is an important part of our more general ability to treat other with respect, and it is therefore a prerequisite of civilizations.'[28]

With regard to the vertical relationship between the state and its subjects, things are not different. Citizens expect the state to act with integrity also; that is, that it acts in accordance with a coherent set of basic principles and rules that citizens can recognize as expressing a particular conception of fairness or justice, even if they do not endorse this conception themselves. Ronald Dworkin has also provided us with a particular interpretation (or 'conception') of the norm of equality – an interpretation which relates the idea of human dignity to both the ideal of equality and the ideal of liberty, and tries to construe these three basic ethical notions into a coherent whole.

This is no mean feat. How does Dworkin manage to integrate the idea of human dignity with those of equality and liberty? And, importantly, what does his particular conception of equality mean for the relationship between the modern state and its subjects? Dworkin argues that a legitimate government respects the equal dignity of its subjects first of all by respecting the *personal responsibility* of each citizen for making a success of his own life, 'a responsibility that includes exercising his judgment about what kind of life would be

27 Dworkin, R., *Is Democracy Possible Here?*, Principles for a New Political Debate, Princeton University Press Princeton NJ and Oxford UK 2006, p. 94.

28 Dworkin, R., *Law's Empire*, Harvard University Press, Cambridge Mass. 1987, p. 166.

successful for him.'[29] Thus, respecting equal dignity implies respect for personal responsibility. But this, in turn, implies guaranteeing citizens the liberty to freely decide what would constitute a life worth living for them:

> 'If liberty is valuable because lives led under liberty are more valuable lives, then the egalitarian principle itself requires government to attend to liberty, because it requires government to have concern for the lives of those it governs.'[30]

Liberty, however, implies *equal* liberty: Governments should guarantee equal liberty to all. Liberty and equality are thereby two sides of the same coin for Dworkin. Dworkin argues that we practically all share the idea that our life has intrinsic value to us, but that this 'principle of self-respect' – the objective importance of your life – 'is mirrored in the objective importance of everyone else's.'[31]

Dworkin calls this 'Kant's principle' because it obviously refers to the Kantian idea that we cannot escape, without contradiction, generalizing this idea of a right to personal responsibility and individual liberty. This generalization connects liberty and equality: Citizens are entitled to equal respect for their liberty and equal concern for their particular interests and needs. A legitimate government, therefore, respects the equality of a citizen by also respecting the equal importance of each life to those who live this life.

In short, Dworkin's conception of equality implies liberty and his conception of liberty implies equal liberty and therefore equality. The political rights to particular kinds of liberty, like the right to the freedom of speech, are 'trumps': Such rights cannot be sacrificed for the sake of the policies and compromises that politics habitually trades in.[32] In other words, rights function as a kind of fortification against governmental intrusion, or intrusion by any other powerful party, that jeopardizes the ethical independence and freedom of the citizens.

The *fundamental* human right, according to Dworkin, is the right to be treated by our government with a certain kind of attitude: 'An attitude that expresses the understanding that each person is a human being whose dignity matters. [...] The most glaring example of contempt for this principle lies in blatant prejudice and discrimination.'[33] This fundamental human right, which obviously derives from the principle of human dignity and relates to the right to equal respect and concern, supports the traditional liberal rights to free speech and expression, conscience, political activity and religion. Dworkin argues that

29 Dworkin 2006, p. 10.
30 Dworkin 2000, p. 130.
31 Dworkin 2011, p. 260.
32 Dworkin 2006, p. 31; cp. Dworkin 1977.
33 Dworkin 2006, p. 37.

in modern democracy, the right to freedom of speech is both instrumentally and intrinsically important. Protecting the freedom of speech can be thought to be both effective and efficient in helping us to learn the truth, and to decide whether we are governed well or badly. We associated this instrumental justification with the idea of the free market of ideas earlier.

The second kind of justification supposes, however, that freedom of speech is an essential and 'constitutive' characteristic of a democratic society. Thinking of freedom of speech as a good in itself, as intrinsically valuable, leads to a more principled defense of the right that seeks to protect it. Dworkin argues that this constitutive characteristic has two dimensions. Firstly, freedom of speech is valuable because morally responsible people should be trusted to make up their own minds about what is good and what is bad, or what is true or false: 'Government insults its citizens, and denies their moral responsibility, when it decrees that they cannot bet trusted to hear opinions that might persuade them to dangerous or offensive convictions.'[34]

But there is a more active side to this moral responsibility as well. People should not only be granted to make up their minds about what others have to say, they should also be able to freely *speak* there minds, 'to express [their beliefs and convictions] to others, out of respect and concern for them, and out of a compelling desire that truth be known, justice served, and the good procured.'[35]

Surely both the right to express yourself and the right to judge opinions for yourself are not absolute. In some instances, these rights will have to yield to security in case of emergency – American law generally refers to the 'clear and present danger test' in this context. But, this exception granted, Dworkin considers these rights to be close to absolute as they are closely connected to the second principle of dignity, the principle of moral responsibility.[36] Curtailing free speech is patronizing, governments should not treat its citizens as irresponsible children and decide what they should and should not say or hear.

American law is, however, less restrictive than Dutch law on this matter. Dutch criminal law actually outlaws hate speech and speech that incites violence against particular individuals and groups. People that express their hatred for others in society, that incite violence and discrimination, can pose a serious threat to public order and security. Criminal law is, of course, largely dedicated to deal with such threats.

But is government also allowed to curtail the freedom of speech of citizens under these principles in order to protect the *equal dignity* of fellow citizens? In contrast to American law, Dutch law does try to protect Dutch subjects from speech that incites *discrimination*. Incitement to discrimination can of course also pose a security threat. But it can also be thought to serve an ulterior motive, a purpose that readily follows from Dworkins political

34 Dworkin 1996, p. 200.
35 Dworkin 1996, p. 200.
36 Dworkin 2000, p. 159; 2011, 203, 204.

philosophy as I just sketched it. The Government should treat every citizen with equal respect and concern, but do all Dutch citizens also have an obligation not to discriminate fellow human beings on arbitrary grounds such as race, ethnicity, gender, sexual orientation or religion?

Implicit in discrimination on such grounds is a judgment of inferiority, and 'projecting an inferior or demeaning image on another can actually distort and oppress' Charles Taylor writes – particularly if this demeaning image is *interiorized* by the victim.[37] Discrimination undoubtedly robs its victim of his or her (equal) dignity and is oppressive in the sense that the victim no longer feels free to express, or even *be* who he or she wants to be.

Such an infringement of equal dignity also implies an infringement of equal liberty. Especially if individuals or groups are discriminated on the basis of an identity attached to qualities and characteristics that are *not* chosen and not alterable, like ethnicity and gender, the victims are not only treated as unequal but also limited in their freedom to be and express who they are. Such discrimination has the effect of delimiting the liberty of its victims; they are not only imprisoned in an inferior identity, but the victim of the projection of an inferior identity has a life sentence. And how could the incitement to such discrimination be a valuable contribution to the democratic debate about how the democratic community should govern itself?

This distinction between unalterable characteristics such as ethnicity and gender, on the one hand, and (religious) beliefs and opinions on the other, actually plays a role in the interpretation of the criminal law provisions on hate speech by the Dutch judiciary. The discussion of the unalterable human characteristics cannot be seen as an (albeit rather aggressive) attempt to make people change their minds about what to believe and what not to believe, and therefore the freedom of speech is deemed to be more limited here than the freedom to attack religious ideas or political ideologies. The context is decisive, but under some circumstances, attacking certain ideas can also only be understood as intending to humiliate individuals or groups, and in particular to *exclude* them from the ongoing debate in a modern democracy. Such speech is unacceptable in a modern democratic culture.

Dworkin's political philosophy does imply that we all have the *moral* obligation not to discriminate on such grounds. Dutch criminal law, however, makes this into a legal obligation as well. The provisions on hate speech, incitement to violence and discrimination against individuals or groups cannot be understood as having merely a public order rationale. They can also readily be understood as protecting the individual human dignity of all members of society, and thereby their right to equality and liberty. Modern egalitarian culture forbids us from projecting a demeaning image on such grounds as ethnicity, sexual preferences or religion; the Dutch criminal code even declares it punishable by law.

37 Taylor, C., *The Ethics of Authenticity*, Harvard University Press, Cambridge Mass. 1991, p. 49-51.

The officials of the law should, however, not use this instrument too lightly. The protection of the equal dignity and thereby liberty of one individual or group in society will be experienced as the denial of the dignity and liberty of another. Especially in the political context, 'to defend one's own values or beliefs without attacking or throwing doubt upon those of others with differing view is well nigh impossible.'[38] Moreover, criminal law is *ultimum remedium*, we should always keep in mind that by using this instrument we are not persuading but *forcing* individuals to do what we think is right. Criminal law is about retaliation and deterrence, not about truly convincing people. If the state uses its monopoly on the use of force to patronize one of its subjects, the subject will feel reproached like a child who cannot be trusted to make up his own mind and express himself responsibly. This will be a thoroughly humiliating experience, not only for the suspect but also for all those who strongly indentify with him.

Concluding Remarks

'Indeed, the project of taming the desire for recognition has been so successful in the hands of modern political philosophy that we citizens of modern egalitarian democracies often fail to see the desire for recognition in ourselves for what it is,' Francis Fukuyama wrote in 1992.[39] Indeed, during the last decades of the twentieth century, identity politics seemed dead and buried until Wilders single-handedly revived the politics of recognition. On the one hand, Wilders saved democratic politics from degenerating into a technocracy by defying several politically correct taboos of late twentieth century politics and giving expression to a widely felt fear and anger about what Dutch society was coming to. Many praise him for re-engaging a part of the Dutch electorate that was deeply disappointed in politics generally, and for thereby saving democratic institutions from losing their legitimacy.

On the other hand, Wilders' 'realistic' political style and behavior comes close to being parasitic on the very liberal and democratic culture he wants to defend. The politics of recognition has a logic very different to the logic of liberal democracy. The politics of liberty and equality thrives on an egalitarian culture – on *isothymia* – and history has taught us Europeans that such a culture is highly vulnerable and cannot be expected to survive very long when identity politics degenerates into warmongering. We should remember, I think, that historically *megalothymia* is the default and *isothymia* is the exception. The Americans went to war to make the world safe for democracy. But they were very reluctant to do so for they knew, also by experience, that war destroys whatever makes democracy possible.

38 Aubert, V., *The Hidden Society*, Bedminster Press Inc., Totowa NJ 1965, p. 95.

39 Fukuyama 1992, p. 163.

14 Deliberation can be Rough

Explaining the Democratic Importance of Free Speech

Stefan Rummens

Introduction

Free speech is an essential element of any democratic political system. Although the political role of free speech does not necessarily provide the sole justification of an extensive legal protection of the freedom of expression of citizens, it has been widely recognized as one of its primary rationales. In this regard, the European Court of Human Rights has argued, for instance, that 'freedom of political debate is at the very core of the concept of a democratic society which prevails throughout the [European] Convention [on Human Rights].'[1] Similarly, the United States Supreme Court has argued that '[t]he protection given speech and press was fashioned to assure unfettered interchange of ideas for the bringing about of political and social changes desired by the people.'[2] In the academic debate, Alexander Meiklejohn has famously argued that '[t]he principle of the freedom of speech springs from the necessities of the program of self-government.'[3] More recently, Cass Sunstein has stated that '[i]f we start with the Madisonian ideal, we will insist on the traditional but now disputed idea that the First Amendment is focused first and foremost on political deliberation. I suggest that "political speech" lies at the heart of constitutional concern.'[4]

In view of this close conceptual connection between free speech and the ideal of democratic self-government, it seems surprising that there is almost no interaction between the blooming academic debate on free speech on the hand, and the equally rich academic debate on deliberative democracy on the other.[5] In view of the prominence – or even

1 Lingens v. Austria, Eur.Ct.H.R. (Ser. A, No. 103) §42 (July 8, 1986).
2 *Roth* v. *US* 354 US 476, 484 (1957).
3 A. Meiklejohn, *Free Speech and Its Relation to Self-Government*, New York, Harpers and Brothers, 1948, p. 26.
4 C. R. Sunstein, *Democracy and the Problem of Free Speech*, New York, The Free Press, 1993, p. 122.
5 There are, of course, a few notable exceptions. From the side of the free speech debate, Cass Sunstein explicitly understands democracy in terms of deliberative democracy (Sunstein 1993). Similarly, Maleiha Malik has referred to the importance of 'discourse ethics' as a framework for dealing with extreme speech, 'Extreme Speech and Liberalism', *in* I. Hare and J. Weinstein (Eds.), *Extreme Speech and Democracy*, Oxford, Oxford University Press, 2009, pp. 96-120. From the side of deliberative democracy, the most noteworthy contributions are probably Jane Mansbridge, 'Everyday Talk in the Deliberative System' *in* S. Macedo (Ed.), *Deliberative Politics: Essays on Democracy and Disagreement*, Oxford, Oxford University Press, 1999, pp. 211-

dominance – obtained by the deliberative paradigm within the field of democratic theory and the primary focus of this paradigm on the importance of public deliberation, a more explicit exchange between these two debates could have been expected. I surmise that the near absence of such an exchange can be explained, to a large extent, by the fact that deliberative democracy famously works with an ideal of *reasonable* deliberation between citizens engaging in a civilized and inclusive exchange of arguments with one another. The debate on free speech, in contrast, is not really concerned with this kind of civilized behavior, but faces the challenge, rather, of determining how to deal with forms of expression which are considered to be extreme, hateful or otherwise unsettling.

This contribution aims to demonstrate that, in spite of these different focuses, a more explicit mutual engagement between the debates on deliberative democracy and free speech is important and fruitful. My aim is, more specifically, to start from some of the more recent developments within the deliberative paradigm and to show that the so-called 'systemic' approach to deliberative democracy is well equipped to explain the central role of free speech in the democratic system and, thus, to justify a far-reaching legal protection of the freedom of expression of both citizens and politicians.

The outline of the argument presented here is as follows. After explaining the relatively recent systemic approach to deliberative democracy (section 2), I sketch and endorse a more specific 'concentric' model of the deliberative system, much in line with Jürgen Habermas' two-track model of the public sphere (section 3). I argue that such a concentric model is capable of dealing with the 'paradox of tolerance' in an original manner, whereby extremists are given much leeway at the periphery of the political system but face decreasing tolerance as they approach the more formal centers of decision-making such as parliament and government (section 4). The concentric model of deliberative democracy presented here emphasizes the central epistemic and motivational roles of free speech. As a result, it endorses a far-reaching legal protection of political speech broadly construed (section 5). In the final section, I briefly focus on the implications of this model for the freedom of speech of politicians as well as for the freedom of association granted to political parties (section 6).

What is a Deliberative Democratic System?

The paradigm of deliberative democracy has emerged in political philosophy in the late eighties and early nineties of the previous century. It has been on the rise ever since and

239; and Joshua Cohen, 'Freedom of expression', *Philosophy & Public Affairs*, Vol. 22, No. 2, 1993, pp. 207-263.

has by now become the most prominent paradigm within democratic theory.[6] The basic idea is straightforward. The model assumes that democratic legitimacy is based on mutual justification between citizens. More specifically, the model argues that laws should be based on an agreement which is the outcome of an inclusive and reasonable exchange of arguments amongst all the people affected by these laws.

In the development of the deliberative model over the past decades, it is possible to distinguish – very roughly – between three different stages. In the first stage, philosophers were mainly concerned with developing the normative ideal of deliberative legitimacy. Here, an analysis of the presuppositions of reasonable discourse took center stage. Most famously, Jürgen Habermas' model of the 'ideal speech situation' focuses on the inclusiveness of deliberation and the absence of power relations potentially distorting the 'force of the better argument.'[7]

In the second stage, deliberative democracy took an 'empirical turn,' in which much attention was given to experiments with deliberative mini-publics, whereby a small number of randomly selected citizens come together to actually deliberate on topics of public interest.[8] Here, political scientists aimed to analyze the extent to which the ideal presuppositions of reasonable discourse can be approximated in real life situations, and to assess whether, and how, the quality of deliberation could be improved.

Several theorists have recently identified the emergence of a third stage of investigation, in which deliberative theory is now taking a 'systemic turn.'[9] The main concern here is to think about the best way to institutionalize the deliberative ideal in the context of large-scale contemporary societies. Although mini-publics can approximate the ideal of reasonable deliberation to some extent, their main problem is, of course, that only a very small fraction of all citizens can actually participate in these deliberative gatherings. Because most citizens are excluded, the more generalized use of mini-publics as elements in actual decision-making processes is considered by some theorists to actually undermine the realization of the original deliberative ideal.[10] Advocates of the systemic approach suggest that we should

6 J. Habermas, *Between Facts and Norms: Contributions to a Discourse Theory of Law and Democracy*, Cambridge, MIT Press, 1996; J. Bohman and W. Rehg (Eds.), *Deliberative Democracy: Essays on Reason and Politics*, Cambridge, MIT Press, 1997.

7 Habermas 1996; id., 'Discourse Ethics: Notes on a Program of Philosophical Justification' *in* id., *Moral Consciousness and Communicative Action*, Cambridge, Polity Press, 1990, pp. 43-115.

8 J. Bohman, 'Survey article: the coming of age of deliberative democracy', *The Journal of Political Philosophy*, Vol. 6, No. 4, 1998, pp. 400-425; M. Delli Carpini, F. L. Cook and L. Jacobs, 'Public deliberation, discursive participation and citizen engagement: a review of the empirical literature', *Annual Review of Political Science*, Vol. 7, 2004, pp. 315-344; R. Goodin and J. S. Dryzek, 'Deliberative impacts: the macro-political uptake of mini-publics', *Politics and Society*, Vol. 34, 2006, pp. 219-244.

9 J. Parkinson, *Deliberating in the Real World. Problems of Legitimacy in Deliberative Democracy*, Oxford, Oxford University Press, 2006; J. Parkinson and J. Mansbridge (Eds.), *Deliberative Systems*, Cambridge, Cambridge UP, 2012.

10 C. Lafont, 'Deliberation, participation, and democratic legitimacy: should deliberative mini-publics shape public policy?', *The Journal of Political Philosophy* , early view, doi: 10.1111/jopp.12031.

first and foremost look at the deliberative quality of the democratic system as a whole, rather than focus on the deliberative quality of individual sites of deliberation. They submit that a deliberative system works on the basis of a division of labor between different institutions and sites, whereby violations of the ideal of rational deliberation at one point in the system could contribute to the rationality of the overall democratic process.[11] A typical example here concerns the inclusiveness of the public debate. In order to bring neglected issues on the public agenda of a political community, it is often necessary for pressure groups to engage in different sorts of political activism. In order to be successful, such activists should probably not be too 'rational' in the strict deliberative sense. Some stubbornness, a willingness to raise your voice and a refusal to 'listen to reason' are often necessary in order to be heard by a larger audience. In cases such as these, the behavior of activists, which seems 'irrational' compared to the standard of ideal speech, can nevertheless contribute to the inclusiveness and, thus, 'rationality' of the wider public debate.

One of the main challenges for the systemic approach is to provide criteria for assessing the deliberative quality of the democratic system as a whole. In a recent contribution, some of the main authors in the field have identified three main functions any adequate system should fulfill.[12] On the *epistemic* level, a deliberative system should produce preferences, opinions and decisions that are adequately informed by a careful consideration of all the relevant facts and arguments. On the *ethical* level, the system should promote mutual respect amongst citizens as autonomous agents. On the *democratic* level, the system should promote an inclusive political process on terms of equality.

Although I do not think there is anything wrong with these three requirements as such, I believe that they are somewhat redundant and incomplete. They are redundant because the first epistemic requirement, if properly understood and developed, seems to encompass the other two. If it is indeed the case – as is widely assumed and as I will further explain below – that an epistemically adequate process of deliberation requires an inclusive political process in which all citizens are respected as autonomous participants, then the fulfillment of the first function seems to presuppose the realization of the other two. At the same time, the three functions identified are incomplete because they fail to fully capture what I would like to call the motivational aspect of legitimacy, i.e. the fact that decisions are legitimate to the extent that they are actually endorsed by citizens.

For the purposes of this article, I will therefore work with two alternative criteria for assessing the deliberative quality of a democratic system. On the *epistemic* level, the legitimacy of a democratic system depends on the extent to which it produces outcomes that are maximally epistemically adequate. This means that outcomes should be based on an

11 J. Mansbridge et al., 'A systemic approach to deliberative democracy' *in* Parkinson and Mansbridge 2012, pp. 1-26 at 2-3; J. Mansbridge et al., 'The place of self-interest and the role of power in deliberative democracy', *The Journal of Political Philosophy*, Vol. 18, No. 1, 2010, pp. 64-100.

12 Mansbridge et al. 2012, pp. 10-13.

adequate process of deliberation in which all the possibly relevant facts and arguments have been taken into account. On the *motivational* level, the legitimacy of the system depends on its ability to generate outcomes which are actually endorsed by citizens. This means that citizens are generally motivated to act in conformity with the requirements imposed upon them by the law.[13]

Before proceeding to explain, in the next section, which kind of democratic system best fulfills these epistemic and motivational requirements, three additional remarks regarding the nature of the deliberative model of democracy are in order. It is, first of all, sometimes suggested that the deliberative model provides a purely proceduralistic model of democracy in the sense that it simply identifies procedural criteria for the reasonableness of deliberation, but puts no substantive constraints on the possible outcomes of such deliberation. Elsewhere, I have argued at length that this is a mistaken understanding of the deliberative ideal.[14] Deliberative democracy, in fact, combines procedural and more substantive elements in a unique way. The model contains a substantive core which can best be identified as a commitment to the equal autonomy of all citizens. Autonomy should thereby be understood in a twofold sense. On the one hand, deliberative democracy is committed to the individual autonomy of all citizens as legally guaranteed by a wide set of individual liberty rights. On the other hand, the model is also committed to the political autonomy of all citizens, which allows these citizens, on the basis of a wide set of political rights, to participate on the basis of equality in the democratic process. Although the idea of autonomy constitutes the substantive core of the model, it is crucial to note that this core is relatively vague and that the model itself does not provide a specific interpretation of the requirements of autonomy. Here, the procedural element comes into play. The model assumes that only the citizens themselves are capable of determining the more specific content of autonomy that is adequate for their specific political community. Therefore, a deliberative democratic process is needed to generate a more specific understanding of, for instance, freedom of religion, and to ensure that it is tailored to the specific historical, cultural and other circumstances of the society at hand. This understanding of democratic deliberation as a 'procedure of elaboration' in which the core idea of autonomy is given a more specific and context-dependent interpretation, is well captured by Jürgen Habermas' understanding of the democratic state as a constitutional project.[15] For Habermas, the universal core of every constitutional democracy consists of an abstract scheme of rights, essentially protecting the individual and political autonomy of all citizens

13 In my recent publication, 'Staging deliberation. The role of representative institutions in the deliberative democratic process', *The Journal of Political Philosophy*, Vol. 20, No. 1, 2012, pp. 23-44, I also discuss a third criterion, i.e. the need for the deliberative system to constrain non-discursive power. This third function will not play a role in the present discussion.

14 S. Rummens, 'Debate: the co-originality of private and public autonomy in deliberative democracy', *The Journal of Political Philosophy*, Vol. 14, No. 4, 2006, pp. 469-481.

15 Habermas 1996, chapter 3.

in an impartial manner. This abstract scheme of rights is given more precise content on the basis of actual democratic processes in which constitutional requirements, ordinary laws as well as actual policies determine the ways in which citizens wish to mutually recognize each other as autonomous agents. Although the abstract scheme of rights is universal, the more specific contents of constitutions, laws and policies are – appropriately so – colored by the more specific social, cultural, economic and other elements that characterize individual societies.

The need to take into account contextual elements also explains, secondly, why deliberative democracy requires the *actual participation* of citizens at large. Advocatory or vicarious deliberation by philosophers or policy-makers is not sufficient for both epistemic and motivational reasons.[16] On the *epistemic* level, deliberation is supposed to take into account the needs, preferences and values of all citizens as 'concrete others' – to use the felicitous expression introduced by Seyla Benhabib.[17] Impartial decision-making requires us to take into account contextual elements which would disappear if we were to understand others as noumenal selves or as agents behind a veil of ignorance as Kant or Rawls would have it. Indeed, if we want to devise social policies capable of dealing with, for instance, the needs of unemployed single parents, it is crucial to actually involve the people targeted by these policies, because only they themselves are capable of explaining their needs and of identifying policies that might actually alleviate some of their main concerns. Similarly, a proper elaboration of the freedom of religion will necessarily be colored by the experiences of the religious people actually living in our society. Regulations regarding the much debated head scarf, for instance, cannot be made without involving all the parties concerned in the actual decision-making process. Elsewhere, I have emphasized that deliberation as an epistemic process involves two crucial elements. On the one hand, deliberation aims to *track* all the relevant issues, concerns and values of all citizens affected by certain policies. On the other hand, deliberation also aims to confront the often conflicting needs and values of different citizens and to *transform* or *filter* these preferences in such a way that a reasonable and impartial agreement can be constructed which gives, to use Habermas' expression, 'equal concern to the interests and values of all citizens affected.'[18] On the *motivational* level, the actual participation of citizens is required because people need to be assured that their own concerns have adequately been taken into account. Ideally, their participation in the debate thereby provides them with a better understanding of the often conflicting but also often legitimate concerns of others and allows citizens to indeed undergo a

16 S. Rummens, 'Democratic deliberation as the open-ended construction of justice', *Ratio Juris*, Vol. 20, No. 3, 2007, pp. 335-354.

17 S. Benhabib, *Situating the Self: Gender, Community and Postmodernism in Contemporary Ethics*, Cambridge, Polity Press, 1992, pp. 158-170.

18 Habermas 1996, pp. 154, 167.

transformation at the level of their preferences which motivates them to accept the outcome as a reasonable and impartial one.

The deliberative model is, thirdly, often understood as a highly consensualistic model of democracy, which ideally assumes that laws should be based on a consensual agreement amongst all citizens. It is true, of course, that the ideal of consensus plays an important role in many versions of the deliberative model. As I have argued, elsewhere, however, a full appreciation of the context-dependent nature of deliberation reveals that an adequate model ought to recognize that deliberation is a necessarily open-ended endeavor.[19] If the purpose of deliberation is to take into account contextual elements, and if human beings are historical creatures living in an ever-changing society, then deliberation cannot and should not come to an actual closure. New needs, new challenges, new preferences will always emerge and should lead to a reconsideration of existing laws and regulations. The essentially open-ended nature of deliberation implies, in my view, that actual consensus should not be seen as a desirable outcome of real life deliberations. Ongoing disagreement can play a highly beneficial role in society in the sense that it keeps everybody alert and keeps us aware of the fact that a fully just society can never be attained. An appreciation of this open-endedness has implications, moreover, for our understanding of the epistemic and motivational requirements imposed on an adequate deliberative system. Although the idea of consensus remains a regulative (and, hence, counterfactual) ideal in the sense that legislation should aim for an impartial realization of the ideal of autonomy, the epistemic function of any adequate deliberative system should be understood, at the same time, to include a requirement for the system to contain mechanisms preventing the premature closure of the debate. The motivational requirement, in turn, should not be understood to mean that every citizen should always agree with the content of every single political decision. It means rather that every citizen should be able to sufficiently identify with the democratic system as a whole, and appreciate the democratic process as one in which her concerns are sufficiently taken seriously even if, necessarily, some or even most of the decisions are not fully in line with her own considered preferences.

DELIBERATIVE DEMOCRACY AS A CONCENTRIC SYSTEM

Although the ideal of reasonable face-to-face deliberation as the basis for democratic legitimation is relatively clear, the institutionalization of this ideal in large scale societies of millions of citizens seems deeply problematic. In the literature, three main models of institutionalization have been presented. As already indicated in the previous section, much theoretical and empirical attention has been given to the idea of *mini-publics* as

19 S. Rummens, 'Deliberation interrupted. Confronting Jürgen Habermas and Claude Lefort', *Philosophy & Social Criticism*, Vol. 34, No. 3, 2008, pp. 383-408.

proxies for large scale deliberation. The idea is that the outcome of a reasonable deliberation amongst a group of randomly selected citizens will approximate the ideal of a much more inclusive deliberation and will be able to detect, not the public opinion of citizens as it exists, but the opinion that the public would have if it would have had the opportunity to extensively deliberate on some issue. In order to connect these small scale deliberations in mini-publics with the larger democratic process, many ideas have been suggested and tried out, ranging from mini-publics that simply contribute to the ongoing informal public debate to mini-publics that prepare or even replace actual decision-making by elected officials.[20]

Although the rough overview in the previous section has focused on these mini-publics, two other models for the institutionalization of the deliberative model have also been presented in the ongoing debate. One of these emphasizes the importance of *deliberative networks*.[21] This model dovetails with the recent growth of more horizontal governance networks, both on the national and the transnational level, as increasingly complementing or even replacing more traditional and centralized government institutions. The idea is that these more decentralized networks have a big democratic potential because they represent a form of policy making that is geared towards the inclusion of all possibly relevant stake-holders in the decision-making process. Deliberative democrats of this strand emphasize the importance of including these stake-holders in adequately deliberative manners. Horizontal governance networks should connect a wide range of deliberative sites in which all possible stakeholders or their representatives can participate. In this context, some theorists have argued that the European Union, with its wide range of consultation procedures and its decentralized decision-making processes, provides a highly promising example of such a deliberative network.[22]

The third and final model of institutionalization is perhaps the most traditional one, in the sense that it retains a central role for *parliamentary institutions*. Here, the prime example is perhaps Habermas' two-track model of the public sphere.[23] This model makes a distinction between the informal public sphere at the periphery of the political system, and the formal public sphere of the formal decision-making institutions such as, primarily, parliament and government. The idea is that public deliberation in the informal sphere, which encompasses contributions of civil society organizations, the media and the deliberations of ordinary citizens, should ideally generate concerns, ideas and arguments that are able to influence and shape decision-making in the formal core of the system.

---

20 Goodin and Dryzek 2006; A. Fung, 'Survey article: recipes for public spheres: eight institutional design choices and their consequences', *The Journal of Political Philosophy*, Vol. 11, No. 3, 2003, pp. 338-67.

21 J. Bohman, *Democracy across Borders: from Dêmos to Dêmoi*, Cambridge, The MIT Press, 2007; J. Cohen and C. Sabel, 'Directly-deliberative polyarchy', *European Law Journal*, Vol. 3, 1997, pp. 313-42.

22 J. Cohen and C. Sabel, 'Sovereignty and solidarity: EU and US' *in* K.-H. Ladeur (Ed.), *Public Governance in the Age of Globalization*, Aldershot, Ashgate, 2004, pp. 157-175.

23 Habermas 1996, pp. 306-308, 352-359.

In my view, these three models or modes of institutionalization are not mutually exclusive. The task of the systemic approach to deliberative democracy probably consists in developing a configuration of different and interacting modes of deliberation which together constitute a deliberative system with a high overall deliberative quality. Although I believe, in this regard, that mini-publics and deliberative networks can play a role in enhancing the overall legitimacy of our democratic system, I have also already argued that, in my view, the more traditional parliamentary institutions will continue to play an essential role in any adequate deliberative system for the foreseeable future.[24] This essential role of parliamentary institutions is, however, not always fully recognized by participants in the academic debate. The main reason for their importance is the need for the *actual participation* of the citizenry at large in the deliberative decision-making process, as explained in the previous section. Here, both the mini-public and the network-approach seem problematic from both an epistemic and a motivational perspective. On the epistemic level, first of all, the inclusiveness of deliberation seems hard to guarantee on both approaches. It seems clear that a selection by lot of a limited number of participants in the mini-publics will not always suffice in assuring that all the relevant concerns and perspectives will be voiced by the selected group. Although the stake-holder approach of the network model seems to make a more systematic effort to include all possibly relevant concerns, it is clear that here too, access to the network will be easier for well-organized subgroups with more social and cultural capital than for other groups. The example of European decision-making might provide a case in point.

The more serious problem in my mind, however, lies not on the epistemic but on the motivational level. For outsiders who are not able to actually participate in the deliberations, both mini-publics and deliberative networks appear as *black boxes*. Although outsiders are expected to accept that the outcomes generated by these sites have a high deliberative quality, they have no idea of the kind of arguments that have been raised, which policy alternatives were on the table and whether thereby their own concerns have indeed been adequately presented and defended. In circumstances such as these, it is not surprising that these outsiders, who remain unaware of all the arguments discussed and are thus unable to undergo any form of preferential transformation themselves, fail to identify with the process and its outcomes and therefore fail to endorse their legitimacy. Here again, the widely felt 'democratic deficit' with respect to the so-called inclusive European decision-making procedures might provide a case in point.

If we compare mini-publics and networks on the one hand with the parliamentary two-track model on the other, the latter has some qualities which, in my view, make it vastly superior in terms of the actual participation of citizens. Here, two structural features of the model play a key role. The first feature is the *concentric nature of the decision-making*

24 Rummens 2012.

process in the parliamentary system.[25] Thereby, new concerns and ideas are usually put on the public agenda by participants in the informal public sphere at the periphery of the system. Social, cultural, ecological, feminist and other issues have, in the past, been raised by civil society actors and organizations introducing new ideas and possible solutions. Growing awareness amongst the wider public ensures, after a while, that some of these concerns and ideas are taken up by the more formal decision-makers in parliament and government, where they can potentially influence and shape new legislation and policies. On the *epistemic* level, this concentric structure supports the twofold 'tracking' and 'filtering' function of the deliberative system. New concerns and ideas can be tracked by the wide and inclusive nature of the informal public debate at the periphery. As ideas make their way through the deliberative system towards their potential implementation in policies and legislation – a process which often takes many years or even decades – they are confronted with other and competing concerns and interests. Ideally, this complex process leads to an outcome in which all possibly relevant values and interests have been given due concern and which, therefore, approximates something like an 'impartial' outcome. On the *motivational* level, the connection of formal decision-making in the center with the informal public sphere at the margins aims to ensure that all possibly relevant voices can be heard and taken into account. Thereby, one of the main concerns of deliberative democrats is the maintenance of an open and inclusive public debate and the empowerment of hitherto marginalized groups and agents with the aim of giving them the capacity to make themselves heard.

The second structural feature of the parliamentary system concerns its *narrative or dramaturgical logic*.[26] Here, I refer to the fact that the organized competition between political parties gives focus and structure to the wider political debate in society. Because, necessarily, there are only a limited number of recognizable political players and a limited number of issues that can attract media attention, the public debate acquires a kind of narrative or dramaturgical structure, whereby a limited number of ideological positions are played out against each other and have to engage – through the political actors representing them – in a public and adversarial exchange of arguments concerning a limited set of specific issues. This dramaturgical structure ('the political theatre') gives the public debate a unique kind of wider *visibility* that you cannot have with mini-publics or deliberative networks. The media-coverage of an adversarial exchange between a limited number of political players allows the wider audience of citizens to become familiar with the issues at stake and the arguments defended by the different parties. This exchange will allow them to think some of the issues through for themselves, and thereby to potentially

25 Habermas 1996, pp. 306-308, 352-359; S. Rummens and K. Abts, 'Defending democracy: the concentric containment of political extremism', *Political Studies*, Vol. 58, 2010, pp. 649-665.

26 Rummens 2012; J. Boswell, 'Why and how narrative matters in deliberative systems', *Political Studies*, Vol. 61, 2013, pp. 620-636.

transform their own ideas and, finally, to identify themselves with one or more of the positions advocated on stage. The fact that this adversarial play on stage usually does not lead to some form of consensus between all parties but generally remains caught in a majority-minority dynamic is thereby not problematic, but, contrary to common wisdom within the deliberative paradigm, actually highly beneficial from the point of view of the deliberative system as a whole. Indeed, the fact that decisions are made by a majority over and against an opposing minority has benefits on both the epistemic and the motivational level. On the *epistemic* level, the oppositional logic of the representative system not only makes visible a 'space of political reasons' that allows citizens to familiarize themselves with issues and options, it also gives an important temporal continuity to the debate. In contrast with what happens in mini-publics or deliberative networks, outvoted minority positions remain present on the political stage and can act as sort of 'epistemic reservoirs.' They represent concerns and policy options that have, for now, not been chosen but that, nevertheless, remain present as future possibilities. The minority signals that not all citizens are satisfied with the current state of affairs and that at least some citizens fear that there are concerns which have not yet been adequately taken into account. The ongoing presence of these outvoted concerns also has a crucial *motivational* importance. If citizens disagree with the majority decision, they can still feel represented on the political stage by the outvoted minority positions. Although their concerns did not win the vote this time, they remain visibly present and could perhaps, on some future occasion, gain majority support. The visible presence of minority positions thereby allows for the ongoing identification of citizens with the democratic system as a whole even on occasions where they fail to identify with the actual majority decision. In this context, many authors have indicated that the growing difficulty of providing for a visible opposition within the political system (as a result of the growing importance of supposedly consensualistic governance networks) is one of the major reasons for the increasing success of populist, anti-establishment and Euro-skeptical parties. If opposition is no longer possible within the political system, opposition will turn against the system as a whole.[27]

My emphasis on the importance of the visibility generated by oppositional dynamics in the parliamentary system is, as yet, not widely shared within the deliberative paradigm and also departs from Habermas' much more consensualistic understanding of the two-track model of the deliberative system. I believe that it is precisely the systemic turn in deliberative democracy that allows us to understand, contrary to ordinary wisdom, that oppositional dynamics are not at odds with the deliberative ideal, but actually contribute to its adequate institutionalization in large scale societies. It is, in my mind, one of the

27 C. Mouffe, *On the Political*, London, Routledge, 2005, pp. 64-76; A. Føllesdal and S. Hix, 'Why there is a democratic deficit in the EU: A response to Majone and Moravcsik', *Journal of Common Market Studies*, Vol. 44, 2006, pp. 533-62 at 549; P. Mair, 'Political opposition and the European Union', *Government and Opposition*, Vol. 42, 2007, pp. 1-17 at 6.

main advantages of the systemic approach that it allows to defuse to a large extent the ongoing debate between advocates of deliberative democracy and defenders of the so-called 'agonistic' model of democracy, which remains – in the current debate – one of its main competitors.[28] Although theorists of agonistic democracy will probably be reluctant to acknowledge this, their critique on the rationalistic and consensualistic nature of deliberative theories can, in my view, to a large extent be incorporated into the deliberative approach by recognizing that 'adversarial politics' and supposedly 'irrational' forms of contestation can contribute in important ways to the 'overall' reasonableness of the deliberative system as a whole.

Dealing with Extremism: The Guideline of Decreasing Tolerance

We have now been talking at length about the best way to institutionalize the deliberative ideal in large scale societies, and the way in which the parliamentary system, more specifically, has much to contribute to the realization of the epistemic and motivational functions of an adequate deliberative system. The reader might wonder how this analysis intends to contribute to our understanding of the importance of the legal protection of citizens' freedom of expression. Here, the preceding reference to the affinities between the deliberative and the agonistic models of democracy already opens up a first connection with the academic debate on free speech.[29] If political debate is not necessarily geared towards consensus but can be aimed at staking out new or hitherto neglected points of view in the political space of reasons, a deliberative model has an interest in allowing and even supporting as much as possible the free expression of political ideas in the public sphere.

Nevertheless, the reference to the importance of a more agonistic exchange of ideas does not yet suffice to fully connect with the debate on free speech. In this context, it is important to notice that the agonistic model of democracy is in itself not yet a model for dealing with extremist forms of political contestation. Although the agonistic model stresses the importance of political disagreement, the model also recognizes that a stable liberal democratic regime requires agreement on a shared normative framework. In this regard, Chantal Mouffe – perhaps the most renowned advocate of agonistic democracy – refers to the need for a shared commitment to the 'ethico-political values of liberty and equality for all.'[30] These values provide the criterion for making a crucial distinction between 'agonistic adversaries,' i.e. legitimate contestants in the political domain committed to the core values of liberal democracy, and 'antagonistic enemies,' i.e. extremists who do not share this commitment and should therefore be considered as outsiders posing a threat to

28 Mouffe 2005; id., *The Democratic Paradox*, London, Verso, 2000.

29 Compare, in this regard, Malik 2009.

30 Mouffe 2000, pp. 102-104; 2005, pp. 31-32, 121-122.

the regime itself.[31] In spite of the central importance of the distinction between agonism and antagonism, it is surprising that Mouffe has little to say about how democratic regimes should deal with their antagonistic enemies. In view of our present concern, this is precisely the point of interest. Free speech legislation is not primarily concerned with the public expressions of citizens already committed to freedom and democracy. The problem of free speech most urgently arises with reference to citizens using their freedom of expression to advocate extremist ideas challenging these core values.

Here, the debate on free speech faces the well-known 'paradox of tolerance.'[32] A liberal democratic regime is committed to the value of tolerance and the maximal recognition of citizens' freedom to do as they please. At the same time, it is unclear to what extent this tolerance should be extended to people who do not share this commitment to tolerance and who set out to undermine some of the core values of liberal democracy itself. In the literature, two main answers to this paradox can be distinguished. Militant conceptions of democracy emphasize the normative substance of democracy and advocate intolerance towards the intolerant.[33] On this conception, the core democratic values ought to be defended by actively suppressing extremist ideas and groups in the public sphere. Proceduralistic conceptions of democracy, in contrast, emphasize the procedural aspects of democracy and advocate much wider tolerance vis-à-vis the intolerant.[34] Democracy is essentially a procedure for making legitimate decisions and all political actors respecting some minimal procedural requirements should be allowed to participate in this process on an equal footing.

It is one of the core strengths of the concentric model of democracy as explained before that it is able to transcend the opposition between militant and proceduralistic models of democracy. As already indicated, the deliberative model combines substantive and procedural elements in a unique manner. In combination with the concentric design of the two-track public sphere, this implies, as already emphasized by Maleiha Malik, that 'the process of engagement with extremists can be "slowed down" and "expanded".'[35] In this regard, Koen Abts and I have advocated what we call a *guideline of decreasing tolerance for extremists*.[36] This means that extremist political actors should be given significant leeway to express their ideas at the periphery of the political system. However, to the extent that these actors or their ideas come closer to the political centers of actual decision-making,

31 Mouffe 2000, pp. 13, 49-57, 98-105; 2005, pp. 14-21.

32 J. Rawls, *A Theory of Justice*, Boston, Harvard University Press, 1999, pp. 190-194.

33 For an overview of the recent literature on militant democracy, see G. Capoccia, 'Militant democracy: the institutional bases of democratic self-preservation', *Annual Review of Law and Social Science*, Vol. 9, 2013, pp. 207-226.

34 M. Fennema and M. Maussen, 'Dealing with extremists in public discussion: Front National and "Republican Front" in France', *The Journal of Political Philosophy*, Vol. 8, No. 3, 2000, pp. 379-400.

35 M. Malik, 'Engaging with extremists', *International Relations*, Vol. 22, No. 1, 2008, pp. 85-104 at 93.

36 Rummens and Abts 2010.

tolerance for the intolerant should gradually decrease and our attitudes towards extremists should become increasingly restrictive.

Deliberative democracy is a procedural theory in the sense that the precise content of legislation and policies should be generated in the public debate. This means that the debate should be open to the input of citizens as much as possible. This openness is mainly guaranteed by the periphery of the political system, which provides – with a term used by Habermas – the 'context of discovery' in which all the possibly relevant concerns, facts, issues, interests and values of all possibly affected citizens can be tracked down.[37] Of course, the deliberative model is, at the same time, also committed to the substantive values of liberty and equality. This means, of course, that the input of the deliberative process at the periphery should be filtered out and transformed as the deliberation proceeds through the system in order to yield 'impartial' laws and policies. In Habermas' terminology, as we move from the periphery to the center, the 'context of discovery' becomes a 'context of justification'[38] in which we should look for ways of dealing with citizens' concerns that are respectful of *all* citizens indiscriminately and, therefore, compatible with the core values of individual and political autonomy.

I submit that the guideline of decreasing tolerance is appropriate from the systemic perspective of deliberative democracy in the sense that it is in line with the epistemic and motivational functions of the deliberative system. On the *epistemic* level, the guideline is, as already indicated, compatible with the idea that the system as a whole should 'track' and 'filter' all relevant concerns. Although the deliberative model has a substantive core, the specific content of the requirements of autonomy cannot be determined in an a priori manner by experts, philosophers, policy makers or judges. It would, therefore, be inappropriate to impose a priori constraints on the contents of the arguments that can be introduced into the debate. Only an actual democratic debate can decide whether the concerns and arguments raised are relevant and should be given any weight in the design of new laws and policies. The openness of the debate thereby also extends to 'extremist' contributions which are manifestly at odds with the core values themselves. It is always possible (and even likely) that these manifestations are epistemically relevant in the sense that they have some kind of *signaling function*, testifying to some deep concerns of at least parts of the citizenry with the current state of affairs. It is generally very unwise of policy-makers not to listen to the voices of dissatisfaction. Of course, listening to extremists' concerns does not mean that politicians should simply endorse the extremist 'solutions' advocated. The deliberative process, as an epistemic process, remains, at the same time, a transformative and 'filtering' process in which the concerns of citizens should be weighed against the legitimate concerns of others. In practice, this means that politicians (as well as citizens)

37 Habermas 1996, p. 307.
38 Habermas 1996, p. 307.

engaged in public deliberation should assess to what extent non-extremist measures (i.e. measures compatible with the equal autonomy of all citizens) could alleviate some of the concerns introduced by the extremists.

On the *motivational* level, the guideline of decreasing tolerance seems well designed to give the extremist voice as much recognition as possible without disavowing the core commitment to the substantive value of autonomy. In contrast with the militant models of democracy, the deliberative model does not aim to exclude the extremists' voice from the public sphere. Every citizen is given the almost unconditional right to enter the political debate and make her case. The model recognizes that every contribution has a potential epistemic relevance and should therefore be given due consideration. To that extent, even extremists should not feel completely excluded from the system. At the same time, of course, this openness towards the extremist has clear limitations. In contrast with the proceduralistic model, the deliberative model remains a substantive model that recognizes that legitimate decisions should meet certain substantive criteria. Therefore, it is not the case that every political actor who can rally support is thereby, ipso facto, advocating legitimate positions. Here, the deliberative model should side with the militants in their resolve to uphold the core values of liberty and equality.

As explained here, the guideline of decreasing tolerance avowedly still remains very abstract. It mostly aims to provide some guidance in developing more specific strategies for dealing with the extremist enemies of (deliberative) democracy. Importantly, the guideline assumes that an effective anti-extremist strategy will require a comprehensive approach in which different political actors are dealt with through a diversity of means. With regards to these means, a wide range of options is available, including legal forms of repression, administrative measures, intelligence controls, civic education and social control through civil society. In terms of the targeted actors, it should be clear that individuals at the periphery of the system should be given a maximum of leeway. As individuals become more organized in the form of civil society organizations or even political parties, and to the extent that their potential impact on the actual political process increases, the measures of containment should become stricter. Nevertheless, it is important to keep in mind that legal restrictions are only one possible way of dealing with extremism and often only a measure of last resort. To the extent possible, extremism should be dealt with on the basis of less repressive means in order to keep the democratic process as open as possible. As Koen Abts and I have argued with regards to political parties, for instance, the curtailment of party financing or a so-called 'cordon sanitaire' imposed by other parties could provide adequate political rather than (more repressive) legal means for putting civilizing pressure on political actors approaching the centers of decision-making.[39]

39 Rummens and Abts 2010.

Rough Deliberation: The Political Importance of Protecting Free Speech

Although the previous section has argued that the deliberative model provides guidance in the determination of a series of possible measures for dealing with extremists in the democratic system, it is clear that legal restrictions are and should be part of the range of available measures for this purpose. In this section, I propose to have a closer look at the implications of the concentric model of the deliberative system for a proper understanding of the nature and limits of our legally protected freedom of expression.

As already indicated in the introduction, many theorists as well as Courts consider the maintenance of a healthy democratic regime to constitute one of the main reasons for our political and legal concern for the protection of free speech. As should be clear from the previous arguments, the systemic approach to deliberative democracy advocated here fully endorses this concern. It is not my intention to claim that the protection of democratic self-government provides the sole justification for a wide protection of citizens' freedom of expression. More direct arguments related, for instance, to the respect for citizens as autonomous individuals could probably provide additional arguments in this regard.[40] Be that as it may, concerns for the preservation of a healthy and dynamic democratic system should in any case weigh heavily when considering possible restrictions on our freedom of expression. It is thereby useful to keep in mind that, according to the deliberative model, the adequate protection of the autonomy of citizens presupposes the existence of an open democratic system in which the specific contents and conditions of such protection can be decided. In this sense, the democratic system and the freedom of expression function as conditions of possibility for the overall protection of the autonomy of citizens. Therefore, if the implementation of restrictions on the freedom of expression is considered on the basis of arguments referring to other aspects of citizen's autonomy – such as, for instance, their freedom of religion – it is safe to assume that in almost all circumstances priority should be given to the protection of free speech. Attempts to protect religious freedom by curtailing one of its conditions of possibility seem generally ill-advised.

In the previous section we have argued that there are important epistemic and motivational reasons for considering the protection of contributions to the public debate as a primary constitutional concern. It is essential that the democratic system is capable of tracking all possibly relevant concerns and arguments and it is essential for the commitment of citizens to the democratic regime that they know and experience that they have the opportunity to raise their concerns, no matter what these might be. Therefore, Stefan Sottiaux and I have argued elsewhere that the law should give the fullest protection possible

40 For a very brief overview of possible justifications of free speech, see C. Young, 'Does freedom of speech include hate speech?', *Res Publica*, Vol. 17, 2011, pp. 385-406 at 389-394.

to political speech.[41] It is thereby important to understand the category of political speech in a broad manner. In this context, the wide definition of political speech presented by Cass Sunstein seems to be on the right track. He defines it as speech 'both intended and received as a contribution to public deliberation about some issue.'[42] In our understanding, this definition fits well with the concentric model of democratic deliberation because it is compatible with an extensive understanding of the political nature of speech in terms of its origin, form and content. In terms of *origin*, it is important to emphasize that political speech is not restricted to the contributions of actual politicians. Ordinary citizens play an essential democratic role as participants in the informal public debate. Precisely because it is important to capture and track all possibly relevant facts and arguments, the political relevance of speech does not depend on the political nature of the context in which it is raised. Debates in civil society, in bars, in parks, in academic settings can all have political importance and should be protected as such. In terms of *form*, it is noteworthy that the political meaning of speech does not depend on whether or not the contribution takes the shape of a well formulated discursive argument. All kinds of activities, symbolic acts, artistic or other expressions can also have a political meaning. In terms of *content*, it has already been indicated that almost every message could have a potentially relevant political meaning and that it is therefore not acceptable to impose a priori legal constraints on the possible content of political speech.

The systemic approach to deliberative democracy defended here thus acknowledges that 'deliberation can be rough.' Public deliberation cannot and should not be conceptualized simply in terms of a reasonable and civilized exchange of arguments. There are crucial epistemic and motivational reasons for recognizing the democratic importance of rough deliberation, including those forms of expression most civilized people would consider highly inappropriate or even repugnant. In this context, Cass Sunstein has already made the point that even racist speech can play a relevant role in the public debate:

> 'A great deal of public debate produces anger or resentment on the basis of race. If we were to excise all such speech from political debate, we would have severely truncated our discussion of such important matters as civil rights, foreign policy, crime, conscription, abortion and social welfare policy. Even if speech produces anger or resentment on the basis of race, it might well be thought a legitimate part of the deliberative process.'[43]

41 S. Sottiaux and S. Rummens, 'Concentric democracy: resolving an incoherence in the European Court of Human Rights' case law on freedom of expression and freedom of association', *International Journal of Constitutional Law*, Vol. 10, No. 1, 2012, pp. 106-126. The argument presented here closely follows the argument in sections 4 and 5 of this paper.

42 Sunstein 1993, p. 130.

43 Sunstein 1993, p. 186.

In a similar vein, Jane Mansbridge, who is one the prominent authors within the deliberative paradigm and, notably, one of the first promoters of the systemic approach within that paradigm, has argued that offensive or even hurtful forms of speech can have political relevance because they might help us to understand the underlying concerns of people using them:

> 'In a public forum and in everyday talk, there are justifiable places for offensiveness, noncooperation and the threat of retaliation – even for raucous, angry, self-centred, bitter talk, aiming at nothing but hurt. These forms of talk are sometimes necessary (...) to achieve authenticity, to reveal (...) the pain and anger, hate, or delight in another's pain, that someone actually feels, when expression or knowledge of those feelings furthers the understanding that is the goal of deliberation.'[44]

Of course, the precise limits of the protection of free speech cannot be directly deduced from the deliberative theory of democracy. In fact, the theory implies that also in the case of free speech legislation, the precise limitations and constraints can only be determined on the basis of the democratic process itself. Thereby, cultural and other differences between societies could legitimately lead to differences in terms of the precise contents of regulations. Nevertheless, in spite of the fact that a priori philosophical arguments fail to fully determine the appropriate extent of the protection of free speech, the theory clearly points towards the need for a very wide ranging protection, including forms of extremist expressions or hate speech.

As a result, the theory, as it stands, already contains sufficiently normative content to allow for a critique of certain existing forms of legislation or juridical practices. Although a more comprehensive analysis of existing practices is beyond the scope of this contribution, two examples can be mentioned. First, the existing Dutch legislation concerning group defamation on the basis of race or religion and the legislation regarding incitement of hatred[45] seems very problematic because it purports to stifle political speech for the purpose of preventing very general and vaguely defined forms of 'harm.' Secondly, the existing jurisprudence of the European Court of Human Rights regarding Article 10 of the European Convention on Human Rights seems problematic because its reviews of hate speech bans increasingly simply refer to content-based arguments whereby any form of speech at odds with the core values of the Convention is considered to be unworthy of legal protection.[46]

44 Mansbridge 1999, p. 223.

45 137c Sr and 137d Sr, respectively. The (in-)appropriateness of this legislation is extensively discussed in several contributions in the first part of the present volume.

46 See Sottiaux and Rummens 2012 for a more extensive argument in this regard.

Of course, the presumption of deliberative theory in favor of wide ranging protection of free speech does not automatically imply that the only acceptable model is the American model, whereby the Supreme Court is extremely protective and allows for almost no restrictions on free speech.[47] Here, in-between positions are clearly conceivable. Whichever position legislators and courts wish to develop, however, some general guidelines following from the theoretical perspective defended here should be taken into account. First, the political nature of speech provides a weighty reason for its protection. Thereby, the political character of speech should be broadly understood, as explained, in terms of origin, form as well as content. Secondly, although restrictions on free speech might be justified under certain circumstances, these restrictions should not simply be based on the content of speech but should refer to the harmful consequences of certain speech acts. Speech directly inciting violence or discrimination, for instance, should not be acceptable. However, in this context, it is important for legislators and judges to refer to forms of 'harm' that are precisely enough defined, severe enough to warrant restrictions and adequately (causally and directly) connected to the speech acts under consideration. Thirdly, harm to the democratic system itself might provide a reason for imposing restrictions on freedom of speech. Hereby, the guideline of decreasing tolerance implies that restrictions could only be legitimized in case the speech acts under consideration indeed pose a real threat in the sense that there is a genuine possibility that the speaker's action will facilitate the unfiltered impact of extremist views on actual policies or legislation. Cases such as these will normally be extremely rare.

Politicians and Political Parties

To conclude the argument presented here, it is worthwhile to also briefly consider the implications of the concentric model for the freedom of speech of politicians as well as for the leeway that should be given to political parties for expressing extremist views. With regards to politicians, two arguments with opposite thrust could be made, whereby both of these arguments also seem in line with the concentric model. On the one hand, it is fair to say that politicians are closer to the centers of decision-making than ordinary citizens. Following the logic of the concentric model, this proximity would provide a reason for being more restrictive vis-à-vis politicians in comparison to ordinary citizens. On the other hand, however, politicians play a very specific role in the political system in the sense that they are supposed to represent the views of significant parts of the population, whereby electoral support provides a measure for this wider endorsement. In view of their specific

47 For a recent comparative analysis of the American and European jurisprudence, see E. Bleich, 'Freedom of expression versus racist hate speech: explaining differences between high court regulations in the USA and Europe', *Journal of Ethic and Migration Studies*, Vol. 40, 2014, pp. 283-300.

role, it has been argued that politicians should not receive less but rather more protection in terms of their freedom to express their political views. In view of the seeming soundness of *both* of these arguments, however, it is probably best to conclude that there are as yet no compelling reasons for giving politicians either more or less freedom of expression than other citizens. The suggestion here is therefore to place both politicians and non-politicians on a par with eachother.

The main threat of politicians to the democratic system arguably resides not in their individual person but rather in the fact that they are part of an organized political party that is engaged in the mobilization of electoral support for a political program. To the extent that the threat resides with the party rather than with the individual politician, Stefan Sottiaux and I have argued that the guideline of decreasing tolerance implies that strategies for dealing with extremism should primarily focus on the former rather than the latter.[48] When targeting political parties, however, it should be kept in mind that legal restrictions or actual party bans are again a measure of last resort. As mentioned, other means such as the curtailment of party financing or a political 'cordon sanitaire' provide alternative and less repressive means for dealing with extremist parties. In view of the dramaturgical role of political parties discussed above, whereby political parties contribute to the generation of a visible ideological landscape and the public constitution of a space of political reason, the existence of smaller extremist parties should not in itself be considered a threat to the political system. It is only when these parties become sufficiently strong to actually have a significant impact on the quality of policies and legislation that the most drastic measures could become appropriate. In this context, we have argued that the jurisprudence of the European Court of Human Rights with regard to the protection of the freedom of association under Article 11 of the European Convention on Human Rights is more adequate than its jurisprudence regarding Article 10 on freedom of expression.[49] In the famous *Refah* case, for instance, the Court upheld the decision by the Turkish government to dissolve the *Refah* party on the basis of the threat the party posed to the survival of the Turkish democratic regime.[50] As we have argued, the Court thereby developed an adequate test for assessing party dissolution which not only focuses on the content of the party program, but which gives central importance to the actual threat posed by the political party. The lesson here should be that adjudication on free speech as well as on freedom of association should indeed take into account these contextual elements and

48 Sottiaux and Rummens 2012, section 5.

49 Sottiaux and Rummens 2012, section 2. Compare also S. Sottiaux, 'Anti-democratic associations: content and consequences in article 11 adjudication', *Netherlands Quarterly of Human Rights*, Vol. 22, No. 4, 2004, pp. 585-601.

50 *Refah Partisi (the Welfare Party) and others v. Turkey*, 31 July 2001 (Third Section); *Refah Partisi (the Welfare Party) and others v. Turkey*, 13 February 2003, Reports 2003-II (2003) (Grand Chamber).

focus on the genuine threat posed to the democratic system. It is this threat alone which constitutes a legitimate constraint on the political use of these two basic freedoms.

Conclusion

In this paper, I have tried to make a connection between the flourishing academic debates on both free speech and deliberative democracy. I have tried to show that the recent systemic turn in deliberative democracy implies that advocates of deliberative democracy should no longer simply focus on reasonable and civilized forms of deliberation as the source of democratic legitimacy. A systemic approach, which looks at the deliberative quality of the deliberative system as a whole, can explain how seemingly uncivilized and irrational forms of behavior can still play a meaningful and important role within the wider deliberative system. Throughout my argument, I have focused on the epistemic as well as the motivational functions that an adequate democratic system should fulfill. On the basis of these criteria, I have argued that a far reaching protection of political speech, including extremist forms of speech which most of us would consider inappropriate or even repulsive, is a necessary condition for the maintenance of a dynamic and inclusive deliberative system that tracks all relevant concerns of citizens, and is able to maintain at least some form of loyalty even amongst those citizens who disagree with some of the core values of our liberal democratic regime.

15 The New Censorship

A Case Study of the Extrajudicial Restraints on Free Speech

Paul Cliteur, Tom Herrenberg and Bastiaan Rijpkema[*]

The central assumption of this contribution is that the limits of free speech are, to an increasing extent, not established by the legislature or the judiciary, but by terrorist organizations and terrorist individuals – in such a way that it amounts to a new kind of censorship. At least, this is the case with regard to a particular kind of speech: Religious criticism or religious satire. Freedom of speech is nowadays 'freedom of speech in an age of theoterrorism.'[1] This means that freedom of speech is accompanied by many factual constraints which are *real* limits on the free speech for the persons concerned, namely, those targeted by terrorist assault. The general public feigns ignorance, however, along with leading politicians. In a study of five major cases: The Carrell Affair, the Cartoon Affair, the Rushdie Affair, the Terry Jones Affair (better known as the Koran-burning pastor), and the Youssef Affair (better known as the creator of the *Innocence of Muslims* video), we hope to clarify the predicament our civil rights seem to be in.

The three authors of this contribution have all done research on one or more of these cases. Cliteur has studied the Carrell, Cartoon and Rushdie Affairs,[2] Rijpkema has studied the case of the American maverick Koran-burning pastor Terry Jones,[3] and Herrenberg has studied the most recent case, that of Mark Basseley Youssef, who was the creator of an insignificant satire on the prophet Mohammed which, months after it was posted on the Internet, was the center of controversy in many parts of the world.[4] In all of these cases,

* We want to thank the participants in a colloquium at the department of Jurisprudence, Leiden University, for the critical discussion of an earlier version of this chapter. In particular we want to thank: Yoram Stein, Machteld Zee, Roy van Keulen, Janneke Vink, Zhang Tu, Sarah Strous and Mirjam van Schaik.

1 The term "theoterrorism" is used for terrorism which finds its source and justification in a conception of God. We cannot, within the context of this contribution, explain and justify why we think this is useful vocabulary and have to refer to: Cliteur, Paul, "The Challenge of Theoterrorism", in: *The New English Review*, 30 May 2013, full text: www.newenglishreview.org/Paul_Cliteur/The_Challenge_of_Theoterrorism/.

2 Cliteur, Paul, "Van Rushdie tot Jones: over geweld en uitingsvrijheid", in: Afshin Ellian, Gelijn Molier and Tom Zwart, Eds., *Mag ik dit zeggen? Beschouwingen over de vrijheid van meningsuiting*, Boom Juridische uitgevers, The Hague 2011, pp. 67-89.

3 Rijpkema, Bastiaan, "Vrijheid van meningsuiting in de val tussen religieus extremisme en utilitarisme", in: *Nederlands Juristenblad*, afl. 44/45, 14 December 2012, pp. 3106-3111.

4 Herrenberg, Tom, "Politici, de vrijheid van meningsuiting en *Innocence of Muslims*", in: *Nederlands Juristenblad*, afl. 33, 27 September 2013, pp. 2255-2259; Herrenberg, Tom, "Vrijheid van meningsuiting in de multiculturele samenleving: evaluatie van twee tegenstrijdige interpretaties", in: *Civis Mundi*, 14 January 2014.

threats and (attempted) murders were the results, while western politicians tried to appease the anger of violent crowds and reassure their colleagues in other parts of the world that they did 'not agree' with the expressions. The defense of free speech that some of them presented was so weak that it bordered on making excuses for having a constitution, a democracy, and freedom of the press. The present contribution tries to tie together the research done on the several individual cases.

The Netherlands is an interesting country to start our study of this perplexing phenomenon. The Netherlands is central to our subject, because what took place here could be considered as the catalyst: The cancellation of fourteen seconds of satire by the German-Dutch show master Rudi Carrell in 1987. From here, it seems the story unfolds automatically to the predicament we now find ourselves in. So let us start with this memorable piece of satire in 1987.

THE CARRELL AFFAIR IN GERMANY[5]

On New Year's Eve, 1987 (*Sylvester* in German), German television broadcast some highlights from the 'comedy show'[6] of Rudi Carrell (1934-2006). Carrell was a Dutch-born entertainer who became one of the most beloved show masters on German television. Successes in his home country led him to seek new challenges. In 1965, he moved to Germany. The *Rudi Carrell Show* (1965-1972) and *Rudi's Tagesshow* (1981-1987) were huge successes. Carrell's audiences made up about two-thirds of all German TV viewers. On at least one occasion, in 1987, he drew a viewership of twenty million people.[7] The item in question, which was watched by an audience of 20.5 million people,[8] was the cause of a diplomatic controversy with enormous ramifications. It was a spoof, broadcast on Sunday 15 February, 1987, in which Carrell used cinematic tricks to make it appear as if women were throwing their underwear at the feet of Iran's Ayatollah Ruhollah Khomeini.[9]

Only seconds after Carrell's show aired, Reinhard Schlagintweit (*b.* 1928), the civil servant of the German government responsible for contact with the Middle East, received a call.[10] On the phone was Mohammad Djavad Salari (*b.* 1951), the Iranian ambassador in Bonn since 1984. He was very angry. Was Schlagintweit aware that the 'highest supervisor of all Muslims' ('*das geistliche Oberhaupt aller Muslime*') had just been insulted? Not only

5 Parts of the following discussion of the Carrell Affair appeared in: Cliteur, Paul, "The Rudi Carrell Affair and its Significance for the Tension between theoterrorism and religious satire", in: *Ancilla Iuris*, 2013: 15, pp. 15-41, full text: www.anci.ch/paul_cliteur.

6 "Risque spoof on Khomeini sparks Iranian uproar", in: Associated Press, 17 February 1987.

7 "Rudi Carrell", in: *Britannica Online Encyclopedia*.

8 "Tehran expels two W. Germans", in: *The Washington Post*, 18 February 1987.

9 See for an analysis of Carrell's humor: Lixfeld, Hannjost, "Witz und soziale Wirklichkeit: Bemerkungen zur interdisziplinären Witzforschung", in: *Fabula*, Vol. 25, nr. 3-4, September 2009, pp. 183-213.

10 "Carrell-Affäre: nicht klug", in: *Der Spiegel*, Nr. 9, 23 February 1987, pp. 25-27, p. 25.

had the Iranian people's religious feelings been hurt, but those of Muslims 'all over the world.'[11]

We have to study the argument disclosed in this conversation carefully, since it is characteristic of a way of thinking which is widespread, and at the heart of the phenomenon we are discussing in this essay. What does Salari contend? He claimed that criticism of Khomeini (a respected cleric from *his* perspective, a brutal dictator from another) was not only the criticism of one specific dictator but an insult to a whole country. And not only an insult to a whole country, but also to its citizens. And not only to its citizens, but also to the religion those citizens are supposed to share: Islam. And not only the specific fundamentalist interpretation of Islam put forward by the Iranian theocracy, but Islam *tout court*. So by a simple sleight of hand, criticism of one specific dictator became criticism of one fifth of the world's population. In the Iranian culture, Salari indicated, it was 'unthinkable' to mock Ayatollah Khomeini.[12] And, most importantly, he promised that there would be consequences, though he did not specify them.

The Consequences of Carrell's Spoof

One of those consequences proved to be the closure of the Iranian consulates in West Berlin and Hamburg which, in itself, was not a great problem. Another consequence was that an Iran Air flight from Frankfurt to Tehran was delayed for six and a half hours due to an Iran Air personnel strike in protest against the show.[13] Which was not a great problem either. Tehran had ordered the strike, as Saeed Kamyak, the airline's operations director for West Germany, indicated. Yet another consequence of Carrell's perceived insult was that on 18 February, Iran ordered two West German diplomats to leave Iran in retaliation for Carrell's spoof of Khomeini.[14] Another inconvenience, perhaps, but not something that would unsettle the way the world is organized. Furthermore: Germany's ambassador, Armin Freitag, was summoned to the Foreign Ministry and handed a 'strongly worded protest note on the insulting program.'[15] Also, on 18 February, Iranian students staged a protest at the West German embassy, chanting anti-U.S. and anti-West German slogans. The students demanded an official apology from Bonn about Carrell's spoof.[16] In addition, the Goethe Cultural Institute in Tehran was closed in retaliation for the broadcast of Car-

11 Ibid., p. 25.
12 Ibid., p. 26.
13 "West German spoof of Khomeini sparks Iranian protests", in: Associated Press, 17 February 1987.
14 "Tehran expels two W. Germans", in: *The Washington Post*, 18 February 1987; "Iran expels two German diplomats in retaliation for TV spoof", in: Associated Press, 17 February 1987.
15 "West German spoof of Khomeini sparks Iranian protests", in: Associated Press, 17 February 1987.
16 "Iran miffed over Khomeini spoof on German TV", in: *Tampa Bay Times*, 19 February 1987.

rell's '*Tagesschau.*'[17] Last but not least: Carrell was threatened[18] and received police protection from the German government. *That*, so it has become more and more manifest in the past decades, proved to be something new and extremely unsettling: A German citizen, being threatened on German soil, by a foreign dictator.

THE FOLLOW UP IN THE NETHERLANDS

As might be expected, the Dutch took great interest in the (until then) German Carrell Affair, and the broadcasting corporation VARA wanted to show in its program 'Behind the News' (*Achter het Nieuws*) the fourteen-second clip that had caused all the commotion. This is the ABC of journalism, is it not? Let people decide for themselves what they think about the fourteen-second spoof that had caused so much uproar in a neighboring country, the journalists of VARA must have thought.

It was announced that the footage would air on 23 February 1987, eight days after the German broadcast, but something unusual happened: The Dutch minister of foreign affairs, Hans van den Broek (*b.* 1936), personally called the broadcasting corporation. During his telephone call on 23 February, a few seconds before the network was due to broadcast the program containing the contested item, the minister tried to convince the host, Paul Witteman (*b.* 1946), *not* to air the item discussed. It would be 'too dangerous' for Dutch nationals living in Iran. The reporter, understandably surprised to have the minister of foreign affairs on the phone, took an unusual approach to this dilemma: He invited the minister to call again a few minutes later, when the show was live, and explain his reasons for asking the program to censor the spoof. To the surprise of many, perhaps, the minister agreed, and as a result, all of the considerations about giving in to pressure from Iran (or not) were aired openly on Dutch television. Delicate discussions on what to do when faced with such tricky dilemmas, usually held behind closed doors, were now laid out for all to see. With the wisdom of hindsight we may ask: Was this perhaps one of the most fateful publicly aired dialogues of modern times?

Why fateful? Because now, it was there for all to see: The fourteen seconds of satire were eventually *not* broadcasted on Dutch television (for that was the result of the open discussion) out of fear for an unclear threat from a dictator abroad.

In Iran, a great triumph was booked on that memorable evening of 23 February 1987: An Iranian dictator had successfully intimidated a small country in Europe, a country allegedly committed to the rule of law and democracy. But also, apparently, a country that

17 "Iran angered by ayatollah under undies", in: *The Globe and Mail*, 21 February 1987.

18 Religious fanatics threatened with attacks ("Religiöse Fanatiker drohten mit anschlägen"). See: "Grösstes Witz-Archiv Deutschlands – Aufgewärmte Slips", in: *Der Spiegel*, 27 October 1997.

was quick to relinquish all that when confronted with a much stronger antithetical perspective: The theocracy, led by God's one and only representative on earth.

DUTCH PARLIAMENTARIANS STRUGGLING WITH THE ISSUE

On 26 February, 1987, the minister of foreign affairs, a member of the Lubbers II coalition, comprised of the liberal party and the Christian Democrats, justified the steps he had taken before the Dutch Parliament.[19] During that session, the minister of foreign affairs repeated what he had said during the conversation with Witteman, and claimed that he had only pointed out to the broadcasting corporation what the 'consequences' of the transmission of the program could have been. He explained that he had learned from the Dutch embassy in Tehran that re-airing the clip on Dutch television would be experienced in Iran as a 'profound insult to Khomeini.'[20] This could cause an outburst of 'anger' from the 'Iranian public.' The security of the people working at the embassy would not be guaranteed, and diplomatic relations could be severed (this is the worst thing that could happen to a country from the perspective of a diplomat, one may surmise). These considerations, Van den Broek explained, persuaded him to 'seek contact' with the broadcasting corporation. The minister further claimed that he had left the decision, and the responsibility for it, up to the corporation (apparently implying that, from his perspective, the broadcaster would be responsible for any consequences, rather than the ministry of foreign affairs or the Iranian government). The Dutch minister even declared that he had not experienced any 'pressure from the Iranian side.' All things considered, he said he 'could understand' the position of the Iranian government.[21]

The Dutch Parliament did not strongly criticize the minister for his telephone call to the Dutch broadcasting corporation. The Labor faction declared 'understanding' for what the minister had done.[22] The Christian Democrat representative stated that 'an insignificant piece of satire should not affect the relationship between two countries.'[23] The Liberal Bolkestein (from the VVD, so in the coalition with the Christian-Democrats at that time) also backed the minister of foreign affairs, reasoning that the security of Dutch people abroad had to be safeguarded.[24] Yet, he confided that the whole affair made him feel

19 Before a huge commission in which all the political fractions of the Dutch representative were present: The so-called commission of foreign affairs ("vaste Commissie voor Buitenlandse Zaken"). See for proceedings of the meeting: "Verslag van een mondeling overleg", in: Tweede Kamer, 1986-1987, 19 700, hfdst. V, nr. 79, pp. 1-3.

20 TK 1986-1987, p. 1.

21 Ibid., p. 2: "Daaraan voegde hij toe dat hij de gang van zaken niet heeft ervaren als druk van Iraanse zijde, en dat hij zich, de situatie daar in ogenschouw nemende, de houding van de Iraanse regering kon indenken".

22 Ter Beek (PvdA), in: TK 1986-1987, p. 2.

23 Gualthérie van Weezel (CDA), in: TK 1986-1987, p. 2.

24 Bolkestein (VVD), in: TK 1986-1987, p. 2.

somewhat uneasy. He feared that this affair could set a 'dangerous precedent.'[25] The only Member of Parliament who seemed to adopt a straightforward critical stance on the minister's intervention was from the socialist faction. She claimed that there was certainly pressure from the Iranian side, and warned that a threat of outbursts from the Iranian people had to be seen as 'blackmail.'[26]

The Carrell Affair was soon forgotten. In the history of Dutch media it was even considered to be a funny event. The suggestion given by the journalist, Witteman, for the minister to call in to openly 'discuss' the moral quandary before a television audience was even seen as a good joke. He had brought a member of the government to discuss what to do with freedom of the press in a kind of popular plebiscite. Was this not the epitome of democracy? Or had, with the non-transmission of the program something more serious happened in the world?

The Rushdie Affair[27]

Was the Carrell Affair indeed a 'dangerous precedent' as Bolkestein feared (without drawing the necessary conclusions from his, in itself, interesting intuition)?

In 1989, two years after the Carrell Affair which ended so gloriously for the Iranian dictator, Khomeini tried to take a further step. This time not to intimidate a Dutch-German show master, but to have an ex-Muslim murdered who had written a blasphemous novel about the prophet of Islam. He declared:

> 'I inform all zealous Muslims of the world that the author of the book entitled *The Satanic Verses* – which has been compiled, printed, and published in opposition to Islam, the Prophet, and the Koran – and all those involved in the publication who were aware of its contents, are sentenced to death.
> I call upon all zealous Muslims to execute them quickly, wherever they may be found, so that no one else will dare to insult the Muslim sanctities. God willing, whoever is killed on this path is a martyr.

25 In 2008, so more than twenty years later, Hans van den Broek, now a "minister of state" (an honorary title conferred upon ex-politicians on the basis of great merit), called upon the government to sue Geert Wilders for making the anti-Islam film Fitna. Again, the ex-minister of foreign affairs feared that Dutch citizens living abroad would be harmed as a reaction to Wilders' film. See: Koelé, Theo, "Kabinet moet Fitna verbieden", in: *De Volkskrant*, 26 March 2008. So over the years Van den Broek's position on these matters has been fairly consistent.

26 Van Es (PSP), in: TK 1986-1987, p. 3.

27 The discussion of the Rushdie Affair in the next sections relies in part on: Cliteur, Paul, "Van Rushdie tot Jones: over geweld en uitingsvrijheid", in: Afshin Ellian, Gelijn Molier en Tom Zwart, Eds., *Mag ik dit zeggen? Beschouwingen over de vrijheid van meningsuiting*, Boom Juridische uitgevers, The Hague 2011, pp. 67-89.

> In addition, anyone who has access to the author of this book but does not possess the power to execute him should report him to the people so that he may be punished for his actions.'[28]

Writing and publishing a novel 'in opposition to Islam, the Prophet, and the Koran' is under the Universal Declaration of Human Rights, as issued by the United Nations in 1948, an elementary human right. Article 18 declares:

> 'Everyone has the right to freedom of thought, conscience and religion; this right includes freedom to change his religion or belief, and freedom, either alone or in community with others and in public or private, to manifest his religion or belief in teaching, practice, worship and observance.'

But for the faithful this Article is far more controversial than many liberals realize. Rushdie had 'changed' his religion! He had become an 'apostate,' as is the right of everyone living under a regime of human rights.[29] This was not the case in Iran, however.[30]

But there is a second remarkable element in this declaration (a fatwa) by Ayatollah Khomeini. Here, a comparison with Galileo might be illuminating. In the year 1632, Galileo published a book of dialogues on the Copernican and Ptolemaic systems, in which, in the words of Bertrand Russell, 'he had the temerity to place some remarks that had been made by the Pope into the mouth of a character named Simplicius.'[31] The pope was furious. Galileo was living in Florence at that time and was on good terms with the Grand Duke. But the Inquisition sent for him to come to Rome to be tried. The Grand Duke would be threatened if he would continue to shelter Galileo. Galileo however, did not make it easy for them; he claimed he was too old (seventy years) to travel. Besides, he was ill and going blind. But the Inquisition was not so easy to shake off, as one might expect (they had more

28 Ruhollah al-Musavi al-Khomeini, 14 February 1989, quoted in: Pipes, Daniel, "Two Decades of the Rushdie Rules", in: *Commentary*, October 2010, pp. 30-35; Pipes, Daniel, *The Rushdie Affair: The Novel, the Ayatollah, and the West*, Second Edition with a postscript by Koenraad Elst, Transaction Publishers, New Brunswick (USA) and London (UK) 2003, p. 27. Ayatollah Khomeini "knew no English and had apparently never read the novel", writes Bernard Lewis in: "Religion and Murder in the Middle East", p. 105.

29 See on this, Jespersen, Karen, & Ralf Pittelkow, *Islamisten en naïvisten: een aanklacht*. With an introduction provided by Afshin Ellian, Nieuw Amsterdam, Amsterdam 2007, a book translated into French (Jespersen, Karen, & Ralf Pittelkow, *Islamistes et naivistes: un acte d'accusation*, Editions du Panama, Paris 2007), but unfortunately not into English. An impressive recent book is: Marshall, Paul, and Shea, Nina, *Silenced: How Apostasy and Blasphemy Codes are Choking Freedom Worldwide*, Oxford University Press, Oxford 2011.

30 And also not the situation in other parts of the world where religious extremism gains significance. See: *Freedom of Thought 2012. A Global Report on Discrimination against Humanists, Atheists and the Nonreligious*, International Humanist and Ethical Union, London 2012; *Freedom of Thought 2013. A Global Report on Discrimination against Humanists, Atheists and the Nonreligious*, International Humanist and Ethical Union, London 2013.

31 Russell, Bertrand, *The Scientific Outlook*, Routledge, London and New York 2001 (1931), p. 12.

uncooperative candidates at stake to deal with)[32] and Galileo was commanded to come to Rome as soon as he would recover, which he did, in due course, and where he, as we all know, recanted.

Now, Khomeini was no pope. And Rushdie was in another situation than Galileo. Rushdie's 'Grand Duke,' Margaret Thatcher, would not have delivered her heretic, blasphemer or apostate to the supreme leader of Islam, as one may expect.[33] But Khomeini was a much too resourceful man to acquiesce in this predicament. So he took recourse to the same tremendously successful instrument he had tried with so much success with the Dutch: Intimidation.

In the case of the Dutch, only the *possibility* that violence might occur was sufficient for the Dutch government, and the Dutch broadcasting corporation, to back down on freedom of the press. In case of the arrogant British (a former world power, after all) a somewhat stronger medicine might be needed. This was the fatwa. As Mohamed Arshad Ahmedi writes in his *Rushdie: Haunted by His Unholy Ghosts* (1997), since that moment 'even non-Muslims around the world were going to add a new word to their vocabularies no matter what language they spoke – this word was Fatwa.'[34] Khomeini, in the words of his declaration, 'called upon all zealous Muslims to execute them quickly.' Two years later, in 1991, the Japanese translator of Rushdie's *The Satanic Verses* was found slain at a university in northeast Tokyo.[35] The translator, Hitoshi Igarashi (1947-1991), was also a Japanese scholar of Arabic and Persian literature. The assailant, who was never caught, was probably executing the orders of the religious scholar, whose reputation the Iranian government took great pains to defend: Ayatollah Khomeini. Such killings evince not only an enormous religious zeal (something Khomeini refers to in his declaration: He exhorts 'all zealous Muslims' to execute, what Hitchens has called his 'bribed assassination scheme')[36] but also an overwhelming respect for the interpretations of religion by religious leaders. From a modernist perspective, the interpretation of Holy Scripture by a religious scholar is not taken as the final word for religious believers. In that sense, we are 'all

32 In 1632 Galileo had, of course, what happened with Giordano Bruno fresh in his mind: Bruno was caught and burned at the stake at the Campo dei Fiori in Rome in 1600.

33 Although she may have been tempted. In his conversation with Rushdie, the French philosopher Bernard-Henri Lévy indicated that he had heard Margaret Thatcher saying that Rushdie deserved this, and also that Prince Charles was chuckling in Paris about the Rushdie Affair, saying that Rushdie was quite expensive for the British crown. See: Lévy, Bernard-Henri, *Avec Salman Rushdie: Questions de principe six*, Le Livre de Poche, Librairie Générale Française, Paris 1999, pp. 78 and 96. That Prince Charles is also rather expensive for the British crown without having any significant talent for *anything at all* probably did not cross his mind.

34 Arshad Ahmedi, Mohamed, *Rushdie: Haunted by His Unholy Ghosts*, Islam International Publications Limited, Tilford UK 2007 (1997), p. 39.

35 Weisman, Steven R., "Japanese Translator of Rushdie Book Found Slain", in: *The New York Times*, 13 July 1991.

36 Hitchens, Christopher, *God is not Great: How Religion Poisons Everything*, Twelve, New York, Boston 2007, p. 28.

protestants now; even Catholics are.' From a pre-modern perspective, though, which now makes its resurgence in theoterrorism, following the religious leaders is an absolute command, indispensable for personal salvation.

There is one aspect that many missed in Khomeini's declaration and, in a certain sense, this proved also fateful to the Dutchman Theo van Gogh in 2004. Khomeini, referring to the book *The Satanic Verses*, did not only incite the murder of the *author* of the book, Salman Rushdie, but also called for the death of 'all those involved in the publication who were aware of its contents.' Italian *translator* Ettore Capriolo was attacked with a knife on 3 July 1991 in Milan, and the Norwegian *publisher* William Nygaard was wounded by gun shots on 11 October 1993 in Oslo. As Ramine Kamrane writes on the publisher and translator: 'They were no Muslims.'[37] Only Rushdie was Muslim, or at least regarded as one.

The Murder of Theo van Gogh

This was something that Theo van Gogh must have missed, when he decided to work together with Ayaan Hirsi Ali on the film *Submission* in 2004, a movie dedicated to the plight of women in countries where Islam occupies an important influence. Van Gogh considered himself to be the 'village idiot' of Amsterdam. He was no apostate. He had never been a believer. He was not a Muslim; he was an atheist. So the whole repertoire of punishments religious fanatics have in store for apostates, heretics and blasphemers (so faithfully executed by the Christian state on behalf of the Inquisition)[38] would not be applicable to him.

The murder of the Dutch film director, film producer, columnist, author, actor, journalist, public intellectual and – most important of all – 'contrarian' Theo van Gogh (1957-2004),[39] abruptly ended the dream of a multicultural paradise that the Netherlands was in the eyes of many progressive and well-meaning leftist intellectuals and politicians.

Van Gogh was born in The Hague, the Netherlands, but lived in Amsterdam, the capital of the country. He was also killed in Amsterdam, on the streets, in broad daylight. He was the son of Johan van Gogh (*b.* 1922), who had worked for the Dutch intelligence agency. Theo's uncle (1920-1945), also called Theo, was executed as a resistance fighter by the Nazis during the occupation of the Netherlands in the Second World War. His

37 Kamrane, Ramine, *La Fatwa contre Rushdie: une interprétation stratégique*, Éditions Kimé, Paris 1997, p. 30.

38 Bennassar, Bartolomé, *Brève Histoire de l'Inquisition: L'intolerance au service du pouvoir*, Fragile, Gavaudun 1999; Green, Toby, *Inquisition: The Reign of Fear*, Macmillan, London 2007.

39 The word 'contrarian' is deliberately chosen because, although a category in itself, the closest analogy to Van Gogh would perhaps be the British-American public intellectual Christopher Hitchens. See his: Hitchens, Christopher, *Letters to a Young Contrarian*, Basic Books, New York 2005.

great-grandfather, also called Theo, was the famous art dealer (1857-1891), younger brother of the world-renowned artist Vincent van Gogh (1853-1891).

Theo van Gogh's life was full of personal quarrels and vehement intellectual clashes with people he deemed to be politically correct (in particular the mayor of Amsterdam, Job Cohen). In the last years of his life he was much impressed by the ideas and work of two other notorious Dutch opinion makers: Pim Fortuyn (1948-2002) and Ayaan Hirsi Ali (*b.* 1969). Fortuyn was a Dutch politician who was murdered by a left-wing activist, Volkert van der Graaf (*b.* 1969). Van der Graaf deemed Fortuyn to be a 'danger' who had to be stopped (i.e. eliminated). One of Fortuyn's political issues was criticizing Islam for its anti-Enlightenment stances, in particular with regard to homosexuality (Fortuyn was an ostentatious homosexual himself who openly avowed his sexual preferences). His most controversial statements were about the 'backward nature' of Islam (in Dutch: *achterlijk*).[40] Hirsi Ali is a Somalia-born writer who, after becoming an atheist,[41] criticized her former religion, Islam, of anti-feminist proclivities.[42] She made a film together with Van Gogh on this issue, which on 29 August, 2004, was shown on Dutch television.[43] The title of the film, *Submission*, refers to the literal translation of the word 'Islam,' but also to the submissive attitude the believers exemplify with regard to the central ideas of their belief, which makes progress difficult, if not impossible. For Van Gogh, Hirsi Ali and Fortuyn, progress in the sense of Enlightenment was only possible by relinquishing religion.[44]

---

40 Poorthuis, Frank and Hans Wansink, "De islam is een achterlijke cultuur", Interview with Pim Fortuyn, in: *de Volkskrant*, 9 February 2002. Fortuyn's ideas on Islam are explained in: Fortuyn, Pim, "Tegen de islamisering van onze cultuur. Nederlandse identiteit als fundament", in: *De grote Pim Fortuyn omnibus*, Speakers Academy, Van Gennep 2001, pp. 197-283. Fortuyn was influenced by: Goodwin, Jan, *Price of Honor: Muslim Women lift the Veil of Silence on the Islamic World*, A Plume Book, Penguin 2003 (1995). See on his life and ideas in general: Snel, Bert, *Pim 1: De politieke biografie van Pim Fortuyn als socioloog en als politicus 1990-2002*, Uitgeverij Van Praag, Amsterdam 2012; Snel, Bert, *Pim 2: Pim Fortuyn en zijn partijen, Leefbaar Nederland, Leefbaar Rotterdam, Lijst Pim Fortuyn*, Prof. Dr. W.P.S. Fortuyn Stichting 2013.

41 She tells her life-story in two autobiographical books: Hirsi Ali, Ayaan, *Infidel: My Life*, The Free Press, London 2007 and Hirsi Ali, Ayaan, *Nomad: From Islam to America, A Personal Journey through the Clash of Civilizations*, The Free Press, London 2010.

42 She made her entrée in Dutch intellectual circles in 2001 with an article under the title "Allow us a Voltaire". She means: allow us, Muslims, also critical minds as Voltaire. Do not condemn us, Muslims, to obscurity by criticizing the Enlightenment thinkers who criticize religion. See: Hirsi Ali, Ayaan, "Gun ons een Voltaire", in: *Trouw*, 24 November 2001, also in: Vink, Jaffe and Chris Rutenfrans, *De terugkeer van de geschiedenis*, Uitgeverij Augustus, Amsterdam 2005, pp. 79-85. She further developed her criticism in: Hirsi Ali, Ayaan, *The Caged Virgin: An Emancipation Proclamation for Women and Islam*, The Free Press, New York and Sydney 2006. Her work shows some similarities with that of Taslima Nasrin (France), Necla Kelek (Germany), Maryam Namazi (United Kingdom). See: Cliteur, Paul, "Female Critics of Islamism", in: *Feminist Theology*, 2011, 19(2), pp. 154-167.

43 Hirsi Ali, Ayaan, *Submission*, broadcasted in "Guests of the Summer" ("Zomergasten") on 29 August 2004, with an introduction by Betsy Udink, Uitgeverij Augustus, Amsterdam 2004.

44 At least Islam. Fortuyn had sympathy for Catholicism. Hirsi Ali and Van Gogh were straightforward atheists and had no sympathy for any religion whatsoever. Hirsi Ali was influenced by the Dutch atheist Herman Philipse. See: Philipse, Herman, *Verlichtingsfundamentalisme?* Open brief over Verlichting en fundamen-

Since the terrorist attacks of 9/11, Van Gogh made criticism of Islam an important part of his polemics. His last film, titled '06/05,' was dedicated to the life and to the murder of Pim Fortuyn, who was killed on that date. In 2003, Van Gogh wrote a book titled *Allah weet het beter* (Allah knows Better).[45] In circles of artists and writers, Van Gogh was exceptional because he did not subscribe to the left-wing views of many of his colleagues. But he was also hated for this. And for his personal attacks, which were – it has to be admitted – often beyond the pale.[46]

The irony is that for many people his death, and especially the way this came about, actually proved what he had not been able to convey during his lifetime: That radical Islam was a mortal danger to the social cohesion of Dutch society (and, frankly, all democratic and liberal societies).

2 November, 2004

On 2 November, 2004, Van Gogh was murdered by the home-grown jihadist Mohammed Bouyeri (*b.* 1978)[47] while cycling to work in the morning. After shooting the filmmaker eight times with a handgun, the killer tried to decapitate Van Gogh with a knife. Bouyeri also stabbed two knives in the chest of his victim, one with a note in which he spelled out his extremist message to the world, and in particular to western democracies, to Jews and to Ayaan Hirsi Ali. Hirsi Ali proved to be untouchable for the killer, while Van Gogh was a soft target. Van Gogh was an easy targer for two reasons. The first reason was that he had no police protection, like Hirsi Ali did have. Van Gogh used to make jokes about the Amsterdam police who had offered him protection, but only during and after his public performances: 'I hope that Al Qaeda respects the office hours,' Van Gogh used to say. The second reason is that he himself, as we indicated, believed that he was not in the same way a target for terrorist attacks as Hirsi Ali was, because *she* was a Muslim (or rather an apostate Muslim) and *he* was a Dutch writer with no ties to Islam. So in his case, there was no 'apostasy.'[48] According to his understanding of Islamist ideology, there would be no

talisme aan Ayaan Hirsi Ali, Mede bestemd voor Piet Hein Donner, minister van Justitie en coördinerend minister in de strijd tegen terreur, Uitgeverij Bert Bakker, Amsterdam 2005.

45 Gogh, Theo van, *Allah weet het beter*, Xtra Producties, Amsterdam 2003.

46 A portrait of Van Gogh is painted by his friends Holman and Pam in: Holman, Theodor, *Theo is dood*, With a foreword by Gijs van de Westelaken, Mets en Schilt, Amsterdam 2006; Pam, Max, *Het bijenspook: over dier, mens en god*, Prometheus, Amsterdam 2009.

47 Buruma, Ian, *Murder in Amsterdam: The Death of Theo van Gogh and the Limits of Tolerance*, Penguin, New York 2006; Eyerman, Ron, *The Assassination of Theo van Gogh: from Social Drama to Cultural Trauma*, Duke University Press, Durham and London 2008; Llosa, Mario Vargas, "Schießen, schneiden, stoßen: Theo van Goghs schrecklicher Tod", *Die Welt*, 4 November 2006; Chorus, Jutta, & Olgun, Ahmet, *In Godsnaam: Het jaar van Theo van Gogh*, Uitgeverij Contact, Antwerp/Amsterdam 2005.

48 Ibn Warraq, Ed., *Leaving Islam: Apostates Speak Out*, Prometheus Books, Amherst, New York, 2003; Marshall, Paul, and Nina Shea, *Silenced: How Apostasy and Blasphemy Codes are Choking Freedom Worldwide*, Oxford

reason to harm him, let alone kill him. He was, after all, 'the village idiot.' But this proved to be a fatal mistake of not only Van Gogh himself, but also of the Amsterdam police and Dutch authorities in general. The murder took most people by surprise. Especially the politically correct elite that Van Gogh had so vehemently criticized. Now they felt embarrassed, although not many people (frankly, no one) changed their attitudes openly. For Dutch society, though, the murder proved a watershed. The anti-Islam party of Geert Wilders had huge electoral success (like Fortuyn's party had done before).[49] It is difficult to imagine this taking place without this 'spectacular' murder. A few weeks after the murder of Van Gogh, on 24 November, 2004, Wilders created a foundation aimed at publicizing his ideology and attracting financial support. This organization was the forerunner of the foundation currently named 'Friends of the PVV' (*Stichting Vrienden van de PVV*), which is, of course, closely related to Wilders' political party: the Party for Freedom (*Partij voor de vrijheid*, or *PVV*).

The murderer of Van Gogh, Mohammed Bouyeri, was apprehended almost immediately after his deed and was convicted on 26 July, 2005, to a life-long prison sentence without parole.[50] This severe sentence was in part the result of the fact that the murderer showed no remorse at all. On the contrary, he used the public trial to explain the jihadist ideology in a manner that must have been a painful experience for many people who had denied any danger.

After the murder, a confusing and heated debate on the 'causes' of this tragedy erupted. This made evident a deep rift in Dutch society. On the one hand, there was the multicultural and politically correct Dutch elite who pointed accusatory fingers at Van Gogh's brutal and outrageous criticism of vulnerable minorities in Dutch society. On the other hand, there were the people that pointed to the nature of jihadist ideology. The two groups could not agree on the causes of the new religious terrorism that seemed to be taking hold.

FROM VAN GOGH TO THE DANISH CARTOON AFFAIR

We ended the Rudi Carrell Affair with the speculation that it is plausible to suppose that there is a connection between the Carrell Affair and the subsequent Rushdie Affair. It is not improbable that Khomeini's success on the evening of 23 February, 1987, having seen a minister of foreign affairs on Dutch television trying to convince a Dutch journalist *not* to criticize his person and regime by re-airing a controversial spoof, has had some effect

University Press, Oxford 2011; Marshall, Paul, Ed., *Radical Islam's Rules: The Worldwide Spread of Extreme Shari'a Law*, Rowman & Littlefied Publishers, Inc., Lanham etc. 2005; Sookhdeo, Patrick, *Freedom to Believe: Challenging Islam's Apostasy Law*, Isaac Publishing, Three Rivers (Michigan) 2009.

49 For a biography of Wilders, see: Fennema, Meindert, *Geert Wilders: Tovenaarsleerling*, Uitgeverij Bert Bakker, Amsterdam 2010.

50 Rechtbank Amsterdam, 26 juli 2005 (Moord op Theo van Gogh).

on the Rushdie Affair one year later. But, let's admit it, this is speculation. We do not have access to the Iranian state archives, nor do we have information from Khomeini himself, or those around him, that the Dutch and the English cases are connected.

The connection between the murder of Theo van Gogh and the next great clash between democratic values and theoterrorism is better documented. Why were the Danish cartoons made? This had something to do with the Van Gogh case. Flemming Rose (*b.* 1958), culture editor of the *Jyllands Posten*, the daily that published the cartoons, was surprised by the fact that in January 2005, the *International Film Festival* in Rotterdam refused to show the film *Submission* by Theo van Gogh and Ayaan Hirsi Ali due to security considerations.[51] The organization feared 'that the screening might trigger further acts of religious violence.'[52] Rose considered this to be odd. Would this not imply that free press gave in to threats of violence? Under those circumstances, was freedom of expression not in fact abolished or at least severely limited?[53] That was Rose's question.

Another incident that provided food for thought was that writer Kåre Bluitgen (*b.* 1959) found it impossible to contract an illustrator for a children's book because nobody dared to make a picture of the prophet Mohammed.[54]

This was the background of the cartoon affair. This is important, because if it is true, there were no pestering xenophobic intellectuals trying to target innocent religious minorities, as was contended in many commentaries.[55] The people who organized the cartoon experiment were concerned. They were concerned about the erosion of civil liberties.

But it soon appeared to Rose that it proved much more difficult than expected to convince people that there was something important at stake. There was no problem at all, many said. Subsequently, the idea arose to 'test' whether there really was a problem. A real empirical test, like the way science tries to prove or disprove something.[56] To test whether cartoonists exerted self-censorship, he asked forty-two cartoonists to give their view on the prophet Mohammed. Only twelve of those actually sent in a cartoon. It was not clear in advance who would present a critical view on the prophet and who would take a more

51 Troost, Nanda, "Nooit zal ik zwijgen", in: *de Volkskrant*, 9 January 2010, www.volkskrant.nl/vk/nl/2694/Tech-Media/archief/article/detail/977464/2010/01/09/Nooit-zal-ik-zwijgen.dhtml.

52 "Fears prompt withdrawal of Van Gogh film", in: *The Guardian*, 27 January 2005, www.theguardian.com/film/2005/jan/27/festivals.rotterdamfilmfestival.

53 Rose, Flemming, "Why I Published Those Cartoons", in: *Washingtonpost.com*, Sunday, 19 February 2006.

54 Kim, Sebastian C.H., "Freedom or Respect: Public Theology and the Debate over the Danish Cartoons", in: *International Journal of Public Theology*, 1 (2007), pp. 249-269.

55 For example, one of the princesses of Orange, Mabel, stated in an interview that one should not publish something with the sole aim to insult, harm or humiliate other people. See the remarks by Princess Mabel quoted in: Albrecht, Yoeri, and Pieter Broertjes, "Ik kan niet tegen onrecht. Het veelkoppige monster van de onvrije democratie", in: *de Volkskrant*, 10 March 2007.

56 See on the scientific method: Russell, Bertrand, *Religion and Science*, Oxford University Press, London New York Toronto 1935, pp. 7-19.

laudatory stance. The experiment was simply to establish how many people, if any, *would dare* to make such a cartoon. And so the twelve cartoons that would cause such turmoil on the international scene came into being: the cartoons 'that shook the world,' to quote the title of Jytte Klausen's book.[57]

The British, the Danish, the Dutch, and the Americans

So far we have dealt with the Dutch, the British and the Danish confrontation with theoterrorism. The Dutch were the first to be tested. And they failed. The British were the second. They fared a little better, perhaps also because of the indefatigable Rushdie himself, who showed great talent in mobilizing the artistic scene to support his case.[58] Rushdie also had great talent in making clear that this was not about *himself* or about *one book*, but about books in general, about what is called the 'principle of free speech.'[59] His case gave rise to some of history's most beautiful defenses of freedom of speech and freedom in general, including Jeremy Waldron's early commentary,[60] and an essay by the always thoughtful Karel van het Reve.[61] These were the 'Milton's' of our time.[62]

Now it was America's turn to be tested by the religious fanatics. Let us first state what we do *not* mean by being 'tested' in this context. First, the United States had, of course, 9/11. This was indeed a manifestation of religious fanaticism of the most violent sort. But it was not a 'test' in the sense that it is discussed in this contribution. A 'test' in the sense discussed here means that there is a dilemma with regard to the question: What action should we undertake? Give up on your principles in exchange for temporary peace, or defend fundamental ideas: Freedom of speech, freedom of conscience, freedom of religion, *et cetera*? The Cartoon Affair was a real dilemma for the Danish politicians. What to do?

---

57 Klausen, Jytte, *The Cartoons that Shook the World*, Yale University Press, New Haven and London 2009.

58 A collection of support from fellow writers is: MacDonogh, Steve, Ed., In Association with Article 19, *The Rushdie Letters: Freedom to Speak, Freedom to Write*, Brandon Book Publishers, Kerry, Ireland 1993; Chervel, Thierry, Hrsg., *Redefreiheit ist das Leben: Briefe an Salman Rushdie*, Piper, München, Zürich 1992. French support for Rushdie is to be found in: Abdallah, Anouar, et al., *Pour Rushdie: Cent intellectuels arabes et musulmans pour la liberté d'expression*, La Decouverte, Carréfour des littératures, Colibri, Paris 1993.

59 Rushdie, Salman, "Coming After Us", in: Lisa Appignanesi, Ed., *Free Expression is No Offence*, Penguin Books, London 2005, pp. 21-29; Rushdie, Salman, "Do we have to fight the battle for the Enlightenment all over again?", in: *The Independent*, 22 January 2005; Rushdie, Salman, "In Good Faith", 1990, in: Salman Rushdie, *Imaginary Homelands: Essays and Criticism 1981-1991*, Vintage Books, London 2010 (1991), pp. 393-414; Rushdie, Salman, *Joseph Anton: A Memoir*, Jonathan Cape, London 2012.

60 Waldron, Jeremy, "Rushdie and Religion", first published under the title "Too important for Tact" in: *The Times Literary Supplement*, 10 March 1989, pp. 248 and 260, and reprinted in: Waldron, Jeremy, *Liberal Rights: Collected Papers 1981-1991*, Cambridge University Press, Cambridge/New York 1993, pp. 134-143.

61 Reve, Karel van het, "Achterlijke artikelen", in: *Elsevier*, 4 March 1989, also included in: Karel van het Reve, *Verzameld Werk*, Vol. 6, Van Oorschot, Amsterdam 2011, pp. 350-353.

62 Milton, John, *Areopagitica*, 1644, in: John Milton, *Complete Poems and major Prose*, Edited with notes and introduction by Merritt Y. Hughes, Hackett Publishing Company, Indianapolis 2003 (1957).

Grovel for the fanatics and make excuses about cartoons in newspapers? Try to have the cartoons suppressed, and the makers convicted on some trumped up case about 'blasphemy,' 'insulting a group of people because of their religion' or similar legislation? The Dutch were put to the test in a similar fashion: What to do? Broadcast fourteen seconds of (un)necessary satire on a brutal dictator, or try to pass on this dilemma to others (as the Dutch did *de facto* with the British, who would become the next victim of the zealous fanatics Khomeini had ignited). 9/11 was not a situation of that sort. And neither was the Iran hostage crisis of 1979-1981. Here, Iran seized sixty-six American citizens at the U.S. embassy in Tehran, holding fifty-two of them for more than a year. The crisis, which took place during the chaotic aftermath of Iran's Islamic revolution (1978-1979) and its overthrow of the Pahlavi monarchy, had a dramatic effect on the domestic politics in the United States, it poisoned US-Iran relations for decades, and proved a deadly blow to the popularity of the Carter administration. But in the hostage crisis, the free speech dilemma was not present. It is only recently that the Americans have made their entrance into the brave new world where freedom of speech or the First Amendment is the target. This happened in the Terry Jones Affair and the Youssef Affair.

THE TERRY JONES AFFAIR[63]

The controversy surrounding Jones started in July 2010, when he used Facebook to announce an 'International Burn a Quran Day,' to be held at his church on 11 September, 2010, in honor of the victims of the terrorist attacks on the World Trade Center in New York, exactly nine years before.[64] Jones' idea was eccentric, but not entirely new. On 14 January, 1989, in the town of Bradford, in northern England, another book-burning was organized: Salman Rushdie's *The Satanic Verses*. As Kenan Malik (*b.* 1960) writes in *From Fatwa to Jihad: The Rushdie Affair and its Legacy* (2009), the novel was tied to a stake before being set alight in front of the police station. 'It was an act calculated to shock and offend,' Malik writes.[65] And it did more than that: 'The burning book became an icon of the rage of Islam.'[66] After Terry Jones had announced his plans, assistant pastor Wayne Sapp uploaded a video to YouTube in which the church's intentions were explained, and

63 The material on Terry Jones in the following sections is in part a translation of an article that appeared (in Dutch) in the *Nederlands Juristenblad*, the abovementioned: Rijpkema, Bastiaan, "Vrijheid van meningsuiting in de val tussen religieus extremisme en utilitarisme", no. 44/45, 2012, p. 3106-3111.

64 "Florida Church Plans Koran Burning on 9/11 anniversary", *Agence France Presse*, 31 July 31 2010; see also: "Who is Terry Jones? Pastor behind 'Burn a Koran-day'', 7 September 2010, *ABC News*, http://abcnews.go.com/US/terry-jones-pastor-burn-koran-day/story?id=11575665#.UHCaKs2OL94.

65 Malik, Kenan, *From Fatwa to Jihad: The Rushdie Affair and Its Legacy*, Atlantic Books, London 2009, p. ix.; Thomas, Dominique, *Le Londonistan: Le djihad au Coeur de l'Europe*, Éditions Michalon 2005, p. 34.

66 Malik, Ibid., p. ix.; Weller, Paul, *A Mirror for our Times: "The Rushdie Affair" and the Future of Multiculturalism*, Continuum, London, New York 2009, p. 2.

– to add force to the announcement – included some images of a burning Quran.[67] On 21 July, the *Religious News Service* re-aired the announcement,[68] and in the following days the news spread to, among others, England,[69] the Netherlands[70] and France.[71] A few days later, on 31 July, the first terrorist threat was made; members of the 'Al Falluja Jihadist Forum' threatened to 'spill rivers of your (American) blood.'[72]

So, when the leader of a small church of about fifty members[73] in a – by American standards – fairly small town like Gainesville[74] announced that he intended to burn a Quran, this announcement apparently reached the Netherlands (in this case the, in terms of readership, rather insignificant newspaper, *Reformatorisch Dagblad*) within the same month.[75] Modern means of communication make the world more closely knit. Marshall McLuhan (1911-1980) described this phenomenon as early as 1962 and coined the now well-known notion of the 'Global Village.'[76] Unfortunately, in times of ongoing terrorist threats, we are inclined to say that our stay in the 'Global Village' is becoming increasingly less pleasant than the idea of a 'village' might suggest. The reality of our time is that what happens in one country is most likely to have effects in other countries.[77] Contemporary terrorism *is* transnational by its nature and recognizes no international boundaries. This 'new reality' was confirmed once again in the Terry Jones affair.

In September 2010, the media attention started to gather momentum and the responses to Jones' plans also intensified. After protests broke out in Indonesia[78] and Afghanistan,[79]

---

67 "Why couldn't we look away?", *St. Petersburg Times*, 11 September 2010.
68 Ibid.
69 "Church will burn Koran on 9-11", *The Guardian*, 27 July 2010.
70 "Kerk roept op tot Koranverbranding", *Reformatorisch Dagblad*, 28 July 2010.
71 "Une église de Floride propose de bruler le Coran le 11 septembre", *Agence France Presse*, 31 July 2010.
72 "Florida Church Plans Koran Burning on 9/11 anniversary", *Agence France Presse*, 31 July 2010.
73 Estimations vary. According to the local newspaper *The Gainesville Sun* the church has 50 members, see: "Petraeus: Dove World's Quran burning may have global impact", *The Gainesville Sun*, 7 September 2010, www.gainesville.com/article/20100907/ARTICLES/100909663.
74 Gainesville has approximately 125.326 inhabitants (2011), see: http://quickfacts.census.gov/qfd/states/12/1225175.html.
75 "Kerk roept op tot Koranverbranding", 28 juli 2010, *Reformatorisch Dagblad*, www.refdag.nl/kerkplein/kerknieuws/kerk_vs_roept_op_tot_koranverbranding_1_493456.
76 See McLuhan, M., *The Gutenberg Galaxy: the making of typographic man*, Toronto: The University of Toronto Press, 1962, inter alia, p. 21 and 31. Globalization as such, of course, began much earlier. See e.g. Roberts, J.M., *The Penguin History of Europe*, London: Penguin Books 1996, p. 340-341.
77 See Cliteur, P.B., *Het Monotheïstisch Dilemma*, Amsterdam: De Arbeiderspers 2010, p. 78 and also Singer, P., *One World: The Ethics of Globalization*, New Haven & London: Yale University Press 2004, p. 7.
78 "Protest rallies against "Burn a Quran day" continue", *Asia-Pacific News Agencies*, 5 September 2010.
79 "Afghans attack NATO outpost; Muslims worldwide outraged at threat to burn Quran", *Montreal Gazette*, 10 September 2010.

government officials from, among others, Jordan,[80] Pakistan,[81] Egypt,[82] and Iraq[83] also condemned the proposed burning.[84] Iran blamed Israel.[85]

WHAT TO DO: DEFEND FREE SPEECH OR GIVE IN TO TERRORISM?

The same type of reaction that in 1987, in the aftermath of the German Rudi Carrell Affair, was presented by the Dutch minister of foreign affairs in the discussion before the Dutch television audience, was now ventilated by a man with high military rank: U.S. General David Petraeus (*b.* 1952), at that time the ISAF commander in Afghanistan. He condemned the proposed burning of the holy book, and warned of possible consequences. This is what he said:

> 'It could endanger troops and it could endanger the overall effort. It is precisely the kind of action the Taliban uses and could cause significant problems. Not just here, but everywhere in the world we are engaged with the Islamic community.'[86]

Following Petraeus, the burning was condemned by a diverse parade of celebrities and government officials, from actress Angelina Jolie (*b.* 1975)[87] and the 'Veterans of Foreign Wars of the United States,'[88] to the U.S. embassy in Kabul,[89] the Lieutenant General of the UN-training mission in Afghanistan William Caldwell (*b.* 1954),[90] Secretary of State Hillary Clinton (*b.* 1947),[91] and NATO Secretary General Rasmussen (*b.* 1953).[92]

Pastor Jones, however, indicated he wanted to have a reaction from the White House. The president seemed reluctant, though, to make official declarations on the issue. And

80 "Jordan condemns US pastor's planned Koran burning", *The Jordan Times*, 10 September 2010.
81 "Worldwide outrage at planned Quran burning", *Al Arabiya*, 8 September 2010.
82 Ibid.
83 Ibid.
84 For an overview of countries that condemned the burning, see: www.csmonitor.com/World/Global-Issues/2010/0909/11-countries-speaking-out-against-Koran-burning-in-Florida/India.
85 According to Iranian Foreign Minister Manouchehr Mottaki the burning was "orchestrated by the Zionist regime after being defeated in its efforts against Muslims and the Islamic world", see: "Worldwide outrage at planned Quran burning", *Al Arabiya*, 8 September 2010.
86 "Petraeus Says Quran-Burning Protest Will Endanger Troops", *Wall Street Journal*, 6 September 2010.
87 "Angelina Jolie", *The Hamilton Spectator*, 10 September 2010, www.thespec.com/whatson/article/254810--angelina-jolie.
88 "VWF Strongly Against "Burn a Koran Day"", *Targeted News Service*, 7 September 2010.
89 "Petraeus: Koran burning plan will endanger US troops", *BBC South Asia*, www.bbc.co.uk/news/world-south-asia-11209738.
90 "U.S. Afghanistan commanders condemn Koran-burning plan", *Reuters*, 6 September 2010.
91 "Clinton condemns Quran-burning plan", *CNN U.S.*, 8 September 2010.
92 "Pressure mounts in U.S. against Koran-burning plan", *Reuters*, 7 September 2010.

how could he? Part of the First Amendment, which protects free speech, is that it is up to the American citizen to choose his own, sometimes unsympathetic, means to get his message across. Book burning, although an archaic approach, used to be practiced widely[93] not only in Greek and Roman culture,[94] but also in Christian Europe. It received a bad press because of the Nazis, whose book burning, initiated by Joseph Goebbels, was still fresh in our minds. But can you forbid this? There were certainly no legal grounds to do so. Besides, how could this be seen as the task of the president? In the American democracy, with the separation of powers, establishing the limits of free speech and developing criteria as to which means are legitimate for expressing your opinion, is the prerogative of the legislative or the judiciary, but certainly not the executive.[95] What the theoterrorist aims to do (and if not 'aims to do,' he certainly effectuates this) is forcing the executive to transgress its bounds. Again, this can be seen as a success. If a foreign dictator can make a democratically legitimated politician in another country seek refuge in an attempt to stifle the press, this can be seen as a triumph of dictatorship over democracy. If the president of the greatest democracy in the world is forced to call an American citizen to ask him not to use his constitutional right attributed to him in the national constitution, this is not only a triumph of dictatorship, but also a humiliation of democracy with great symbolic significance. The president and his advisors must have been aware of the delicacy of the situation. But, apparently, the president feared the turmoil and looming catastrophe even more than a violation of the constitution. First, a White House spokesman declared that the White House subscribed to Petraeus' warning.[96] (Again, a breach of the normal situation: A president who agrees with a civil servant). Then things accelerated. Two days after the White House statement, U.S. President Obama (*b.* 1961) appeared on 'Good Morning America,' where he explicitly called on Jones to refrain from the Quran burning. The President said the following:

> 'What he's proposing to do is completely contrary to our values as Americans; that this country has been built on the notions of religious freedom and religious tolerance. And as a very practical matter, as commander-in-chief of the armed forces of the United States, I just want him to understand that this stunt that he is talking about pulling could greatly endanger our young men and women in uniform who are in Iraq, who are in Afghanistan. We're already seeing protests against Americans just by the mere threat that he is making.'

---

93 Fishburn, Matthew, *Burning Books*, Palgrave, MacMillan 2008.

94 Cramer, Frederick H., "Bookburning and Censorship in Ancient Rome: A Chapter from the History of Ideas of Speech", in: *Journal of the History of Ideas*, Vol. 6, No. 2 (Apr., 1945), pp. 157-196.

95 One could question how 'involved' judges should be in the lawmaking process, see for instance: Rijpkema, Bastiaan, 'Rechterlijke toetsing is een bijzonder slecht idee', in: *de Volkskrant*, 18 February 2014.

96 "Quran burning plan a "concern": White House", *CBC News*, 8 September 2010.

And, when asked what he was worried about, Obama replied: 'Well, look, this is a recruitment bonanza for al-Qaida.'[97]

That same day Jones declared – despite the pressure from the White House – that he was still determined to burn a Quran on 11 September.[98] A few hours after Obama's appearance on 'Good Morning America,' Jones received a direct phone call from U.S. Secretary of Defense Robert Gates (*b.* 1943). Can you, as a largely unknown maverick pastor, force one of the most senior government officials to negotiate with you about what you will do and say? Yes, apparently you can. During a brief conversation, Gates pointed to the potential dangers to American forces and urged Jones to cancel his plans.[99] Here, the Dutch minister of foreign affairs, Van den Broek, calling to the Dutch television program and advocating a cancellation of the fourteen seconds of criticism of Ayatollah Khomeini, comes to mind.

The comparison between the American president and the American Secretary of Defense trying to dissuade Jones from burning a Quran, and the Dutch minister of foreign affairs trying to influence the media, is interesting, because there are several similarities. During the televised conversation in 1987 between the Dutch minister and the Dutch anchorman of the program, the journalist suggested that by not showing the Khomeini spoof, they, the people from the broadcasting corporation, could do some 'kind of favor' to the minister. Van den Broek, however, did not think Witteman was delivering him any service: 'I only provide the information you need in order to take *your own responsibility* in this matter.' Witteman disagreed and answered: 'But you understand, of course, because you are an eminent person, what kind of influence the minister of foreign affairs expounding such a view has. No matter how much we value our freedom of the press.'

Perhaps the journalist should have answered: 'Excellency, with all due respect, what you suggest is that we change roles. Is it not *my* responsibility to report on what happens in this world and *your* responsibility to protect us against evil?' What the minister effectively did was foster the impression that he, as an organ of the state, could 'inform' the broadcasting corporation of the evils of the world in which we are living, and that the broadcasting corporation had to bear the burden of not making this world unsafe. By a majestic sleight of hand the minister reversed the tasks and responsibilities of the most important actors in this play.

But with his remark, the journalist was also onto something. Apparently, the minister, in pretending only to 'give advice' to the broadcasting corporation, tried to make people believe that he acted in his private capacity: As an ordinary civilian 'giving advice' to a reporter. And he expected the broadcasting corporation to adopt the role of the state by

97 For a transcript of the interview, see "Opinion Roundup: Burning the Quran", *National Public Radio*, 9 September 2010.
98 "Florida Pastor Determined to Carry Out Quran Burning", *AOL News*, 8 September 2010.
99 "Obama's Pentagon chief calls Florida pastor", *USA Today*, 10 September 2010.

doing what is necessary to guarantee the security of Dutch citizens. Primarily on the territory of the state, but also abroad. If the state cannot bear that, indeed great, responsibility, the state ceases to be a state. It becomes a 'failed state.'

Now, it may be argued that it is wildly over the top to insinuate that the United States, the United Kingdom, or the Netherlands are 'failed states' because they have not been able to avert some terrorist attacks. The Netherlands is not Somalia, is it?

This is true. But this teasing exaggeration may perhaps sharpen our understanding. What constitutes a 'failed state' is difficult to ascertain. For some religious minorities living in Saudi Arabia, the state is failing to protect their interests and guarantee their personal safety.[100] Christians in that country have a different opinion about the state than the majority of Sunni Muslims.[101] And how does the Danish state look from the perspective of Kurt Westergaard, living under 24/7 protection for almost ten years already? He is still alive, the optimist retorts, which is true, but at what personal cost for the cartoonist? And how do the bereaved of Theo Van Gogh look at the Dutch state? As a monument of decency and effectiveness, or at least with some ambivalent feelings about its monopoly on the legitimate use of force?

One may still insist that the notion of the 'failed state' is too rhetorical to use in this context. In that case, we are willing not to use it. As long as the general message comes across that there is an element of perspective in the concept of 'failed state,' this is fine.

Let us underline: It is the state, not the broadcasting corporation, which has a responsibility to guarantee the security of the citizens. What the state may require from its citizens (and from private organizations) is to behave in accordance with the law. This was, effectively, what the television corporation was doing. It was, obviously, not illegal to report on a journalistic event in Germany. Not only was it not illegal, it was precisely what journalists are supposed to do. What the minister asked from the broadcasting corporation was to suspend or annul their primary function (i.e. to inform the public) because the state failed (or anticipated this failing) to fulfill its primary function. When an incumbent minister asks a television host – during a live show – not to broadcast a specific fragment, this is not simply the 'supplying of information,' but a request that a presenter – especially 'on the spot' – can hardly refuse.

100 See Morawiec, Laurent, *Princes of Darkness: The Saudi Assault on the West*, Rowman and Littlefield, Lanham 2005 for a chilling portrait.

101 See on this: Shortt, Rupert, *Christianophobia: A Faith under Attack*, Rider, London 2012; Marshall, Paul, and Nina Shea, *Silenced: How Apostasy and Blasphemy Codes are Choking Freedom Worldwide*, Oxford University Press, Oxford 2011.

THE MARK BASSELEY YOUSSEF AFFAIR[102]

The second American affair that sparked a row was the Youssef Affair. Mark Basseley Youssef[103] is a Coptic Christian who was born in Egypt, but emigrated to the United States later in his life. He is the *auctor intellectualis* of a short video that became known as *Innocence of Muslims*.[104] Roughly speaking, the video consists of two parts. The first part pictures an angry mob of Muslims rioting in the streets of modern-day Egypt. In the second part, the video shifts to the past and focuses on the prophet Mohammed. This part includes scenes in which Mohammed is talking to a donkey, womanizing, and advocating slavery. Moreover, he is called 'a murderous thug' and is, in general, pictured as a warlord. While this video undoubtedly offended many Muslims, it is no more offensive in nature than, for example, anti-Semitic stories that have appeared in Arab media about Jews demanding the blood of a child for their matzos, or about a Jewish conspiracy to rule the world – occasionally regarding the *Protocols of the Elders of Zion* as the brightest star of indisputable science.[105] Apart from this similarity, the greatest difference with those expressions is, obviously, that violent eruptions occurred in the wake of *Innocence of Muslims*. It was reported that 21 countries were the scene of protests or attacks on American and other Western targets in the first week after the video attracted serious attention.[106]

Just as with the affairs discussed earlier in this chapter, several political leaders found it difficult to defend freedom of speech in this case. The highest official of the foremost international organization, United Nations Secretary-General Ban Ki-moon (*b.* 1944), commented that:

> 'All human beings have the inalienable right to freedom of expression, freedom of assembly. These are very fundamental rights. But, at the same time, this freedom of expression should not be abused by individuals. Freedom of expression should be and must be guaranteed and protected, when they are

102 The following discussion of the Mark Basseley Youssef Affair is based in part on: Herrenberg, Tom, "Politici, de vrijheid van meningsuiting en *Innocence of Muslims*", in: *Nederlands Juristenblad*, No. 33, 27 September 2013, pp. 2255-2259; Herrenberg, Tom, "Vrijheid van meningsuiting in de multiculturele samenleving: evaluatie van twee tegenstrijdige interpretaties", in: *Civis Mundi*, 14 January 2014.

103 Also known as Nakoula Basseley Nakoula.

104 Google, the parent company of video-sharing website YouTube, was ordered by the 9th U.S. Circuit Court of Appeals in February 2014 to remove the video from YouTube. This was due to a copyright claim by one of the actresses in the video.

105 For examples of anti-Semitic expressions, see: "New Trends in Arabic Anti-semitism", vimeo.com/16779150; "Cartoons from the Arab World", www.tomgrossmedia.com/ArabCartoons.htm; "Egyptian Scholars: 'The Protocols of the Elders of Zion' Is the Constitution of Freemasonry, Whose Goal Is Jewish Domination of the World", www.memritv.org/clip/en/3039.htm.

106 "Violent protests over US–made film spill into more Islamic nations", *The Daily Telegraph*, 18 September 2012. Although *Innocence of Muslims* sparked controversy in September 2012, it was uploaded on YouTube two months earlier.

> used for common justice, common purpose. When some people use this freedom of expression to provoke or humiliate some others' values and beliefs, then this cannot be protected in such a way. So my position is that freedom of expression, while it is a fundamental right and privilege, should not be abused by such people, by such a disgraceful and shameful act.'[107]

What is most striking is that Ban Ki-moon's preconditions for protected speech (i.e. the obscure 'common justice' and 'common purpose' requirements) are completely outside the recognized human rights framework and cannot be found in the key human rights instruments adopted by Ban Ki-moon's *own* organization: the United Nations.[108] Even if we would take Ban Ki-moon's requirements as mandatory for protected speech, we are left with the question: What would count as a 'common purpose' or as 'common justice'? It is everything but obvious that ridiculing symbols of power, whether they are political, religious, or economic in nature, fails to serve a 'common purpose,' bearing in mind that critique – which can, of course, take many forms – enables mankind to progress.[109] Ban Ki-moon also referred to a specific kind of reprehensible behavior: 'Humiliation.' A person who humiliates 'makes someone feel ashamed and foolish by injuring their dignity and pride.'[110] When exactly is freedom of speech used 'to provoke or humiliate some others' values and beliefs'? Would Ban Ki-moon say that someone who strives for the legal prohibition of male circumcision on religious grounds 'humiliates' the values of others? Or would a capitalist mocking Marx and Engels count as such? Did Marx in turn 'humiliate' religious people when calling religion 'das Opium des Volkes'? Did Monty Python's *Life of Brian* 'humiliate' Christians?

---

107 www.un.org/News/Press/docs/2012/sgsm14518.doc.htm.

108 Article 19 of the Universal Declaration of Human Rights (1948) reads: "Everyone has the right to freedom of opinion and expression; this right includes freedom to hold opinions without interference and to seek, receive and impart information and ideas through any media and regardless of frontiers"; Article 19 of the International Covenant on Civil and Political Rights (1966) reads: "(1) Everyone shall have the right to hold opinions without interference. (2) Everyone shall have the right to freedom of expression; this right shall include freedom to seek, receive and impart information and ideas of all kinds, regardless of frontiers, either orally, in writing or in print, in the form of art, or through any other media of his choice. (3) The exercise of the rights provided for in paragraph 2 of this article carries with it special duties and responsibilities. It may therefore be subject to certain restrictions, but these shall only be such as are provided by law and are necessary: (a) For respect of the rights or reputations of others; (b) For the protection of national security or of public order (ordre public), or of public health or morals"; Article 20 of the International Covenant on Civil and Political Rights reads: "(1) Any propaganda for war shall be prohibited by law. (2) Any advocacy of national, racial or religious hatred that constitutes incitement to discrimination, hostility or violence shall be prohibited by law".

109 See on the importance of critique: Clifford, William Kingdom, "The Ethics of Belief", in: Stephen, Leslie and Frederick Pollock, Eds., *Lectures and essays by the late William Kingdon Clifford*, Macmillan and co., London 1901, pp. 163-205. Clifford is discussed in: Cliteur, Paul, *The Secular Outlook: In Defense of Moral and Political Secularism*, Wiley-Blackwell, West Sussex (UK) 2010.

110 www.oxforddictionaries.com/definition/english/humiliate.

And what is the legal status of 'humiliation' precisely? Does Ban Ki-moon propose to introduce a new right, the right 'not to be humiliated in your beliefs'? And where to include that in the Universal Declaration of Human Rights?

Although his remarks were a threat to the free exchange of opinions, Ban Ki-moon appeared to be in good company. In his response to *Innocence of Muslims*, president of the European Parliament, Martin Schulz (*b.* 1955), 'condemned strongly not only the content but also the distribution of such a movie, which is really humiliating the feelings of a lot of people all over the world.'[111] The problem is not that Ban Ki-moon and Schulz took a stance against 'humiliation,' but that they stretched the meaning of that word to such an extent that it comes close to an attempt to immunize such an influential symbol as a prophet from criticism. But, then again, that might very well be their aim, since Schulz literally '[criticized] any attempt to ridicule Islam,'[112] while Ban Ki-moon said, referring to *Innocence of Muslims* and the *Danish cartoons*: 'This must stop…'[113] We would be ill-advised to follow these two leaders in their vision on free speech, for if we did, the possibilities of persuading others on topics of public concern would be enormously reduced.

Concluding Remarks: The Future of this Conflict

This contribution is dedicated to an important modern phenomenon: The tension between theoterrorist threat and civil liberties, in particular, the freedom of speech and the freedom of press. The aim of analyzing the five 'affairs,' the Carrell Affair, the Rushdie Affair, the Cartoon Affair, the Jones Affair, and the Youssef Affair, is to show a common pattern. We are inclined to affirm that these five cases, usually seen (or rather dismissed) as 'incidents,' as having no relation with each other, are somehow connected. It seems not unreasonable to speculate (we concede: This is speculation; there is no hard historical proof) that the Carrell Affair was the beginning of the Rushdie Affair, and from there, the situation developed. One may also say: It is highly unlikely that the successes of the Iranian regime in intimidating the Netherlands did *not* have some impact on the self-esteem of the Iranian leaders and stimulate them to take bolder steps (which they actually did two years later in the Rushdie case). The idea that the Carrell Affair was a specifically local matter with no impact on the Iranians ('Why would they be interested in a silly little country most people cannot even locate on the map?') is not very convincing. The Iranian government took an interest in what was said about Khomeini *in Germany*, and on the basis of this firm histor-

111 www.youtube.com/watch?v=FSd2JK78C48, at 2:28.

112 "Schulz on the violent attacks against diplomatic missions", 15 September 2012, www.europarl.europa.eu/the-president/en/press/press_release_speeches/press_release/2012/2012-september/html/schulz-on-the-violent-attacks-against-diplomatic-missions.

113 www.un.org/News/Press/docs/2012/sgsm14518.doc.htm.

ical fact, it seems likely that they also took an interest in what was being said about them *in the Netherlands*.

Theoretically, it is possible that at some point in the future material will pop up (from government archives or otherwise) which will prove such a historical connection. A pipe dream would be, of course, an entry in some sort of diary, kept by Ayatollah Khomeini, or someone close to him, with a tenor like this: '24 February 1987. Great success in intimidating Dutch infidel nation without firing a shot, or having to kidnap anybody. Unfortunately, proud and stubborn German government did not apologize for disgraceful spoof on German TV, but show master himself so afraid that he tried to appease us. Success with intimidating the Dutch government stimulates us to think about further steps to take in intimidating decadent infidel nations.'

It is certainly very likely that the intuition of the Dutch minister of foreign affairs was entirely right with regard to the seriousness of the situation. But having the right diagnosis does not mean you also have the right therapy. And if crisis management was the strategy, we may ask: Was it also wise to *openly call* the Dutch broadcasting corporation, thereby showing to the whole world, and also to the theoterrorists, how eager the Dutch government was to appease the terrorists?

From a formal constitutional point of view this was problematic, of course. In a democracy, a member of the government (and acting on behalf of the government as a whole)[114] is not supposed to call the media, and try to influence the way those media report on matters of politics or anything else. But that is not the main point we want to make in this chapter. This would turn our questions into a manifestation of some sort of scholarly *Prinzipienreiterei*. The point we want to raise, is whether 'only giving advise' to the media by politicians is such an innocent practice. Most people think it is. They have the feeling: 'Why is it wrong to call to the media and friendly *ask* them to take their responsibilities seriously'? The Dutch minister of foreign affairs did not *prohibit* the Dutch media from broadcasting the program critical of Khomeini. There was no *compulsion* involved. Only a call to 'reasonableness.' President Obama also did not *force* pastor Jones to relinquish his plans to burn the Korans. He only made a reasonable appeal for him to not do this. What could be better than to have a president who so humbly enters into a social discussion with some reasonable arguments? A plan to burn a holy book *is a lunatic plan*, is it not? Why be so 'puritanical' in constitutional matters?

The answer is: We do not primarily approach this matter from the angle of what is constitutionally right or not. Our point is: We think those kinds of phone calls could, in all likelihood, have adverse effects. Those phone calls could very well, contrary to the

114 In a parliamentary democracy the minister acts on behalf of the government. See: Visser, R.K., *In dienst van het algemeen belang: ministeriële verantwoordelijkheid en parlementair vertrouwen*, Boom, Amsterdam 2008, p. 19; Driessche, I.A., *Politieke ministeriële verantwoordelijkheid: het Nederlandse begrip in vergelijkend perspectief*, Kluwer, Deventer 2005, p. 147.

intuition of most people, not make this world a safer place, but more *un*safe instead. After all, behavior that gets rewarded, gets repeated. Obama, Petraeus, Clinton, Ban Ki-Moon, Schulz and all other politicians who engage in such seemingly innocent discussions on what would be a feasible way to behave in such matters, accomplish the complete opposite of what they think and hope. What they accomplish is that terrorists will think they are on the right track. Imagine what a success it is, from the side of terrorist politics, to have the president of a free country openly calling a citizen to *request* this citizen to relinquish his constitutional rights and behave the way people are supposed to behave in dictatorships, i.e. to 'know in advance,' and in their behavior anticipate the preferences of the dictator and, although enshrined in the constitution as your right, 'freely' to forfeit that right, allegedly on the basis of reasonableness and decency (which are in reality considerations of fear; and, what is worse, fear *for all to see*).[115]

This is precisely what terrorists aim to do: To unsettle the structures in a foreign country by means of intimidation. They force a government to do things it would not do without that intimidation (as the definition of 'terrorist aim' in Article 83a of the Dutch Penal Code rightly points out).

Now, what governments usually do not do voluntarily is give a piece of territory to a group of citizens who have decided that, because they have their own language and culture, they want to secede from the national polity.[116] That group of separationists decides, potentially, to resort to arms. What a government usually does not do voluntarily is to denigrate the system of values they have chosen to regulate their community. Usually, governments believe in their constitution, in their human rights, in their system of democracy. So if in the culture wars, between democracy and theocracy, theocratic terrorists manage to force a democratic government to publicly distance itself from, for example, the First Amendment of the American constitution (as Obama *de facto* did in our view) or the Universal Declaration of Human Rights and the International Covenant on Civil Rights and Political Rights (again, as Ban Ki-Moon *de facto* did in our view) this demonstrates *ad oculos* to the citizens in theocratic countries that their system is manifestly better than the democratic system. If you really believe in democracy and the rule of law, you would never speak in such flippant terms about those ideals, would you not? For theocratic leaders this is very important. The significance may be seen as purely 'symbolic,' but symbols play an important role in politics.

The message theocratic leaders want to communicate to their population is: People living in democracies may have televisions, smartphones, luxurious holiday resorts and

115 As Alan Dershowitz writes: *Why Terrorism Works: Understanding the Threat, responding to the Challenge*, Yale University Press, New Haven and London 2002. The difference between "fear" and "fear for all to see" is essential from a Machiavellian perspective, of course.

116 Buchanan, Allen, "Theories of Secession", in: Brooks, Thom, Ed., *The Global Justice Reader*, Blackwell Publishing, Malden, Oxford, Carlton 2008, pp. 94-115.

fancy cars, they still live in a spiritually arid environment with their wives and daughters walking around like prostitutes, while the vilification of the prophet is standard procedure by both governments and citizenry, and even their leaders have to confess that *au fond* their system is inferior to the state where God (Allah) illuminates our path.

This ideological warfare with sometimes violent outbursts may be with us for some time to come. Especially in an increasingly religious world. There is – so it seems – still no solution for this problem. What these five cases also show is that there seems to be no significant difference between the response of politicians in a relatively insignificant country as the Netherlands and their colleagues in the supposedly most powerful country on earth, The United States of America. The reactions of relatively inexperienced politicians as the members of the Dutch government do not differ significantly from important players on the world stage as Obama, Gates, Ban Ki-Moon and Martin Schulz. Whether this can be seen as 'good news' or an embarrassment is left to the reader to judge.

We should not make the mistake to think that the cultural expressions we talk about in this chapter are not important enough to defend. This is the most obvious with the book-burning pastor, of course. Book-burning, although a practice of all times and all places,[117] is a practice that since the Nazi-period is so much associated with Joseph Goebbels committing German anti-Nazi authors to the flames that we cannot possibly see pastor Jones as some sort of victim. We associate him with one of the darkest pages in human history, as an unsympathetic lunatic, at best. This is, to a somewhat lesser degree, also the case with the other cultural manifestations we have talked about. People cannot take the shows of Rudi Carrell very seriously. It's dubious humor and not high-standing art, one would think. That the cartoons were made 'with the sole purpose to hurt,' to 'pain' people,[118] is a tenacious prejudice not many people are willing to set aside for gaining a better-informed judgment about the background of the matter.[119] Rushdie is reprimanded for being a haughty and self-obsessed person.[120] Mark Basseley Youssef is a fraud, a man with a criminal record. So why advocate the 'rights' of such a bunch provocateurs, criminals

117 Cramer, Frederick H., "Bookburning and Censorship in Ancient Rome: A Chapter from the History of Ideas of Speech", in: *Journal of the History of Ideas*, Vol. 6, No. 2 (Apr., 1945), pp. 157-196; Fishburn, Matthew, *Burning Books*, Palgrave, MacMillan 2008.

118 To mention only one example out of many: Seidenfaden, Tøger, "Hard secularism as intolerant civil religion: Denmark and the Cartoon Case", in: Porsdam, Helle, Ed., *Civil Religion, Human Rights and International Relations: Connecting People Across Cultures and Traditions*, Edward Elgar, Cheltenham, UK, Northampton USA 2012, pp. 178-192.

119 Most people do not know what the stance of the editor of the Jyllands Posten who commissioned the cartoons is: Flemming Rose. See: Khader, Naser, and Flemming Rose, "Reflections on the Danish Cartoon Controversy", in: *Middle East Quarterly*, Fall 2007, pp. 59-66. This is one of the most uninteresting articles for most people to read: Rose, Flemming, "Why I Published Those Cartoons", in: *Washingtonpost.com*, Sunday, February 19, 2006.

120 This point was made by one of the smartest people of our time whose smartness did not transpire in this contribution to the discussion on the fatwa: Dummett, Michael, "Open Letter to Rushdie", in: *The Independent*, 11 February 1990.

and, at best, reckless men, in such a fanatical way? Is this not to take Enlightenment too seriously, thereby transforming it into Enlightenment-fundamentalism?[121] Would that not take our 'Voltairian,' 'I disapprove of what you say, but I will defend to the death your right to say it' a little too far?

As we said, we think this is a mistake. The problem is, what starts with insignificant trifles will end with serious matter: With Galileo,[122] Bruno[123] and Servet.[124] We are already there, in fact, when we see that it proved possible to stifle several dissident voices in the fields of religious sensibilities and religious criticism. Yale University Press did not include the Danish cartoons in scholarly work.[125] A book on, mind you, *cartoons in general,* does not contain the most notorious cartoons of our time.[126] When BBC director general Mark Thompson was asked by the historian Timothy Garton Ash whether he, Thompson, would *not* air a show about the prophet Mohammed that was 'comparably satirical' to *Jerry Springer: The Opera,* which was broadcast by the BBC in 2005 and received tens of thousands of complaints for its 'irreverent treatment of Christian themes,' Thompson said: 'Essentially the answer to that question is yes.' Thompson argued: 'Without question, "I complain in the strongest possible terms," is different from "I complain in the strongest possible terms and I am loading my AK47 as I write".'[127] Salman Rushdie never made a *The Satanic Verses II* (and no publisher would have published it, to be sure). Kurt Westergaard never made a second cartoon comparable to his first one. So, it seems that – for the time being – theoterrorist intimidation is still fairly successful.

There are glimmers of hope, though. Humorous satire proves to be such a powerful force[128] that new manifestations keep popping up (one may think of the Jesus and Mo

121 This is the tenor of: Gray, John, "A Clash of ideologies: 'the Enlightenment' versus Islamism", in: *The National,* 2 July 2010; Gray, John, "Evangelical atheism, secular Christianity", in: Gray, John, *Gray's Anatomy: Selected Writings,* Allan Lane, Penguin Books, London 2009, pp. 292-307; Gray, John, "Monolithic secularism unsuited to today's Europe", Interview with John Gray by Nathan Gardels, in: *New Perspectives Quarterly,* 28 April 2004.

122 Forced to abjure his theses in 1633 before the Inquisition in Rome. See: Russell, Bertrand, *The Scientific Outlook,* Routledge, London and New York 2001 (1931), p. 18.

123 Burned at the stake in Rome. See: Rowland, Ingrid D., *Giordano Bruno: Philosopher/Heretic,* Farrar, Straus and Giroux, New York 2008.

124 Burned in 1553 on the instigation of Calvin. See: Zweig, Stefan, *Castellio gegen Calvin oder Ein Gewissen gegen die Gewalt,* Fischer Taschenbuch Verlag, Frankfurt am Main 1983 (1936).

125 Klausen, Jytte, *The Cartoons that Shook the World,* Yale University Press, New Haven and London 2009 did not comprise the cartoons itself although the author, for scholarly reasons, had wanted to include them in the book. The publisher refused.

126 Navasky, Victor S., *The Art of Controversy: Political Cartoons and the their Enduring Power,* Alfred A. Knopf, New York 2013.

127 "Mark Thompson: BBC director general admits Christianity gets tougher treatment", *The Telegraph,* 27 February 2012, www.telegraph.co.uk/culture/tvandradio/bbc/9107689/Mark-Thompson-BBC-director-general-admits-Christianity-gets-tougher-treatment.html.

128 Davies, Christie, "The Danish cartoons, the Muslims and the new battle of Jutland", in: *Humor,* 21-1 (2008), pp. 2-7; Morreall, John, *Comic Relief: A Comprehensive Philosophy of Humor,* Wiley-Blackwell, Malden/Oxford 2009.

cartoons). Who would have thought that after the Cartoon Affair, a new satire of the prophet would appear on the Internet? Who could predict that *book-burning* would ever force us to fundamentally consider our commitment to civil liberties? This can be seen as fruitful – at least intellectually.

Of course, we do not want to say that we are fond of *all* satire – certain manifestations are certainly of poor quality. We also do not consider book-burning an elevated form of artistic expression; far from it.

But that is not what this is all about. All of the time, everywhere, new controversial expressions, films, works of art, scholarly treaties and essays are being produced. It is highly unrealistic to think that governments can 'regulate' the production and diffusion of these works and ideas. They could not effectively do so in the Enlightenment, and cannot do so now. The Internet adds to that. This means that every 'solution' to a crisis is always temporal. The Dutch minister of foreign affairs will have had the feeling that he 'solved' the problem. He did not. At least, he might have 'solved' a crisis – in crisis management-style – but he did not solve the underlying problem. He passed it on to the British. And the British passed it on to someone else. Now, in the Jones Affair and the Youssef Affair, the Americans are struggling with the problem.

Governments should understand that imposing limitations on free speech – regardless of its relative effectiveness in the short run, mainly the success of catapulting the threat to your neighbors – erodes the foundations of a free society. They should realize that *extrajudicial* limitations ultimately amount to the same as their legal counterparts: They not only unduly restrict the exercise of free speech but deregulate the whole system of government. This 'new censorship' is not about explicitly limiting free speech, that is, by force of law, but about restricting it in a more subtle manner, using all sorts of 'requests,' 'suggestions,' condemnations, and allegations to make people relinquish their free speech rights themselves. This is something Europe, and especially, the bulwark of free speech, the United States, should be deeply concerned about. And *this* is what is at stake in such seemingly frivolous things as the jokes of Carrell, Rushdie's novel, the cartoon of Westergaard, the film of Van Gogh, the actions of Terry Jones, and the video of Mark Basseley Youssef.

Notes on the Contributors

Dr. Ambrogino G. Awesta obtained his master's degree in International and European Public Law (Cum Laude) at Tilburg University (2010), and his master's degree in Jurisprudence and Philosophy of Law at the University of Leiden (2011). From 2010 to 2014, he has been employed as a lecturer by the Department of Jurisprudence of Leiden Law School, where he has also completed his PhD dissertation *Freedom of Expression in a Pluralistic World Order* (2014).

Prof. dr. Paul Cliteur is professor of Jurisprudence at Leiden Law School and author of *The Secular Outlook* (Wiley-Blackwell, Chicester 2010), *Het Monotheïstisch Dilemma* (De Arbeiderspers, Amsterdam 2010) and (together with Dirk Verhofstadt): *Dirk Verhofstadt in gesprek met Paul Cliteur* (Houtekiet, Amsterdam/Antwerp 2012). He was also a professor of Philosophy at the University of Delft and guest-professor at the University of Gent (Belgium).

Prof. dr. Afshin Ellian is professor of Jurisprudence at Leiden Law School. He is the author of several writings on freedom of speech and has co-edited the following recent works: *Terrorism: Ideology, Law and Policy*, Ellian, Molier and Suurland (Eds.), Dordrecht 2011: Republic of Letters Publishing; *The State of Exception and Militant Democracy in a Time of Terror*, Ellian and Molier (Eds.), Dordrecht 2012: Republic of Letters Publishing.

Prof. dr. Amos Guiora is professor at the S. J. Quinney College of Law, University of Utah and has published extensively both in the U.S. and Europe on issues related to national security, limits of interrogation, religion and terrorism, and the limits of power, multiculturalism and human rights. He is the author of *Legitimate Target: A Criteria Based Approach to Targeted Killing; Freedom from Religion: Rights and National Security* (first and second editions); *Global Perspectives on Counterterrorism* (first and second editions); *Fundamentals of Counterterrorism; Constitutional Limits on Coercive Interrogation; Homeland Security: What is it and Where is it Going; Tolerating Intolerance: The Price of Protecting Extremism* (Oxford University Press 2013) and *Geopolitics and Security: Sovereignty, Intervention and the Law* (Taylor & Francis 2013).

Mr. Tom Herrenberg is a PhD candidate at the Department of Jurisprudence at Leiden Law School. His research interests lie in the field of human rights, with particular emphasis on freedom of expression.

Dr. Arie-Jan Kwak is assistant professor at the Department of Jurisprudence at Leiden Law School. His research interests ranges from legal professional ethics, the methodology of legal science to the philosophy of law and jurisprudence. Kwak recently published articles on law and literature and Ronald Dworkin. A representive publication is 'Vrijheid boven alles; over de rechtsstaat op een hellend vlak', in: *Justitiële Verkenningen*, 2007, pp. 23-34. He has also edited a volume on legal and religious interpretation: Kwak, Arie-Jan, Ed., *Holy Writ: Interpretation in Law and Religion*, Ashgate, Farnham/Burlington 2009.

Dr. Koen Lemmens is an associate professor of public law at KU Leuven and is the Belgian national director of the E.MA Human Rights and Democratization (European Inter-University Centre for Human Rights, Venice, Italy). He received his PhD from the European University Institute, Florence, Italy (2003), with a doctoral thesis on the limits of freedom of the press. He is an attorney at the Brussels bar, specialized in procedures before the European Court of Human Rights, and held teaching positions at the Vrije Universiteit Brussel and Universteit Antwerpen. He has taught extensively at all levels, with specialist modules focusing on human rights (mainly the ECHR-level), comparative (constitutional) law and legal theory.

Dr. Jan-Peter Loof is assistant professor of constitutional and administrative law and lectures constitutional law and human rights at the Institute for Public Law of Leiden Law School. He also is Commissioner (board member) at the College voor de Rechten van de Mens, the national human rights institute of the Netherlands. Next to that, he is chairman of the board of the School of Human Rights Research (in which seven Dutch universities co-operate in research and education in the field of human rights) and editor-in-chief of the *Nederlands Tijdschrift voor de Mensenrechten/NJCM-Bulletin* (the leading Dutch human rights law journal). His field of research includes the development of international human rights standards, the effects of these standards within the municipal legal order and the mechanisms for implementation of these standards within the national constitutional and administrative systems. He wrote a PhD thesis (2005) on the limitation and derogation of human rights during states of emergency and other national security crises.

Dr. Gelijn Molier is associate professor at the department of Jurisprudence of Leiden Law School. He has written extensively on freedom of speech. Recent works he has co-edited include *Terrorism: Ideology, Law and Policy*, Ellian, Molier and Suurland (Eds.), Dordrecht 2011: Republic of Letters Publishing; *The State of Exception and Militant Democracy in a Time of Terror*, Ellian and Molier (Eds.), Dordrecht 2012: Republic of Letters Publishing; *Mag ik dit zeggen? Beschouwingen over de vrijheid van meningsuiting*, Boom Juridische uitgevers, The Hague 2011.

Prof. dr. Remco Nehmelman is full professor Public Institutional Law, Utrecht University (The Netherlands). In his research he focuses on constitutional issues such as parliamentary immunity, the role of a Senate in a bicameral system and questions concerning the relation between the central state and decentralized public bodies (e.g. municipalities, provinces, water authorities). He is also a member of the Dutch Council for Public Administration (Raad voor het openbaar bestuur). The Council is an advisory body of the Dutch government and parliament and advises on the structure and functioning of the government.

Dr. Aernout Nieuwenhuis is associate professor of Constitutional Law at the University of Amsterdam. He has written many articles on fundamental rights issues, in particular on freedom of speech, and is the author of *Over de grens van vrijheid van meningsuiting: theorie, rechtsvergelijking, discriminatie, pornografie, Ars Aequi, Nijmegen 2006.*

Mr. Bastiaan Rijpkema received his LL.B. at Erasmus University Rotterdam and his LL.M. in Jurisprudence and Philosophy of Law (cum laude) from Leiden University. He is now a PhD candidate at the department of Jurisprudence in Leiden, where he also teaches legal theory. His dissertation deals with the relationship between democracy and the rule of law. His main research interests lie within the field of jurisprudence and political philosophy. Together with Cliteur he wrote 'The Foundations of Militant Democracy', in: Afshin Ellian & Gelijn Molier, Eds., *The State of Exception and Militant Democracy in a Time of Terror*, Republic of Letters Publishing, Dordrecht 2012, pp. 227-273. He also reissued the inaugural address of the Dutch constitutional scholar G. van den Bergh and wrote an introduction for this book: *Wat te doen met anti-democratische partijen? De oratie van George van den Bergh*, Elsevier, Amsterdam 2014.

Dr. Stefan Rummens is associate professor of Moral Philosophy at the Institute of Philosophy of KU Leuven (Belgium). His research mainly concerns metaethics and political philosophy. Regarding the latter, his interests include topics such as deliberative democracy, European democracy, populism, extremism and free speech. He has published articles in a number of international journals, including *The Journal of Political Philosophy, Political Studies, European Law Journal* and *I.CON.*

Prof. dr. Henny Sackers graduated from Radboud University Nijmegen, the Netherlands, in 1989, with a specialisation in criminal and administrative law. After graduation, he worked at the department of Criminal Law and Criminology, Radboud University, as an assistant professor. In 2008 he was appointed professor of administrative criminal law. He is also a deputy judge at the District Courts Arnhem and 's-Hertogenbosch. The research conducted by Henny Sackers focuses on several matters of enforcement of public law, including topics such as blasphemy, religion offences and group discrimination. Recently he published a book on the Dutch arms legislation (The Weapons and Ammunition Act).

Dr. Marloes van Noorloos is assistant professor of criminal law at Tilburg University in the Netherlands. In 2011, she defended her PhD thesis *Hate speech revisited. A comparative and historical perspective on hate speech law in the Netherlands and England & Wales* at Utrecht University (Intersentia, 2011). She has published various articles about hate speech, freedom of expression and freedom of religion (e.g. 'The politicisation of hate speech bans in the twenty-first century Netherlands: law in a changing context', *Journal of Ethnic and Migration Studies* 2014/2; 'Criminalising defamation of religion and belief', *European Journal of Crime, Criminal Law and Criminal Justice* 2014/4).

Mr. Max Vetzo is a law student at the Utrecht Law College (honours programme in law, Utrecht University). He currently studies law at the University of Cambridge as an exchange student. His main interests lie in the fields of constitutional law and criminal law. In 2014 he was a member of the delegation that won the 'Grondwetstrijd' with their proposal to reform the amendment procedure of the Dutch Constitution.

Prof. dr. Tom Zwart is Professor of Human Rights at the Faculty of Law, Economics and Governance of Utrecht University. He also serves as the Director of the Netherlands School of Human Rights Research, established by the seven leading Dutch universities, which consists of around 250 researchers from diverse disciplines. He specialises in the Asian and African approach towards human rights, the relation between international criminal law and local culture, and human rights and cultural values. He has been a visiting professor at a number of universities around the world, including the University of Cambridge, Sciences-Po, the University of Haifa and Tsinghua University. He has advised national and international governmental bodies on human rights, including the EU, the Council of Europe and the UN Human Rights Council. Prior to taking up his position at Utrecht, Zwart served as Head of the European and Legal Affairs Department of the Dutch Home Office, and as senior counsel to the Dutch Deputy Prime Minister.